MW00608400

*Sanctified*
*Trial*

# Sanctified Trial

## The Diary of Eliza Rhea Anderson Fain, a Confederate Woman in East Tennessee

Edited by John N. Fain

Voices of the Civil War
Peter S. Carmichael, Series Editor

The University of Tennessee Press / Knoxville

The Voices of the Civil War series makes available a variety of primary source materials that illuminate issues on the battlefield, the homefront, and the western front, as well as other aspects of this historic era. The series contextualizes the personal accounts within the framework of the latest scholarship and expands established knowledge by offering new perspectives, new materials, and new voices.

Copyright © 2004 by The University of Tennessee Press / Knoxville. All Rights Reserved. Manufactured in the United States of America. First Edition.

Frontispiece: Portrait of Eliza Fain, attributed to Samuel Shaver. Originally oil on canvas but later cut down, mounted on board, and extensively retouched. From the private collection of John and Ann Fain.

This book is printed on acid-free paper.

Library of Congress Cataloging-in-Publication Data

Fain, Eliza Rhea Anderson, 1816–1892.
    Sanctified trial : the diary of Eliza Rhea Anderson Fain, a Confederate woman in east Tennessee / edited by John N. Fain. — 1st ed.
    p. cm. — (Voices of the Civil War)
Includes bibliographical references (p. 385) and index.
ISBN 1-57233-313-8 (acid-free paper)
    1. Fain, Eliza Rhea Anderson, 1816–1892 — Diaries.
    2. Tennessee, East — History — Civil War, 1861–1865 — Personal narratives.
    3. Tennessee, East — History — Civil War, 1861–1865 — Social aspects.
    4. Women — Tennessee — Rogersville — Diaries.
    5. Rogersville (Tenn.) — Biography.
    6. Rogersville (Tenn.) — History, Military — 19th century.
    7. Rogersville (Tenn.) — Social conditions — 19th century.
    8. United States — History — Civil War, 1861–1865 — Personal narratives, Confederate.
    9. United States — History — Civil War, 1861–1865 — Social aspects.
    I. Fain, John N. II. Title. III. Voices of the Civil War series.
    E605.F14 2004
    973.7'13'092--dc22

                        2004005630

# Contents

## The Diary of Eliza Rhea Anderson Fain, a Confederate Woman in East Tennessee

# Illustrations

## Photographs

*Following Page 278*

# Documents

# Maps

# Foreword

In the wake of the Confederacy's collapse, East Tennessee's Eliza Fain turned to God just as she had done in 1861 when the United States was on the brink of disunion. Even in the confusion that followed Abraham Lincoln's election, she saw the hand of Providence unmistakably at work, elevating the South as the last bastion of Christendom. Fain perceived, as did many white Southerners, that the abolitionists ruled the North and that these godless missionaries of antislavery controlled a Republican party determined to destroy the South. Supporting secession and fighting in defense of the South, Fain concluded, was a religious duty that provided Southerners with an opportunity to show their enemies the power of their faith and the righteousness of their cause.

With the Confederacy's destruction in 1865, however, Fain was in shock. She could no longer claim divine favor for the Confederacy when its armies were surrendering throughout the spring of 1865. A tormented Fain accepted the cold reality of defeat, but she agonized over the war's consequences, desperately searching for a higher purpose in a conflict that she had always believed would prove that Southerners were God's chosen people. Perhaps God wanted the North and South to be reunited, she reasoned, but she could not conceive of the possibility that slavery was a sin that had earned the Confederacy divine wrath. On May 17, 1865, in a diary passage remarkable for its candor and honesty, Fain wrote that the

Confederate cause was just and moral because of the institution of slavery, and that history would ultimately vindicate the Southern people for defending human bondage. Slavery "has caused the best blood of the South to flow," she wrote. "I believe the Bible teaches [that] slavery is right. If this is true every soldier of the Confederate Army who has fallen is a martyr for the truth and no great truth of God's Holy Word has ever been sustained without the seal of the blood of the Christian being affixed."

Virtually every page of *Sanctified Trial* is filled with such passionate and thoughtful entries. Few journals offer such richly textured descriptions of the spiritual and emotional chaos that so many Southern women endured during the war. Fain offers more than just a record of her feelings or a mundane chronicle of her daily activities; her words reveal how those on the home front wrestled with the political and religious issues of the day. From the inception of the conflict, she insisted that more than political independence was at stake. The war was, in Fain's mind, an epic struggle that would ultimately demonstrate that a slave society was a fundamentally Christian one. Such an assumption, however, did not lead to religious fanaticism. She did not see the conflict as a crusade against a Northern infidel who deserved to be exterminated. If anything, Fain's religious sensibilities infused her with a spirit of moderation toward her enemies in 1861. As a Christian she could not easily justify the slaughter of human beings, even if they were demonic abolitionists. More than anything else, she desired peace and goodwill between the two sections. On April 24, 1861, she wrote: "Let us not sin against our Northern brethren, but O let us feel towards them as thou requires, if an enemy hunger let us feed him if he thirsts let us give him drink. O let us not be overcome with evil; but overcome evil with good."

This spirit of compassion that animated Fain's words in 1861 gradually disappeared as she encountered the brutality of war. Mounting Southern casualties, the incarceration of her sons in prisoner-of-war camps, and the rise of guerrilla war in her own community embittered her toward the North. East Tennessee was a land of divided loyalties, where Unionists, pro-Confederate forces, and bush-whackers committed heinous crimes against civilians. Unionist bush-whackers frequently targeted Fain because of her membership in the slaveholding class and because her husband and sons served in the Confederate army. In March 1865 a guerrilla force composed of local Unionists terrorized her family for a final time. The unit's leader pounded on the front door until Eliza, who did not have time to put on her stockings or shoes, finally answered. When she opened the door, the man boldly announced: "Good Morning Mrs. Fain, I am here and I intend to tear up and burn down your house." Although he did not uphold his promise, he allowed his men to pillage freely, taking the family silver and foodstuffs. Fain, it appears, remained calm throughout the ordeal as she felt the protective shield of God. That evening an embittered Fain confided to her diary that "the Lord has said 'Vengeance is mine, I will repay saith the Lord.'" "This," she grimly added, "is sufficient for me to know."

Fain's desire for retribution was more than a cry for vengeance. Her demands for a harsher war against the North must be under-stood as part of her fierce loyalty to the ideological and political interests of the planter class. Union victory meant the destruction of slavery, and Fain realized that this would destroy a society devoted to hierarchical social relations where she and members of her family stood on top. For her, death was preferable to the destruction of this way of life. When Fain learned that Lee had evacuated Richmond on April 2, 1865, she reassured herself by writing that "I believe he [Lee] is a Christian and would as soon think he would renounce his life as willingly as his Christian principle. I know he reads his Bible and feel if he does he feels this war is to establish the true doctrine of God's Holy Word in regard to slavery."

Although Fain's commitment to slavery cemented her loyalty to the Confederacy, she still feared that white Southerners would earn God's disfavor if they failed to uphold their duties as Christian masters. White men taking liberties with their female slaves consti-tuted an unforgivable sin in Fain's opinion, and the amalgamation

of the races, she warned, might result in the Confederacy's downfall. From her reading of the Bible, Fain believed that God had the
power to either build or tear down a nation. An obedient country
would forever endure, but if Southerners practiced evil or succumbed to temptation, Fain worried, God would destroy her
beloved Confederacy just as He had uprooted the people of Judah
for their disobedience. "Does the South feel and know for the sins
she has been visited?" she asked. Fain admitted that too many
Southerners had not sufficiently repented and continued to commit
"the dark and heinous crime of amalgamation, where men have
enslaved their own flesh and blood." Fain was particularly outraged
that Southern ministers refused to denounce this "transgression"
from the pulpit, that organized prayers had not been offered "to our
Father" so that racial mixing would end, and that Christians generally refused to openly take a stand against this sin. At the end of the
Civil War, Fain exclaimed in her diary: "The more I see the more
deeply am I impressed each day of my life that God is pouring out
his wrath upon the South on account of the amalgamated race who
have been born in a state of slavery. O white man of the South has
it ever entered in thy soul to count the cost of this terrible sin.
Think of Manassas, Richmond, Shiloh, Franklin and many other
bloody battlefields where the noble, the pure and good have fallen
and then see what it is for a nation favored of God as no other has
been to mix blood with a race whom God for reasons unknown to
us has doomed to a state of servitude."

Fain's discussion of racial mixing and the Confederacy's
standing with God is one of the most significant contributions of
*Sanctified Trial.* Her critical observations should not be interpreted
as guilt over human bondage, much less an indictment of slavery.
She was convinced that the institution was divinely sanctioned.
Her only doubts centered on the failure of some whites to live up to
their obligations as Christian masters. Historian Eugene Genovese
has brilliantly shown that most slaveholders shared Fain's perspec-
tive on the war, believing that God was testing Southerners to bring

slavery up to biblical standards or to face His wrath. Expecting Southerners to reform slavery to a higher Christian standard caused a great deal of anxiety in Fain, for it encouraged her to think long and hard about the moral condition of the nation. It is clear that religion did not make her unthinking, but highly critical of the world around her.

This is what makes Fain's diary such an amazing primary source. When she found defects in the behavior of her fellow Southerners, Fain often blamed these sins for battlefield defeats or other problems on the home front. In some instances she even succumbed to bouts of depression when the war seemed to favor the North, but Fain never despaired, always managing to regain her equilibrium through pure and simple faith. In the case of Fain and probably countless other slaveholders, religion could simultaneously be a pillar of strength as well as a weak joint in the foundation of Confederate nationalism. The trauma of Confederate defeat shattered Fain's self-identity as an upper-class woman and slaveholder. Union victory and emancipation, she believed, had unleashed a class of uneducated poor whites and former slaves on the downtrodden South. Fain's ensuing loss of power and prestige as a slaveholder essentially stripped her of paternalistic feelings towards African Americans. Throughout the war Fain had expressed a sincere concern for the welfare of slaves who she did not believe could handle "the responsibilities" of freedom. But following Appomattox, she no longer softened her racial and class elitism through the language of paternalism. She openly resisted black autonomy and expected freed people to return to a subservient position that resembled their lot in slavery. "May the poor deluded child of Africa learn wisdom," she wrote on June 29, 1865, "and choose slavery such as they had with us to a liberty which has in it no provisions for their soul or body."

Fain could never reconcile herself to black freedom, nor could she accept that Union victory signified the inherent wrongness of the Confederate cause. Vindication for the South, she predicted, would eventually come, but it would not occur on the battlefield. God would redeem the mission of a Confederate nation if white Southerners patiently endured the humiliating trial of Reconstruction with Christian fortitude. With the advent of Northern military rule, Fain was sure that the South's hierarchical world of white over black and rich over poor would dissolve into racial anarchy and mob rule. Only then would all of humankind see the immorality of Northern aggression against the South. A divine reward would certainly follow, Fain predicted, and "our Father in his own good time and way will vindicate Southern character and bring us forth as one of the tried, refined and purified people of the earth."

Fain came to terms with defeat without having to condemn the people that she supported or the principles that she upheld during a long and bloody civil war. In this way, she kept alive the dream that the South would reemerge as a Christian slave society ruled by faithful men over a people who dutifully served their master in heaven as well as on earth. The fact that her dream survived the war testifies to the strength of Fain's Christian faith and to the powerful influence of the South's proslavery theologians. Few published accounts reveal the intense spiritual battles that Confederate women endured while their men were off fighting in the armies. Quite simply, this is essential reading for anyone interested in the religious dimensions of the Civil War. Moreover, Fain's honest self-examinations and her critical observations of the world around her make *Sanctified Trial* one of the most powerful and engaging diaries to come from a Southern woman. Any reader of this journal will certainly agree that Eliza Fain deserves to be placed alongside Mary Chesnut and Catherine Edmondston as one of the most important commentators on the Confederate experience.

Peter S. Carmichael

University of North Carolina at Greensboro

# *Preface*

I discovered the diaries of Eliza Rhea Anderson Fain in my parents' home, which had formerly been the home of Eliza's granddaughter Elizabeth Fain. How did the volumes get there? Eliza Rhea Anderson Fain had a daughter, Sallie, who married Sam Fain, a distant cousin, after the Civil War. Eliza lived with Sam and Sallie for a while after the death of her husband, Richard, in the large home that Sam built in 1875 in Mossy Creek, Tennessee (now known as Jefferson City). After the Civil War, Eliza was supported for the most part by her son-in-law, a prosperous merchant, farmer, manufacturer of cotton yarn, and land speculator. Sam and Sallie had five children, and the youngest, Elizabeth, graduated from the University of Tennessee in 1901. None of the children ever married, and they kept almost everything they had inherited from their parents. Elizabeth Fain was the last of this line, and from about 1943 until her death in 1953, she lived mainly with my family, who were her only relatives in Jefferson City. My father, Dr. Samuel Clark Fain, is the son of Dr. Samuel White Fain, a first cousin of Elizabeth Fain.

Elizabeth Fain never mentioned the diaries, which were kept in a cheap wooden trunk with other items. As a child I thought that the large box in her room must have held bars of gold because of the way Cousin Elizabeth treated it when she lived with us. Later I learned that it contained various family portraits—of Eliza, of her mother, Elizabeth, and of her husband's father—which an artist named Samuel Shaver had painted. The box also contained hand-tinted photographs of Elizabeth's parents.

Elizabeth Fain was a woman whose religious faith and opposition to alcohol were similar to those of her grandmother. Elizabeth obtained a graduate degree in history from Columbia University and taught for many years at a Presbyterian college in North Carolina. She never married and always left important decisions to her bachelor brother John. There is a family story about Mary C. Fain, my grandmother, who had been left a widow with five small children. A domineering matriarch, Mary once asked Cousin Elizabeth about the nature of some new construction on their property and was incensed when Elizabeth replied, "Brother hasn't said." The clear indication was that Elizabeth would not ask John about the matter and that she always deferred to him as the patriarch. Upon her death, Elizabeth Fain left the bulk of her estate to the University of Tennessee to fund scholarships in the College of Agricultural Sciences. She did this in memory of her brother John, who had also obtained his undergraduate degree there.[1]

The home of Elizabeth Fain was left to my siblings and me, with our parents having life occupancy. The trunk containing many letters, the diaries of Eliza Fain, and the military papers of Eliza's husband was in a closet off one of the upstairs bedrooms. Most of these documents, including the diaries and many historical artifacts, constitute the John N. Fain Collection, which is now part of the Calvin M. McClung Historical Collection at the East Tennessee History Center in Knoxville. The McClung Collection is maintained by the Knox County Public Library System. Eliza's diary has been microfilmed along with many of the other Fain papers, and these are also held in the McClung Collection.

1. During the 2002–3 academic year, the Fain endowment provided scholarships totaling $12,500 for six students from Jefferson County, Tennessee, according to a letter dated July 10, 2003, from Dennis Jones, the director of planned giving for the Institute of Agriculture at the University of Tennessee.

I became interested in the diary in the early 1970s and over a twenty-five-year period prepared a typescript of the most interesting one-third of the diary. Most of the entries in the period before or after the Civil War are religious meditations or summaries of sermons by preachers. Approximately 9 percent of my initial transcription covered the years from 1835 through 1859; 29 percent covered the period from 1860 through 1870; and the remaining 62 percent covered the period from 1871 through 1892.

Daniel Stowell used the diary as one of the sources for his book *Rebuilding Zion: The Religious Reconstruction of the South, 1863–1877* (New York: Oxford University Press, 1998). In addition, he also wrote an article specifically devoted to information obtained from the diaries; this appeared as a chapter entitled "'A Family of Women and Children': The Fains of East Tennessee during Wartime" in *Southern Families at War: Loyalty and Conflict in the Civil War South*, edited by Catherine Clinton (New York: Oxford University Press, 2000).

Daniel also converted the original typewritten transcription, which was started before the days of personal computers, into one electronic format and offered helpful advice on preparing the diaries for publication.

I am also indebted to Sheila Johnston, George Webb, and Donahue Bible for assistance in obtaining relevant information about people and events in and around Rogersville.

# Editorial Policy

Eliza Rhea Anderson Fain started keeping a diary in 1835 and continued doing so until nine days before her death on January 19, 1892. The diary, when discovered eighty years after Eliza's death, consisted of approximately 3,750 manuscript pages in twenty-eight volumes with about a million words. In some years, especially after the Civil War, she appeared to have had no paper and did not keep a diary. Most of the volumes are recycled store account books, bank account books, commissary record books from the Civil War, and the like, given to her by her husband or relatives. The diary entries were not always kept in chronological order, for when Eliza ran out of paper she would sometimes put entries for a particular day in earlier sections where there was space. The paper and ink were of good quality, and nearly all the entries remain legible. However, the handwriting is sometimes crowded, making it hard to read and difficult to decipher the spelling of some proper names. Some names are actually spelled incorrectly; for example, she wrote "Eckles" when referring to General John Echols.

The major concern in bringing the diary into print was selecting those sections that would be of interest to a general audience. Approximately 13 percent of the original diary was chosen for publication and emphasizes life during the Civil War. I have omitted the less interesting sections devoted to sermons she heard in church, accounts of the deaths of family members, or religious reflections. Sometimes, Eliza would conclude or interrupt the daily entry with a prayer, and these were removed if they were not relevant to the narrative. Nothing has been added, but considerable amounts of soporific text have been deleted. Entire entries for some days have been omitted if they had no apparent relevance to the Civil War. Ellipses have not been added to denote deleted passages since these would have been so frequent as to impede the narrative flow.

Eliza Fain observed no consistency in spelling, capitalization, punctuation, or usage. I have attempted to regularize spelling and correct misspelled words and place names. One example is the word "wagon," which she sometimes spelled as "waggon" according to the British style. Some words are not in current usage, and these are spelled as they were written. Long entries have been broken into sentences and paragraphs. Periods and commas are provided for sentences where Eliza used dashes or no punctuation at all. As was common for that era, the daily entry for one day would often consist of one long paragraph with very long sentences. A logical sentence structure was imposed, and some muddled sentences were deleted when it was difficult to understand what was being said.

Eliza's views regarding slavery and the Southern cause are not acceptable to most people today. They are presented exactly as she wrote them in order to provide insights into why so many people in the South supported secession and slavery. Eliza was no reluctant Confederate and, until the South's defeat, never wavered in her belief that slavery and secession were supported by her God.

Eliza often recorded favorable rumors about military actions in her diary, and historical inaccuracies are noted but have not been deleted. Eliza never returned to her diary to mark out sections of it, but a few times she commented at a later date on what she had recorded in prior years. Such passages are included here.

The text is divided into seven chapters. There is a chapter for each year of the war, one for the Reconstruction period, and an epilogue. The chapter headings are based on excerpts from the diary in that year and were chosen to reflect a key event of the year. The title for this book comes from an entry on April 4, 1865, when Eliza is reflecting on her visitation two days before by bushwhackers. They threatened to burn her home but in the end robbed her of food, silverware, a horse, and anything else of value that they could carry away. She describes this experience as "a sanctified trial," which pretty well sums up her experiences during the Civil War and illustrates the key role of her religious faith.

# Introduction

The impact of the Civil War on East Tennessee was quite different from that in the Deep South since the majority of the population in East Tennessee opposed secession. In contrast, most of the citizens in West and Middle Tennessee favored secession, so Tennessee as a state joined the Confederacy. When Tennessee seceded from the Union, it was impossible for East Tennessee to become a separate state because the easy routes of access into the area were through the secessionist states of Virginia and Georgia. Thus, East Tennesseans were unable to separate themselves from Tennessee as West Virginians did from Virginia. The Civil War in East Tennessee not only pitted neighbor against neighbor but also involved alternating control by the Union and Confederate armies in the area around Rogersville, located in upper East Tennessee just below the Virginia state line.[1]

The supporters of secession in East Tennessee were largely, but not exclusively, the wealthier merchants, farmers, and professionals of the towns and cities. There were few planters in the area since the climate was unsuited for the growing of cotton or rice. The majority of the Unionists were from the rural and mountainous regions and tended to be less affluent. However, the citizens also

1. James W. Patton, *Unionism and Reconstruction in Tennessee 1860–1869* (Chapel Hill: Univ. of North Carolina Press, 1934); Noel C. Fisher, *War at Every Door: Partisan Politics and Guerrilla Violence in East Tennessee* (Chapel Hill: Univ. of North Carolina Press, 1997).

split along party lines, with many Whigs opposing secession and many Democrats favoring it.[2]

The most prominent Unionist in East Tennessee was probably William G. "Parson" Brownlow, whose contempt for the aristocratic secessionists suggested that the Civil War in East Tennessee was also a class struggle.[3] Brownlow could have been speaking of the Fains when he said that the well-to-do secessionists were descended from foreigners who came to this country as indentured servants but had "taken their start in life by peddling on pins and needles, by spading up gardens for other people, or by entering other people's lands and, by hook or by crook securing their titles."[4]

Richard Fain's great-grandfather, Nicholas, came from Ireland to Chester County, Pennsylvania, in about 1753 with few assets. In 1766 he petitioned the court to obtain a peddler's license and moved down the Shenandoah Valley into Virginia.[5] In 1782 Nicholas and his son Captain John Fain (Richard's grandfather) obtained land grants in East Tennessee. John was killed by Indians in Tennessee on

2. As Kenneth W. Noe and Shannon H. Wilson point out in their introduction to *The Civil War in Appalachia: Collected Essays* (Knoxville: Univ. of Tennessee Press, 1997), there is no consensus among scholars as to why mountaineers chose to support the Confederacy or the Union during the Civil War. What is clear is that East Tennessee was one part of the Confederacy where the majority of the voting citizens openly opposed secession and continued to do so throughout the Civil War. In contrast, the mountaineers in Alabama, Georgia, South Carolina, North Carolina, and Virginia who were against secession before the war became reluctant Confederates during the war. See Daniel W. Crofts, *Reluctant Confederates: Upper South Unionists in the Secession Crisis* (Chapel Hill: Univ. of North Carolina Press, 1989).

3. Parson Brownlow was a Methodist preacher and newspaper editor in Knoxville, Tennessee, who believed in Methodism, temperance, slavery, and the Union. He was a skilled debater whose partisan harangues skewered his opponents with cruel wit. Brownlow was well known for his verbal attacks on anyone who disagreed with his religious or political views. During the Civil War he waged unrelenting verbal warfare on Confederate sympathizers in East Tennessee without any hint of Christian charity. E. Merton Coulter, *William G. Brownlow: Fighting Parson of the Southern Highlands* (Chapel Hill: Univ. of North Carolina Press, 1937); Stephen V. Ash, ed., *Secessionists and Other Scoundrels: Selections from Parson Brownlow's Book* (Baton Rouge: Louisiana State Univ. Press, 1999).

4. *Brownlow's Knoxville Whig and Rebel Ventilator,* February 20, 1864.

5. Max Fain, *Nicholas Fain of Tennessee* (Atlanta: M. Fain, 1980), 4–62; military papers and related documents of Richard G. Fain, John N. Fain Collection, Calvin M. McClung Historical Collection, East Tennessee History Center, Knoxville. This set of documents will hereafter be referred to as the Fain Collection.

August 8, 1788, and his son, another Nicholas, became the first mayor of Rogersville, Tennessee, and a wealthy merchant-farmer. Most merchants and planters in pre–Civil War America were born into the upper class. However, as Elisha P. Douglass has pointed out, an exception to this pattern of business history occurred from 1780 to 1820 on the frontier, where "the number of businessmen coming from humble origins increased markedly."[6] The second Nicholas Fain, Richard's father, was one of these individuals.

East Tennessee was a bitterly divided region both during and after the Civil War. The struggle for political control started in 1860 with the election of Abraham Lincoln as president and only ended with the collapse of Radical Republican rule of Tennessee in 1869. Few people in East Tennessee were against slavery, and even Parson Brownlow supported the institution. The divisions in East Tennessee probably had little to do with slavery since slaves were a small minority of its population (less than 10 percent). There were also many Unionists in the hills and mountains of Northern Alabama, Western North Carolina, and Eastern Kentucky, but they lacked the political leadership provided to those in East Tennessee by Parson Brownlow and Andrew Johnson. Furthermore, the Civil War largely bypassed these regions, whereas East Tennessee was the scene of many battles during the conflict.

During the period from 1865 through 1869, the Radical Republicans under Brownlow, primarily from the lower class, were in political control of everything except the courts, and they drove out many of the secessionists during a reign of terror and intimidation.[7] The Radical Republicans attempted to confiscate the property of the former Confederates so that landless Unionists could profit from their opposition to secession, but these efforts were unsuccessful. By 1870 the social structure had largely returned to what it had been prior to the Civil War, and rule by "aristocratic

6. Elisha P. Douglass, *The Coming of Age of American Business: Three Centuries of Enterprise, 1600–1900* (Chapel Hill: Univ. of North Carolina Press, 1971), 10.

7. Fisher, *War at Every Door*; Patton, *Unionism and Reconstruction in Tennessee*.

elites" of the conservative Republican variety in East Tennessee was considered preferable to rule by freed slaves and poor whites.[8] Even after the end of Reconstruction in the South, the Republicans continued to be the dominant political party in East Tennessee. The primary determinant of party preference was the side that one's father and grandfather had supported during the Civil War.

Rogersville is the county seat of Hawkins County and is located in the northeast corner of Tennessee just below the Virginia state line. In June 1861 Hawkins County was divided on the secession issue, with only 40 percent of the voting population favoring separation from the Union.[9] Rogersville lies on the north side of the Holston River and was a prosperous town prior to the completion in 1858 of the railroad that ran from Bristol to Chattanooga on the south side of the river. The mainline railroad bypassed Rogersville, which, like other East Tennessee towns in similar situations, fell into a period of economic decline that has continued to this day. The businessmen and other leaders of Rogersville attempted to prevent this decline by building a spur railroad called the Rogersville and Jefferson that ran for ten miles from Bulls Gap on the main railroad to the river at Rogersville. Eliza Fain's husband, Richard, was president of this railroad.[10] Since a bridge across the river had not been built when the Civil War began, access to the railroad required a four-mile trip, by

8. Fred Arthur Bailey, *Class and Tennessee's Confederate Generation* (Chapel Hill: Univ. of North Carolina Press, 1987). It should be noted that Oliver P. Temple, in *East Tennessee and the Civil War* (Cincinnati: Robert Clarke, 1899), attempted to rewrite history by ignoring the brief rule of Tennessee by the Radical Republicans. Temple claimed that the majority of the Republicans in East Tennessee were conservative, cautious, and anti-revolutionary farmers who owned their own land, while the Democrats were the party of the poor and laboring people. Temple ignored the fact that in the rest of the South the Republicans were mostly former slaves and Yankee carpetbaggers at this time. What still remains to be explained is how the former Whigs, who were conservative property holders, managed to take over the Republican Party in 1869 from Parson Brownlow and his coalition of former slaves and landless Unionists.

9. W. Todd Groce, *Mountain Rebels : East Tennessee Confederates and the Civil War, 1860–1870* (Knoxville: Univ. of Tennessee Press, 1999), 40; Fisher, *War at Every Door*, 188–90.

10. H. F. Cummings, *Report to the General Assembly on the condition of the railroads in Tennessee* (Nashville: E. G. Eastman, 1859), 72–73. This report lists Richard G. Fain as president of the railroad.

foot or by horse, from the home of Eliza and Richard Fain through Rogersville to the river. A ferry was used to cross the river.

During the Civil War, Rogersville was primarily under Confederate control, although it periodically came under occupation by Union troops. At other times it appears to have been ruled by Unionist guerrillas or bushwhackers, such as William Sizemore's band. Eliza was lucky that none of her men were at home when Sizemore ransacked her home on April 5, 1865, and that she lost only her horse and possessions. Eliza was told that her home would be burned, but her moral and physical presence probably kept her daughters from being raped and her home from being destroyed. It has recently come to light that the same group of raiders killed five men later the same day at Rice's Upper Ferry four miles southwest of Rogersville.[11]

The home of Eliza and Richard Fain, located two miles east of Rogersville, was a two-hundred-acre farm near the stage road that later became Highway 11W. In 1877 the farm was advertised for sale with these words: "the above farm has a two story frame dwelling with an ell for dining room and kitchen, stable, cribs and other out houses; good springs; about 100 acres cleared, and balance wood land; a small creek running through the farm."[12] Richard had built the large house in 1845 on land inherited from his father, who had built a

11. For an account of Sizemore's guerillas and another band led by Bill Owens, see Donahue Bible, *From Persia to Piedmont: Life and Death in Vaughn's Brigade* (Mohawk, Tenn.: Dodson Creek Publishers, 1993). William O. Sizemore led a group of independent raiders that seized food, horses, cattle, hogs, grain, and any other marketable commodity that in turn could be sold to the quartermasters of whatever army was occupying Hawkins County. Sizemore's group primarily harassed secessionists. Captain Bill Owens operated a band that served as scouts for General John C. Vaughn's command and protected Southern sympathizers. Owens enlisted in the Confederate Army in 1861 and served for one year as a private in Company D of the Thirty-first Tennessee Infantry Regiment. He then returned to Hawkins County and led a guerrilla force of secessionists that included former Confederate soldiers. There is no evidence that the title "captain" meant anything more than that he was the leader of the group. On April 5, 1865, a seven-man squad of this band was ambushed at the ferry by Sizemore's guerillas; five of the seven were killed. Bill Owens was not with the squad at the time but appears to have been in North Carolina attempting to obtain horses.

12. Advertisement of items for sale by Sam N. Fain (Eliza's son-in-law), printed broadside dated 1877, from the private collection of John and Ann Fain. For reasons that are unclear, the farm was apparently never sold. If it was sold, it was repurchased by Powell Fain, since he lived on the farm after the death of Eliza.

brick home nearby that still stands. However, Eliza and Richard's family home in Rogersville, which later became the home of their son Powell Fain and his wife, burned to the ground in 1897.

Eliza and her husband were both members of families that had sustained themselves as merchants and clerks in the small towns of East Tennessee. Although Eliza and Richard were part of the slaveholding elite and a prominent family, they were not one of the wealthiest families in Rogersville. The 1860 census lists thirty-four families with greater financial assets.[13] Clearly they were members of what might the called the second tier of wealth in Rogersville before the Civil War. Eliza and her family were relatively impoverished after the Civil War. However, their relative social position remained intact since freed slaves and landless whites were left with nothing. The Fains lost the economic value of their few slaves but retained their home and their two-hundred–acre farm. The property contained no first-class farmland, and today it consists of forested hills, pasture, and suburban developments. Before the Civil War, farming on the Fains' land was performed by slaves, and afterwards it was done by Eliza's sons and by former slaves working as hired hands.

Eliza Rhea Anderson Fain was born on August 1, 1816, to Elizabeth Rhea and her husband, Audley Anderson, in Blountville, Tennessee, in Sullivan County; she died on January 19, 1892, at the age of seventy-five in Rogersville, Tennessee, in Hawkins County. Eliza's father had died when she was only two. Eliza's mother subsequently lived with her brother Samuel Rhea in Blountville until her marriage to Nicholas Fain in 1832. Samuel Rhea was a prosperous and very pious Presbyterian who functioned as her surrogate father. Eliza was educated at the Knoxville Female Academy and joined the Blountville Presbyterian Church at the age of

13. This conclusion is based on an analysis of the 1860 census records for Hawkins County. Richard Fain listed total assets of ten thousand dollars; his brother Hiram listed assets of five thousand dollars. Free Schedules of Hawkins County, Tennessee, *Eighth Census of the United States, 1860* (Washington, D.C.: National Archives and Records Administration, Microfilm Publications), RG029, M653, Roll 1255.

seventeen. She married her stepbrother Richard in 1833, some eighteen months after her mother had married Richard's father.

Eliza Rhea Anderson Fain and Richard G. Fain, a graduate of the United States Military Academy at West Point, were part of the emerging commercial-professional elite living in East Tennessee towns. Like others of their class, they were strong supporters of secession and never wavered in their commitment to the Confederacy.[14] Eliza was an exceptionally literate woman for her day, having attended an academy in Knoxville for a few years before her marriage. She was a great believer in education, and in an 1867 letter to her husband she wrote of their children, "To have them educated and valuable members of society has been my highest desire so far as earth is concerned."[15]

Eliza's mother's family, the Rheas, were pious Presbyterians who appeared to worship both God and learning in about equal parts. In his book *Historic Sullivan* (1909), Oliver Taylor had this to say about Blountville, where Eliza was born and raised: "The Rheas, Andersons, Fains, Dulaneys, Maxwells, Tiptons, Rutledges and Gammons are some of the settlers who came here with liberal educations, and this, with the wealth many acquired here, enabled them to dispense a hospitality that was rare in its refinement and culture—the percentage of illiteracy was less in the early days of the county than it was for a few generations following."[16] Eliza and Richard were members of this cousin network of Scotch-Irish Presbyterians who dominated business and culture in East Tennessee in the period from its settlement to the Civil War.

Eliza was a devout evangelical Presbyterian. In 1837 a religious revival among Presbyterians greatly affected Eliza and resulted in the formation of a "New School" Presbyterian church in

14. For background information on the experiences of East Tennessee Confederates during the Civil War, the best available source is Groce, *Mountain Rebels*.

15. Eliza Fain to Richard Fain, December 1, 1867, Fain Collection.

16. Oliver Taylor, *Historic Sullivan: A History of Sullivan County, Tennessee* (Bristol, Tenn.: King Printing Co., 1909), 140.

Rogersville. Eliza and Richard left the "Old School" church and joined the "New School" Presbyterians, who were more oriented towards outreach and mission.[17] However, by the time of the Civil War, the majority of the members of the "New School" church, along with its minister, were against secession and aligned with the Northern Presbyterian denomination. Consequently, Eliza and her husband began worshipping at the other Presbyterian church, where the majority of the members were secessionists.

Eliza Fain derived her strength and character from her faith, which enabled her to face down "bushwhackers" and survive the privations of the war. Eliza attempted to live her life based on the dictates of Southern Presbyterianism, which derived from the beliefs of the Puritans and Calvinists as interpreted by evangelical Protestants of the nineteenth century. They emphasized that life was to be based on eternal principles, not gratification of undisciplined desires. This does much, for example, to explain Eliza's opposition to dancing and drinking.

17. In her diary entry for January 23, 1837, Eliza wrote, "Since last Sabbath my mind has been in the most distressed state on account of my great sins and the alienated state of my affections from the Lord that I have ever experienced. Doubt and the most alarming thoughts have taken possession of my soul." This is from a section of her diaries that are not included in this text. The complete diaries, however, are now contained in the Fain Collection at the McClung archive and are also available there on microfilm.

R. Clay Crawford wrote in his reminiscences of Rogersville in the *Rogersville Herald* in 1901 that he well remembered the exciting time when this split occurred in the Presbyterian church: "I was too young to fully understand the proceedings, but I know the excitement ran high. The speakers were very bitter and personal in the debates and some of the meetings were quite disorderly. At times the moderator found it impossible to preserve order in the assembly, and I really expected the meeting to erupt in a free fight. I am under the impression that some blows were struck either in the church or outside on account of what occurred within. A large part of the congregation seceded and built the church [that still stands in Rogersville]." Reprinted in *Reminiscences of Rogersville*, ed. Sheila Johnston (Rogersville, Tenn.: Privately published, 1994).

This account of the division among Presbyterians in Rogersville is supported by a pamphlet on the history of the "New School" Presbyterian Church in Rogersville that was erected in the 1840s after the split. (The pamphlet was privately published by the Rogersville Presbyterian Church in the 1920s, and a copy is contained in the Fain Collection.) In the graveyard beside the church are monuments to Eliza and Richard Fain. The two Presbyterian churches reunited some years after the war when the worst of the bitterness had subsided, in part because there were not enough Presbyterians left to support two churches.

Eliza lived her faith through personal example and good works, but the standards she set were so high that she was continually disappointed in the actions of most of her children. Only one daughter seemed to meet her expectations, but eventually four of her sons became pillars of their communities, married, and raised families. Two of these sons seem to have been honorable men who married the women they impregnated, as indicated by the recorded dates of their marriages and the births of their first children. One daughter made an unhappy first marriage, and Eliza had to help her raise her sons. Another daughter never married, and the other daughters died as young adults.

Eliza subscribed fully to the paternalistic racism that characterized the South in the first half of the nineteenth century. Her husband owned eight slaves (four of whom were children under the age of twelve at the start of the Civil War) and rented another slave. Eliza and Richard supported the view of evangelical Protestants in the South that slavery was not a moral evil.[18] The historian Donald G. Mathews could have been describing Eliza and her husband when he wrote that "Evangelical Protestantism in the Old South enabled a rising lower-middle/middle class to achieve identity and solidarity, rewarding its most committed religious devotees with a sense of personal esteem and liberty."[19] Citing passages in the Bible, the preachers attempted to rationalize slavery as being divinely ordained. Evangelical Protestants in the South actually argued that slavery and Christianity were compatible. Such arguments demonstrate the remarkable ability of Protestantism in the South to accommodate its theology to prevailing social mores—a tendency that continues to this day.

Eliza's diary demonstrates that evangelical Protestants in the border regions could be just as fervent supporters of secession as

18. Bertram Wyatt-Brown, "Modernizing Slavery: The Proslavery Argument Reinterpreted," in *Region, Race, and Reconstruction: Essays in Honor of C. Vann Woodward*, ed. J. Morgan Kousser and James M. McPherson (New York: Oxford Univ. Press, 1982), 27–50.

19. Donald G. Mathews, *Religion in the Old South* (Chicago: Univ. of Chicago Press, 1977), xv.

the planters of the deep South. In contrast, the equally pious evangelical Protestants of the North were convinced that slavery was incompatible with the Bible. In his second inaugural address on March 4, 1865, Abraham Lincoln noted that both sides "read the same Bible, and pray to the same God; and each invokes his aid against the other." Eliza's diary is a profound demonstration of why the secession movement in the South, which was initiated by wealthy and mostly secular planters in South Carolina, had the support of the much larger churchgoing middle class of the South, whose numbers included relatively few slaveholders.

Although Eliza's husband and five of her sons served in the Civil War, none died in the conflict. During the postwar period, however, her husband and five of her children died of what appears to have been tuberculosis (or "consumption," as the disease was commonly called at the time). The malnutrition accompanying their poverty after the war probably contributed to their deaths from consumption.

For most of the war, in the absence of her husband and four oldest sons, Eliza had to manage a household that included nine slaves, two adult daughters, and six younger children. Eliza was clearly a matriarch running a large establishment on limited means, and the reality of her life was far from the image of the Southern plantation mistress.[20] As her diary entry of June 2, 1861, indicates, Eliza was up to the task of managing a farm and a household of seventeen people despite the misgivings of Gus, a thirty-one-year-old male slave. Only once does Eliza reveal any disagreement with her husband, and that was over farming arrangements involving Richard's brother. In the end she defers to her husband, and throughout the diaries she always adheres to the view that the chief end of woman is obedience to God and her husband. Eliza also had to manage her household during the postwar period, as her husband never appears to have

---

20. See Anne Firor Scott, *The Southern Lady: From Pedestal to Politics, 1830–1890* (Chicago: Univ. of Chicago Press, 1970); and Drew Gilpin Faust, *Mothers of Invention: Women of the Slaveholding South in the Civil War* (New York: Random House, 1996).

recovered physical or mental strength. But even when she was running the show, Eliza was the type of woman who conformed her life to the image of the husband as lord and master.

Eliza had once been a supporter of the view that slaves should be converted to Christianity, then freed and sent back to Africa as missionaries. In fact, her family had sent two former slaves to Liberia in 1842.[21] Eliza's mother and Sam Rhea, her

21. Eliza's account of sending these persons to Liberia appears in a small leather-bound book that is now part of the Fain Collection. In this book, on April 7, 1842, she wrote: "We started to Liberia, Africa two colored persons Dick and Ruth. They were sent under the care of the colonization agent W. Levi Walker. They were induced to emigrate through the influence of Sion Harris a colonist from Liberia who had emigrated there about 13 years since from this part of the state and had returned for the purpose of inducing the descendants of the Rev. George Erskine to emigrate. Dick was accompanied by his wife Polly who belonged to Mrs. Deaderick. We sincerely trust that their removal may be the means of good to themselves and usefulness to dark and degraded Africa. They were members of the church. May the God of all Grace so enlighten and sanctify them that they may manifest to the heathen around that there is truth and reality in the religion of Jesus Christ." Eliza also recorded that Dick and Ruth sailed from Norfolk, Virginia, on July 7 and arrived in Monrovia after a trip of forty-four days. Dick, however, died only seven days after his arrival. Eliza based this information on a letter from a former slave named Baccus to Samuel Rhea of Blountville. Samuel was Eliza's surrogate father, and according to Oliver P. Temple in *East Tennessee and the Civil War* (107), Samuel freed those of his slaves who wished to go to Liberia; Baccus was clearly one of those freed persons.

In the proceedings of the convention of the Friends of African Colonization held in Washington May 4, 1842, it is recounted that eighty-six emigrants had arrived in Norfolk from Tennessee. The report further stated: "They possess good characters; some are artisans, some agriculturists, some are prepared to be teachers and a few to preach the Gospel. Among them are the friends and relations of that valuable and heroic citizen of Liberia, Zion Harris, who is now in this country pleading the cause of the Colony. The death of the Rev. Mr. Erskine, his father-in-law was the affecting incident. Willing and ready to die he left one request, that his son, would, should providence permit, once visit Tennessee and bring to Africa the surviving relatives left behind." Sion and Zion Harris are clearly the same person, and the report went on to state that "Harris returns to Africa with thirteen of his kindred." See "The American Colonization Society Website," http://ourworld.cs.com/ceoofamcolso/id24_m.htm.

For further information about Sion Harris, see Durwood Dunn, *An Abolitionist in the Appalachian South: Ezekiel Birdseye on Slavery, Capitalism, and Separate Statehood in East Tennessee, 1841–1846* (Knoxville: Univ. of Tennessee Press, 1997) 33–34, 187–88. Sion Harris is described as a former slave and carpenter-farmer from Knox County who went to Liberia in 1830. Sion married Martha Erskine, the daughter of George Erskine, a former slave who had been freed and educated by Dr. Isaac Anderson at Maryville College in East Tennessee. Rev. George Erskine had been sent as a Presbyterian missionary to Liberia in 1820. The abolitionist Ezekiel Birdseye attended a camp meeting of Presbyterians in Maryville where Sion Harris spoke for ninety minutes. Birdseye said that Sion impressed everyone as having natural talents of a high order.

uncle and surrogate father, appear to have been especially strong proponents of the view that slaves had been brought to American shores by God to be Christianized so that they could return to their own land as missionaries.[22] This scheme proved to be impractical. Few blacks preferred a return to Africa, and Southern opinion had turned to the view that slavery was divinely ordained as well as a practical arrangement. However, the management of slaves was not always easy, and in her diary entry of November 28, 1842, Eliza wrote of the great and numerous trials her mother had endured: "Her principal source of trouble are blacks. She has a hard set to deal with." It was no picnic to be the mistress of slaves, for the slaves, having scant motivation to do otherwise, often did as little as possible. Although a pious mistress preferred to use cajolery in dealing with slaves, coercion was often necessary, and this was something most women were reluctant to use. Many white women in slaveholding Southern households felt that the curse of slavery was on them rather than on the slaves and that their legal status was little better than that of slaves.[23]

Eliza Fain was far from unique in keeping a diary during the nineteenth century. Hiram Fain, her husband's brother, lived near Eliza and Richard and kept a diary from 1850 to 1870. This single volume primarily reported the weather but contained comments on events during the Civil War. The wartime section of the diary has been published, and it shows that Hiram held views about secession and the Civil War that were similar to those of

22. Eliza had this to say in her diary on December 30, 1860: "Last Friday was the annual return of my sainted mothers birthday. She would have been 73. I have often thought of her peace loving spirit. Had she lived to see this day she would have been greatly troubled for our loved country. She had always believed and instilled into the minds of her children that this land was destined by God for the evangelization of much heathen country and especially Africa. She seemed to think that God in his wisdom and goodness to that fallen benighted land had permitted them to be brought here to Christianize them and let them go to their own land as pioneers of Christianity there. Could she have lived to see this day it would have seemed dark and dreary." Eliza Fain Diaries, Fain Collection.

23. See Catherine Clinton, *The Plantation Mistress: Woman's World in the Old South* (New York: Pantheon Books, 1982).

Eliza.[24] There are numerous references to Hiram and his family in
Eliza's diaries and vice versa. At one point during the war, Eliza
became somewhat upset with Hiram over a financial matter but
eventually deferred to her husband, who sided with his brother.
Nan Kinkead, a friend of Eliza's daughters, also kept a
diary during the Civil War. While this diary remains in private
hands, a fictionalized account based on it has been published.[25]
There are numerous references to Nan Kinkead in Eliza's diary
and to the Fains in the book entitled *Miss Nan: Beloved Rebel*. The
diaries of two other young, female Confederate sympathizers
from East Tennessee, Ellen House[26] and Myra Inman,[27] have also
been published. Ellen House's diary starts in 1863 with the
Yankee occupation of Knoxville and recounts her expulsion, only
fifteen months later, by the Union forces. At that point she
moved to Georgia, where she remained for nine months until the
end of the Civil War. Myra Inman lived in Cleveland, Tennessee,
near Chattanooga; she started her diary at age thirteen in 1859
and concluded it in 1866. Myra was, like Eliza, a dedicated Christian and a member of a prominent but not especially wealthy family
whose social life was centered around their church. In her diary
Myra mentions visits to Mrs. Leonard Ross (Martha Fain) by
her family in early 1863 but does not note that these were
deathbed visits. Martha Fain Ross died on February 14, 1863,
leaving six children. Eliza mentions Mrs. Ross's death in her
diary entry of April 12, 1863, observing that Martha had made
an unhappy choice in her marriage. Martha was a daughter of

24. John N. Fain, "The Diary of Hiram Fain of Rogersville: An East Tennessee Secessionist," *Journal of East Tennessee History*, no. 69 (1997): 97–114. The original diary is now part
of the Fain Collection.

25. Margaret Lyons Smith, *Miss Nan: Beloved Rebel* (Johnson City, Tenn.: Overmountain
Press, 1994).

26. Daniel E. Sutherland, ed., *A Very Violent Rebel: The Civil War Diary of Ellen Renshaw House*
(Knoxville: Univ. of Tennessee Press, 1996).

27. William R. Snell, ed., *Myra Inman: A Diary of the Civil War in East Tennessee* (Macon, Ga.:
Mercer Univ. Press, 2000).

John Fain of Dandridge, a distant cousin of Eliza's husband, and is buried in Dandridge.

It was quite common for nineteenth-century women to keep diaries, and these were often dismissed by their descendants as being of little consequence. This was certainly true in the case of Eliza Fain, whose diary was ignored and apparently never read by her descendants. It was kept because her descendants never discarded any family letter or other document that they had inherited. After the death of Elizabeth Fain in 1953, the contents of the home were cleared by my mother who consulted an expert about what to do with the early-nineteenth-century items. He advised her to keep them, which she did in an upstairs closet until I discovered them.

The theoretical analysis of women's diaries in the light of postmodernism is only now beginning. Discussing the importance of such diaries, the literary scholar Amy Wink has noted that they reveal how women can "act creatively and individually even within the limited and culturally imposed structure."[28] Wink has also argued that women's diaries are the most authentic form of autobiography; this is especially so with Eliza's diary, which was not censored or reworked in later years into a more polished memoir. Wink, in commenting on the Civil War diary of Cornelia Noble, said that it expressed a "culturally coded conception of the divine righteousness of the Confederate Cause,"[29] and this description also appears to apply to the diary of Eliza Fain. However, while a perception of the Southern cause as divinely ordained worked fine so long as the South appeared to be winning the war, the defeat of the Confederacy forced Cornelia Noble—as it did Eliza Fain—to realize that secession may not have been God's will after all. Wink has suggested that Southern women diarists during this transitional time applied the traditional powers of domesticity and piety to their acceptance of defeat. It was easier for these women to continue

28. Amy L. Wink, *She Left Nothing in Particular: The Autobiographical Legacy of Nineteenth-Century Women's Diaries* (Knoxville: Univ. of Tennessee Press, 2001), xxxiii.

29. Wink, *She Left Nothing in Particular,* 109.

supporting the religious, patriarchal, and paternalistic social order with which they were familiar than to "alter the foundations of their socially constructed identity."[30]

Eliza Fain adjusted to the demise of the Confederacy without losing her faith or agonizing for years about why her God had allowed the defeat of the South. Such adjustment was especially difficult for secessionists in divided regions, where they were now alienated from many of their former friends and where control of their churches and communities was in the hands of local Unionists. Eliza was fortunate in that she was able to attend a Presbyterian church controlled by former Confederates. In Rogersville, there were two Presbyterian churches whose differences before the war were mainly theological. During the war, the churches were divided as well over the secession issue, with Unionists attending one church and Confederates attending the other. Similarly, in Dandridge, Tennessee, where my great-grandfather lived, the local Presbyterian church came under the control of Unionists. After the war, my great-grandparents left that church to join a Presbyterian church where they did not have to stand up publicly and ask forgiveness for the sin of having supported secession.

Eliza was a practical woman, and as the de facto matriarch of a large family, it probably took all her effort just to survive after the war. There was little time for agonizing over defeat, and the Fains of Rogersville and Dandridge preferred to forget as much as possible the lost dreams of the Civil War. I cannot remember ever hearing about the Civil War from my parents, Cousin Elizabeth, or my grandmother who lived in Dandridge. That does not mean, however, that they had forgiven the North or that they would vote for a Republican candidate for office. However, political control of East Tennessee remained in the hands of the descendants of former Unionists, and the best policy in those circumstances was to say as little as possible to one's children about the Civil War.

---

30. Wink, *She Left Nothing in Particular,* 121.

Eliza's adjustment to the defeat of the South seems to have been influenced by her cousin Jonathan Bachman, who was the minister of her Presbyterian church from 1865 to 1873.[31] The Reverend Bachman then left Rogersville to become the pastor of the First Presbyterian Church in Chattanooga, where he served for more than fifty years building a large and successful church. Jonathan Bachman had been attending Union Theological Seminary in New York City at the start of the war but returned to the South to become a captain in the Confederate Army until he surrendered at Vicksburg. Bachman was a leading proponent of the view that ex-Confederates and ex-Unionists should work together in Chattanooga to industrialize the South and let bygones be bygones. It was said of him that he was a leader not only of his church but also of the town and that "he advanced to all, no matter what denomination or former view, the idea of harmony among men, faith in God and a patriotic belief in a reunited country."[32]

The diary of Eliza Fain is unique both because of its length (about a million words written over fifty-seven years) and because it was written by a mother of twelve who fully subscribed to the church-based culture of the antebellum South. Furthermore, Eliza was neither a young girl nor a plantation mistress as were most of the female authors of published diaries from the Civil War era. The life of the plantation mistress was modeled on the more secular life of the Jeffersonian South, which in turn was patterned on that of the English country set with its emphasis on the virtues of urbanity, nicety, and distinction.[33] The most famous Civil War diary by a woman is that of Mary B. Chesnut, a member of the

31. John Trotwood Moore and Austin P. Foster, *Tennessee: The Volunteer State, 1769–1923*, vol. 4 (Nashville: S. J. Clarke, 1923), 742–47; Charles D. McGuffey, ed., *Standard History of Chattanooga, Tennessee* (Knoxville: Crew & Dorey, 1911), 423–27.

32. Charles E. Govan and James W. Livingood, *The Chattanooga Country, 1540–1951* (New York: E. P. Dutton, 1952), 300.

33. Marjorie S. Mendenhall, "Southern Women of a Lost Generation," in *Unheard Voices: The First Historians of Southern Women*, ed. Anne Firor Scott (Charlottesville: Univ. Press of Virginia, 1993), 92–109. This essay was originally published in *South Atlantic Quarterly* in 1934.

secular plantation aristocracy of South Carolina by both birth and marriage. However, her account, as originally published, was actually written in the 1880s and is a polished memoir based upon her diary.[34] In contrast, Eliza Fain's diary is a somewhat hurried and rough account by a busy mother and farm manager who wrote down her thoughts at the time and never went back to rewrite her entries or edit them.

Like Mary Chesnut, Eliza was married at seventeen and was raised in a patriarchal slave society. However, Mary did not have any children and moved in the highest social circles. In contrast, Eliza gave birth to thirteen children and lived in what was, even then, a backwater town far from centers of wealth and influence. There are few published diaries from this era that provide the insights of a middle- or upper-class mother who was also a pious evangelical Protestant but who supported secession as fully as any plantation mistress. It was these women whose husbands and sons provided the bulk of the truly committed soldiers that enabled the South to fight for four long years.

Eliza began her diary when she was nineteen, and she continued to make entries until nine days before her death at age seventy-five. There are no private remarks about sex in the diaries as this was a taboo topic in the nineteenth century. She never mentions anything about being pregnant except for one complaint about back pain, which occurred shortly before the birth of her last child. Apparently considering offspring an inevitable consequence of marriage, Eliza had thirteen children, all but one of whom survived childhood. That Eliza herself survived childbirth so often is amazing for an era when deaths from childbirth were common. One of Eliza's sisters, for example, had died at age nineteen shortly after giving birth to her first child. Most healthy married women at

34. For recent scholarly editions of the Chesnut diaries, see C. Vann Woodward, ed., *Mary Chesnut's Civil War* (New Haven, Conn.: Yale Univ. Press, 1981), and C. Vann Woodward and Elisabeth Muhlenfeld, eds., *The Private Mary Chesnut: The Unpublished Civil War Diaries* (New York: Oxford Univ. Press, 1984). The former book contains the 1880s text, while the latter presents Chesnut's diaries as originally written during the Civil War years.

this time averaged a child every two years until they either died or reached menopause. Yet Eliza never once mentioned being either excited or disappointed that she was pregnant again. On August 10, 1846, she did comment that she had suffered five hours of "excruciating torture" just prior to the birth of her son Powell. Eliza seems to have approached marital sex with either dignified acquiescence or enthusiastic cooperation. The latter feeling is perhaps apparent in her entry of July 24, 1836, when, as a young mother of age twenty, she commented on her husband's absence: "I have received several letters from my husband since he left, to be separated from him is quite painful."

It is unclear why Eliza did not want to write anything down of an intimate nature except in coded messages, but one reason may have been that the many large and bulky volumes of her diary could not be easily kept under lock and key. Furthermore, as a diarist Eliza was always in control of what she wrote, and her diary appears to be the carefully crafted expression of a public face that emphasized obedience to one's husband and worship of one's God. Eliza's life was centered around her church and her family. Moreover, life was not meant to involve frivolities such as dancing, and temperance was considered necessary for salvation. While it is not entirely clear why Eliza became so upset when her sons Sam and Powell, son-in-law Amos Smith, and nephew Sam Gammon overindulged in alcohol during and after the Civil War, it is true that alcoholism was severely condemned by evangelicals. But it is also true that after the war many of the former Confederate soldiers were, with good reason, despondent about the future; thus, it is hardly surprising that some of them turned to alcohol as a consolation.

In her diary, Eliza places a special emphasis on miscegenation as a factor in the demise of slavery and the defeat of the South, although it is not entirely clear why she thought this was so. It may well have had something to do with her religious faith and a conviction that the strict moral code she observed applied equally to white men and to slaves. As a devout Presbyterian, Eliza believed that slaves had souls and must follow the same moral standards as their owners. She also felt that if it was the will of God for women to observe fidelity in their marriage vows, it was equally incumbent upon their husbands and sons to follow the same standards, and this included sex with female slaves. As Edwin Mims has noted, many a spotless Southern woman became "unwillingly aware of the loose morals of her men in their relations with women of another race."[35] And in such relations sexual coercion was often a factor. Just as powerless female slaves were forced to do the cooking and housework for the woman of the house, so, too, were they vulnerable to the sexual attentions of the male masters. For an upright Victorian woman like Eliza, sex outside of marriage was as wrong for men as it was for women, whether free or slaves. And since she was apparently aware that Southern men often engaged in such relations, this may explain why she saw miscegenation as critical to slavery's downfall. It was perhaps easier for her to believe that illicit sexual conduct had corrupted slavery in the South than to accept the notion that the institution itself was against the will of God.

There is some evidence to suggest a sexual competition between Eliza and the slave woman named Polly. Richard Fain could possibly have been the father of Hill and Lewis, Polly's two sons. Although no information has been found to date regarding their paternity, they are described in the 1860 census as mulattoes, while Polly, their mother, is described as a black female. It is also possible that George or John Fain (the unmarried brothers of Eliza's husband) could have been their fathers. Polly was six years older than Eliza and accompanied her from Blountville to Rogersville.

Further insight into the miscegenation issue is offered by the diary of Gertrude Thomas, another devout nineteenth-century Southerner who was very much concerned with moral rectitude.[36]

35. Edwin Mims, *The Advancing South: Stories of Progress and Reaction* (New York: Doubleday, Page & Co., 1926), 240.

36. Virginia Ingraham Burr, ed., *The Secret Eye: The Journal of Ella Gertrude Clanton Thomas, 1848–1889* (Chapel Hill: Univ. of North Carolina Press, 1990).

Gertrude deplored interracial sex, and this appears to be a coded protest against her husband's adulterous relationship with one of their slaves. Wives were powerless in these situations, but that did not mean that they accepted the sexual double standard so prevalent in the South at this time. Eliza's feelings were no doubt similar to Gertrude's. While Eliza's faith could justify slavery, that did not extend to husbands, fathers, or sons having sexual relations with female slaves. This may reflect ambivalence about slaves as property, since Eliza thought that slaves should have religious instruction, marry, and follow the same moral codes that applied to slaveholders.

After the end of the Civil War, the section of Tennessee where Eliza lived was dominated by Unionists who made life as difficult as possible for former Confederate supporters. Many of the former Rebel soldiers in East Tennessee left during the immediate postwar period, when "Brownlowism" was at its height, and never returned. It appears that those who could leave East Tennessee did so, moving to Atlanta, Memphis, Jerseyville in Illinois, or other towns where they were less subject to persecution. Richard Fain left Rogersville to work as a clerk for a wealthy relative in Mossy Creek. This relative, Sam Fain, married Richard and Eliza's daughter Sallie, and they took Eliza into their home after Richard's death.

Read today, Eliza Fain's diaries offer a richly textured view of a world long vanished. In particular, her record of the Civil War years reveals a woman of unwavering piety and principle—a strong-willed matriarch determined to hold her household together in the midst of the most severe trials the young country had yet faced. Her opinions and observations have much to tell us about the impact of war in a region of deeply divided loyalties, about the sustaining power of religious faith, about the views and rationalizations of slaveholders, and about the way everyday life was lived almost a century and a half ago.

# Principal Characters in the Diary

Biographical details about various individuals to whom Eliza Fain refers in her diary are provided below. The information about the Fain family and their slaves is based on the Fain family genealogy records in the Frank B. Fain Collection and on the papers of Richard and Eliza Fain in the John N. Fain Collection; both sets of papers are held in the McClung archive in Knoxville, Tennessee. The information about the military service of Richard and his sons comes from these papers and from their military service records in the National Archives, which are available on microfilm. The military service information was further verified by consulting *Tennesseans in the Civil War*, Parts 1 and 2 (Nashville: Civil War Centennial Commission, 1964–65); the multivolume *Roster of Confederate Soldiers, 1861–1865*, ed. Janet B. Hewett (Wilmington, N.C.: Broadfoot Publishing Co., 1995–96); and *The Blue and Gray from Hawkins County, 1861–1865: The Confederates*, ed. Sheila Weems Johnston (Rogersville, Tenn.: Hawkins County Genealogical & Historical Society, 1995). Information about the military service of other individuals mentioned in the diaries came from these sources, as well as from the *Roster of Union Soldiers, 1861–1865: Kentucky–Tennessee*, ed. Janet Hewett (Wilmington, N.C.: Broadfoot Publishing Co., 2000), and the *Roster of Union Soldiers*,

*1861–1865: Ohio,* 4 vols., ed. Janet Hewett (Wilmington, N.C.: Broad-foot Publishing Co., 1999). All of the obituary information mentioned below came from undated clippings archived in the John N. Fain Collection; their publications of origin could not be determined.

## Eliza's Husband and Children

Richard Gammon Fain, the husband of Eliza, was born on March 6, 1811, in Rogersville, Tennessee, and died on September 11, 1878, in Mossy Creek, Tennessee. Richard married Eliza Rhea Anderson on December 17, 1833. He graduated from the United States Military Academy at West Point, New York, in 1832 as a brevet lieutenant, First Artillery. He served in the Indian campaign in the Northwest until he resigned in December 1832. In 1836 he was involved in the Cherokee removal. He joined the Confederate cause in 1861 as commissary general of the Provisional Army of Tennessee. In September 1861 he accepted the rank of major as commander of the Brigade Commissary in Knoxville Tennessee, where he was part of General Felix Zollicoffer's command. In May 1862 Richard became the organizing colonel of the Sixty-third Regiment of Tennessee Volunteers, but because of ill health he resigned his commission in November 1863.[1] Richard was pardoned by President Andrew Johnson in October 1865 and took the oath of loyalty to the United States. On July 5, 1869, he was re-enrolled as a voter in Hawkins County.

Richard was a merchant and bank officer in Rogersville, clerk and master of chancery court, and president of the Rogersville and Jefferson Railroad before the Civil War. From 1839 to 1841 and

1. According to records in the National Archives, the Sixty-third Tennessee Regiment was also known as the Seventy-fourth and as Fain's Regiment. The archives also contain a letter dated October 20, 1863, and written from Missionary Ridge, in which Richard Fain tendered his resignation. That letter included a statement from an army surgeon about Richard: "I certify that I have carefully examined Co. R. G. Fain 63rd Tenn Regt and find him unable to perform the duties of this office because of chronic disease of the liver and peculiar irritability of the system which prostrates him on the least exposure. I therefore recommend his discharge from service." *Compiled Service Records of Confederate Soldiers Who Served in Organizations from the State of Tennessee* (Washington, D.C.: National Archives and Records Administration, Microfilm Publications), RG109, M268, Roll 347.

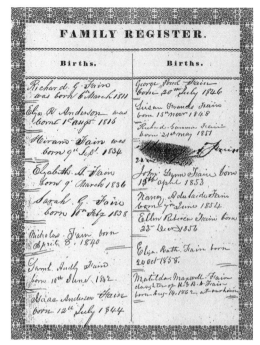

A page from Richard and Eliza Fain's family Bible, on which they recorded their dates of birth as well as those of their thirteen children and first grandchild. From the John N. Fain Collection, East Tennessee History Center.

from 1842 to 1845, he was postmaster of Rogersville. His postwar experiences are best summed up by this line from his obituary: "When the war closed it found him broken in health and broken in fortune but he struggled on manfully until death came."

Eliza and Richard had thirteen children. They are listed below in order of their birth. All of the children except John Lynn reached adulthood, but five of them died of tuberculosis between the ages of twenty-one and thirty-five. One daughter remained single, but the other seven children married at the average age of twenty-nine, giving Eliza twenty-seven grandchildren. Sallie married a distant cousin, Sam Fain, whose piety and wealth made him the ideal son-in-law. None of Eliza's sons ever seemed to meet her expectations and, except for Powell and Hiram, married Yankee girls. What is known about each child is summarized below.

Hiram, the oldest child of Eliza, was born on September 9, 1834, and died on January 5, 1869, in Rogersville Tennessee. He was named for an uncle who lived in Rogersville. Hiram died at age thirty-four, leaving a pregnant wife, Bettie Lyons (born on October 15, 1839; died on February 13, 1884), and three small children under the age of six: Matilda (Maxie), born in 1862; David, born in 1865; and Sam, born in 1867. The fourth child was Anna Rhea, born on August 27, 1869. Hiram and Bettie Fain are buried in marked graves at the New Providence Presbyterian Church cemetery some ten miles east of Rogersville. Hiram and Bettie were married in 1859; she was the daughter of David Lyons of Surgoinsville. Hiram enlisted in June 1861 in the Confederate service as a quartermaster (general staff, assistant commissary subsistence). In 1862 he joined the Sixty-third Tennessee, which his father had organized, and served until April 1864 in the commissary division. In August 1864, holding the rank of assistant commissary, he was transferred to Gracie's brigade by order of General Archibald Gracie. Upon returning home from the war, Hiram pursued farming, but he died four years later from tuberculosis that he may have contracted while in the army. There is no indication that Hiram's widow, Bettie, ever remarried; the 1880 census lists her as living in Hawkins County with her four children.

Elizabeth, or Lizzie, the oldest daughter of Eliza, was born on March 9, 1836, and died in 1904 in Rogersville. She was also known as "Liz" and seems to have been the unmarried daughter who lived with her mother and, subsequently, her brother Powell until her death. There is no evidence that Lizzie was ever gainfully employed during her lifetime.

Sallie, Eliza's second daughter, was born on February 10, 1838, in Rogersville, Tennessee; she died on November 12, 1912, in Mossy Creek, Tennessee. Sallie taught school, and after the war she was hired by a distant cousin, Sam Fain of Mossy Creek (now Jefferson City), to be a governess for the children of his deceased sister, Martha Fain Ross, who were living with him. Sam was an affluent bachelor and forty-six years old when he married Sallie in 1867. Sam appears to have provided a job for Richard Fain as long as he was able to work and subsequently provided the majority of support for Eliza until her death. Sam and Sallie had five children: Lida, Martha, John, Frances, and Elizabeth. John became a college professor, as did Elizabeth. Martha was for many years the secretary to Dr. Charles W. Dabney, president of the University of Tennessee and later the University of Cincinnati. None of these children ever married.

Nicholas, the second son of Eliza, was born on April 8, 1840, in Rogersville, Tennessee; he died in 1900 in Carrollton, Georgia. Nicholas was named for his grandfather but went by Nick. During the Civil War Nick joined the Nineteenth Tennessee Infantry Regiment (C.S.A.) in May 1861 and served as a private in Company K, known as the Hawkins County Boys. In October 1862 Nick joined Company B of the Sixtieth Tennessee Mounted Infantry Regiment with the rank of second lieutenant. His brigade was captured near Vicksburg in May 1863. Nick, along with his first cousin Sam Gammon, who served as the captain of his company, were subsequently held prisoner at Johnson's Island until February 1865. Nick left Rogersville after the war and moved to Carrollton, Georgia. He married Annie Kingsbury on March 21, 1878. Seven months later, their first child, Mary, was born on October 26, 1878. They had two other children, Richard and Kate.

Sam, Eliza's third son, was born on June 10, 1842, and died on August 26, 1874, in Rogersville, Tennessee. Sam joined Company K of the Nineteenth Tennessee in May 1861. In 1862 he joined the Sixty-third Tennessee as a private when it was organized by his father; he was promoted to first sergeant in January 1863. Sam accompanied that unit to Virginia in 1864. He returned to Rogersville in January 1865 and was serving in a home guard when he sustained a serious injury to his leg.[2] After the war Sam was a grocery salesman working out of Baltimore. He never

---

2. Sam had attempted to transfer to the Twelfth Tennessee Cavalry Battalion but was not approved. In late March a cousin serving with the Sixty-third Tennessee wrote to him, saying that he could return to the Sixty-third and "all will be fine," as the soldier who was supposed to have switched places with him after he left had never shown up. However, because the letter was mistakenly addressed to Sam in care of the Twelfth Tennessee, he probably never received it. In any event, the war ended only a month later. The letter to Sam is contained in the National Archives (*Compiled Service Records . . . Tennessee*, Roll 52).

married and died of consumption. Sam is buried in a marked grave at the old Presbyterian cemetery in Rogersville.

Ike, the fourth son of Eliza, was born on July 12, 1844, in Rogersville; he died in June 1917 in Chariton, Iowa. Joining the Sixty-third Tennessee when it was organized by his father, he initially held the rank of sergeant in Company C but was demoted to private in December 1862. Ike first served as an orderly for his father, but in June 1863 he was appointed forage master. He did not go to Virginia with the Sixty-third Tennessee in 1864 and was removed from the regimental roll by Colonel Abraham Fulkerson. Ike then joined a local cavalry unit, Company A of the Twelfth Tennessee Cavalry Battalion, serving near Rogersville for the remainder of the war. Ike had a hot temper and was accused of being involved in the murder of William Bird, a Union sympathizer, while part of the home guard in 1861. Near the end of the war, he was accused of the theft of three horses from William Alvis, a local resident, and briefly jailed for his alleged involvement in the Bird murder in 1866. Ike was later arrested for his role in a July 1867 riot in Rogersville and left town afterwards for Iowa. On November 23, 1876, Ike married Mattie James in Chariton, Iowa, and they had four children: Lillie Belle, Richard Rhea, Olive Earnestine, and Jessie, who died as a child. Ike's obituary from the Chariton newspaper described him as one of the town's most prominent citizens.

Powell, the fifth son of Eliza, was born on July 7, 1846, and died on July 1, 1914, in Rogersville. Powell lived nearly all of his life in Rogersville, where he was a salesman for various businesses and postmaster for a brief period. He appears to have been a popular and genial man and was thought by his mother to have a drinking problem. However, his obituary describes him as a widely and favorably known Christian gentleman and a member of one of the area's pioneer families. He served in the Sixtieth Tennessee (C.S.A.) near the end of the war. On January 15, 1880, Powell married his first cousin and nearby neighbor Sarah (Sallie) Fain. A daughter of Hiram Fain, Sallie was born on April 7, 1854, and died on March 14, 1929, in Rogersville. She and Powell had seven children: Will Rhea, Sam

Nicholas, Robert Rogan, Nelle, Richard Gammon, Hiram Bradford, and Lady Julia. The couple lived in the home of Richard and Eliza Fain until it burned in 1897.[3] Powell is buried in a marked grave in the new Presbyterian cemetery in Rogersville.

Fannie, the third daughter of Eliza, was born on November 15, 1848, and died of tuberculosis on June 17, 1914, in Rogersville. Fannie's first marriage was rather unhappy. She married Amos Smith, aged thirty-eight, on September 19, 1876. Amos had been a lieutenant in Company B of the Nineteenth Tennessee. They had two sons, Lee Jackson and Richard Fain Smith. Apparently, Amos had great difficulty holding a job, and judging from Eliza's comments in her postwar diaries, he seems to have been an alcoholic. After the death of Amos, Fannie married R. V. Campbell of Rogersville. According to her obituary, Fannie was for many years a member of the Rogersville Presbyterian Church and lived a consistent, devoted Christian life. Fannie is buried in the new Presbyterian cemetery in Rogersville in a marked grave.

Dick, the sixth son of Eliza, was born on May 21, 1851, in Rogersville; he died in 1922 at Carrollton, Illinois. Dick went to Jerseyville, Illinois, in 1872 where he taught school for four years. He stayed in the area and subsequently entered the mercantile business and pursued farming. His obituary describes him as follows: "Mr. Fain was a genial, courteous, kindly gentleman. He held strictly to his own ideas of right and wrong, but accorded to others the right to their own views." In other words, he was as sure of the rightness of his opinions as his mother had been during the Civil War. Dick married a Yankee woman, Julia Brace, and her descendants said that she was never quite accepted by her husband's family. Dick and Julia were married in Carrollton, Illinois, on April 25, 1880. They had one son, Brace, born on December 25, 1880.

3. In 1914, shortly after Powell's death, Sallie applied for a pension that Tennessee provided to indigent widows of former Confederate soldiers. In that application she declared that her husband had no property; this indicates that Powell had either never purchased Eliza's farm or had sold it prior to his death. Tennessee Confederate Pension Applications—Widows, Tennessee State Library and Archives, Nashville, Case 5520, Roll W30, microfilm.

John Lynn, the seventh son of Eliza, was born on April 15, 1853, and died on April 25, 1853, in Rogersville.

Nannie, Eliza's fourth daughter, was born on June 7, 1854, and died of tuberculosis on May 13, 1876, in Rogersville. Her death is described in Eliza's diaries, and her obituary described her in flowery Victorian words: "She was one of the wise virgins and was ready to meet and welcome the Immortal Bridegroom and go with Him to the mansion of eternity. She had lived a pure and harmless life, and while her death is a sad loss to society, she is the gainer by the change." Nannie is buried in a marked grave in the old Presbyterian cemetery in Rogersville.

Ellen R., also called Ella, was the fifth daughter of Eliza. She was born on December 23, 1856, in Rogersville. She died of tuberculosis on December 30, 1879, in Mossy Creek, Tennessee.

Eliza, also known as Silla or Lillie, was Eliza's sixth daughter. She was born on October 25, 1858, in Rogersville; she died of tuberculosis on April 3, 1882, in Mossy Creek. Her obituary states: "For some time past Miss Lillie had been declining under the slow but sure ravages of consumption." This statement is probably an accurate description of what the last few years of life were like for not just Lillie but also her sisters Ella and Nannie. Ella and Lillie are buried along with Richard and Eliza Fain in the new Presbyterian cemetery in Rogersville. There is an imposing monument marking their graves.

Samuel Rhea (Sam) Gammon, who was born on January 26, 1837, and died in August 1879, was actually Eliza's nephew. His mother, Eliza's sister Nancy, had died six weeks after his birth, and he looked on Eliza as his surrogate mother. In the diaries it is sometimes difficult to tell whether references to Sam are to her son or her nephew. Never married, Sam was the organizing captain of Company B in the Sixtieth Tennessee Mounted Infantry. After the war ended, Sam taught school in Jerseyville, Illinois, for a year, then moved to Memphis, where he was a lawyer for thirteen years. There are numerous references to Sam in the postwar diaries, and many have to do with his drinking problem, which is referred to obliquely in his obituary: "That he had faults is only to say he was a man, but even these were against himself more than others." Sam Gammon is buried in the old Presbyterian cemetery in Rogersville beside his cousins Nannie and Sam Fain.

## *Other Relatives of Eliza Fain*

Audley Anderson, Eliza's father, was born on March 11, 1785, and died of measles on April 5, 1818, in Blountville, Tennessee. He married Elizabeth Rhea on January 30, 1812, and, upon his death, left his wife and four daughters: Fanny Rhea, Rebeckah Maxwell, Eliza Rhea, and Nancy Audley. The Andersons were a prominent family in Sullivan County, and Audley was a merchant in Blountville prior to his death. Audley was the son of John Anderson, who married Rebeckah Maxwell on January 12, 1775. John's parents, William and Elizabeth Campbell Anderson, were both emigrants from Ireland.

Elizabeth Rhea, the mother of Eliza, was born on December 28, 1779, and died on April 4, 1853, in Blountville, Tennessee. The oldest of nine children, she was the daughter of Joseph Rhea Jr., an Irish emigrant, and Frances Breden. Elizabeth was twenty-two years old when she married Audley Anderson. After her husband's death in 1818, she lived with her unmarried brother, Samuel Rhea, a wealthy merchant and pious Presbyterian in Blountville, Tennessee. Sam Rhea moved out of the house after marrying Ann Rutledge in 1826 but returned after Ann's death in 1827 with their infant son, Samuel Rhea Jr. Elizabeth Anderson and her daughters (especially Eliza) raised Sam Rhea Jr. until his father married Martha Lynn on January 8, 1832, five months before Elizabeth married Nicholas Fain of Rogersville. The Rhea family was one of the most distinguished pioneer families of East Tennessee. Elizabeth Rhea's uncle, John Rhea, had been a prominent figure in eighteenth-century Tennessee.

Nicholas Fain of Rogersville, the father of Eliza's husband, was born on February 4, 1782; he died on July 2, 1849, in Rogersville. He was the son of Captain John Fain, who was married to Agnes McMahan and later killed by the Indians. Nicholas's grandfather, also named Nicholas Fain, came to Pennsylvania in about 1753 from Ireland. The first Nicholas Fain was of French Huguenot extraction, and his wife was Elizabeth Taylor, an English woman. The younger Nicholas married Sallie Gammon on June 26, 1806. Sallie's father was a prosperous early settler, and after his marriage Nicholas Fain worked in the mercantile business in Blountville with his father-in-law. In 1814, however, Nicholas moved to Rogersville and continued in business until about 1843, when he retired to Springvale, the brick home he had erected in 1829 two miles east of Rogersville on a large farm. Nicholas Fain built the first brick house in Rogersville and was the first mayor of the town, as well as postmaster from 1823 to 1839. Although he was reportedly educated for the law, Nicholas probably accumulated much of his wealth from land speculation, horse trading, and storekeeping.

Sallie Gammon, the mother of Eliza's husband, was born on January 19, 1875, and died on April 25, 1831, in Rogersville, Tennessee. She was the first wife of Nicholas Fain and the daughter of Richard Gammon of Sullivan County, who was born in 1750 in London, England. Richard Gammon married Sarah Gamble in 1781. Nicholas Fain married Eliza's mother, Elizabeth Anderson, on May 1, 1832, almost eighteen months before Richard and Eliza were married on December 17, 1833. In a letter (now contained in the John N. Fain Collection) dated May 5, 1832, to his sister Eliza, Richard said that he had just learned of his father's impending marriage to a widow with two unmarried daughters. One sentence reads: "I anticipate much pleasure indeed in the company of the sisters during my stay at home in July." Rogersville chronicler R. Clay Crawford said many years later that Eliza and Richard had been married with their parents in a double wedding, but that was just an embellishment of a good story.

Many of the names mentioned frequently in Eliza's diaries are those of her relatives. Especially prominent are her sisters, who all married between the ages of sixteen and eighteen. Three of the sisters (including Eliza) had eleven, twelve, and thirteen children, while the fourth sister, Nancy, died at the age of nineteen shortly after the birth of her first child. Eliza died at age seventy-five, while the other two sisters, Fanny and Becky, lived for forty-four and forty-nine years, respectively, which was not unusual in those days for mothers of a dozen children. Eliza had a total of twenty-six nieces and nephews on her side of the family, while her husband had twenty-seven, for a combined total of fifty-two. Also, Eliza had sixty-three first cousins on her mother's side of the family, the Rheas.

Fanny Rhea Anderson, Eliza's oldest sister, was born on November 8, 1812, at the home of Joseph Rhea; she died in 1856 in Nashville, Tennessee. In 1930, when she was about the age of eighteen, she married W. R. McAlister and lived with him in Nashville. Fanny had thirteen children, and one of her grandsons, Harry Hill McAlister (1875–1959), served as governor of Tennessee from 1933 to 1937.

The other of Eliza's older sisters, Rebeckah (Becky) Maxwell Anderson, was born on September 8, 1814, and died on March 21, 1863, in Blountville, Tennessee. She married William Gammon in 1831 at age seventeen and had eleven children.

Nancy Audley Anderson, Eliza's younger sister, was born on February 28, 1818, and died on March 3, 1837. She was sixteen years old when she married Abraham (Abram) Looney Gammon on June 17, 1834, and died not quite three years later. Six weeks before her death, she gave birth to a son, Samuel Rhea Gammon.

Hiram Fain, a brother of Eliza's husband, was born on May 19, 1807, and died on January 12, 1879, in Rogersville, Tennessee. On April 5, 1842, Hiram married Mrs. Sarah Petty, who was born on February 12, 1819, and died on September 17, 1901. Hiram and Sarah lived in Springvale, which was up a lane from the frame house of Richard and Eliza Fain. Their oldest son, Ernest (called "Pete"), was born on January 29, 1844, and died in 1918 in Rogersville. He served in the Sixty-third Tennessee and married Sallie Glover on March 30, 1869, in Bartlett, Tennessee. Their first son, Clarence, was born on November 9, 1869. Ernest later married Amanda Carter on February 23, 1885. Lucie Fain, Hiram and Sarah's second child, was born on October 9, 1846, and died on February 13, 1910. Lucie first married Henry Smith and later Will Price. The facts about Hiram and Sarah Fain's other children are as follows: Nicholas was born on August 5, 1848, and died on October 30, 1863; Ida was born on December 20, 1851, and died on November 30, 1902; Sarah (Sallie), was born on April 9, 1854, married Powell Fain (Eliza's son) on January 15, 1880, and died on March 14, 1929; Cornelia Fain was born on January 2, 1857, and died on November 15, 1863; and Tom (Tomy) Fain was born on April 6, 1861, and died on December 10, 1863.

Nancy Fain, a sister of Eliza's husband, was born on July 19, 1809, and died in 1880. Nancy married James McCarty, aged twenty-seven, on October 4, 1826, when she was only seventeen, against the wishes of her mother. Nicholas Fain even sued his son-in-law once and in his will left Nancy's share of his estate in trust. James McCarty died in 1855. He was sheriff of Hawkins County three times between 1826 and 1848. He and Nancy had the following children: Sarah, born in 1827; Annis, born in 1829 and married to Lewis Poats in 1855; Mollie, born in 1832; Jennie, born in 1834; Nick, born in 1836 and a member of the Nineteenth Tennessee; Alice (called "Bug"), born in 1838; Kyle, born in 1842 and a member of the Nineteenth Tennessee; Mike, born in 1844 and a member of the Sixtieth Tennessee Mounted Infantry (C.S.A.); and Buena Vista, born in 1846.

John Hammer Fain, a brother of Eliza's husband, was born on May 23, 1813, and died on August 29, 1853. John was a bachelor who lived with Richard and Eliza for at least a few years prior to his death at age forty. He apparently had a drinking problem and is said to have died of dissipation complicated with consumption.

His share of his father's estate was also left in trust, indicating that Nicholas did not feel that John was a responsible person.

Eliza Ruth Fain, a sister of Eliza's husband, was born on April 15, 1815, and died on February 24, 1872. Eliza Ruth married George Powel (1807–1873) on August 11, 1836. George was the son of Judge Samuel and Mary Rutledge Powel, one of the leading families of Rogersville. George Powel was a successful businessman whose reported wealth of eighty thousand dollars for the 1860 census made him the second richest man in Rogersville after Charles McKinney, whose assets totaled ninety-five thousand dollars. George was educated for the law and lived in Rogersville, where he was circuit court clerk from 1840 to 1852, then master of chancery court from 1855 to 1858. George served as a representative to the General Assembly of Tennessee as did his brother Samuel Powel. George and Eliza Ruth Powel had nine sons and one daughter. The oldest, Richard Powel, was born on April 4, 1837, and married Sally Blevins (1838–1923) on September 9, 1857; he served as a captain in Company C of the Sixty-third Tennessee. Sam Powel was born on January 13, 1839; he married first Mec (or Meg) Walker (1843–1878) and later V. Walker (1840–1915), both daughters of Colonel John Walker. Sam was a second lieutenant in Company K of the Nineteenth Tennessee. Fain Powel, born in 1840, married Ann Armstrong, then Addie McDeermid; he was rejected for Confederate military service. Tom Powel, born on September 1, 1842, married Becky Earnest, a second cousin, and was a second lieutenant in the Sixty-third Tennessee. George Rutledge Powel, born on June 4, 1844, died of fever on October 22, 1862, while serving as a sergeant in the Sixty-third Tennessee. The other children were Ed Powel, born in 1846; Mollie Powel, born in 1848; Bob Powel, born in 1850; Charles Powel, born in 1853 or 1854; and Jim Powel, born in 1855.

George Gammon Fain, a brother of Eliza's husband, was born on December 4, 1816, and died on October 3, 1877. George was a store clerk or teacher for most of his life. Although he never married, there is a mention in Eliza's diaries that he fathered a daughter who was born in about 1845. He also appears to have sired at least two other children by a woman named Moring Sillivan (or Morning Sullivan), who might have been a common-law wife. The son went by the name of John Graham Fain. George enlisted as a sergeant in December 1861 in Company D of the Fourth Tennessee Cavalry (C.S.A.), eventually serving in Henry M. Ashby's Second Tennessee Cavalry Regiment. He was later discharged for nervous debility.

The Reverend Sam Rhea Jr., a first cousin of Eliza and the son of the brother of Eliza's mother, was born in 1827 and died in 1865. Sam was more like a brother than a cousin to Eliza, having spent his early years in the care of Eliza's mother. Educated at the University of Tennessee and Union Theological Seminary in New York, Sam Rhea became a missionary to Persia (Iran). His father supported him financially while he served in the mission field. His memoirs were published after his death, and Eliza was distressed by his antislavery and pro-Union positions.

Jonathan (Johnny) Bachman was a first cousin of Eliza and the orphaned son of Fannie Rhea Bachman, a sister of Eliza's mother. He was born in 1837 as one of ten children. Cousin Johnnie studied at Blountville Academy, then at Emory and Henry College, followed by Union Theological Seminary. He resigned from the seminary to enter the Confederate army as a private in the Nineteenth Tennessee, Company K (C.S.A.), along with Sam and Nick Fain. In the summer of 1862 Jonathan organized a company for the Sixtieth Tennessee (C.S.A.) and was its captain. This regiment surrendered at Vicksburg in 1863, and Jonathan became a paroled prisoner of war. Subsequently he became a chaplain, and at the close of the war he was elected pastor of the New Providence and Rogersville Southern Presbyterian Churches. In 1873 he became pastor of the First Presbyterian Church of Chattanooga, where he served for more than fifty years. His son, Nathan Bachman, was for a time a United States senator from Tennessee in the twentieth century.

# *African Americans Mentioned by Name in the Diary*

In the 1860 slave census,[4] the following eight individuals were listed as property of Richard Fain: a sixty-year-old black male, a thirty-year-old black male, a twenty-one-year-old mulatto male, an eleven-year-old mulatto male, an eight-year-old mulatto male, a five-year-old mulatto female, a three-year-old mulatto male, and a fifty-year-old black female. The mother of the three youngest children had been the wife of Gus (apparently the thirty-year-old male listed above); she was named Mary and had died on February 25, 1858. Eliza and Richard Fain also rented another slave named Caroline; thus, five adult slaves and four slave children were living with them at the start of the Civil War in 1861. The known facts about these individuals, as well as other African Americans who are mentioned in Eliza's diary, are as follows:

Ahab came as a slave from Nicholas Fain and is first mentioned in 1846. He died in 1870. Eliza provided the clothes for his burial. He is apparently the sixty-year-old male listed in the 1860 census.

Amy Martin is first mentioned in 1864. A pregnant free woman, she was allowed to live for a while in one of Eliza's cabins. When her child died shortly after she gave birth, Amy was asked to leave. Eliza was upset with what she considered to be Amy's immoral conduct and lack of industry. Amy apparently continued to live near the Fain farm after the war, for in an 1876 diary entry Eliza notes that Amy had come by to ask for soap grease.

Caroline, also known as Carrie, was rented in 1858 from a Margaret Watterson for fifty-two dollars a year for housework. Caroline's father was known as Uncle Joe. Caroline married Frank McCarty in 1859, a slave in one of the Heiskell households

---

4. Slave Schedules of Hawkins County, Tennessee, *Eighth Census of the United States, 1860* (Washington, D.C.: National Archives and Records Administration, Microfilm Publications), RG029, M653, Roll 1282.

Sale agreement for the 1854 purchase of a slave named Gus by Richard Fain from Alexander Hale for nine hundred dollars. From the John N. Fain Collection, East Tennessee History Center.

(see opposite). She left with Frank on April 11, 1865, but they clearly did not venture far, since numerous payments to them for work were recorded in the postwar period.

Cindy, the five-year-old female mulatto in the 1860 census, was also known as Lucinda, Linda, Liz, Gen, or Erin. She was born on March 27, 1855, to Mary. Cindy left in August 1865 but reappeared in 1873 with a three-week-old infant who died a week later. Cindy died in 1883, leaving two children, and was buried by the Fains.

Augustus, or Gus, was purchased in 1854 from a man named Alexander Hale for $990 and was apparently the thirty-year-old black male of the 1860 census. Gus left the Fains in the summer of 1865 but evidently stayed in the vicinity, since there were numerous payments to him for work in the postwar period.

Hill, the twenty-one-year-old male mulatto of the 1860 slave census, was a son of Polly (see below). Born in about 1839, he was sent to live with a cousin in 1857 because the Fains could not manage him. However, Hill worked for the Fains after the war, and in 1874 Ike Fain sent him his (Hill's) photograph.

Jim, the eight-year-old mulatto male of the 1860 slave census, was born on January 12, 1853, to Mary.

> *Hired of A. Watterson, administrator of the estate of Margaret Watterson, deceased, Caroline, a slave belonging to said estate for the term of twelve months next ensuing; for value received in said Caroline's services, we promise to pay unto said A. Watterson the full sum of fifty two dollars, at the expiration of the above term of service. And further subject to the following conditions, viz said slave Caroline is to be kept in Hawkins County, Tenn. Necepary & timely medical aid & attention is to be given to her, said Caroline in cases of sickness &c. befalling her, during said term of service at the charges of the hirer and he is also to furnish her with all necepary & comfortable clothing in addition to her above wages; during said term, without any charges to the said estate. Witnep our hands & seals.—*
>
> *March 1st 1861.*

Rental agreement for the slave Caroline in 1861. Richard Fain agreed to pay fifty-two dollars per year to the estate of Margaret Watterson and furnish Caroline with "necessary and comfortable clothing." According to the 1860 census, Margaret Watterson owned twenty-four slaves. From the John N. Fain Collection, East Tennessee History Center.

Lewis was another of Polly's sons and appears in the 1860 slave census as the eleven-year-old male mulatto. He left the Fain household in 1863 with Federal troops.

Margaret Brice or Fain, a former field hand, was a homeless freedwoman who apparently came to live with her mother, Polly, in 1865 on Eliza's place.

Mary Martin was apparently a free black woman since there are documents indicating that she was owed various amounts prior to 1861 to sew clothes for the Fains and some of their slaves. This Mary was the daughter of Peggy Martin and a sister of Amy Martin. Peggy Martin died in 1863.

Nate, was born on August 23, 1856, and appears in the 1860 census as the three-year-old male mulatto. He was a son of Mary, the deceased wife of Gus.

Peggy Martin, the mother of Mary and Amy Martin, died on October 2, 1863, and was apparently a free black woman.

Polly was the fifty-year-old black female listed in the 1860 slave census. She came with Eliza from Blountville and was the mother of Lewis and Hill.

Of the African Americans described above, the following were living in Eliza's household as of January 1863: Ahab, Caroline, Cindy, Gus, Hill, Jim, Lewis, Nate, and Polly.

## *Rogersville Residents Mentioned in the Diary*

William Bird was a sixty-year-old man mentioned in the December 26, 1861, entry of Eliza's diary, where she gives an account of his death at the hands of local Confederate soldiers. Exactly why he was killed is unknown, although it might have related to a dispute that arose prior to the war. Sam and Ike Fain may have been involved in his death because in August 1866 Ike was arrested by William O. Sizemore, a former Unionist guerilla who had become the constable and special deputy sheriff for Hawkins County. The capias issued by the circuit court charged Ike with "being present, aiding and abetting in the murder of old man Wm. Bird." Ike was jailed but later released, after which he moved to Iowa. When Reconstruction ended, most such cases were dropped because of the difficulty in obtaining convictions, and this was apparently the case with Ike.

Abraham Fulkerson was the lieutenant colonel of the Sixty-third Tennessee Infantry Regiment, which was organized in 1862

*Map, Facing Page:* The Rogersville area of East Tennessee, taken from "A Geological Map of Tennessee" by J. M. Safford published in 1869. Rogersville is located in the relatively narrow Holston River Valley between the Bays Mountains and the Clinch Mountains. It is evident why the railroad—and later the interstate highway system—bypassed Rogersville in favor of the relatively wide central valley between the Bays Mountains and the Great Smoky Mountains (identified as the Unaka Chain on this map). Morristown is at the junction of the two railroads identified on this map, but at the time of the Civil War the line between Tazewell and Newport had not yet been built. The point at which the railroad crosses the mountains just below the Bays Mountain Group is the location of Bulls Gap; however, the branch railroad that connected Bulls Gap to Rogersville is not shown on the map. From the private collection of John and Ann Fain.

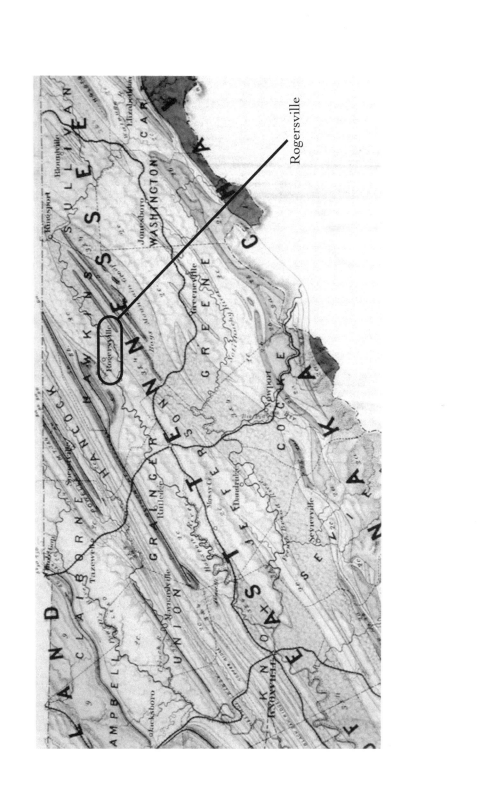

Rogersville

with Richard Fain as its colonel. Shortly before the Battle of Chickamauga, Fulkerson took over the command after Richard resigned because of ill health. The unit took 404 men into this battle, and half were killed or wounded. The next year the regiment went to the Virginia front. Three hundred men fought in the Battle of Drewry's Bluff in 1864, but again half were killed or wounded. Colonel Fulkerson was captured, and for the remainder of the war he was imprisoned at the Federal prisons of Morris Island, Fort Pulaski, and Fort Delaware. The regiment remained under the command of General Robert E. Lee, but only twenty-eight men were with the regiment when they surrendered at Appomattox.

Fulkerson was a graduate of the Virginia Military Institute and was wounded in the Battle of Shiloh while serving as a major in the Nineteenth Tennessee Infantry Regiment. He was also severely wounded in the Battle of Drewry's Bluff. After the war he moved to Bristol, Virginia, where he practiced law and lived until 1902. He was elected to the Virginia legislature and in 1880 to the United States House of Representatives. In a history of the Sixty-third Tennessee Regiment that he wrote twenty years after the war, he had this to say: "The demons of war took possession of innocent and quiet homes, and reveled there until long after peace had been restored elsewhere. And yet, while there is much to deplore in the animosities engendered and the excesses perpetrated in this fratricidal war, we have reason to be proud of the courage and manhood exhibited by the citizen soldiers who went forth and confronted death at each other's hands for what they conceived to be the right. The descendants of the men who turned the tide of war at King's Mountain, New Orleans and Buena Vista should not be enemies of each other. Let us beat our swords into plowshares, and our spears into pruning hooks, and learn war no more; or, if we must fight, let it be with a common foe, shoulder to shoulder, in all time to come."[5]

5. Abraham Fulkerson, "Sixty-third Tennessee Infantry," in *The Military Annals of Tennessee, Confederate: First Series: Embracing a View of Military Operations*, ed. John Berrien Lindsley (Nashville: J. M. Lindsley, 1886), 584–95.

Frank Fulkerson was a nephew of Abraham Fulkerson and served during the Civil War in the Sixty-third Tennessee. He was born in 1825 and died in 1894. He was married to Elizabeth Hale and later to Penelope (Neppie) Neill. He was an elder in the Rogersville Presbyterian church and among the close friends of Eliza and Richard Fain.

C. W. Heiskell enlisted in Company K of the Nineteenth Tennessee as a private. However, he was soon elected captain of the company and eventually became colonel of the regiment. He married Eliza Netherland, who was a daughter of John Netherland, a prominent Rogersville citizen and unsuccessful Whig candidate for governor in 1860. Heiskell was a member of the Presbyterian Church and after the war moved to Memphis, where he became a prominent attorney and circuit court judge.

Joseph B. Heiskell was C. W. Heiskell's brother and son of Judge F. H. Heiskell. He was elected to the first Confederate Congress. After his capture in Rogersville by Union troops, he was kept a prisoner for the remainder of the Civil War. He was one of the former Rebels who were warned to leave Rogersville, but when he moved to Memphis, the Unionists used the murder-warrant procedure in an attempt to bring him back to Rogersville. A deputy came from Rogersville to arrest him, but a sympathetic judge intervened by arresting Heiskell for treason and then releasing him as soon as the deputy left town. After Reconstruction J. B. Heiskell became attorney general of Tennessee.[6]

Nan Kinkead was among the Fains' nearby neighbors and a friend of Eliza's daughters. She also kept diaries that became the basis of a book entitled *Miss Nan: Beloved Rebel* by Margaret Lyons Smith. There are numerous references in the Kinkead diary to the Fains, and Eliza's diary also mentions Nan many times. Rowena Kinkead (sometimes called Row) was Nan's sister and another friend of Eliza's daughters. The Kinkeads lived four miles east of Rogersville, and like the Fains they were Confederate supporters.

6. Helen M. Coppock and Charles W. Crawford, eds., *Paul R. Coppock's Mid-South*, vol. 2 (Memphis: Paul R. Coppock Publication Trust, 1992), 116–20.

Absalom Arthur Kyle, born in 1812, was a well-known Whig lawyer in Rogersville and knew Andrew Johnson. Before the war he served as a district attorney general for the First Judicial Circuit of Tennessee, and for this reason Eliza referred to him as "General" Kyle. There is no record of his having served in the military on either side during the war. A conservative Unionist who opposed secession, Kyle served as Richard Fain's lawyer when Richard applied for a pardon after the war.

W. C. Kyle was a Union supporter, but there is no record of any military service by him. His wife, Alice Kyle, was a friend of Eliza's and a member of the Presbyterian Church. Though described by his son as a merchant and slave trader before the war,[7] Kyle opposed secession and was a Hawkins County representative to Unionist conventions in 1861.[8]

George and Orleana Merrimon were neighbors of the Fains who are described as living two and a half miles east of Rogersville, probably between the Fains' home and the river. Their farm adjoined those of the Fains, Amises, Hales, and McKinneys. George had ten slaves consisting of five couples, and it is said that after the Civil War he gave each couple two acres and helped them to build cabins. The Merrimons had nine children. Two of their sons were killed in the war while serving on opposite sides. Their oldest son, William Merrimon, was born on May 6, 1839, and married Kitty Bates on February 12, 1861. He first served in Company B of the Sixtieth Tennessee Mounted Infantry of the Confederate army. He was captured at the Battle of Big Black and released in February 1864, at which point he returned to service but this time as a Union soldier (a decision that reportedly upset his wife). He died on March 5, 1865. Polly Merrimon was born on November 25, 1840, and married Thomas Hamblin in 1857. James Peyton (Jim) Merrimon was born on July 16, 1842, and died at the Battle of Drewry's Bluff in 1864 while

---

7. *Goodspeed's History of Tennessee, Illustrated*, East Tennessee Edition (Nashville: Goodspeed Publishing Co., 1887), 1230.

8. Temple, *East Tennessee and the Civil War*, 170, 353.

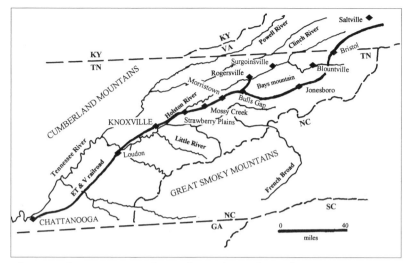

This map of East Tennessee during the Civil War shows the East Tennessee and Virginia Railroad as well as the Rogersville and Jefferson, which connected Bulls Gap to the Holston River near Rogersville. Map by John Fain.

serving in the Confederate army. The other Merrimon children were Mary Jane, who was born on December 13, 1843, and died on August 21, 1863; Susan, who was born in 1843 and died in 1849; George Wiley, who was born in 1849; Jessie, who was born in 1851; and Martha Ann, who was born in 1853.[9]

William O. Sizemore was the leader of a lawless band of Union sympathizers who are frequently mentioned in Eliza's diaries. Bill Sizemore was born in 1833 in the Clinch Valley, just north of Rogersville and was living in Rogersville in 1860 with a wife and three children. He was a shoemaker but listed no assets in the 1860 census. He enlisted on July 8, 1861, as a private in Simpson's Company of the Confederate army, but he obtained a discharge on October 24, 1862, claiming that he was over thirty-five years of age. However, he was in fact only twenty-nine, and his widow later said that he was discharged to make shoes. It actually appears that he had become disillusioned with military life and lied to get a release. Sizemore subsequently

9. Merrimon Family Papers, Hawkins County Public Library, Rogersville, Tenn.

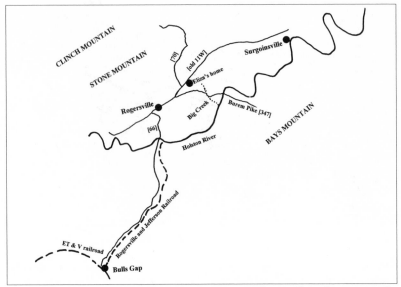

Rogersville and vicinity, with modern highways noted as well as the Rogersville and Jefferson Railroad at the time of the Civil War. The railroad bridge across the Holston River had not been completed at this time. Map by John Fain.

became the leader of a group of Unionist guerrillas. He may have served as a recruiting officer and scout for the Union army, as his family claimed after the war, but no existing official record indicates military service to the Union.

In the immediate postwar period, Bill Sizemore ran a hotel and was an officer of the law until he was killed on October 11, 1867, by Irodell Willis, one of his two chief aides during his time as a guerrilla leader. In 1866 Willis and Sizemore had become involved in lawsuits against each other. During the following year, Sizemore and some of his followers came to the home of Irodell Willis's mother, demanding to see him. When Willis's mother refused to tell them where her son was, she was so severely beaten that she died on August 19, 1867. Her son killed Sizemore to avenge her death.[10]

10. Donahue Bible, letter to John N. Fain, June 25, 1998. Bible is a local historian living in Mohawk, Tennessee. His work on General John C. Vaughan's brigade, *From Persia to Piedmont*, is a good source of information about Sizemore.

*The Diary of Eliza Rhea Anderson Fain,
a Confederate Woman in East Tennessee*

# *Chapter 1*

## *The Desolating Hand of Civil War Begins: 1861*

The secessionists started the year with high hopes for success in their attempts to defy the government of the United States. Their irrational zeal resulted in the start of the Civil War when hot-headed South Carolinians attacked Fort Sumter in April. Eliza supported the cause of secession with great enthusiasm and was happy to see her husband and three of her sons join the Confederate army after the fall of Fort Sumter. She had three younger sons who were seventeen, fifteen, and ten in 1861. However, as her diary entry for May 18 indicates, she was already aware that the Civil War would be an awful scourge.

Monday January 14, 1861
I have been reading tonight from the New York Observer, the Sentinel of the Country. All as yet seems to be hostile with no concession on the part of the North and no giving way in the South. O what is to be the result. I do fear South Carolina is not placing her trust in the mighty God of Israel. I see her legislature was in session on Sunday the 30th of Dec. I cannot feel a people safe who thus trample under foot the fourth commandment.

Thursday morning January 24, 1861

Gloomy this morning with a mist falling. Yesterday quite a cold day and sleeting the greater part of the day. I at home so happy with the loved of this precious place. Our political world still wears the aspect of hostility and want of love and patriotism. Today all is so dark and foreboding. Could the South present one unbroken phalanx to the North of love and peace in our own midst we would not long doubt the results. We as a people of the South have shown to the North the most unmistakable evidences of love and forbearance. What have we not done to conciliate and now the blow has been struck which forever seals our destiny in the election of a sectional President who takes into his hands the reins of our Federal government. He will appoint a cabinet of his own selection which the South cannot approve of. We are asked to submit to this rule without any definite arrangement for our rights as free born citizens. I for one feel indignant at such a thought. I love my country, I love her constitution. I love everything connected with her whole history, but the disposition I see in one portion of her to usurp entire control. I cannot find it in my heart to say I submit. Are we not inheritors of the same precious legacy bequeathed by our noble Southern ancestry. Shall we just lie still and become the dupes of northern fanaticism. Treat us as brethren or let us go so that we may treat each other as brethren of the same parentage. I was so distressed by a thought suggested by my husband. He told me that some of our own Southern born citizens were trying to set into motion the ball of discontent and dissatisfaction by saying we are not going to fight for their negroes. My soul sinks and exclaims have we traitors of that kind in our midst for if true in love of country have they counted the cost of such an expression. I feel no one living in the South could give vent to such expressions unless influenced by motives of the darkest dye or have spoken unwittingly not knowing the effect of such words in our community.

O Lord may I not become so excited as to lose sight of thy cause for it is that which I so much condemn in the North. I do feel they have tempered with thy holy word wresting and perverting its truths to such an extent that no ism however absurd is to be set aside if it will only subserve the machinations of wicked men.

Feb. 22, 1861

The sun has risen brightly upon our distracted country ushering in the 129th anniversary of our illustrious Washington (born Feb. 22, 1732) and is it true more than a century has passed since the birth of our nations father. His name has been transmitted to posterity so familiarly; how hard to realize that his life was passed; and he numbered with the triumphant throng before I had an existence; it may be said of him more than any human being; he lives always in our midst. The history of his boyhood, youth and manhood are familiar to almost every schoolboy or girl who have studied history.

We do feel he was an object of God's special care for the upbuilding of our mighty Republic. I have been deeply impressed with the thought could thy spirit Immortal Washington hover over our country and see and know the condition we are now in. Me thinks if nought could disturb the happiness of a redeemed spirit; thine would be in anguish; to see thy children for whom thou hast done so much; and to whom thou didst bequeath the richest legacy ever given to man; just on the verge of one of the most terrific revolutions ever recorded by man; and with no possible prospect on this day (so far as I know) of a peaceful adjustment. What didst thou sacrifice so much for: was it not that we might be a free people; that each section of our country might enjoy undisturbed her peculiar institutions; that each should have an equal right in all things pertaining to our form of government and that we should love one another.

March 4, 1861

On yesterday I attended church with my beloved husband and heard to me a most excellent sermon. Today is the inauguration of President

Lincoln. The struggle has come; the issue is being felt—may we O Lord know our duty. May we faithfully perform looking to Jesus who is our blessed saviour through the deep and dark scenes of life.

April 16, 1861

Raining, cold and dark; to human eye the prospect for farming is gloomy beyond anything I have known. The ground has been so wet for two weeks ploughing has not been thought of. I went into my garden yesterday. The beans that I had planted the 8th of March were lying in the ground some had sprouted others much swollen, whether they will come up or not I cannot tell. I replanted my beans, peas where missing. Put in a row of beans by the row of snowdrops. Had Hill & Jim[1] to working out my onions. O my Father do not frown upon us, but give us a season and may we yet have a plentiful harvest.

Our natural world is presenting the same gloomy phase with our political. Days are dark in the extreme in the history of our country. All overtures of peace from the South have been rejected. President Lincoln's assurance to the South of the evacuation of Fort Sumter are now regarded as false and being a delusion to lull the vigilance of the South and to enable the North to make all preparations for an attack. Will such duplicity be successful? It may be but I do not feel it can; for I have felt from the first the position of the North has been wrong. I feel they have set aside the word of God and in its stead have substituted their own wisdom for the upholding of their own selfish ends. Thus O God giveth to none thy power to govern or rule. Man is still at thy bidding and in thy power; thou canst say thus far and no further canst thou go; and may we O God feel willing yea glad that thou holdest the reins in thy own hands. Fort Sumter was attacked by the Confederate troops under the command of G. Beauregard on Friday morning at

---

1. Hill, born in about 1839 and a son of Polly, and Jim, born in 1853 and a son of Mary, were slaves belonging to Eliza and Richard Fain.

4. Gen. Anderson it is said has surrendered. May it O God close the scene of deadly strife and may we be willing for each section to have their rights without molestation.

April 18, 1861
After many days of cloud with scarcely an hour of sunshine; once more we are permitted to see in all its brightness the grand luminary of day shedding his reviving influence all around. May our loved land behold the rising of the reconciled face of the great son of righteousness. Never before in our country's history have we been called to witness such dark foreboding hours. Where, O where infinite eternal all wise God is it to cease. Are we bent on self destruction—is there no help with thee O my father in these dread hours to stay this overwhelming calamity I do beseech thee my God not to leave us to ourselves but show thyself in the vindication of whatsoever thou sees is right.

Fort Sumter has been taken without any serious loss of life. Only one as I understand and he killed so foolishly. General Anderson in firing a salute wounded some four or five killing this one. May we not hope O God that thy protecting care and power having been so signally manifested on this occasion will still be thrown around to preserve life. On Friday morning 4 o'clock Ft. Sumter was attacked—surrendered on Saturday at 1. The Fort greatly injured, the United States troops were lying outside the bar without any possible chance of succoring Anderson. May the South feel whose arm has been made bare in this engagement. My only hope is in Israel's God—if he is for us the united armies of the world conspire in vain for our destruction.

The horrors of battlefield scenes has been deeply impressed in my mind during the last 10 days. Nick has read to me the account of Napoleon (by Abbat) crossing the Alps to surprise and divert the Austrian troops from their intended destruction of the French Empire. The dreadful slaughter on the plains of Marengo fills me with feeling I have no language to express. Austria in Bonaparte's view might have saved that dreadful loss of life had she been willing to yield to what was right. But she felt I have the power now is my time to conquer. But did the God of Heaven so view it — methinks not for if ever man was aided from on high to accomplish a victory does it not seem to human view that Napoleon was at this time; the crossing of the Alps is one of the most wonderful displays of mans recklessness ever recorded; and one of the greatest displays of the protecting preserving care of God ever manifested to man. I have been greatly struck with what appears to me to be a striking contrast in the history of Austria with the North of the present time. The South have sued for peace upon all terms; consistent with the maintenance of her dignity of character; as a part of a free self governed people; how has she been treated with duplicity, intrigues and cunning which her high toned peace loving men, were not able to detect. Now what alternative has she left? None but to defend herself trusting in God, as I do hope she may do. May we be kept in peace O God because of our trust in thee.

April 24, 1861
How troubled I do feel sometimes. My whole soul seems to sink within me, O my Father can we not look to thee, is there no balm in Gilead, is there no physician there to heal our deadly difficulties. O hide not thyself from us, make us to know thee aright, let our trust be in thee; let us not sin against our Northern brethren, but O let us feel towards them as thou requires, if an enemy hunger let us feed him if he thirsts let us give him drink, O let us not be overcome with evil; but overcome evil with good, we do feel O God that we have been treated by the North in a most shameful manner, but we feel thy children are there and as such we love them and would not raise our hands to do them an injury. But ask of thee to give them wisdom from on high that they may know thee as a God of love. O why, may we not love one another; will Christianity, what we have always regarded as the purest Christianity, lie still and see the polluters of the earth rise and take possession of our happy country.

Can they see the laws of God violated in the most shameful manner, the Bible set aside for a higher law and feel I can bear all this but disturb not my repose. Let me know and feel I am a Christian. I care not for my brethren—O may this feeling never pervade the Southern Mind. I do feel this has been one of the sins of Northern Christians. They have felt because my brother or sister in the South is a slaveholder therefore I am holier than thou, I cannot hold fellowship with thee instead of having the 13 chapter of 1 Corinthians indelibly impressed and acting up to that they have rejected us and set at naught the word of God.

O could our Christian friends North come and live with us for a few months I do think it would greatly change their feelings toward us. Let a Northern woman come into one of our black peoples homes and there see stretched on a bed of sickness one of our servants—man, woman or child and see us in tender solicitude bending over the sufferer doing all that we can to relieve their sufferings, and then know the great anxiety we are often suffering in regard to their spiritual well being methinks you would turn from the spot and say if this is slavery so let it continue unmolested by me until the great head of the church sees fit to change it if it is his will. Our happy land that which has been the song and pride of so many hearts will never, while we live, be looked on as it has been. The world will soon know we do not love one another, O how sad how sad.

April 29, 1861

Peace is still a stranger in our beautiful land. Of all places of the earth none seems to have been so lavishly decorated as our own fair, yea fairest Republic but I fear the desolating hand of civil war. O can it be; my heart is stricken whenever those words arise in my mind *Civil War*. O dreadful thought. Shall the Christian brother rise against the Christian brother and stain his hands and heart in the blood of those for whom a dear Redeemer has made so costly a sacrifice. To me this is something so startling, so strange. I cannot, I never have been able to see the why or the wherefore of such a course. It is not for the good of our colored population. Every movement of Abolitionists have only been detrimental to that race physically, intellectually and morally. Poor creatures, O God wilt thou in thy good Providence not take this great matter into thine own hands. O may we of the South feel the high missionary ground upon which thou has placed us. Let us be faithful, let us ever feel they are a portion of thy creation for whom we of the South have the strongest anxieties for their eternal safety. We know O Father they have precious never dying souls. We know for them our dear Redeemer agonized on Calvary. We know too our heavenly Father they are capable of loving thee and of becoming the humblest of thy followers. May they prove loyal in this mighty conflict.

My heart was made to feel sad on yesterday at the Methodist church by the remarks of Mr. Graves in reference to our colored population. Some person had found fault about their assembling themselves for religious meetings fearing lest some tampering spirit might be at work and cause them to turn their hands against us. I do not think at present it is best for them to meet in that way. I do feel if they are only sincere in their feelings to thee there will be no difficulty for them to admit amongst them responsible white men. O no they will feel glad to have men go for their assemblies and say I know their sincere desire is to serve the living God. For my own part I cannot say I have had an hours uneasiness concerning them since the first of our political differences. If all are as these I have around me; I am not afraid of one of the Ham's[2] descendants on this side of the Atlantic.

## May 12, 1861

I have bid my sons farewell a few minutes since.[3] I do feel my soul is moved to its very depths of grief. I do feel I have given my sons not

2. In the Bible, Ham was the second of Noah's three sons, and some people in the South erroneously thought that Africans were descended from Ham. The views on this question of Presbyterians in the South, especially those of their leaders, are covered in Stephen Haynes, *Noah's Curse: Race and the American Imagination* (New York: Oxford Univ. Press, 2002), 6–14.

3. Nick and Sam joined Company K of the Nineteenth Tennessee Infantry Regiment (C.S.A.) in May 1861 and received training in Knoxville.

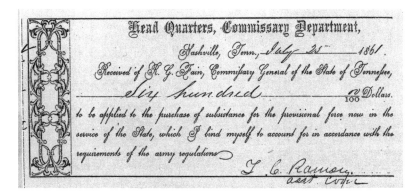

A receipt for supply funds retained by Richard Fain in his role as commissary general of the "Provisional Army of Tennessee." Briefly in 1861, the state had a Commissary Department, which functioned until July 31, 1861, when its responsibilities were transferred to the Confederate government in Richmond, Virginia. From the John N. Fain Collection, East Tennessee History Center.

to make war upon an enemy but to act in self defence to resist the invasion of a foe to civil liberty and who would in a short time become the usurper of religious freedom. Who would soon take our Holy Bible and mutilate it until the word of God would become the traditions of men.

I have felt this morning, have Christian mothers North laid their sons with the same loyalty of feeling upon their country altar that we mothers of the South have done. I feel it can hardly be possible. Our homes are here, they have been endangered by the intemperance of those who know nothing of us — only by misrepresentation. A designing political aristocracy have determined our overthrow. No means are to be left untried for the accomplishment of this object. The name traitor, rebel and other odious epithets are heaped upon us and for what — because we have dared to resist an oppression threatening the extinction of the whole Southern population. I do feel so troubled at the thought of such tyranny and feel will a righteous God give us up to such utter desolation. I feel he will not.

May 18, 1861

Yesterday morning I bid my beloved husband farewell. How hard to part from those so dear at all times, but how peculiarly trying at this time, when everything in our political world wears an aspect of such gloom and darkness. To me, this deadly struggle is a mystery on the part of the North, what do they want. It cannot be possible Christians in the North wish to become usurpers of our homes and drive us as exiles into foreign lands. It cannot be to ameliorate the condition of our colored people. When every step they take but enhances the wretchedness of their condition by making them enemies to the best earthly friends they can have. It seems to me passing strange their unjust interference. May our Father enable us to see our sins as a nation and repent in deep contrition of heart. May mercy prevail and our loved country saved from the horrors of that awful scourge Civil War.

My dear loved one has gone to act as Commissary General[4] for Tennessee troops. May he be enabled to fulfill the duties of his office promptly, efficiently and with fidelity. Let his trust be in Israel's God. I feel much worn down have been passing through scenes of such excitement for several days and will add on to troubles of the mind too great physical exertion. My garden and other domestic cares press heavily. Had my sheep sheared yesterday — today in my garden.

Sabbath June 2, 1861

Darkness, darkness all is dark as yet so far as our difficulties with each other are concerned. The troops from the North are still advancing. Troops are moving in from the South to meet and repel this attack with a determination and energy equal to that manifested by the bands of the Revolution. Surely we of the South do

4. Richard Fain graduated from the United States Military Academy at West Point in 1832 but had worked as a merchant since that time. His business experience probably led to his appointment as commissary general of the Provisional Army of Tennessee, which was soon incorporated into the Confederate army.

feel we are struggling for Liberty just as that devoted band felt; when they resisted British tyranny. Was not the great head of the church moving forward in that mighty work, is it not to his almighty arm we owe the existence and preservation of our Republican form of government until the present moment. When I say Republican I do not mean Black Republican. O no that seems to be as hostile to liberty as ever English rule has been. They seem to feel I am willing to set aside the Bible with all its holy precepts to man if, by so doing I can but exalt the North in her sectional feelings and prejudice.

My soul is troubled to its greatest depth. My husband, my sons are gone. The rests of the Holy Sabbath are broken up by this unholy strife. The sacredness of the home circle has been invaded—perhaps never again to be as it has been; our family altar has been broken down. We kneel in silence to the God of Battles and ask of him to give us victory if it is consistent with his will and the great interests of the church. Why O why have our Northern brethren meddled with our domestic institution of slavery; how little they know of the deep anguish many of us feel in regard to our servants for their immortal souls. And I do feel the judgements of Almighty God will rest upon the heads of the Northern people for their unjust interference and thereby thwarting our plans for the elevation of our colored people in a moral point of view. My servants have been so loyal to me ever since these difficulties have commenced. My soul rises in gratitude to that being in whose hands are the hearts of all men. They see my troubles and seem to wish to do everything they can to make one happy, no words, no looks of indifference do I have from them. I have just written passes for Gus and Lewis[5] to go to town to attend preaching this evening. This has been made necessary by the interference of Northern men.

Poor Gus he seems so troubled; said to me: Miss Liza I never have felt so troubled when Master Richard was from home.

---

5. Gus, born in about 1830, and Lewis, born in about 1849, were slaves belonging to Eliza and Richard Fain.

We all seem to be so broken up. These things are solace to a troubled heart coming from one, who has been a member of my family many years; and for whom I have such kind feelings. One who has been expected to take the assassins knife or deadly tread to embrace his hands in the blood of my family and lay our home in ashes. Has not the cry of the oppressed South gone up into the ears of the Lord of Sabaoth and will he not be avenged speedily. Masters and slaves have both been oppressed. I have felt so greatly troubled during the past week. There seems to be so much dissatisfaction among our people. Some are still clinging with a strange infatuation to what they regard as the Union side of the question. When in reality our Union has long since been obliterated if not done away with. Why wish to stand connected with those who regard us as sinners of such deep dye? Have not our churches been broken up by its deadly venom. Have not the most solemn compacts been violated. Have we not been denounced as being of inferior mould. And do we yet wish to cling to people for whom we cannot have that respect we should feel. With pain I hear of the movements in our midst which will give comfort and encouragement to our enemies.

On last Friday morning before day I was awakened from my sleep with a feeling of indescribable grief. I rose early my purpose fixed to write to a friend who was throwing his influence on the side of the North. I sat down and addressed to him a few lines which I do trust may lead him to think should he receive them. I sent the letter to a particular friend with the request after reading it for her to do as she thought best with it. I love her as a Christian and have such confidence in her Judgment. I shall feel perfectly satisfied with her disposal of it. After sending my letter my soul was still troubled. I sought a place of retirement with my Bible.

June 6, 1861
Troubles are still thickening around us. This evening received from my loved husband the lengthiest letter I have yet received

dated June 4. I have been thinking all day of the pleasures I should feel in welcoming him home but his letter has rather driven the hope from me. They are expecting orders every day to march to Virginia.

I see from the Union of the fourth an account of the death of one of Virginia's heroic sons. His blood has moistened the soil of Fairfax. His name is Capt. John Marr[6]—how sadly we feel to hear of the death of our brave sons. O God may they die looking to Jesus. I would love to know whether this the first martyr to the cause of the South was a believer in Jesus. If he was I do feel it will be the blood of righteous Abel crying to God for vengeance on his wicked brother.

I received this evening a printed letter from the editor of the Mothers Magazine soliciting so earnestly for remittances from his southern patrons saying he has never felt like taking sides against the South, has ever felt they knew better how to manage their affairs than they of the North could do it for us. O that all our Northern friends had felt thus and let us alone to do our work which God has given us in regard to the benighted of the earth. I feel he is sincere for I have never that I recollect of seen anything interfering with our institution of slavery in the magazine which has been almost a constant monthly visitor for more than 20 years.

## June 16, 1861

At home sweet home although so sadly broken up. My helpless little darling daughters lying around me on the floor giving vent to the girlish impulses of the heart not knowing or comprehending the deep sources of grief which disturbs my peace on this calm, beautiful Sabbath morning. My husband has been permitted to revisit his home. O my husband you little know the place you occupy in my heart dearer than all the world. He came Saturday

---

6. Captain John Quincy Marr was killed on June 1, 1861, in a skirmish at the Fairfax County Court House in Virginia. Since he was the first Confederate officer killed in the war, a monument was erected in his memory on the courthouse grounds in 1904.

the 8th[7] and remained until Tuesday morning the 11th at 6:00 o'clock when I set out with him to Knoxville. We arrived at Knoxville around 11 having had a comfortable ride, Eliza Ruth Powel[8] and Sandy going with us. Put up at Lamar house and after dinner went out in omnibus to fairgrounds to visit my dear my darling boys. Never will I forget the feeling I had when I came in sight of and entered the gates leading to tents. I had often imagined to myself the look of the tented field but never until that day had any realization of its appearance and never, while I live, can I forget the expression of gladness beaming from the sunburnt face of that noble band of volunteers who went from our midst as many of them gathered around to welcome us in their midst. My heart was so cheered by their happy faces. I do feel so glad I went to see them. My only regret I had so little time with them. We did not have a chance to talk to our loved sons about anything connected with the great interest of the Soul. I feel there are many connected with the nineteenth regiment of East Tennessee[9] who are good young men. My loved friends from Sullivan

7. On June 8, 1861, an election was held in Tennessee to ratify the ordinance of secession. It passed by a vote of 32,923 in favor and 14,780 against. In Hawkins County the vote was 845 for and 1,260 against secession. Citizens of the Holston River Valley region of Hawkins County and Rogersville were predominantly for the South, while those residing in the mountains were predominantly Unionists. According to local historian Sheila Weems Johnston, there were actually more soldiers from Hawkins County who fought for the South than for the North. Johnston's three volumes on Hawkins County and the Civil War have been published under the general title *The Blue and Gray from Hawkins County, Tennessee, 1861–1865* (Rogersville, Tenn.: Hawkins County Genealogical & Historical Society, 1995); she devotes separate volumes to Confederate soldiers, Federal soldiers, and the battles.

Looking at the geographic lines along which the citizens of Hawkins County were divided reveals economic divisions as well. The Rogersville residents who supported the Confederacy tended to be prosperous members of the merchant and professional classes. The Union supporters of the mountain regions, which had relatively poor land, tended to be less affluent farmers. However, this pro-Union sentiment does not appear to be especially linked to antislavery sentiment but, rather, to class differences. And while some individuals in the Upper South supported secession only with hesitation, others (like Eliza Fain) never wavered in their loyalty to the Southern cause. See Groce, *Mountain Rebels;* and Crofts, *Reluctant Confederates.*

8. Eliza Ruth Powel was Richard's younger sister and had sons serving with the Confederate army in Knoxville.

9. This unit was originally the Second Regiment of Tennessee Volunteers but served in the Civil War as the Nineteenth Tennessee Infantry Regiment (C.S.A.).

are many of them in this Regiment; Cousins Johnny Bachman and Sam, John and Jimmy Rhea, Joe and Bob Rhea sons of Cousin J. D. Rhea, Will Gammon sister R's son, cousin J. Crawford and perhaps many others I did not know. Abram Gammon is there as captain. My heart rises in gratitude and love to God for giving to our Southern homes husbands, sons and brothers who go forth so cheerfully, so nobly for the maintenance of civil and religious freedom.

My first born son[10] who left yesterday to take his place to aid in the prosecution of the war. May he feel the deep responsibilities resting on him as an older brother. O Lord let him ever remember he is born to die and that he is a child of the covenant. O my God thou knowest whether or not I have laid my husband and my sons on the altar of Southern Freedom from a right motive. Last Thursday (13th) was a day set apart by the President of the Confederacy as a day of fasting and prayer to God.

June 21, 1861

The many little exciting incidents in my visit to my sons in Knoxville[11] have not been put down in my little book for want of time upon a weekday. On Tuesday 11th in the evening we went out to the

---

10. Hiram was born in 1839 and married Bettie Lyons in 1859. Hiram served in the quartermaster section of the Confederate army.

11. Nick and Sam Fain served in what became Company K of the Nineteenth Tennessee. W. J. Worsham, the regiment's drummer boy, wrote a history of the unit entitled *The Old Nineteenth Tennessee Regiment, C.S.A.* (1902; reprint, Oxford, Miss.: Guild Bindery Press, 1992). The book is an excellent eyewitness account of the Civil War in the West. The regiment started out with 1,060 men; however, despite additional recruits that were added during the war, the unit surrendered in Bentonville, North Carolina, with only 64 enlisted men. The regiment suffered heavy casualties in the Battles of Fishing Creek, Shiloh, Stones River, Chickamauga, Chattanooga, the Atlanta Campaign, Franklin, and Nashville.

Worsham confirmed that the regiment was made up of companies recruited along the railroad line in East Tennessee from Bristol to Chattanooga. It was organized at the old fairgrounds a mile east of Knoxville. According to Worsham, the Nineteenth Tennessee served in Colonel W. S. Statham's brigade at the Battle of Shiloh in 1862. This brigade suffered the second highest casualty rate of any Confederate brigade involved in that engagement. The Nineteenth itself had 33 soldiers who were killed or who died shortly after the Battle of Shiloh, as well as 30 men wounded. Nick and Sam, after their original one-year enlistments had expired, resigned from the Nineteenth in order to enlist in the Sixtieth and Sixty-third Tennessee Infantry Regiments that were organized in 1862.

encampment. Colonel Cocke riding on horseback came to the gate first and there we had to stand until a permit from the officer of the day let us pass. As we drove along between the tents my eyes turned first to one side and then to the other to see the loved faces; at length they began to appear and never while I live will I forget the cordial welcome of that noble band of volunteers. They all seemed so greatly rejoiced to see us—but the blackest set of sunburnt faces I have ever seen together. I felt you now look like you perhaps may be able to stand some hardships. Could not sit still every drilling of a company every tap of the drum brought me to my feet. Mr. Haynes[12] made a very nice little speech that evening to the boys and spoke of the noble stand old Tennessee had taken the Saturday before with her sisters of the South. What was in the prospective for her as one of the most richly endowed of all states for manufacturing purposes. She must rise and her noble stalwart sons were then assembled to vindicate her rights and if need be to lay down their lives for the accomplishment of her determination to shake off from the earth the tyrant Lincoln and his bloody minions if nothing else would do. After he got through the Athens band struck up Dixie in sweet and acceptable order.

On Wednesday morning Ruth, Richard and I rose early to take a short walk before breakfast to see if our eyes would rest on a recognizable spot.[13] Sallied forth in the direction of the river turned into a cross street to see if we could find where Mrs. Craighead lived with whom Eliza Ruth boarded many years ago but alas time changes all things. Not a remembered spot could be found so came back to breakfast.

12. Landon Carter Haynes (1816–1875) was a spellbinding orator and a staunch supporter of secession. In October 1861 he was elected by the Tennessee legislature to be one of the two representatives in the Confederate States Senate.

13. Eliza and Eliza Ruth (a sister of Richard Fain and one year older than Eliza) both attended the Knoxville Female Academy, a boarding school for girls that opened in 1829. The school later became the East Tennessee Female Institute, and in 1846 the charter was amended so that degrees could be given. Mary Rothrock, ed., *The French Broad–Holston Country: A History of Knox County, Tennessee* (Knoxville: East Tennessee Historical Society, 1946), 256–57.

We left the hotel about 10 or 11 o'clock (after finding no chance to see our boys that day until after dinner) and made our way to the Deaf and Dumb Asylum through the kindness and attention of Mr. Samuel Shaver.[14] Met our kind friend Phoebe who seemed to be wonder stricken at the sight of Richard and I. Here we dined having such a kind invocation from our dear friend Mr. Park.[15] I have always loved Mr. Park since my daughters went to school to him. Mr. and Mrs. Park took so much pleasure in showing us the school the buildings. In the schoolroom where he examined the pupils was a little boy who struck us as a wonderful specimen of a deaf & dumb child. His name was Joseph Perr from the district (I think) who was truly a wonderful little boy. I was so thankful as I look on that once neglected portion of our people to see and know the wonderful improvement which a few years had produced in their favor. They looked so happy seemed to be doing so well.

Mr. Shaver had promised to get a buggy and take us out after dinner to see our dear boys. Being as we thought too long in coming for us we set out on foot for our boarding place, had not gone far before he met us. We got up and were soon moving briskly in the direction of the camp. We arrived found all well—had not been a great while on the ground before a dispatch was out for our loved boys with their company and Capt. Willets to put themselves in moving condition and go to the depot and take a train at 7 o'clock to take them to Loudon bridge.[16] We felt sad Ruth and I wanted to go where they were packing but my husband thought best for us not to go.

---

14. Samuel Shaver was a portrait painter who lived in Rogersville before the Civil War. (See Prentiss Price, "Samuel Shaver: Portrait Painter," *The East Tennessee Historical Society's Publications*, no. 24 [1952]: 92–105.) He painted a portrait of Eliza, as well as portraits of Eliza's mother, Richard's father, and many members of the Powel family. Shaver's wife was a sister of Eliza Ruth Powel's husband, and Eliza Ruth was the sister of Richard Fain.

15. James Park was the minister of the Old School Presbyterian Church in Rogersville from 1853 to 1859; he then moved to Knoxville as president of the Tennessee School for the Deaf and Dumb. He later served for many years as minister of the First Presbyterian Church in Knoxville.

16. This railroad bridge crossed the Tennessee River in East Tennessee between Knoxville and Chattanooga. Confederate troops guarded the structure because it was perhaps the single most important bridge in East Tennessee with regard to rail movements.

July 10, 1861

Had a letter from Nick yesterday. He says Capt. Heiskell did not seem displeased with him for staying over his time—spoke jokingly of putting him on extra duty. He went back 1st of July, Monday. They are now encamped on Cumberland Mountain. As they stand sentinel upon the fastness of the mountain may their thoughts be turned by thy Holy Spirit to the great importance of placing a sentinel at the door of their hearts to be on the lookout for the approach of the adversary of soul. My dear Sam seems to have forgotten he has ever known a mother's love or a mother's care.

July 11, 1861

On the 2nd of this month—Tuesday night—I saw for the first time the comet supposed to be the comet[17] which appeared during the reign of Charles the fifth and caused the abdication of the throne by him. I was so struck by the grandeur and beauty of the sight, had known nothing of the expectation of a comet—was walking through my yard listening for the return of Powell and Gus who had gone to the river (for molasses and sugar) when my attention was directed towards the heavens and what a beautiful sight struck my view. My first thought was could it be a world on fire. I thought then of the predicted conflagration of our own dwelling place and wondered will the destruction of our world be visible to the inhabitants of other worlds. Still visible tonight but losing much of its brilliancy. O that I understood astronomy. I feel could I know all that man can know my knowledge would be poor and imperfect but I have always had a great thirst for astronomical study. I think no science can awaken with the heart of man such unbounded admiration for the power and glory of a creative God.

17. The comet was also mentioned on July 7, 1861, by Hiram Fain, Richard Fain's brother, in his personal journal (Fain, "The Diary of Hiram Fain," 101). The comet was named in 1556 for King Charles V of Spain, the chief European power at that time. The comet had also been observed in 1264 and 975 C.E.

July 23, 1861

I have said farewell again this morning to my best, my dearest earthly friend. My loved Richard more precious than any other living being on earth. Heart doubly sad this morning—husband gone—hours of darkness rapidly approaching. The news from Virginia calculated to elate the heart in one point of view but in another to make it feel so sick of the wickedness of man. The news was received yesterday of a great battle between the Southern and Northern troops commencing Friday morning 19th at daylight still going on Sunday night. According to the dispatch the Southern seems to be driving them back into their own land.

The dark and lowering clouds of civil discord seem to threaten the destruction of our loved East Tennessee. A man came to brother Hiram Sunday night saying a difficulty was likely to occur at Sneedville—that the Union men were or had taken H. Rose's company of volunteers prisoners. I felt excited; but my darling husband seemed to think there was nothing serious about it. I fear this morning it is going to be more serious trouble than we thought for the specie of the bank was sent off this morning with my husband and others. I cannot help feeling uneasy but trust all may be ordered aright.

This evening brings a confirmation of the truth of yesterdays news. Our troops are said to be moving forward with great success though a heavy loss of life. The report this evening says 25,000 of the enemy and 10,000 of our own.[18] Is it not O my Soul a dreadful thought such a loss of noble life. O Lord how are we to live in this manner and feelings of deadly hate. Stay O Lord this terrible strife. I have not felt well this evening my bowels troubling me much. We are so troubled in mind. The thoughts of home difficulties trouble me much. Should we be involved in civil troubles here it will be to

---

18. At the first Battle of Bull Run (or Manassas, as it is also known), the casualties were actually three thousand for Union troops and two thousand for the Confederates. (See Shelby Foote, *The Civil War, a Narrative*, vol. 1 [New York: Random House, 1958–74], 84). The many inaccuracies in Eliza's comments about the war are interesting in themselves because they reflect how news reached the hinterlands of the Confederacy.

us a most dreadful calamity. Our servants may turn their hand against but I have never felt uneasy on that ground. God, O God thou knoweth the hearts of all men. I have felt so grateful as I have thought of thy kindness in quelling a rebellious spirit in our blacks (if any ever has existed).

July 28, 1861

My Sabbaths are days now of such intense feeling and I cannot keep from asking questions concerning the well being of those who have left all in our Southern homes to go forth for what I feel is civil and religious liberty. This morning brother George got back from Knoxville having gone down on Wednesday to make some arrangements about their company. He tells me on that day he travelled with some who were going back from Virginia who had been spectators of the deadly conflict this day week (21st) ever memorable to one who was on that train with the remains of a darling son who had fallen to rise no more—a Mississippian though George did not know his name. I asked George if he thought his father seemed much distressed. He said he seemed so much elated at the success of our armies he did not seem to feel the death of his child much. I have always felt to the truly patriotic heart there is no cause where we could lose our sons which would carry with it an alleviation of sorrow so much as the thought of Liberty, Liberty.

Fain [Powel][19] came out today and took dinner. He told me he had travelled to New Market with 5 soldiers belonging to the 7th Regiment of Georgia one of the suffering regiments I suppose in the fight. The Capt. had his right arm wounded from a Minie ball. A little fellow who Fain said did not look larger than Powell had received two slight wounds from musket balls in his left arm. They spoke of it as a terrible fight, say their colors had been levelled three times before being seized by Johnston. He says he thought they would have killed

19. Nicholas Fain Powel, who went by the name Fain Powel, was Eliza's nephew, born in 1840. According to Sheila Johnston (*Blue and Gray from Hawkins County: The Confederates*, 243), Fain was rejected for military service in the Confederate army due to physical disability.

him by running over him—got in the embrace of the enemy once so closely he thought they would take him prisoner but I suppose his diminutive size for once was a good advantage. He got a chance and took to his heels as hard as he could go to the place where his flag was flying. They say the Northerners fought bravely, poor fellows I feel so sorry such brave hearts should be devoted to so bad a cause. I feel glad I am not where these scenes of excitement would be before my eyes; I feel I can hardly bear it when I am just to hear of it. I have felt from the very first such deep interest in our Southern cause, could not for one moment ever censure the descendants of the Huguenots for the stand South Carolina has taken will be the instrument and made use for the preservation of liberty. I do feel it would be hard for me to fight on that day but I suppose all is lost sight of in regard to day by the assembled hosts some I know would think of the fourth commandment but alas how few; how few. Such is the desolation of war morally, intellectually and physically.

O that our soldiers may be preserved from the awful sins which generally attend military strife. May they learn to be merciful, let them should Northern prisoners fall into their hands treat them as they too have been taught the commandments of God. They too have been dedicated in faith to the God of Israel. Let the South show to the North we have no desire to injure you or covet aught you possess. I fear the leaders of this difficulty have resting on their heads the awful violation of several of God's holy laws. I have felt they have lost sight of his word and of all the feelings of true patriots. I still feel the North has within its bounds those whose hearts are burning with true patriotism, but whose mouths are closed by a military despotism. For such I feel so deeply. Poor Maryland,[20] often have I thought of you and Missouri; the pentup fire must burst forth with a tremendous blaze.

This day was set apart by the congress of the Southern Confederacy as a day of devout thanksgiving to Israel's God for his most

---

20. Whether the citizens of Maryland and Missouri were as upset as Eliza suggested is unclear, but neither of these states seceded from the Union.

signal and merciful interposition at Manassas. O is there a heart in all our Southern land who feels I cannot respond to that call, I feel dead must that heart be to every true principle of patriotism. I have not felt well for several days from suffering in my head—vertigo.

Sabbath August 18, 1861

I do so feel this morning crushed at the thought of the great desecration of thy holy day. My family seem to be moving onward with the downward tide. O Lord, I know nothing but grace, grace can stay this welling tide of iniquity. Today contrary to my feelings, as he knew and in direct opposition to every moral feeling of his own soul, Isaac went to town and made a purchase of a pair of shoes. I knew it not until the deed was done.

O the baneful influences of military life over the soul. It is this I dread more than all things else. I fear that the hearts of my sons will be estranged for all that is good. Sam is at home today; but cannot remain long in one place—been at Uncle Hirams, Mrs. Powels, Ebbing Springs church[21] and now gone to town (3 o'clock), seems to be so restless. I fear he has not read his Bible much since he left home.

The scenes of the 21st battle are vividly impressed upon the minds of those who now travel upon our trains. Fain has again been down the country saw on the trains several wounded. One who had both hands taken off, another one his hand. He preserved the bomb which had deprived him of his hand. O how many poor soldiers have been crippled for life, how deplorable the results of war—cruel, cruel war. Our Southern people have many of the Northern wounded soldiers to care for. I do hope the command of God to an enemy may be thought of and closely obeyed. If thine enemy hunger feed him, if he thirst give him drink. Our duty to an enemy when in health how much more to be observed when in distress.

---

21. This Methodist church is still in use. It was named for a nearby spring known as Ebbing and Flowing Spring, which flows at regular intervals of two hours, forty minutes.

September 1861

[Account of a trip to Nashville.] We got on comfortably to the river in Col. Walker's hack, crossed the river were soon seated in our comfortable train. Moved on quite pleasantly to Gap, waited a short time when the train which was to bear us from our home to the west came up. What a sorrowful sight I was called to witness as I entered the car. Our noble soldiers returning wounded and sick and maimed for life. My heart was sad indeed at the sight. One noble soldier who sat on the front seat with an arm which looked from its bandaging and splinting as though it had been sorely shattered looked up to us and with all the true dignity of our Southern gentleman remarked ladies I would give you my seat but I am not able to stand. My soul almost involuntarily replied I do not wish your seat. I regret that I did not find out his name. I took a seat at the other end of the car beside a lady who got on at the Gap. She was from Sullivan county and had married a Mr. Stillman who was a northern man but true to the cause of liberty. They were talking of going to his northern home but I hardly think they will reach that place until peaceful times roll round.

We traveled nicely but crowded until we reached the collision which had taken place that morning between a freight and gravel train. Here was commotion and a delay which lost the connection. I had seen on the train before getting off here the quartermasters wife and son from Yorktown. She was quite unwell and her little boy very sick. I have seldom felt such a warm sympathy for a passing fellow creature. She had been dispatched to her mother who was sick and rapidly failing. She was hastening on with all the thrilling anxiety of a daughters heart when told she would be delayed; she seemed so troubled. I do hope she was permitted to see her mother. On that train was a noble little boy whose name was George Bowen (his mother Mary Gillespie) his face struck me as familiar. His mother was one of the little children of early life I had loved in Greeneville whilst a schoolgirl. How could I help loving her noble boy who had gone as a soldier in his country cause so early in life. He was returning unhurt although exposed to the enemies fire. He had his trophy with him (a Yankee gun). I could not help thinking his mother has prayed for him. His Capt. Wm. Rogers was near seemed to be very proud of him. He Rogers an invalid from rheumatism. I asked him how he had gotten away from his mother. His reply was noble, she gave her consent—I would not have run away from her. Noble boy may your life be a useful one.

About 2 o'clock on Thursday 5th of Sept., with him who is dearer to me than all else, left Knoxville for Nashville. A. Gammon, John Rhea and other friends on the train had a pleasant trip. A.G. & Co. stopping that night at Loudon. We travelled over that long and dangerous road between Chattanooga and Nashville. Got at Chat. a cup of coffee which with our provisions we had along made our supper. After supper Richard went out into another car to smoke staid so long I felt uneasy. I did not know what to do. I imagined many things and amongst others felt afraid someone had knocked him in the head but after a while he came and I was relieved. Took breakfast at Murfreesboro and arrived at Nashville about 7 o'clock and in a short time was surrounded by the loved friends of Nashville.[22]

Oct. 13, 1861

On Wednesday 25th Sept Sam came home from camp sick. I felt so glad to have him at home. My heart would have been so distressed at the thought of a son sick in camp. He is now well for which I do trust and feel so thankful. On last Thursday 10th Abram Gammon came. I was so glad to see him. He is still quite unwell but better than when he came. I do hope he will soon be well for I do feel he would be such a great loss to his company.

October 27, 1861

O my Father in Heaven let a feeble worm of the dust make a record of mercies received during the past week. This day week I

---

22. Eliza's sister Fanny married W. R. McAlister of Nashville in 1830. She died in 1856 after giving birth to thirteen children. Eleven of the children were alive at this time. Richard probably had business related to his brief service as commissary-general of the Provisional Army of Tennessee.

was surrounded by the sight of home, husband, sons, friends. My husband came on Sat. 19th, left Monday morning at 6 in company with a dear cousin Sam Bachman for Knoxville, arrived safely for which I feel I am so thankful. On Tuesday morning Abram Gammon, Nick Fain, Sam Fain and J. K. P. Gammon left us for their Kentucky camp. I felt so sad at parting from them for ought we know it is the last look we may ever have on their loved faces. Abe was much better but still quite unwell, felt so sorry to see him go before he was well. Sam Fain entirely rested looking so well.

Sam Powel had not been to see me but I felt he was excused having on the 15th linked his destiny with the noble Mec Walker. He of course must give to her the hours of his stay at home. May his life be saved from the demoralizing influences of camp life and let him return to the embraces of her who has given all up all for his sake. Fain Powell also recently married on the 16th to the lovely Ann (Fain is the friend of my dear son Nick); so delicate and frail looking I fear she may not long be a partner of his joys and sorrows.

I have failed to note in my little book a painful but interesting event and feel I must now put it down. On Thursday morning 19th Sept. near Barboursville, Ky. the master called for the spirit of my loved friend R. D. Powel[23] and in highly exciting circumstances. A march from the ford of troops under the command of Col. Battle had taken place on Wednesday night. They arrived at creek near Barboursville about daylight. The cavalry in advance, the Kentuckians were already in waiting for them and as our gallant cavalry advanced from their hidden places they fired one bullet piercing the right breast of poor Bob. He felt he had received his

---

23. R. D. Powel, known as Bob, was a brother of Eliza Ruth Powel's husband. He was the first lieutenant in Company K of the Nineteenth Tennessee Infantry Regiment. As C. W. Heiskell ("Nineteenth Tennessee Infantry," in *Military Annals of Tennessee, Confederate*, ed. Lindsley, 373) and W. J. Worsham (in *The Old Nineteenth Tennessee Regiment*) have both noted, Bob Powel was said to be the first Confederate soldier killed outside of Virginia; this occurred at first light on September 19, 1861, near Barbourville, Kentucky, when he was felled by enemy fire. His body was returned to Rogersville, where he was buried in the old Presbyterian cemetery, according to Sheila Johnston in *The Blue and Gray from Hawkins County: The Confederates.*

death wound, whether he fell or eased himself from his horse I do not know. But when our poor fellows came along in battle array he raised his head, gave a look but none of them could go to him. That was his last sight of those dear boys he loved so much. Before they were permitted to return that noble spirit was gone to the God who gave it but not without giving a pleasant evidence of his willingness to depart. The young men Jones & Wolfenbarger who were with the wagon came up to him before he was gone. I have heard when the announcement was made to him you must die he replied I am ready. I have ever had such confidence in Bob as a Christian. Well do I remember the long conversations he and I have had together on the subject of religion when his mind was in great darkness and he was so greatly distressed. I have never in all my life had so much religious conversation with anyone. He came often to see me. I felt so glad to see him always. I believed he was a Christian. I still think he was although he may have lost sight as it were for a while; the high requirements which God had made upon him to live for Jesus—yet I believe he was his disciple and feel so merciful it was in a precious Saviour to single out one who was prepared to meet him and spare the impenitent. I asked my sons had they been called on to make a selection of one who they felt had made most preparation for death who would they have selected. They replied Uncle Bob. I then appealed to them to think of the goodness and mercy of God in sparing them and giving them time to prepare to meet a God of love in peace.

Bob's request was to bring him home if they could and bury him. They brought his body to Tazewell before they could get any coffin to lay it in. How sad, O how sad to me is that thought, the body of one we love laid in a wagon and taken over such rough roads so far before it can be laid in its narrow house. Such are the trials which our cruel war brings. They arrived at Rogersville on Saturday morning about 3 o'clock having travelled constantly night and day from the ford. His remains were taken to the church.

**FORM OF OATH.**

I _Richard G. Fain_ do solemnly swear or affirm that while I continue in the service I will bear true faith, and yield obedience to the CONFEDERATE STATES OF AMERICA, and that I will serve them honestly and faithfully against their enemies, and that I will observe and obey the orders of the President of the Confederate States, and the orders of the Officers appointed over me, according to the Rules and Articles of War.

_Rich G. Fain_

Sworn and subscribed before me this _5th_ day of _Oct_ 1861, at _Rogersville Tenn_

_J. R. Armstrong (J.P.)_

Oath of allegiance signed by Richard Fain in October 1861 upon his appointment as a brigade commissary major in the Confederate army. From the John N. Fain Collection, East Tennessee History Center.

## Nov. 10, 1861

This morning finds heart, soul and body in a state of great excitement from the rumor of burnt bridges and strong apprehensions of a rebellious movement on the part of the Union desperados of East Tennessee.[24] I fear at a late hour men of standing who have aided and abetted that feeling may find themselves as well as the rest of us involved in irretrievable ruin.

## Nov. 14, 1861

Last Sabbath evening my beloved husband returned having been so strongly solicited by Mr. McFarland and others to come and see what could be furnished for the reconstruction of the burnt bridges

24. Several railroad bridges were burned by Union sympathizers launching coordinated attacks. The Reverend William B. Carter, a staunch Unionist from upper East Tennessee, conceived of the plan and went to Washington to receive the endorsement of President Abraham Lincoln. Unfortunately for the bridge burners, the Union generals in Kentucky declined to invade East Tennessee at the same time. The net result was a harsh retribution against Union sympathizers in East Tennessee. Temple, _East Tennessee and the Civil War,_ 408; Cameron Judd, _The Bridge Burners: A True Adventure of East Tennessee's Underground Civil War_ (Johnson City, Tenn.: Overmountain Press, 1996).

from our timbers at the river. He went back on Monday and got to Knoxville at 9 o'clock P.M. When shall my home be home again, when will the loved be restored. On last Tuesday morning about 5 A.M. messengers from town came requiring Sam and Ike to go immediately and make preparation for a trip to railroad to succor troops stationed at Watauga Bridge. Before going a great distance they ascertained they had been fired upon whilst out on a scout from Mr. N. Taylor's barn. Some were slightly wounded but no lives lost as I understand. How deplorable is such a state of affairs.

Sabbath Nov. 24, 1861

Gloom, gloom impenetrable gloom hangs over me this morning. My son Ike[25] left home this morning with gun strapped on his back and his provisions in a bag to go to Bays Mountain where it is said a number of our poor deluded and infatuated Union men have collected for resistance to the law and to work wickedly.

Why murder our own brothers. O give me faith to cast my burden upon thee my great and eternal friend. Who does not feel they could weep day and night when we think of the calamities which are upon us, a nation which seems to have been as highly favored as any nation ever could be of High Heaven engaged in fearful conflicts.

On last Tuesday evening (Nov. 19, 1861) Kyle Blevins with a number of men detailed from his own and Capt. Faw's companies were impressing guns and coming to the house of a man by the name of Thomas Colwell. They told him their business, spoke to him of their peaceful intentions and whilst Douglas Young was reasoning the case with his son the old man drew a pistol from his pocket and shot him. The shot taking effect Douglas seemed to be a tiger let loose on his prey, he shot him, broke his gun over his head mashing his skull and then plunged his bayonet through him. Douglas was

25. Ike was only seventeen at this time and not yet in the regular army. He was apparently associated with a group of Southern partisans who killed William Bird. After the Civil War he was arrested and accused of being involved in the murder.

cared for by his friends and taken to a home where he lay until next day about 11 o'clock without any medical attention. After dressing his wound he was placed on a slide and brought to town where he is now at George Powels receiving all the kind attention a poor soldier could desire. A young man by the name of Davolt from Capt. Faw's company was shot about the shoulder and was much hurt but not unable to go home. He wanted to get home. No one like home friends when troubles come upon us.

Dec. 6, 1861
On Wednesday night I was aroused from my sleep with heavy foreboding of evil. As a nation how has the Bible been disregarded by our Northern brethren and of what grievous sins have we of the South been guilty. We are visited with the indignation of the King of Kings and Lord of Hosts. Our land seems to be doomed to the horrors of civil war.

George Powel and Joseph Huffmaster brought home yesterday evening Buck Huffmaster who was shot in going from their camp to Sneedville. He and Ike had started to get Capt. Rose's company to come to their assistance but were waylaid from ambush, shot upon and they were I suppose much alarmed.

Dec. 26. 1861
Since listing the above all things have been made to succumb to military rule. The rebellion has been suppressed and many of the members of it have been arrested. Some have paid the high price of life for life. Old Mr. Bird an old man of 60 years was one of the ringleaders, said to be a bold, daring and fearless man. He was shot on a high spur of that mountain region, disarmed and left by the man who shot him while he went for assistance to bring him down. While he was gone the old man crept off some 150 or 200 yards but he was deterred from making his way beyond the reach of his pursuers by his wounds. Poor old fellow I have felt troubled when I thought of his death and feel upon the leading Union men of East Tennessee rest

the blood of these poor deluded victims. Two more men by the name of Harmon[26] have been hung in Knoxville; implicated in that atrocious and diabolical deed of bridge burning. Methinks Mr. Nelson[27] will surely feel grieved when he thinks of his course. O how fearful to incite men to an unjust, unwarranted rebellion.

Buck and Ike made a narrow escape. Ike told me he never felt so frightened in his life with bullets flying by him and he could see no one. A merciful God preserved the life of my child.

26. Jacob Harmon and his son Henry were hanged in Knoxville on December 17, which brought to five the number of bridge burners executed by the Confederates. The most recent account of the so-called Pottertown bridge burners—the Harmons were potters whose wares are highly collectable today—is the privately printed booklet by Donahue Bible entitled *Their Eyes Have Seen the Glory: East Tennessee Unionists in the Civil War* (Mohawk, Tenn.: Dobson Creek Publishers, 1997). See also Judd, *The Bridge Burners*, and Temple, *East Tennessee and the Civil War*, 366–411.

27. T. A. R. Nelson was a leading East Tennessee Unionist whom Eliza accused of fomenting the bridge burning.

# Chapter 2

## Victory to Our Armies: 1862

This year was the high-water mark for the Confederacy, but it started out badly with the loss of Fort Donelson and the loss at Fishing Creek. Eliza's husband served as organizing colonel of the Sixty-third Tennessee Regiment, which was formed in East Tennessee during the summer of 1862. Three of his sons—Hiram, Sam, and Ike—joined the regiment that summer. East Tennessee remained under Confederate control throughout the year.

New Years morning January 1, 1862
How sadly has the light of this first morning of 62 broken upon me. My sons have left me to go forth to combat the world again—Nick, Samuel Gammon[1] and Ike. Sam and Ike to go to Knoxville and Nick to Cumberland Gap. Samuel Gammon has promised me to drink no more until the war closes but of that I have many doubts and fears.

---

1. Samuel Gammon was the only child of Eliza's sister Nancy, who died six weeks after the boy's birth in 1837. Eliza appears to have functioned as a surrogate mother to Sam.

January 5, 1862 First Sabbath of 1862

My heart has been made to feel this morning the blasting influences of war in a moral point of view. The Sabbath is lost sight of. Man feels the commands of God are to be lightly esteemed.

January 13, 1862

Fearful night—poor soldiers how my heart feels for you this dreary night. Sleet falling until the ground is white and I am alone. Lizzie, Powell and Fan at their aunt Nancys [McCarty] for a supper and dance. My heart is weary of Christmasing. My poor Liz has not seemed to think of anything but dancing and frolicking about since Christmas night. It is a source of deep, deep trouble to me that one who has arrived at her years be so absorbed in the vain unsatisfying pleasures of earth. I do hope that ere long something may deeply impress her of the foolishness of her course. Life is too precious to be squandered, the time of probation so lightly esteemed.

O how sad I feel this night as I sit listening to the merciless elements all of which seem to have conspired to add greater sorrow to my cup. Where are my soldier sons this night? My heart is so grieved when I think of our poor soldiers who have to face the storm of rain, wind and sleet with but little to protect them from its chilling effects.

Feb. 19, 1862

O my Father how fearfully gloomy are these hours to me. Disaster upon disaster seems to be before us. I have under my roof this night two poor soldiers of Floyd's brigade names James and Isaiah Sheck from Lee County Virginia. Poor fellows they bring the news of the fearful reverses at Fort Donelson.[2] Will our God let our enemies triumph over us? Will he give us into their hands? I cannot feel he will. We are in thy hands. O my Father we feel the

2. Fort Donelson protected Nashville from invasion via the Cumberland River. Its loss to the Union army of General Ulysses S. Grant forced the abandonment of Nashville by the Confederate forces. Foote, *The Civil War,* 1: 194–209.

arm of man is weak, feeble and impotent in this great struggle for liberty. Make us humble, make us holy and save our Southern land from ruin and desolation.

One month today since the battle of Fishing Creek[3] where our boys were defeated. To me that was the saddest news ever fell on my ear. I felt my heart break, I was completely bewildered I scarcely knew what to do with myself. Had it not been for a visit to my husband in Knoxville I would have felt much like giving up but a kind providence has given me this night a greater command of my feelings.

My son this night is far from me near the enemy lines perhaps engaged in deadly conflict. The battle of Fishing Creek was fought on Sabbath 19th of January between Gen. Zollicoffer's brigade of the South and the forces of Gen. Thomas Schoepf of the North and there fell our brave, our noble general. How much I lament his loss. There too fell the brave, noble Carroll Carmack with his face to the foe. Poor Carroll, never will I forget the joyousness of your manner when you bid me farewell. As I said to you Carroll be a good boy your reply I am always that. There too fell Baily Peyton and Fogy Noble chivalric sons of the South. O what sad homes our country affords this night. I do plead O my Father for a victory that will make our enemies feel they cannot conquer us. These poor boys who are tonight laying on the floor in my room feeling they could not sleep on a bed have left behind on the battlefield the remains of an older brother—Andrew Sheck. How sad will that mothers heart be when these come in to know one is not and will never return.

Sabbath Morning Feb. 23, 1862

This morning Powell came from town (having gone down yesterday evening for the mail and the rain prevented his coming back) bringing me the sad news of the investment of Nashville by the federal forces. To me this is gloomy exceedingly gloomy intelligence.

---

3. The Battle of Fishing Creek, also known as Mill Springs or Logan Crossroads, was a military disaster for the Confederate forces under the popular General Felix Zollicoffer. Foote, *The Civil War,* 1: 177–80.

I have been thinking of the gloom hanging over that beautiful city this morning. There where the ear was greeted every sabbath morning with the cheering sounds of sabbath bells calling on it inhabitants to praise the Lord. All is now hushed, the Sabbath will scarcely be known in the city. My sister sleeps sweetly in that thickly populated graveyard with five of her precious lambs. How much my heart desires to know this day the situation of that dear family.

March 4, 1862
One year today since the Monarch of Tyranny was permitted to take his seat in the Presidential chair.[4] What scenes have been recorded by the Angel of time in the short space of one year. The immortal spirits which have been launched into eternity, the groans of the wounded, the restless moments of those whose health has given way in the camp and the sorrowing hearts of those whose homes have been broken up (never to be home again). All have been done through the instrumentality of Lincoln and his deluded followers. But we needed a scourge and in that man we have been given one of earths dark tyrants. His name will go down to unborn generations with an odium unparalleled in history. The man or men who would have consented to be run as sectional candidates over such a Republic as this deserve the mark of Cain upon them. They have been the murderers of many brethren. I do not feel that the life of any one would give to me one pleasant moment. I do not want the life of any one as an expiation; but I do want peace. O that we may soon have peace in our borders and our persecutors driven to their own land. O that we may worship our God according to the dictates of our own consciences. The Northern people have long sought the trammelling of the consciences of the South. Had they let us alone what a home would many portions of the South present to the world today.

Our servants (whom many have felt it was their duty to educate and train in the nurture and admonition of the Lord) have

4. The reference is to Abraham Lincoln.

been neglected at the unceasing upbraiding of conscience. O how many tears have Christians of the South been caused to shed on account of this unjust interference. When we think that they have been instrumental in entailing upon the South slavery; we cannot refrain from giving vent to our feelings and exclaiming they know not what they do. Our Bible which is so precious has made the way clearer. Methinks had the Bible reader of the North not perverted his understanding and conscience by the influences of a higher law we might this day have been the most prosperous nation upon the face of the earth and our influence felt to the remotest parts of the earth. The South was willing, yea anxious to have the slave granted the privileges of moral improvement and of moral elevation. Had the North cooperated with the South in this great work without trying to throw the firebrands of discontent and murder amongst us what a beautiful home of peace, industry and plenty would we today have shown to the world. May the will of our Father in heaven be done—all is in his hands.

March 17, 1862

My beloved husband left this morning for Knoxville. I always feel so sad when he goes away. How long is this separation to continue?

Today an Irishman by the name of Johnny Goggin came out to get some boneset for Peter Joist. I talked to him about our condition and told him of the duplicity and cunning of the Northern folks. I brought up the objection to the Southern folks for not letting the Northerners bury their dead at Manassas. I asked him if he knew the reason. He did not. I told him we recognized their flag of truce and gave a permit to bury their dead when they turned into throwing up fortifications. I do feel so sorry to think we have intelligent men in our midst who will try to make the unlearned believe such statements are true. Where and what will be the result of such double dealing?

Last night we were called on by five of our noble Southern soldiers belonging to Floyd's brigade to stay all night. Their names

Samuel Burchett, John Rutherford, Elisha G. Burchett, Jonathan Munsey and John A. Shoop.[5] Truly I have not seen five better behaved men anywhere. No smell of liquor, nothing at all but the perfect gentleman. I do trust their lives may be spared to see the independence of our Southern land established and they permitted to enjoy the liberty which Washington and his brave men achieved and Jackson with his noble forces maintained.

## March 18, 1862

How sad I feel this evening. Tears are falling as I write. The thought has been upon me what if in the providence of God the North shall be successful. We cannot dwell together for the breach is greater than it ever has been. We could not live together in the church and can we after this unholy war dwell together in our political government? I feel never without enslaving and oppressing the larger portion of the South; as poor down trodden Ireland has been oppressed. What is to become of these poor creatures in our midst who are part of our household and for whom we feel such a strong attachment?

5. John A. Shoop, Samuel Burchett, Elisha Burchett, and John J. Rutherford all served in Company B of the Fiftieth Virginia Infantry Regiment. John Shoop (also spelled Shoup) was captured in 1864 and spent the rest of the war in prison. John Rutherford later became a sergeant, Samuel a first lieutenant, and Elisha a captain. However, Elisha deserted from the army as his unit proceeded to the Battle of Gettysburg. The Jonathan Munsey to whom Eliza refers may have been John G. Munsey, a member of the Forty-fifth Virginia Infantry; he died on June 6, 1862, of disease. These soldiers were all part of the brigade of former Virginia governor John B. Floyd—a unit that consisted of the Forty-fifth, Fiftieth, and Fifty-first Virginia Infantry Regiments, which were organized in southwestern Virginia. The brigade was one of the few units to actively engage the enemy at Fort Donelson, where they were part of a breakout attempt. General Floyd was in charge of the Confederate forces at Fort Donelson and supported the surrender to General Grant. However, when two steamboats full of new recruits arrived at the scene, he ordered these troops into the fort, turned over command to General Simon B. Buckner, loaded his brigade onto the boats, and fled to Nashville. At the time Eliza encountered them, these soldiers were presumably on their way home with their general. For this debacle, Floyd was relieved of his command on March 11, 1862, although he did not actually surrender it until March 19. Eliza seemed to be unaware that these soldiers, along with those she mentioned in her diary entry of February 19, 1862, were returning home in disgrace. John D. Chapla, *50th Virginia Infantry* (Lynchburg, Va.: H. E. Howard, 1997), 42–48.

March 21, 1862

Our days are growing darker—foes within and foes without. The within ones are to be mostly dreaded. We know not how soon a blow may be struck which will result in war in our midst. To me this has always been the appalling thought and I have ever felt the leading intelligent men of the so called Union party (but to me Lincoln adherents) are the men who have plunged our country in ruin. Had we presented to the North one unbroken phalanx with banners whose motto was death before subjugation we might this night have had homes of peace, our land would not be subject to the tread of the usurper, and our Capital still secure with its precious relics of antiquity, documents and the museum collected by and contributed to by our statesmen and veterans of Revolutionary fame. How humiliating to me is the thought our Capital in the hands of enemies who will I fear destroy it. Such are the reverses of war today elated with success, tomorrow cast down and almost heartbroken.

Our fight at Ft. Donelson was one of indomitable courage and bravery on the part of our Southern troops. I do believe had they been reinforced by five thousand fresh troops we might still have held the day and our gallant Buckner with his noble band been today at liberty in our midst. We were too self-confident and had begun to feel our arms were able to cope with superior forces armed with the most approved weapons.

March 27, 1862

This morning my dear Ike left home to go to his post again having come up on Sunday with his captain and others in search of some men who had deserted. Amongst the number was Gus Figg whose name is associated with the murder of old Mr. Bird. He having made the first effective shot at him. I was so sorry to hear of his desertion. He seemed destined to make a noble soldier. I feel he has been the dupe of some men whose advantages have been greater than his own. What a trouble are opposers of their own country as these union men are. To me it is so strange. What can they be thinking of. The reign of Black Republicanism will be short I think. The men who are the controlling spirits do not seem to have the fear of God before them. All is dark as yet but may we not hope a brighter day will soon dawn and our land be free.

Yesterday was the first day of my new cooking stove. Caroline got dinner and thinks it will do well.

## April 20, 1862

Dear Tom the loved friend of so many hearts is numbered.[6] He fell on Monday the 7th mortally wounded at the battle of Shiloh while leading on his brave daring band to a charge upon one of the enemies batteries. He lived until Tuesday evening at 4 o'clock. There too fell the noble son of the widowed mother—Capt. Willet. He died Monday night. Noble sons of the South may your precious blood cry to heaven for vengeance on the dark invading hosts of our fairs land. One of the brothers-in-law of Tom in speaking of him says his face shone on Sabbath and on Monday with unusual brightness and on it was depicted the deep determination of his soul to conquer or die.

I feel so greatly gratified this morning by a statement of Sallie to me which came through Mr. Hooper (one of Tom's friends who came with his body to C.) to cousin Joe. He says Tom seemed to be a changed man from the time of the battle of Fishing Creek.

The great battle of Shiloh was fought on April 6 & 7 in McNairy Co. Tennessee near Purdy.[7] At that battle on the 6th which was the Sabbath fell our gallant and lamented Gen. A. S. Johnston. On Monday cousin Jimmy Rhea was wounded.

6. In the Battle of Shiloh on April 6, two of the ten captains of the Nineteenth Tennessee were killed. The "Tom" to whom Eliza refers was one of those men: Captain Thomas H. Walker of Company I. The other slain captain was Z. T. Willet of Company B. The total casualties for the Nineteenth were approximately 25 percent of the four hundred soldiers engaged in the battle.

7. Shiloh was the deadliest battle of the Civil War up to this date and resulted in enormous casualties. On April 6 the Confederates attacked but failed to rout the Union army under General U. S. Grant. The next day Grant attacked and drove the Confederates back to Corinth, Mississippi. (For a detailed account, see Foote, *The Civil War*, 1: 340–51.) Purdy was the county seat of McNairy County until 1890, when nothing was left but a few homes and deserted buildings. The railroad had bypassed Purdy, and this spelled its doom.

June 28, 1862

Have had today (Saturday) 4 of Starnes cavalry to take dinner with me — Mr. Wade, Ralph Childress and Sommers. Have just had application from Lt. Norton[8] to take care of two sick men. Have told him to try somewhere else but if not successful to bring them to me and I would do what I could for them.

June 30, 1862

Mr. Osborne of Starnes cavalry came here for breakfast for the pickets. On yesterday morning I was in my garden gathering when I heard a voice crying out hallo, halo in such rapid succession. I started and went to the yard fence when a plain looking man accosted me in the following manner. Madam, I wish to make a few shoes at your shop today. I replied very well sir my blacksmith is in the field with the key. He then said to me madam if it will be pleasant and convenient I would like to hold family prayers. I am a candidate for missionary to China. He was mounted as a cavalry man and looking to me so strange and mysterious my first thought was perhaps you are a Yankee spy feigning to be cracked. I said to him what is your name and where are you from. Castleman is my name and I am from Williamson. I then thought he is one of Col. Starnes men who has become suddenly deranged and I told him I would defer having prayers at that time.

After awhile Mr. Childress and Lien Norton came. I told them of my adventure. They told me he was a perfectly harmless man who had acted as he is now doing ever since they went into camp, that his eccentricity seems to arise from his religious feelings. I told them had I known that I would have treated him so differently. So I sent him some tracts and word to come back by Lt. Norton. This morning here he came mounted on butterfly having had three horses since he joined the regiment. The first-named rabbit, the second cricket. Down he got without ceremony and came in. I handed him the Bible and he read the 3rd chapter of Jonah and sang the first verse of *There is a Fountain filled with blood*, prayed with us and then sang *O sing to me of Heaven when*

8. Lieutenant J. W. Norton of Company E, Fourth Tennessee Cavalry (C.S.A.).

*I am called to die.* We had a few words of conversation then he left and went to the shop.

I asked him to come and get his dinner, he came and took his dinner and then must have prayers again. He read part of the 6th chapter of Daniel, sang and then prayed after which he sang another beautiful hymn and left us. I do feel so glad he came back. I believe he is a true Christian.

God has again in the language of our noble Jackson given victory to our armies.[9] The expected battle near Richmond has taken place having commenced last Thursday at 4 P.M. on 26 of June. This resulted in the overthrow of McClellan's whole army; a victory at a heavy expense. O how many of our precious soldiers have fallen. Amongst the number is Col. Sam Fulkerson a noble gallant son of a widowed mother.[10]

## July 6, 1862

Another privilege granted this day of going to the house of God with my loved husband. Quite a number of Col. Starnes' cavalry at church, nice well-behaved men.[11] Mr. Warren belonging to McGregor's company is the man who has brought flour to be baked from the camp. Mr. Collier came after potatoes for his Lt. a few days ago, got his dinner.

## July 15, 1862

Have been highly favored with a visit from my loved husband. He remained with us yesterday, took dinner at home. He has not taken

9. This refers to the Battle of Seven Days, a Confederate victory that came during the last week of June 1862 outside Richmond. In *The Civil War* (1: 490), Shelby Foote describes this victory as one that "had been accomplished at a fearful price," which agrees with Eliza's assessment.

10. Colonel Samuel V. Fulkerson commanded the Thirty-seventh Virginia Infantry Regiment.

11. Colonel James W. Starnes headed the Fourth Tennessee Cavalry (C.S.A.). Major General Edmund Kirby Smith ordered the regiment to join Brigadier General C. L. Stevenson as scouts in Hawkins and Hancock Counties on June 25, 1862. (See *Tennesseans in the Civil War*, vol. 1 [Nashville: Civil War Centennial Commission of Tennessee, 1964], 62.) Colonel Starnes died on June 30, 1863, of wounds received in subsequent actions.

a Monday dinner for many long months. He left this morning with his two guards Nick and Sam Wills going back to Bean Station. Sam going around to try to get a man to take his place in Capt. Heiskell's company. Nick came last Thursday night between 10 & 11, brought a young man named Scott who has come to join Col. Starnes regiment. They got wet and he has not been well and is still with us. Had for dinner yesterday two soldiers named Cosgroves and Shock out after wagons.

August 10, 1862
Last evening my dear husband came home bringing with him loved friends cousins Abe Looney and Hill McAlister. Both are exiled from home by the cruelty and oppressive treatment of Federals who seek to destroy the peace and happiness of all true-hearted Southern men. I hope the day is not distant when our land, loved land of Tennessee, shall be free.

Sept. 21, 1862
This day two weeks was the last Sabbath on earth of two friends whom I have ever loved; aunt Sallie Lucky and cousin Samuel Bachman. Both died of fever. Cousin Samuel was a true hearted Southerner. He took his stand at an early period in the conflict and had a position in the commissary department which he filled to the satisfaction of all so far as I hear. A little circumstance occurred while he was acting commander of the post at Cumberland Gap which showed his strict adherence to the principals of temperance which he ever advocated. The commander of the post asked him to take charge of a barrel of liquor and deal it out for medical purposes assuring him he should not be required to issue it under any other circumstance. After dealing out one barrel another was brought but he prepared and handed in his resignation which the commander of the post refused to accept. He said he would rather release almost any other officer he had than him. This was told me by a friend. He made a will on the 9th of June leaving all to the cause of Christ to

be disposed of as his friends might think best. He sleeps sweetly beside his loved mother, father and dear sisters in the old churchyard at Kingsport.

## Sept. 22, 1862

An extract of a letter from Capt. C. W. Heiskell in regard to our beloved Sam. After commending the bravery of Tom and expressing deep regret to give him up he says I might say the same of Sam Fain. Col. Moore[12] spoke of Sam by name and said he seemed to be one of the coolest men in the fight. Let his father know of this. I have no doubt Gen. Fain will always think hard of me, but this will never deter me from doing what I conceive to be my duty nor will it deter me from giving that record of praise due to his son for his bravery and good conduct in the fight. Sam's conduct in the battle of Baton Rouge according to Col. Moore's account was most praiseworthy so I think his father might give same or get him some Lieut. in his regiment which would relieve me from all awkwardness if I may so speak as to transferring or not transferring him.

## October 12, 1862

This morning called to part with my loved sons Sam and Ike. Sam going to Knoxville to join his division if not transferred. Ike to go to his papa at Loudon. I do hope my dear Sam may be placed under his papa's eye. I much fear the sly monster is beginning to wrap him up or blind him.[13]

---

12. On May 10, 1862, the Nineteenth Tennessee was reorganized. B. F. Moore was elected a lieutenant colonel, while C. W. Heiskell continued as captain of Company K. The Nineteenth fought in the Battle of Baton Rouge, but because of fever and casualties at Shiloh earlier in the year, there were scarcely a hundred soldiers out of the original four hundred in this battle. Heiskell, "Nineteenth Tennessee Infantry," in *Military Annals of Tennessee, Confederate,* ed. Lindsley, 372.

13. Eliza is referring to Sam's love for alcoholic beverages—a problem that beset several of her sons. Eliza was against alcohol in any form and favored total abstinence.

October 13, 1862

On the 3, 4 & 5th of this month a most bloody battle occurred at Corinth between the forces of Van Dorn and Price against Rosencrans and Thomas. The first two days our forces were successful driving the enemy from strong positions. But on Sabbath we had to retreat leaving I suppose our precious dead to be interred by hands who cared not in what manner they were laid away. From what I can learn of Price and Van Dorn neither of them love the Saviour. I am becoming more firmly fixed in my conviction concerning this war that religion will be more intimately interwoven in its history than any which had ever preceded it. The men who have honored God are the men he has chosen to honor on almost every field.

Nick and Sam Gammon left this morning with Nick going on with his company to Haynesville. Sam going as far as Junction; he expects to return and prepare himself for camp life this winter. I do trust he has set his face against his former vices. He drinks no more, he swears no more, may the resolve which he has made be in the strength of Jesus.

Nothing of interest to record this morning in our country's history. Sam returned last night from the labors of the day having seen 68 of his men aboard on their way to H. He went up to see Nan Kinkead. She gave him a good comforter for which I am so thankful. My supply to furnish my soldier boys is scanty indeed but my father raises friends for them and me.

October 16, 1862

Yesterdays mail brings to me the sad news that my husband is ordered to move further from home. A letter from him dated the 14th says I am ordered to Chattanooga to take command of the post.

The news of the fearful conflict at Corinth is confirmed. My soul seems to be deeply impressed that all is not right in that region. There must be a traitor in the camp whose position gave him an opportunity of knowing much in regard to the movements of our army in that region. An extract from the Mobile Register in the Rebel proves to my mind that all is not right. The battle on Friday is said to have been the hottest and most desperate of all. Soldiers who were in the battle of Shiloh says it was more terrible than that memorable conflict. The enemy appears to have been thoroughly posted with regard to all our movements. They knew when a given division passed a given point, what was its strength, the direction of its march how, when and where the attack was to be made; in short everything they wished to know and of course could make all the preparation they desired to meet us.

Our Generals seem to have been entrapped. A snare was laid by which they thought to destroy many of our brave, noble men. They succeeded in doing us much harm but yet the hand of our Father is merciful. It seems while our men were engaging the enemy at Corinth the Feds. were throwing a force of 20,000 to the rear of our forces to cut off their retreat. The Rebel says these fresh troops were met with unexampled bravery and vigor by our men in the sanguinary engagement of Sunday at Pocahontas which resulted in the discomfiture of the foe. Thanks to the genius and experience of Gen. Price our army escaped by an improvised road to a point west of Ripley where they made a stand.

October 17, 1862.

No news of interest yesterday. A battle took place at Perryville, Kentucky in which it is said Gens. Hardee, Smith and Bragg all were engaged. The reports which we have give a very decided victory to the South. They commenced fighting on Wednesday the 8th and continued Thursday and Friday. In the three days we are said to have taken 25,000 prisoners.[14] This is good news and yet to some how sad were those days of battle. They perhaps have lost their earthly stay. General Van Dorn superseded by General Pemberton.

14. The Confederates' failure to win a decisive victory at the Battle of Perryville kept Kentucky in Union hands for the rest of the war. The rumor of twenty-five thousand prisoners had been spread by General Braxton Bragg, who made this claim in his official report of the battle. Foote, *The Civil War*, 1: 742.

This may be a wise appointment but it does seem to me to be an outrage to Gen. Price.

October 18, 1862

Read with pleasure this morning the 89th Psalm and was impressed while reading with what has been my thoughts in days that are past and gone of the high destiny of our once loved but now broken crushed country. We at one time seemed to be as it were the mistress of the world. Our land was the boast of all lands. Ours was the home of the oppressed from other countries. Ours seemed to be the place where God had chosen above all others for the pure unalloyed propagation of Gospel Truth. We (many of us at least) looked upon it as the only place upon earth where "man sat under his own vine and fig-tree with none to make him afraid." We felt we are as Israel of old the chosen people. We are the people whom God intends to use for the Christianizing of all lands. O compare that with the conviction which is now forced upon us in regard to the present prospects of our bleeding republic.

Our Father has seemed to cast us from him as unworthy of the high trust he had committed to our care. His benignant face no longer shines upon us. He seems to have said to all people, nations and tongues let them alone, let them destroy themselves. I exalted them as I had never done any people on earth before. But alas they have turned from me, they have hewn out cisterns which can hold no water. They have tampered with my holy word perverting its truths to suit their depraved consciences; and have in a portion of the republic which I formed set it aside and for its teaching instituted the teachings of a higher law. Therefore I am angry, my wrath is kindled against them. I have visited them with the desolating sword. I have sent grief and mourning into almost every household and I will continue to incite until what was once the lighthouse of liberty civil and religious shall be entirely demolished or its light shall through the cry of my people which still remain in its walls be raised for the honour and glory of my name throughout the nations of the earth.

October 19, 1862

Attended church today in company with my beloved and heard from Mr. R a choice sermon on the danger of fanaticism. His text Acts 26 verses 9 to 11. He spoke of the fanaticism of Paul before his conversion that he was no hypocrite, that he acted in all good conscience but that his conscience had been perverted by his wrong judgment or will. That he was prepared for the execution of any crime if by that he could advance the desired object of his heart. He went on to show that the revolution now going on in our country is to be attributed to the wild fanaticism of the North, that it had caused them to be idolaters, infidels and has driven them into the wildest isms ever known amongst a civilized enlightened people.

October 21, 1862

Home is again made sad. The loved one of my heart and my dear children whom I love have left. My husband for Chattanooga and Samuel G and Powell for Haynesville where Sam and company are stationed. Nick gone to Bean Station to get his bedding. My heart is very sad. I feel like giving up at times and were it not for the thought what is thy duty I would sink down. But I am one who says, who feels this mighty conflict has to be waged. It is to do or die. No alternative left but to go forward trusting in the God of Abraham, Isaac and Jacob.

We have not sought this quarrel. We have, I feel, done all consistent with what is the duty of free born citizens to live in peace with free born citizens but this would not suffice. The North has said you must bow to us or be subjected to the horrors of Civil War. We of course have chosen the latter feeling that we had arrived at that point in our country's history where it was important the South should make a stand if she expected to maintain in the slightest degree the constitutional liberty which had been guaranteed. We have maintained, so far with honor to our Southern arms, but at what a cost. Let the widow, the orphan, the father, the mother, the sister bereft speak forth to the world and what would be the reply. It has cost us our earthly all.

October 23, 1862

On yesterday morning half after 6 the spirit of noble George[15] (Powel) was set at liberty from its clay tenement. His departure from earth was peaceful calm as a child falling asleep upon its mothers bosom.

October 24, 1862

Night all are sleeping around me at 20 minutes after 11. I feel this night lonely, sad and sorrowful. My poor, my deluded boy is I fear travelling so rapidly the broad road to eternal ruin. He came home this evening and his sister discovered the smell of liquor upon him and told me to make him come to me and see if I did not smell it too. I drew him to me and my heart sank within me. I feel this night if weeping a flood of tears could bring him to see his danger that I could weep day and night for my child that his doom might not be that of the drunkard. He told me candidly when I asked him that he had bought a pint and drank it. O horror of horrors is this to me. My soul would plead that my Father would stay him in his down-ward career.

Another source of grief this night is that my first born sent on this evening his wagon with the express understanding that be would be here by dark. He has failed to come. I do not know where he is nor what he is doing and fear he has fallen in with some one who is a poor companion. How grinding to the heart of a mother to think her children do not love and think of her after a life of anxious care and toil to keep up the perishing body.

October 28, 1862

A letter from my dear husband came from Bridgeport dated the 24th that made me feel sad and yet I do hope I shall be resigned. My husband has gone for the feeling it is his duty. He was elected

---

15. Eliza's nephew, George Rutledge Powel, born on June 4, 1844, died of typhus on October 22, 1862, while home on sick leave from the Confederate army.

Official appointment on February 4, 1863, of Richard Fain as the colonel of the Sixty-third Tennessee Regiment, which he had organized the previous year. From the John N. Fain Collection, East Tennessee History Center.

Colonel of a regiment the 30th of July 1862.[16] His regiment was stationed along the railroad until the 14th of October when he received orders to move to Chattanooga. All of the regiment arrived (I suppose) by the 20th but were there not more than two or three days when they removed to Bridgeport where my loved husband joined them on the morning of the 23rd. He found all in a moving condition with men all on the west side of the river while their tents

16. In July 1862 Richard Fain served as the organizing colonel of the Sixty-third Tennessee Regiment and remained in this position until his resignation in November 1863 because of ill health.

and cooking utensils were on the other side. They were moving all over in a small steamboat.

October 29, 1862

All is quiet in our county now. It seems a treacherous calm which will soon be over and a terrible storm upon us. Mr. Huffmaster came to cover my house on the east side with linseed paint and is now working on it.

I had a letter from my husband dated 27th. I have felt troubled this morning in regards to sending to salt works for salt.[17] Brother Hiram had made an arrangement with an order from Mr. Winter for 25 bushels and we were to send together. My wagon, one horse apiece and Lewis or Gus to drive. The more I thought about it the more perplexed I was. The thought of sending either Lewis or Gus was troublesome to me. Lewis is not able to bear exposure and Gus is so clumsy and inactive. I did not like for him to go so far and concluded it was best for them not to go. Brother H. had told me he could make some other arrangement. I do feel somewhat relieved but what the prospect for salt is I do not know. These are the petty trials of life. How poor how mean they appear to have taken so much thought and so much time but such is earth and they that are earthly.

Nov. 19, 1862

I am this morning again made to feel the unrelenting demands of war, cruel war. My son Ike[18] left this morning for his regiment which he expects to meet at Sweetwater—an order having been issued for the regiment to return there for the purpose of forming a brigade under Gen. John Vaughn. He took with him Hiram's horse and will ride

17. The saltworks were in Saltville, Virginia, and functioned as the major source of salt for Confederates in East Tennessee until December 1864, when the works were destroyed. Saltville is about twenty-five miles from the Tennessee state line.

18. Ike (or Isaac), who was now eighteen, joined the Sixty-third Tennessee as a private when it was organized by his father.

him I suppose through. Sam[19] went along to take Nick's horse to Kentucky to sell. I do hope the Lord will go with them. On last Friday evening a difficulty sprung between these brothers which I felt would almost take my life. For some reason they have never loved as brothers. It has always been a great pain to me but the last difficulty caused me more trouble than any which has ever gone before. It all occurred about a horse as Ike wanted to go to town and Sam to N. Charles.

Monday morning the 24th. My loved husband bid me goodbye again this morning to return to Knoxville where he is expecting to meet with his regiment in a few days. They have been brigaded under Gen. Vaughn. He seemed to feel badly but very submissive feeling all things would be right. Since that time the order has been countermanded and his regiment is now an independent one subject to the order of General Smith.

Dec. 2, 1862

Heart is again made sad by having to say farewell to my beloved husband. I feel he has not been treated well by the commanding officer but I hope it may in the end be for his eternal good. His regiment is now ordered to relieve the Florida brigade and march to Cumberland Gap. Poor fellows they cannot like this and suppose they left Knoxville yesterday morning. My husband left them on Saturday after making all necessary arrangements for transportation before he came home to get him a horse. He took with him this morning Buck and hope he may be useful to him. He is a noble little horse. He received a note from headquarters last night demanding of him a report on account of his absence. He felt rather chagrined. On last Tuesday Nick left to join the troops defending Mobile.

19. Eliza's son Sam joined Company K of the Nineteenth Tennessee in May 1861, but in 1862 he became a private in the Sixty-third Tennessee, serving in that unit until the winter of 1864, when he returned home from Virginia. Nick (or Nicholas), a brother of Sam, also served in Company K of the Nineteenth Tennessee as a private. However, in October 1862 he joined Company B of the Sixtieth Tennessee Mounted Infantry, in which his rank was second lieutenant.

Dec. 3, 1862

Gloomy looking this morning and has been raining the greater part of the night gently, beautifully. I do pray that our enemies may gain no advantage over us this winter by their gunboats. My beloved husband returned last night having gone to Morristown yesterday to see about his regiment. They were there and Col. Fulkerson had come and was drilling his men yesterday evening. He is an efficient officer. My husband met at the Gap the corpse of one of his men a Mr. Cooper from the upper end of the county. His brother was with the remains and brought him over to the river. He expected to get a wagon from Mr. Lyons to convey his lifeless remains to the home of his childhood. He died in Knoxville.

Dec. 22, 1862

This day week about 3 o'clock was a day long to be remembered by those who witnessed the scene. It is one which time will not erase from the memory of those who were the actors and sufferers in the horrible tragedy. Some months since an altercation took place between Gen. [John G.] Bynum and Mr. [John D.] Riley which seemed to settle down in a deadly hostility to each other. This is from the statement of others. I never knew anything about the matter of personal knowledge. Time passed along and each seemed to be cherishing the dark malignant passions of the heart. On last Monday both were in town and I know not whether any words passed between them or not. My own impression is that Mr. Riley became afraid of Gen. B. and determined to close the scenes by taking his life or he taking his. He went to G. R. Powel's house and took from the passage a double barreled shotgun loaded heavily with buckshot (say 20 in each barrel) for the purpose of killing a deer. He came on with it to the bank but Gen. Bynum had gone home as I understood to get his horse and came riding along. He halted a short time to converse with cousin A. about going into the salt business after which he rode off and as he was turning the corner Mr. R. demanded him to halt which was done. I heard that Gen. B. had time to rein up his horse and then

Mr. R let loose the contents of one barrel which proved a deadly shot entering in the region of the lungs tearing one lung to pieces. E. Ruth told me 5 holes were to be seen where the shot had entered. He fell from his horse and took aim at Mr. R and shot off three charges from his revolver. One of the shots struck Mr. R. in the leg wounding him severely. I do not know that Gen. B ever spoke. His spirit was gone in less than 10 minutes from its clay tenement. The life of the murdered had been one continuous scene of rebellion and rejection of God. The life of the murderer is still prolonged.[20]

Dec. 22, 1862

The Sabbath before General Bynum's death he attended church with his interesting wife and heard from Mr. R. that solemn sermon. Had he taken the counsel of the minister on that day he might have been living. Upon what small and too human trifling circumstances hung the life of that man. Just the turning of the corner on the street.

On this day week I enjoyed the presence of my loved husband at home; he was quite unwell from cholera morbus but spent the day with me. On Tuesday morning he started for his post having to go by Morristown to answer the writ of habeas corpus served on him for the body of a young soldier belonging to the regiment. He felt under all circumstance the soldier could not get off but went to answer to the call and has since written to me that the government was successful. The soldier returned to his command.

Richard arrived safely at the Gap on Thursday evening and his regiment arrived at Cumberland Gap on the 8th of December having had a cold march from Morristown. This war is trying the souls of the children of the most high God. Let us be faithful, the conflict will soon be over and the prize gained.

---

20. A pencil addition to the diary dated July 14, 1868, notes that the story as written here may be incorrect. There is no record of military service for John G. Bynum. However, he was at one time a district attorney general for the Third District of Tennessee, which explains why Eliza referred to him as "Gen. Bynum."

December 31, 1862

We have heard this evening a confirmation of the news that the Federal raid upon Bristol is true.[21] The bridges at Union and Watauga are destroyed and what other mischief we know not. We have nothing to hope for if they should succeed in placing their troops here. We hope that favors will be shown to us as we have shown to those amongst us who have taken sides with them. On yesterday morning Sam, Ike, Fain Powel, Ernest and Bert Carmack and some five or six others left their homes for the Gap.

---

21. The military excursion by Union cavalry under General Samuel P. Carter is known as Carter's Raid. It passed nine miles northeast of Rogersville on this day. W. G. Piston, *Carter's Raid; An Episode of the Civil War in East Tennessee* (Johnson City, Tenn.: Overmountain Press, 1989).

# Chapter 3

## War Comes to Rogersville: 1863

The year started with the threat of Union occupation, but the Northern cavalry that posed the threat returned to Kentucky. In September, however, the Yankee forces came back to Tennessee under the command of Colonel Israel Garrard, and they remained until November 6, when they were driven from Rogersville by Confederate forces under the command of Brigadier General William E. Jones at the so-called Battle of Big Creek near Eliza's home. At the end of November, Confederate forces under General James Longstreet moved into the Rogersville area and remained until April 1864.

Eliza's son Nick, along with her nephew Sam Gammon, were among the 1,751 Confederate troops under Brigadier General John Vaughn who surrendered during the Battle of Big Black River in Mississippi on May 17, 1863. Union troops under General Michael K. Lawler attacked the Confederates in a bayonet charge that lasted only three minutes. The Confederates panicked, and the entire Sixtieth Tennessee raised the white flag of surrender before the Union troops even reached their line. Many of the soldiers later concluded that General Vaughn and his officers had given up too soon and that the unit should have defended the honor of the South to the last man. Historian Todd Groce has concluded that this demonstrated how low morale had fallen and that the East Tennesseans "simply lacked the will to fight that day."[1] It should be noted that the Sixtieth Tennessee was one of the units raised in East Tennessee after the announcement that all able-bodied men who did not volunteer for military service would be drafted. In all probability, the men who remained eligible for service in the summer of 1862 were those whose enthusiasm for secession left something to be desired. Nick Fain, Sam Gammon, and Jonathan Bachman had enlisted in the Nineteenth Tennessee in 1861 as privates and fought in the Battles of Shiloh and Baton Rouge. All three left the next year to become officers and recruit men for the Sixtieth Tennessee. In any case, the Battle of Big Black River was a debacle for the unit and sealed the fate of Vicksburg.

Nick and Sam may have been eligible for parole under the parole d'honneur system that was developed during the War of 1812. This system required that they swear an oath not to fight again until formally exchanged for captured Union soldiers of equivalent rank. Captain Jonathan Bachman, another of Sam Gammon's first cousins, was captured at Vicksburg and did accept these conditions, allowing him to return to East Tennessee, where he became a preacher. However, this was not the case for Nick and Sam. They went to prison and remained there until a few months before the end of the Civil War.

Eliza does not mention that her husband resigned his commission in the Confederate army in November. Richard Fain was involved in the organization of the Sixty-

1. Groce, *Mountain Rebels*, 101.

third Tennessee Regiment of Volunteer Infantry and elected as organizing colonel in July 1862. The Sixty-third Tennessee fought at Chickamauga and lost half of the 404 men who went into the battle. These were among the greatest losses of any Confederate regiment in a single battle during the Civil War, and it indicates that this unit was unafraid to fight to the last man. Richard, however, was ill with dysentery and missed this battle. Colonel Abraham Fulkerson replaced Richard and later said of him: "Col. R. G. Fain was a graduate of West Point and an accomplished officer but by reason of age and declining health he was incapacitated for active service in the field, and was with the regiment but very little."[2]

### January 3, 1863

It is now Saturday night as I sit by my home fireside with all asleep around me but my two darling daughters Bet and Sallie. Our prayers have been heard and our enemies turned back. On last Monday evening a courier arrived at Rogersville bringing the startling intelligence that a large cavalry force were crossing the mountains at a Gap called Cranks Gap and moving on to Bristol.[3] They were successful in getting through and on to Bristol where they were met by some of our forces. They burnt bridges then came on to Kingsport and lodged on the premises of Mr. R. Netherland. A messenger came from there to inform us they were coming. The news produced considerable stir in our little town. Citizens and soldiers had to leave without much

---

2. Fulkerson, "Sixty-third Tennessee Infantry," in *Military Annals of Tennessee*, ed. Lindsley, 584.

3. This was a Union cavalry unit that consisted of about a thousand men under the command of General Samuel P. Carter. The unit bypassed both Rogersville and Bristol on their way to Blountville and Carter's Depot. Returning to Kentucky, Carter's men came within eight miles of Rogersville on January 1, 1863, when they passed through Looney's Gap in the Clinch Mountains. In twenty days they covered 470 miles on horseback, having suffered casualties of only two killed and four wounded. Although two railroad bridges were destroyed and hundreds of horses stolen, the raid amply demonstrated how difficult it was to attack East Tennessee from Kentucky. Piston, *Carter's Raid*.

time to think. Some to the railroad and others in different directions. Some moving their Negroes while others sent them into the woods and hills to hide as they could.

I could not help contrasting the situation of the true hearted Southerner and the Tory (if I should so speak) when Col. Starnes cavalry made their appearance in our midst all things remained as they had been. The farmer moved on with his daily business as usual and all hands remained at their posts. Not so when the dark hearted invader was heard to have set foot on East Tennessee soil. All who had any valuables began to think what shall I do, where shall I go and where must I hide everything from the robber. The scene we had on New Years Day will long be remembered. We heard they were coming, had got to Surgoinsville and such a moving about of things has not been seen for a great while. After doing the best we could we sat down to await their arrival. Do I say sat down, I mean by that we calmed our selves for our fate but few moments passed without some head being stuck out to see if they were coming. Old Pollys grim visage grew more and more dark and appalling all the while. I spoke of sending Caroline, Lewis and Gus, Hill and Jim over to George Tucks and keeping Ahab, Polly, Cindy and Nate[4] with my own children for my bodyguard but at this Polly remonstrated in a beseeching manner saying if they get hold of me they will beat me to make me tell where things are hid and the others have gone. Poor old Polly knew but little of the whereabouts of what was put out of the way. The day passed and still they came not. Night came and we all felt now they will come and perhaps give the order prepare supper for so many. I would go out every few moments to listen if I could hear the sound of the bugle or the tramp of horses. Between 8 and 9 went into the yard with Nannie

---

4. Polly, aged fifty-three, was a slave and the mother of Lewis, aged thirteen, as well as of Hill, aged twenty-four. Living in one cabin were Gus, aged thirty-three; Caroline, age unknown, a rented slave married to Frank McCarty; and Gus's three children, eight-year-old Liz, eleven-year-old Jim, and six-year-old Nate. The mother of these children was Gus's wife, Mary, who had died in 1858. Ahab was another slave, who was approximately sixty-three years old in early 1863.

following every time. I stood and listened and in a short time I heard the chatter of horses hoofs on the frozen ground. Nannie drew up close saying Mama they are coming and is that them. I thought there were some five or six from the sound and just supposed they were scouts (I learned afterwards there were two).

At length we thought the bugle had sounded and such a scrabbling in our cabins has not been seen before (and I hope will not again). I told them if they had to go they had better bring their things and put them in the house. Old Polly jerked the few duds she had thrown together in a confused bundle and hurried with quick time to deposit them, then with shawl and bonnet on awaited their arrival all night. Old Ahab scouted until between 1 and 2 A.M. Gus, Caroline, Liz, Jim, and Nate slept in their cabin. Hill, Lewis and Jim in Ahab's. Liz and Sallie acted as sentinels in the house. I had set up the night before until 12 thinking they might perhaps be on us that night (and had another thought was perhaps Richard will send me word what to do). At last Liz says to me Mama if they shoot us will we go to heaven. I replied yes my child. She then said they can't hurt us when we get there. I feel this was sent as a solace to my grief that there is a place where the rage of man never comes.

The night of suspense past, the morning came. As I was aroused from sleep my first thought was the host of the Lord hath encamped around me and mine through the night. We were all secure. I rose, dressed myself and went out anxious to know if they had gone on to town. I was not long in suspense as to that, but still on the lookout for them. After a while news came they had crossed the mountains at Looney's Gap and had spent the night with Abigail Anderson. I felt a load is gone, my prayer was may they never return.

About dinnertime brother George came having lodged in about a half a mile at Mr. Sol Sizemores. They have not molested so far as I can hear many people. They have stolen indiscriminately horse and mules from Southerners and Union, might have done more mischief could they have procured easy transport for blacks.

And while this was going on the Lord was with us in Middle Tennessee enabling our brave men to drive back the ruthless invader with a fearful carnage.[5] Many of our noble brave sons have given their lives on their country altar in this deadly conflict. They commenced firing on our pickets on Sunday (so says Kyle McCarty in a letter to me). Never would I if I could get out of it fire the first gun on the Sabbath. In all the battles which have taken place so far as my observation goes those who on the Sabbath began the attack have been defeated with heavy loss.

The battle raged I suppose terribly on Tuesday and Wednesday the 30th and 31st.[6] The last day was the fearful day. Some of our slightly wounded have returned home. Jack Carmack came tonight bringing the sad news of the death of 4 in Co. K of the nineteenth Tenn. regiment and several badly wounded. Jim Huffmaster thought to be mortally wounded as well as Charlie Miller in James Spears company. Charlie Fudge lost an arm and Henry Smith a leg.[7] Marshall was killed as well as the noble Gen. Rains. I regret to hear of his death. Nick was so well acquainted with him and spoke of him so often to me I almost felt that I knew him but he is no more. The next thought which rises was he prepared for death — this is the solemn question. The names of Gen. Rains and cousin Sam Bachman are associated together in my mind because of their

5. This was the Battle of Murfreesboro, also known as Stone's River, an engagement that resulted in twenty-five thousand casualties about equally divided between Union and Confederate forces. The battle failed to repel the dreaded Yankees invaders, and the Confederates under General Braxton Bragg retreated to Tullahoma, Tennessee. Foote, *The Civil War,* 2: 100.

6. The Battle of Murfreesboro claimed casualties of more than thirty-six killed or wounded in Company K of the Nineteenth Tennessee. Heiskell, "Nineteenth Tennessee Infantry," in *Military Annals of Tennessee,* ed. Lindsley, 374–79.

7. In *The Old Nineteenth Tennessee Regiment* (74–75), Worsham lists the four members of Company K who were killed as E. W. Marshall, William Wax, Charles Miller, and Charles Fudge. The wounded from that company included First Lieutenant Jim (J. H.) Huffmaster, who recovered from his wounds and was promoted to captain of the company in April 1863, W. B. Miller, E. H. Jackson, and John Carmack. The regiment's total casualties in this battle numbered 38 killed and 111 wounded. These losses were twice those of any other regiment in the brigade of General Alexander P. Stewart.

stay at Cumberland Gap. One dies on his bed surrounded by the pleasures of the delightful home of a sister and the other feels his life blood flowing out on the battlefield. Both are martyrs to their country's cause.

January 8, 1863

Kentucky Cavalry started back this morning and will cross the mountains at little War Gap. They came across on Tuesday from Jonesville; having gone that far in pursuit of Yankee bridgeburners. They got there in time to see the rear as they were skedaddling. Richard's regiment (the able part) started at dark from Cumberland Gap on Friday under Col Fulkerson and Major Aiken hoping to meet up with the first invaders of this part of East Tennessee but were too late. Had Col. F. been able to have carried out his wishes he would have had them or they him. They returned Sunday evening much wearied.

January 21, 1863

Several days have past since I penned anything on my book and leaves. Our country still in darkness; a faint glimmering light seems to be rising in the far distant horizon. May it prove the dawn of liberty to the South. Today Sallie read for me the message of President Davis. I feel our President is an honor to our people. His message is a document which will be read many years hence with emotion and with gratitude to the God of Heaven who rules and reigns. He has raised up for this time of trouble the man who now stands at the head of our Southern Government. I was not aware of the deep inquiry inflicted by foreign powers upon our struggling country until I heard that message. Our statesmen have been so guarded for fear of being (I suppose) regarded as appealing for aid. President Davis sets forth in language clear and unmistakable the position which some of the powers of Europe occupied in regard to us from the adoption of principles to regulate maritime operations between neutrals and belligerents entered into in 1856 between the 5 great powers of Europe together with Sardinia and Turkey.

1. Privateering is and remains abolished. 2. The neutral flag covers enemy goods with the exception of contraband of war. 3. Neutral's goods with the exception of contraband of war are not liable to capture under enemy flag. 4. Blockade in order to be binding must be effective that is to say maintained by a force sufficient really to prevent access to the coast of the enemy. Had Europe carried out these principles in strict accordance with international law how different would have been the condition of our Southern land. I feel our President is a Christian and that when he implores High Heaven for protection and aid it is from the depths of the Soul. How great the contrast in this respect between the President of the Northern people; but God our Father hath made us to differ.

January 23, 1863

Had last night a letter from my beloved husband; he is asking my advice in regard to his resigning. I do feel could he stand the service I do not want him to resign if he is useful to his country *as I hope and believe he is.* I feel it is important for everyone to stand firm and unshaken at his post. I do trust that wisdom may be given from God my Heavenly Father to him who is my earthly stay to enable him to do that which is best for him to do. O when shall peace again visit our beloved country.

January 25, 1863

Have had today a sweet foretaste of the joy which will be felt when I shall be permitted to join the church triumphant, have set in his earthly sanctuary and listened to a sermon from my loved minister Mr. Robinson from Nehemiah. Mr. R. showed to the mind so conclusively today that whenever the church becomes corrupt anarchy, despotism and misrule follow. Corrupt New England where abolition practices have taken the pulpits of the noble high souled men who once occupied them, has brought a curse upon our country which nothing can overcome but the dissemination and belief of the holy doctrines of the Bible in all their purity.

February 5, 1863

Last night a soldier came riding up and asked for lodging. I hesitated on account of horse provender but the dislike to turn off a soldier triumphed and I told him to set down and come in. He proved to be a nice man by the name of Alfred Davis. His family is living in Edenton, Georgia but his home is in Shreveport Texas and he belongs to Capt. Nelson's partisan Rangers. Mr. Davis is the first soldier that I have met with who could out talk me but to him I surrender the palm. He was pleasant, affable and quite intelligent. I hope be may become a Christian. I feel so much for our precious soldiers that they may be the children of the most high God. Seems to feel neither Yankee men nor bullets were made to kill him. I love to see our soldiers so bold and daring but with it I love to see the confiding trust of a finite in the infinite.

February 14, 1863

The love of home going forth again to battle with camp life. My dear Ike bid us goodbye this morning with rather a heavy heart having left the Gap on the 25th of January in a wagon and got home on the 28th. He walked across from Mrs. Merrimons and seemed to be much fatigued when he got here. He looked so badly, had a severe spell with his bowels and threatened with brain affection. I was so glad he was permitted to come home, so many poor fellows languish for weeks, years and months in those dreaded hospitals with no one to care for them. To me it has always seemed to be wrong to send men to such places if they could be sent home. I feel it is a great loss of life unnecessarily. Men if permitted to come home and receive the kind nursing and attention of home friends might in a short time be restored to health.

My loved husband has been at home on a visit for two weeks having gone to Knoxville during the time and absent from Monday until Friday. I feel so glad when home can be home for a few short days if no longer during these hours of trial and great perplexity. What a happy thought there is a home where neither war, sickness or famine invade. My husband got home on the thirty-first riding on horseback from the Gap.

## April 12, 1863

On the 14th of February cousin Martha Fain Ross[8] died at Cleveland leaving 6 children to the care of the loved of her own home. 5 boys and a little girl named Amelia. Martha had been a child of sorrow having been unfortunate in her selection of a partner for life. Her married life was one of trouble and sorrow but I trust one of preparation for a better and brighter world. She had married against the wishes of her dear family but never troubled them with a rehearsal of her sorrows and trials—feeling I did it why should I trouble them.

God has again given to a worm a glorious privilege; his church has been thrown open in peace and quiet. Mr. R. today spoke of this departure by the North from the word of God being the cause of our present difficulty. He feels and we all feel we have sinned and come far short of living as he requireth and that he has visited us for our sins and has wrecked his heavier vengeance upon the North for the mutilation of his world and their sins. This is a war I feel for the upbuilding of the truth as it is in Jesus. O that our father would hear the cry of the oppressed South. O Father hear the cry of thy children for our honor and for peace.

## April 22, 1863

This day my loved son Sam bid farewell to the loved of home to go back to Cumberland Gap. His uncle Hiram going with him to try and bring Ernest[9] home who had been quite sick from jaundice. Sam came

---

8. Martha Fain was the daughter of John Fain of Dandridge, Tennessee, and a distant cousin of Richard Fain. She had married a salesman from the North, but why Eliza considered her "a child of sorrow" is unclear. However, Martha's unmarried brother, Sam Fain of Mossy Creek (now Jefferson City, Tennessee), took in the orphaned children and after the Civil War hired Sallie Fain, Eliza's daughter, to be their teacher. This arrangement led to the marriage of Sam and Sallie in 1867.

9. Hiram Fain was Eliza's brother-in-law, who lived on an adjoining farm. His son Ernest, aged nineteen, was serving in the Confederate army.

home 28 of March sick with chills. He had intended going back last Monday week but on Sabbath had a chill and on Monday, Tuesday and Wednesday I gave him freely of boneset. I do hope he may have no more. Our poor soldiers who were in Miss. & Louisiana last summer will be sufferers for many days to come. But this is one of the calamities of war; men must go whether the climate suits or not.

On the 25th of February Richard, E. Ruth [Powell], Nancy [McCarty][10] and myself set out for Mossy Creek. We got there about 5 in the evening, raining and no ways comfortable. There we were two miles from factory, raining and no way to go. Richard set his head to work and was not long in getting things under head way, had made inquiry for a vehicle but none could be had. Mr. Hubbard mentioned Mr. Branner's wagon. So in a short time the wagon was at the door, in all mounted and it was a great ride. One of the best drivers held the lines I have ever seen. A man who once belonged to Mr. Roper. We got in between 7 & 8 wet and in an uncomfortable fix but the kindness of friends soon done away with all that was unpleasant. Cousin Mollie and her husband were there. We took our suppers and not long afterwards were comfortably fixed in our beds, got up the next morning, raining and continued to rain the greater part of the day. We did not get to see the cotton crowd. In the evening we went down and bought a few thing at the store and to look at factory which to me was quite a curiosity. So much machinery—so many different places for the cotton to pass before it was thread.

The next morning they sent us in their wagon to the depot. Cousin Will [Fain] giving me a dog and sending it on to the depot. It was part blood hound. We landed at home Friday evening about sundown. Brought no cotton but have received since 4 bales (of thread). Hiram came up with us from Morristown.

---

10. Eliza Ruth and Nancy McCarty were sisters-in-law of Eliza. The purpose of the visit was to buy cotton thread from the factory of two cousins, Sam and Will Fain. They planned to weave the thread into clothing. Sam and Will's father was John Fain, a first cousin of Richard's father, Nicholas Fain.

April 28, 1863

Have felt so much better today. I have been so troubled for several days past about a field which Richard had consented to take of Brother Hiram. We had gone on got it broke up using his teams and ours. It was nearly harrowed and laid off the first way more than half when I said something about a horse first to Nick in the morning. At noon brother H came over to see Samuel about going to the Gap when I said something to him about a horse. He then told me there was a misunderstanding between he and Richard. His understanding from R. was that if he would furnish the team to break up R. would do the rest. My understanding and all of ours was very different. We thought he had furnished a horse and the feed and we did the rest for half of what was made. I felt this is a very liberal offer on the part of R. to H. but I was willing. I felt he had no one to cultivate his field and I was anxious he should have something to go on. But then I came to find out H. regarded it very differently. He said R. was very anxious to get the field and he seemed to look upon it as an accommodation for us to get it. I was much troubled and perplexed when I found out how he looked on the matter so. I felt I cannot get along with but two horses as our dependence. I studied for a while. My own inclination was supported by my children. Liz (who never wanted us to have anything to do with it), Sallie, Powell and I determined in justice to my family to have nothing to do with it. We sent Sallie to see her Uncle H. and tell him I could not take the field on those terms. He seemed to be rather displeased at the decision and said to Sallie he thought it was a late hour to see about it now. He thought I surely wanted to give him trouble just as he was starting after Ernest. Sallie said to him, no Uncle Hiram mama wants you to go after Ernest. Will you be willing to furnish a horse to work when you come back. He told he would furnish a horse when it was convenient but wanted it understood that when his horse went in there it was as a favor. I did not accomplish anything to move him from the stand he had taken. I then got Brother George to go over and see him. He told him what was the usual way of renting for half over the mountain and that he had understood from Richard we were to have his horse to work. But it was of no avail. After he came back I was just determined to give the field up. I thought we might part on terms of good feeling. So perhaps George had made the proposition to Hiram that we would pay him for the use of his team, take the field work it and give him one-third but to this he would not consent. Horses were my trouble, to make this overture and I still thought perhaps I can do some way to get along if we can only have some compromise which will bear on its face justice and equity and be what is right.

After George came back I told the boys to take their ploughs and go to our own field, feeling so certain it was not what Richard intended to. I set down and wrote to my beloved husband making what I felt was a true statement. I then felt whatever R. says that I will do. Samuel and his uncle Hiram set off and I suppose they went to town. I told his uncle I would not take this field so he spoke to Col. W. to take it but afterwards I suppose Sam told him perhaps he was not right about it so he sent back word to Col. W. to do nothing with it until he came back which was done. By him I received a letter from Richard saying to me let the boys go on and put in the field. That if he had made any bargain of that kind he was not particular with him but supposed he would let us have a horse when he could. This he said he was willing to do and had sent me word that he would when convenient let him have a horse. I received the word but just felt if this is the condition, let me not have anything to do with it. But the word of my husband is the law to me so I have nothing to do but just go on and do the best I can. I do hope I may be enabled to do what is right. Had I known there was the least doubt as to the agreement I never would have brought the boys from this field. But I felt my dear husband had made the impression on the mind of all that brother Hiram was to furnish the horse. I knew he thought that it was that way at the time but he would never have any difficulty about anything. I feel that he is a

Christian and I hope that I may never do anything to wound his feelings in any way. I have been much troubled but the Bible is the sure and never failing source of comfort. I take it up on my days of deepest anguish.

## May 5, 1863

Today I went to wool picking at E. Ruth Powels. Annis Poats, Jennie Walker, E. Ruth, Sarah Powel and I were the white wool pickers. There were three or four black ones. I felt Mrs. Powel is rapidly drawing near her Eternal home. She is very feeble and not able to come down stairs. Sallie came home this morning from Knoxville. Staid Thursday night with Bet Kenner. They went down last Friday from the Junction and staid at Kenners then went down Saturday to Mrs. Heiskells.

## May 18, 1863

My Father Uncle is no more.[11] He died on the morning of the 7th (Thursday) at 2 A.M. peaceful and happy. On April 30th he asked to be taken out on the porch and to the back door. He then for a little while looked as far as he could at the fields and woods in front of us. He said that all looked beautiful and that this was his last sight. O how pleasant to die in the Spring. Sweet fields arrayed in living green and river of delight.

 This evening week our great our noble our lamented Jackson was taken from us.[12] For him we mourn but may his death teach us an instructive lesson that God will be honored and if we in any way rob him of the honor and glory due to him alone he will bring us to

11. Sam Rhea, born in 1795, was the brother of Eliza's mother, Elizabeth Rhea Anderson. After the death of Eliza's father, Audley Anderson, in 1818, when Eliza was only two years old, Elizabeth and her four daughters lived with Sam Rhea until 1826, when he married Ann Rutledge. However, Ann died in 1827, leaving an infant son. At this time, Sam resumed housekeeping with Elizabeth and her daughters. They shared a household until 1832, when Sam married Martha Lynn.

12. Eliza's account of the wounding of General Thomas J. "Stonewall" Jackson by his own men at Chancellorsville and of his subsequent death is substantially correct.

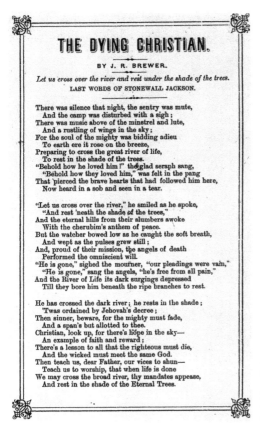

## THE DYING CHRISTIAN.

### BY J. R. BREWER.

*Let us cross over the river and rest under the shade of the trees.*
LAST WORDS OF STONEWALL JACKSON.

There was silence that night, the sentry was mute,
  And the camp was disturbed with a sigh ;
There was music above of the minstrel and lute,
  And a rustling of wings in the sky ;
For the soul of the mighty was bidding adieu
  To earth ere it rose on the breeze,
Preparing to cross the great river of life,
  To rest in the shade of the trees.
"Behold how he loved him !" the glad seraph sang,
  "Behold how they loved him," was felt in the pang
That 'pierced the brave hearts that had followed him here,
  Now heard in a sob and seen in a tear.

"Let us cross over the river," he smiled as he spoke,
  "And rest 'neath the shade of the trees,"
And the eternal hills from their slumbers awoke
  With the cherubim's anthem of peace.
But the watcher bowed low as he caught the soft breath,
  And wept as the pulses grew still ;
And, proud of their mission, the angels of death
  Performed the omniscient will.
"He is gone," sighed the mourner, "our pleadings were vain,"
  "He is gone," sang the angels, "he's free from all pain,"
And the River of Life its dark surgings depressed
  Till they bore him beneath the ripe branches to rest.

He has crossed the dark river ; he rests in the shade ;
  'Twas ordained by Jehovah's decree ;
Then sinner, beware, for the mighty must fade,
  And a span's but allotted to thee.
Christian, look up, for there's hope in the sky—
  An example of faith and reward ;
There's a lesson to all that the righteous must die,
  And the wicked must meet the same God.
Then teach us, dear Father, our vices to shun—
  Teach us to worship, that when life is done
We may cross the broad river, thy mandates appease,
  And rest in the shade of the Eternal Trees.

A broadside tribute to Stonewall Jackson, found among the diaries of Eliza Fain. From the private collection of John and Ann Fain.

see the evil of our ways. Have the people of the South not been guilty of idolatry in regard to our good Generals. Have we not often felt and said if Stonewall is there all will be right. The arm of flesh was omnipotent in our eye. Behold what our Father hath done. He has removed him we feel to himself. He was wounded by his own men having gone forth to ascertain the strength and position of the enemy. Having first given an order to his men to fire on anyone who should approach them. They not knowing of his leaving fired as he returned. His left arm was shattered and his right hand disabled. He fell from his horse. Some of his staff were taken prisoners and his body was passed twice by but was unmolested or undiscovered. I do feel God was kind to us not to let that dear body fall into the hands of a cruel foe. They would have rejoiced, they would have gloated in fiendish revelry over our expiring hero. His ashes will mingle with his native soil but his blood crieth for vengeance on the oppressor.

### May 27, 1863

I often feel so cast down, my family large, my anxiety for their worldly comfort often causes me to feel so depressed feeling ever my great lack as a managing housewife. Feel I am no helpmate to my dear husband; have felt so ever since he came home this time. I am always sorry when I feel this when he is at home. I feel I cannot make his visit as pleasant as I desire.

Yesterday my dear husband went to the Gap[13] or Rogersville Junction in company with Mr. Hayden. The engines authorized to take up our railroad track. He has been stopped in the proceedings by a process in Chancery Court. Mr. Heiskell comes today for Richard to see if something cannot be done to let it remain. He feels it would be a great inconvenience to do without it now. My dear husband in town today.

### May 31, 1863

Today has been a pleasant day. Powell and Dick went to Sabbath School. Tom Powel came back with them but was taken a short time after he came with a chill having quite a high fever after it passed off. How hard for our poor boys who bore the Southern campaign of last summer to have health. I fear many have laid the foundation for premature decay. My heart is filled with intense anxiety about the loved who are at Vicksburg. I do hope the words

---

13. The main line of the East Tennessee and Virginia Railroad running from Bristol to Knoxville came through Bulls Gap (also known as Rogersville Junction). Here a branch line, known as the Rogersville and Jefferson Railroad, connected with the Holston River ferry about a mile from Rogersville. Richard was president of the Rogersville and Jefferson, and there was some controversy about tearing up the tracks. Richard's military papers (see Fain Collection) include a note dated May 22, 1863, authorizing a ten-day leave so that Richard could attend to "important business with the Rogersville and Jefferson railroad and attend Chancery Court to give his bond as Clerk and Master of said court."

of our lamented Jackson may ever stand forth in the hearts of all My trust is in God.

June 1, 1863

My loved husband has again said goodbye to home and friends. O how long are these sad scenes to be kept up by our oppressive foe. I am suffering so much anxiety for those who are far from home. The news from Vicksburg is not cheering having nothing from our own side all Federal news. We have had no news from Vicksburg for 3 or 4 mails. This is a great trouble.

June 2, 1863

I do feel so sad this morning. I have been trying to attend to domestic cares but feel every thing so irksome which I undertake. Days are dark and friends of earth are few. O how unstable is the friendship of this world. We know not how long we shall be able to rely on those who are dear by the ties of kindred. Man is so selfish, he seems to care but little for any one but himself. Yesterday evening E. Ruth came to see me a short time. I love her and have ever loved her. We had a conversation in regard to Richards course about the railroad. She seems to think he did wrong but not from a wrong motive. I feel this is the influence of her husband. I do not think G.[14] has that kind feeling and love for R. which he should have. R. has ever loved G, has been kind, has sought in every way he could consistent with right to have him love him as one of lifes early friends. But it is all to no purpose; he seems to be ever finding something to harrow his own feelings in the wrong way towards him. These thing try me much and my loved husband being from home all the time the trial is so much harder to bear.

14. G. is George Powel, born in 1807. In the 1860 census he was listed as the second richest man in Rogersville. He was married to the sister of Eliza's husband. While a Southern supporter, he was probably more of a pragmatist who was upset about the practical effects that destruction of the railroad would have on business in Rogersville. It appears that Richard favored destruction of the rolling stock, while George opposed it.

My thoughts are turned to friends this day at Vicksburg. All is still dark as to the casualties of the late engagements near Vicksburg. We know not who has fallen but trust the Lord has been there by his spirit cheering the wounded and dying.

June 3, 1863

The Lord is still showing us mercy. We have lain down and slept. No enemy disturbed that quiet repose but the angel of the Lord hath encamped around about us. All have risen in usual health to behold Nature greatly invigorated by the rain which fell while we slept.

My heart is still in trouble for the loved who are in Vicksburg. I think of the sad hearts around me and my own loved ones until I feel at times sick, really sick. I at one time felt Vicksburg will never be the scene of terrible conflict for our enemies felt she is invincible but O Father how differently thou art now making me feel. I was lifted up but now I am cast down. Mothers are this day weeping in suspense. Wives, daughters, and sisters are mourning in silence with that fearful foreboding of evil.

Nan Kinkead was with us last night having staid two nights. She and Liz were in town yesterday. As she left this morning I mentioned I felt if we heard nothing more from Vicksburg I could go no where unless it was to see someone who felt as I felt. I spoke of Mrs. Yeonas. She is so troubled. Liz mentioned the names of Lou Kinkead and Lizzie Miller and I do feel so deeply for those young wives.

June 21, 1863

This day opened upon us in the midst of excitement and perplexing scenes. Yesterday evening the news reached us that the Feds were in the locality of Knoxville and that they had been met and opposed by some of our troops. This evening we have had news that they had been repulsed at Knoxville and had turned in an easterly direction. They have burned the bridges at Flat Creek and Strawberry Plains. Of the truth of this we have yet to hear. Fear it may prove to be true.

O we do tremble at times lest our Father in Heaven should make us feel the horrors of an invasion.

June 28, 1863

We live still in quiet and peace. The invader has turned back and gone. We humbly trust to return no more. What must be the appearance of Vicksburg where the enemy have lain around for more than three months with every now and then a throwing of shells and bombs. Within the last two months they have gained more accessible points for its destruction. O Father may it not fall into the hands of the cruel, the relentless barbarian. This is a place which shall never be forgotten by me. It was somewhere in the regions of this place that my two darling boys Nick and Sam Gammon (as we suppose) fell into the hands of the enemy. Of their fate we know nothing with any certainty. I have the impression on my mind that they must have been in the fight at Edwards Depot on the 15th of May where they were captured. More than a month has passed and yet we are in rather a state of suspense. The only relief which the mind has had from any earthly source was a dispatch from cousin Jimmy Rhea at Jackson on the 19th in which he said that Col. Crawford and staff with the sick (and I think wounded) of Bachmans and Morrows Companies had gotten into Vicksburg; that the regiment was captured and none were killed. I think of my dear boys so often. These are sad days.

June 30, 1863

We have a bountiful wheat harvest. It had seemed to me we were not going to get weather to cut it for the rain has been coming down every day for a week. I felt troubled at the thought of losing that which seems so necessary to the life of man. I awoke night before last and the thought crossed my mind of the wrestling of our lamented Jackson before entering into an engagement. I rose from my bed, kneeled and poured out my soul in prayer to my Father that he would give to us a time in which we might cradle and save our wheat.

I feel he has heard me. They will be able to finish that which is ripe enough to cut today.

Last night I awoke again. The rain was falling fast but my thought was not for the preservation of our grain alone. Having heard by Hiram that the brave, noble band of men from the regiment of my beloved husband had been ordered to Tullahoma I could not sleep.

Hiram came yesterday evening about 8 o'clock. Capt. Clint Lyons with him.[15] He commenced talking about a horse before he got off. The one he was riding (being one of Mr. G. McKinneys whose boy was in town he got the boy to bring him out). I hesitated about letting him have one. Both of mine being in a bad fix for the trip but I feel I have to yield always to Hirams importunities. I perhaps might have held out better had it not been my deep sympathy for Capt. L. He seemed to be so unwell and so anxious to get home. I felt Hiram must go with him. I fear he may have a serious spell of sickness as he was salivating. I felt anxious for them to stay all night but he felt he must get home. He had not been home for four months. Our poor soldiers. I do feel so deeply. Many of whom I fear are laying the seed for premature decay.[16]

## July 5, 1863

This has been a day of rest to me. Indeed I felt so worried this morning. The labors of the past week having very nearly broken me down. My great regret has been throughout this day that I could not read and spend it as I desired. I felt so worn down. I laid down before and after dinner and slept. I feel this evening greatly refreshed.

## July 14, 1863

Fannie, Powell, and Dick went to Sabbath School. E. Ruth (loved friend) came back with them. I felt so glad to see her. She had been

15. Clinton G. Lyons (1829–1900) was a captain in Company A, Twelfth Tennessee Cavalry Battalion (C.S.A.). He was later wounded in the hip at Port Republic and was related to Hiram's wife.

16. This statement probably reflected Eliza's realization that Hiram was showing signs of consumption, from which he died in 1869.

teaching my little girls and hearing the black children say some lessons. She was reading to them the Bible and asking them questions from the Bible and the little catechism for children. For the African race and their descendants I have ever felt a great desire that they might be led to the Saviour. We feel our servants[17] are recognized by God our Father as part of our family over whom we are to exercise our authority to command that they shall obey us in all things with fidelity. As servants who shall receive, with us, from the hands of our Heavenly Father the rich inheritance which is laid up for those who serve him upon earth. The Bible is plain there is no mistaking its holy precepts. Servants are enjoined by it to the strictest integrity of character. Masters are commanded to give to your servants that which is just and equal knowing that ye also have a Master in Heaven.

The Bible will never fail and if as a nation we are right in the holding of the African in bondage it matter not whether we be a nation or nations. Does God our Father sustain us? We of the South are feeling he does.

My dear, my loved husband by this time is on his way to Strawberry Plains where his regiment is encamped. The regiment was ordered on Tuesday or Wednesday night the 16 or 17 of June to leave the Gap and form I suppose a junction with other troops for the purpose of intercepting a company of vandal raiders who succeeded in making their way through some pass near Wartburg. They were marched for 3 or 4 days in the most fatiguing manner but with no success. They were ordered to Knoxville where the vandals had accomplished almost everything for which the raid was made. They destroyed much cotton it was said for Lenoir burned doing I suppose all the mischief to private property they dared take time to do.

A fight at Knoxville but little harm done to either side then they came on up destroying the bridge at Strawberry Plains,[18] at

---

17. It was common for Southerners to refer to their slaves as servants.

18. This refers to the railroad bridge across the Holston River between Strawberry Plains and Knoxville.

Mossy Creek burning the depot and destroying private property. They took several Negroes, mules and horses. I have heard that after the sixty-third regiment found the raiders were gone they sank exhausted to sleep anywhere the body could find room to repose. After this they were ordered perhaps on Monday or Tuesday to go to Tullahoma to reinforce General Bragg but Bragg had concluded to make a retrograde move. This was much, I have no doubt, to the astonishment of many a Confederate soldier and citizen. So the regiment lads after one days work upon the entrenchments or breast works started again covering the retreat of the army with the twentieth and twenty-sixth Tennessee covering it at other points.

July 15, 1863

Days are still dark, very dark. We are made to believe with great reluctance that Vicksburg has fallen. She sustained a brave and noble defense until a scarcity of provisions forced its capitulation. Some accounts say our men agreed to surrender provided they were permitted to come out with their arms. Other accounts say this is false that they had to surrender unconditionally. Her surrender took place on the 4th of July making that day still more memorable. I hope it all may prove a transient rejoicing and that the fall of Vicksburg may be yet made to appear as a great good to our cause. Gen. Lee has made a march into Maryland and Pennsylvania and had a severe battle at Gettysburg, Penn.

July 31, 1863

On last Saturday E. Ruth, Tom Powel, Dick Fain[19] and I set out from town in our wagon for the railroad (old Ahab driving). We arrived at the river in good time, crossed over to depot and took our seats. After waiting until the time for leaving we were on our way to

19. Eliza Ruth Powel and her twenty-year-old son, Tom, accompanied Eliza and her twelve-year-old son, Dick, on the trip to Strawberry Plains. Apparently, the railroad was running at this time since Ahab, Eliza's slave, drove them in their wagon to the river. They crossed on a ferry and caught the branch train to the Junction where they boarded another train for Strawberry Plains.

Junction to visit Strawberry Plains where the regiment of my loved husband was stationed. When we got to the Junction, having had our dinners with us, we thought we would stay in the car but in a short time some soldiers of a North Carolina Regiment stationed at Lick Creek came in. One of them said: "Come in boys take your seats this car is ours this evening." Mr. Wilson got very angry and said; "who told you so. You had better not be too fast." The soldiers replied; "we will show you in a hour or so." Some other words passed when Mr. W. went to loading his pistol. E. Ruth and I tried to act as allayers of difficulty. We told Mr. W. those soldiers were there under exasperating circumstances. Some of these men having been sent to Choptack on Wednesday night or Thursday morning, were wounded by bushwhackers and that the enrolling officer John Hamlin had been killed by them. Mr. W. said if an officer came and told him to go he would go. E. Ruth made inquiry for the officer who came in a short time. Then all was quiet and in less time than an hour they were on their way to town.

About 4 in the evening the freight came along. We were seated in quick time and on our way. We had to leave our box of provisions so hurried. We got to Strawberry Plains about 7 and crossed the bridge. The regiment was camped on the west side. We were cordially welcomed by husband, sons and many friends. We were taken to camp where our supper was prepared by Squire Hudgins. He gave us a very good supper after which we went across the river to Mr. Butlers (who occupies the old Stringfield house). We were kindly received by Mr. and Mrs. Butler and after talking a while we prepared for bed. We had more comfortable quarters than we anticipated having heard of the Yankee devastation there. They have suffered greatly but have still something left which is much more than many have.

On Sabbath morning the beat of the drum and the noise of the train awoke me (I suppose), I was soon up, dressed and ready for going to camp for breakfast. We were there in good time. After breakfast the mounting of the guard, the inspection of arms and the duties of the men on the Sabbath were performed. At 9 or l0 o'clock we set out for the church on the opposite side of the river. We walked to the ferry and then crossed in the boat. Richard, E. Ruth, Doct. Edmonds lady and child and myself formed the company. After a rather tiresome walk we reached the church. Quite a number of soldiers were present and Mr. Crawford preached a very solemn sermon.

Monday we came back to camp for breakfast and had that day a great pleasure granted of seeing my loved cousins J. A Rhea and Johnny Bachman returning from Mississippi with many other soldier friends.[20] On Sabbath a portion of our boys passed us, just saw them on the trains. I felt so rejoiced to know so many were getting home. Although my own loved came not; yet I rejoiced to know so many had escaped the fearful foe to gladden the hearts and make bright the home circle again.

That evening I walked to the brow of the hill and looked on with my loved Husband E. Ruth, Sallie, Dick, Lillie and others at the dress parade. I was pleased and have always loved the military but was doomed that evening to listen to the reading of a painful order that of shooting Wiley Brown for desertion. He had deserted three times and had a son in Co. I of Capt. Gillespie. He seemed much troubled, so I was told, cried the greater part of the night after he heard the order.

I looked on that morning a right drill led by Col Fulkerson and Major Aiken the officers. I was greatly pleased by the martial music and that army made me feel I could almost wish the soldiers life. Woman, I know not what it is and feel when I reflect I desire it not but pray that the day may soon come when the life of the soldier will not be needed, when wars and rumors of wars shall cease. After dinner we left with many sad adieus to the noble braves of Strawberry Plains.

20. Major James A. Rhea and Captain Jonathan W. Bachman of the Sixtieth Tennessee were among the Confederate troops under General John C. Pemberton at Vicksburg who surrendered to General U. S. Grant on July 4, 1863 and were paroled a few days later.

August 2, 1863

Lovely beautiful morning. Peace and quiet reign around. No beat of the drum, no tread of the sentinel, no array of troops, no firing of guns, no booming of cannon. Nothing, nothing which tells of the terrific revolution through which we are now passing is visible to the eye or the ear. But there is a painful consciousness of the fact we all feel scarcely a family in our country is exempt. I might say none, no not one. Those who have not chosen the cause of the South as theirs have gone to the North never again, I fear to feel at ease in our Southern land. To me it is a painful thought that there are those amongst them for whom I have always had a kindly regard.

On yesterday I completed the 47th year of my life. What a life it has been of mercy, my Father has ever been showing to a poor worm. I have entered on my 48th year. I know not what the future may be.

August 9, 1863

Another peaceful Sabbath. I have this day under my roof two of my loved sons: Hiram and Ike. The wife and child of my first born Hiram is with me. How pleasant to be surrounded by those we love. H & B came last Wednesday the 5th after Hiram went home on Monday night. Ike came last night from the plains bringing a letter from my loved husband.

Sept. 6, 1863

The day is dark, very dark. We had a sermon of comfort and consolation from our dear minister from Job. We of the South are passing through deep waters and fiery trials. We have to contemplate this day the devastation of much of our beloved, our beautiful country. The sad thought of making greater inroads upon us harrows our souls with a feeling of inexpressible sadness. How appropriate seemed the selection of the subject of our minister this day.

This day week was a day of excitement.[21] We had news that there was a march of the Federals upon our border. They were effecting entrance through passes in the mountains and were moving in the direction of Knoxville. My loved husband was at home having come from Knoxville on Tuesday August 28 being so unwell he was not able to go with his regiment (which was sent to the bridge at Loudon). He left on Sabbath 30th August taking Lewis with him. They went to Junction but returned in the evening. He staid until Tuesday Sept. 1 when he again left going up on the train to Jonesboro. It is so sad to be shut out from those we love—to feel we can have no communication with them. These are the saddest hours we have been called upon to know since this unholy war first began. I had a letter from my dear Samuel (Gammon)[22] on last Sabbath evening dated August 10th from Johnson's Island near Sandusky, Ohio. I felt so glad to know where they were and that they were well.

Sept 7, 1863

Still in circumstances of mercy. Two weeks today (about 20 minutes before 2 o'clock) the spirit of one of our precious soldiers was released from its clay tenement to dwell I hope with Jesus. His name was Peter Kimberlin from Lee Co. Virginia. He was taken prisoner at Gettysburg then sent to Ft. Delaware where he had a very severe spell of sickness. When hardly able to be moved in accordance with the notions of humanity which have ever actuated the fell foe of the South he was sent on truce boat to Virginia side, from there he went to Petersburg to a hospital. He began to improve and was able to set

21. On August 24 Richard was granted sick leave for fifteen days due to chronic diarrhea, gastric irritation, and remittent fever. On September 4 he was ordered by Brigadier General Alfred E. Jackson at the headquarters of the Fourth Brigade in Bristol to proceed from Bristol to Rogersville Junction "and if possible bring away all the engines and rolling stock of the Rogersville Railroad Branch—and also any other cars that might be there belonging to any other railroad." Military papers of Richard Fain, Fain Collection.

22. Eliza's nephew, Samuel Rhea Gammon, was organizing captain of Company B of the Sixtieth Tennessee Mounted Infantry. Sam was captured along with Eliza's son Nick, then a second lieutenant in Company B, at the Battle of Big Black River near Vicksburg on May 17, 1863.

out for home. Poor fellow had he had a friend to care for him he might still have lived I have no doubt. But he injured himself eating which brought on severe diarrhea accompanied with flux which soon laid low the poor emaciated body of a son of the South. He came to Mr. Merrimon's[23] on Saturday having known some of the family before he left home (he having lived with Mr. Hamlin).

After speaking to Mrs. Merrimon he asked for Jane. When told she was lying a corpse in the room he seemed to be greatly surprised and astonished. Her remains were kept until Sabbath. Mr. Pope made some remarks on Sabbath from this passage (Gal. chapter 6, verse 7). When the coffin came we hurried to get her laid away as the poor body was becoming very loathsome. She had begun to purge at the mouth sometime in the night. Under her head was a place of blood large as a dining plate. She was laid in the graveyard in sight of the home of her childhood. After laying her away our next care was our poor soldier. Sarah Fain[24] remained with him whilst the rest were attending services and burial. He was much worried with his bowels. That morning after we got there Mr. Pope baptized him and took him into the church. He had clean clothes put on him. Sarah and I bathed his feet. Poor fellow he did not want us to leave him any length of time. In the evening Sarah came away. I staid to see what could be done and who would take care of him tonight.

I had sent over for old Ahab but he did not want to go and did not until I came home and just had to beg him to go. I was ashamed to think I had a servant or anyone else about me who was unwilling to sit up with a dying person. At last after much persuasion I got him and Frank off. Had he been a young Negro I could

23. The Merrimons (also spelled Merriman) were adjoining neighbors of Eliza and had nine children. Two of their sons were killed in the Civil War but on opposite sides. Mary Jane was born on December 13, 1843, and died on August 21, 1863, according to Merrimon family papers in the Rogersville, Tennessee, library. Peter Kimberlin served in Company B of the Fiftieth Virginia Infantry.

24. Sarah Fain was the wife of Hiram Fain, the brother of Richard Fain. Hiram and Sarah lived on a farm adjoining Eliza's property, two miles east of Rogersville.

have told him to go but an old Negro gray-headed has privileges which others do not. The soldier lingered along through the long hours of that restless night with but few moments of repose. The morning came, still he lived on in pain after Ahab came home (but just here let me say to the credit of some of the men of Rogersville that Henry Wax, Capt. Henderson and Stokely Mitchell came and set up).

I asked Ahab how he was. He told me the soldier said he was better. A while after breakfast Sarah Fain came along and we went over to see him. As soon as we got in we knew his feeling improvement was but the temporary respite which precedes the march of the grim monster. We found him with no pulse, extremities cold and the clammy sweat upon him. His voice was strong. When we asked him how he was he replied with emphasis better. We worked with him, rubbing warm flannels but had nothing to give him as a stimulus. His bowels were still troublesome. Sarah and I had to attend to him. He wanted us to help him up which we did but he became so exhausted I thought he would die in our hands before we could get him in his bed. We did not attempt to take him up afterwards but used the bedpan.

Cousin Joe[25] came to see him and gave him a dose of medicine and left us to give another in an hour and a half. Dinner came, we set down and whilst we were eating a gentleman came in to speak with him about his son thinking perhaps he had known him at Ft. Delaware. He talked to him sensibly and strong. We came in from our dinner and gave him a portion of his medicine. He threw up his hands in a few moments saying I am gone, I am gone now. I asked him if he was happy. He replied oh yes Jesus has pardoned all my sins. Laying his hand over his heart I asked him if he had any message for his mother and sister. He replied yes but his articulation had become so indistinct and broken he could not utter a sentence. I said to him I must write to them you died happy trusting in

25. Cousin Joe Walker (1831–1891) was a physician in Rogersville; his wife was named Mollie Lynn.

Jesus and that they must meet you in Heaven. He said yes. He continued sensible as long as he could hear. Not long before the breath was gone I asked him if Jesus was precious. He gave a slight nod of the head and in a few moments his spirit was freed from its frail, tabernacle.

On Tuesday evening he was buried on the hill not far from Mr. Merrimons. Mr. Pope was present and sung "And let this feeble body faint or die." His remains were then taken to the grave and laid comfortably in a plain neat coffin made by Mr. F. Jones for which he asked but $7.00. However $11.00 was given by those who stood around. I trust the soldier rests with his Saviour.

Sept. 20, 1863

This is a beautiful morning. I was in rather a perplexed condition. Two soldiers who escaped from Cumberland Gap had found a place of rest at my house Saturday night. In the evening we were much excited by the report of and advance of Federal troops which proved to be nothing but some four or five returning renegades. Fain, Powell[26] and the two soldiers took up the hill. Fain went on down into the hollow where Powell had gone with the horses. Gus who had taken one of our horses into the hollow came back saying: Miss Liza the soldiers are upon the hill and I will look for them and take them where they may all be together. I told him to go. After some time we found out that it was all a delusion. They all came back to the house, got their suppers. Fain and Powell set out for town promising to come back but the rain and the darkness prevented their return. Capt. Reynolds was wounded having had the ball of his thumb on the left hand shot off. He seemed to suffer greatly having been in such a state of excitement for so long and no chance to have it attended to. The wound was very painful. I dressed it with a light starch poultice nicely ground with beef foot oil which seemed to relieve him very much.

26. Powell was the seventeen-year-old son of Eliza, while Fain refers to Fain Powel, who was twenty-two.

Bug, Lizzie the two soldiers and myself set talking until it was nearly midnight. We learned from them they were from Norfolk Va. and that their mother had been imprisoned a month for coming through the line to see her sons, having five in the army. Their father had been through life a seafaring man. He was the captain of a vessel and was a wicked man. I was deeply impressed with the thought as the father is so are the sons and felt grieved to think of the bad influence which an ungodly parent wields. How the influence of a good mother over her sons is lost without the cooperating influence of the father yet she should never grow weary for the promise is hers that in due season she will reap a rich reward if she but continues faithful. Capt. R. said he felt it would be very hard for him to give up his mother.

On Wednesday morning the 9th of September Powell went to town. Whilst there he fell in with one belonging to our army who had been acting in the Quartermasters Department. He belonged to Gen. Polk's corps, was in Knoxville trying to get off the stores when the Yankees came seizing the train and its contents. He told me he could not have made his escape had it not been for the fidelity of the Negro and the kindness of Southern ladies. Knowing nothing of the country he would have been taken had they not assisted him. He was a young man, pleasant and from what I could learn of him a very moral man. His mother, by the fall of Vicksburg, was thrown under Federal rule which seemed to be a trial to him. His name was Roberts. He had settled in Memphis a short time before the war and began to practice law. His mother was pious, a member of the Old School Presbyterian Church. He was suffering greatly from his feet—never having walked much they were soon blistered and became very sore. He rested with us until Thursday morning when Eddie Powel and Powell took him to Mr. William Armstrongs where he succeeded in getting into a wagon. He seemed to be so grateful for any kindness shown him.

I do so love our poor soldiers and feel it is such a pleasure to wait on them. The Yankees are now in our midst having come to Rogersville Friday the 18th.[27] On Tuesday morning there was a dash into Rogersville of some 19 or 20 men who made inquiry of some where William Simpson lived. They seemed to know, rode up and after talking with Mr. Alexander (who went and knocked at the door) they went in making a search but did not tarry long in town. They then came on out taking from Mr. T. Amis' little boy and girl the riding nag of Mrs. A. and a mule, Since which time I learn they have done much mischief. They came back Thursday night the 17th and went into Mr. White's and Simpson's stores taking a good many things. They went in and stopped Mr. J. Amis taking his money.

Mr. Merrimon came to see me to talk to me about it. I told him I believed they were soldiers from neither army but were those loose characters who have been trying to survive by laying out from either side. He seemed to be much frightened but I told him I lay down every night feeling God was my protector. I rose in the morning with the thought that perhaps some were already around my house but still trust in God who I felt could deliver me and mine from the ravenous lion of the North as he had done Daniel from the lion in the den. The 91st Psalm is ever present and David knew in whom he trusted and shall not the believer in Jesus in these hours of darkness and peril lean upon him.

I know that no miracle will be wrought for the preservation of anyone now but I do know that his providential care is so great that it oft times seems to us that he has almost wrought a miracle. When I look at my daughters and feel you may perhaps be subjected to insults I could not bear it, were it not that I have a Father to whom I can go who hath all power over the hearts of man.

27. This marked the arrival of the Seventh Ohio Cavalry of the Union army under the command of Colonel Israel Garrard and the Second East Tennessee Mounted Infantry (U.S.A.) under Colonel J. M. Melton. Also arriving were four guns from the Second Illinois Light Artillery, Battery M. The Union forces encamped about four miles east of Rogersville. *War of the Rebellion: A Compilation of the Official Records of the Union and Confederate Armies* (Washington, D.C.: U.S. Government Printing Office, 1880–91), series 1, vol. 31, pt. 1: 550-66. Subsequent references to this source will be abbreviated *OR* and followed by series, volume, part number, and page reference.

I have been reading the 18th chapter of Jeremiah. In that chapter we have the sovereign power of our God to build up or destroy a nation. We are clearly and explicitly taught that the nation which obeyeth and trusteth in him is the nation which he will sustain. We are taught in it that for the sins of Judah the Lord visited her.

Does not the South feel and know for her sins she has been visited. Take the dark and heinous crime of amalgamation,[28] where men have enslaved their own flesh and blood. Where they have violated the commands of God and where they have as it were introduced into the world another race of being. Do we not feel we are justly visited. Has the Christian South stood up against this sin as she should have done, have our pulpits cried down this grievous transgression as it should have been done, have we prayed to our Father that it might be done away with. Alas, alas we feel we are guilty, we feel our Father is just in giving us this sore chastisement on account of it. We feel the church has not done her duty and we too are suffering. Our sanctuaries have been desecrated by the polluting trend of the dark foe. Our Father we do pray that this cup of bitterness may pass away from us. May the South yet stand forth to the world as a people peculiarly blessed of God. Give us a place amongst the nations of the earth.

This is the third Sabbath day my beloved husband has been shut from home. Days of trial, days of darkness. How long, O Lord shall we be made to feel these hours of anguish. I have heard today that two of our noble ministers have been imprisoned at Knoxville. Mr. Martin and Mr. Harrison. I felt so sad; it may not be true and I do hope it is not. These acts are so intolerant and I feel the South can never expect civil or religious liberty from their hands.

28. Sexual relationships between white slaveholders and their black female slaves often resulted in children. These children were considered to be slaves, and with few exceptions they were not freed by their fathers.

Sept 24, 1863

Yesterday about noon Bug and Nan Kinkead came out having news by Stoke Mitchell that the communication between this place and Nashville was opened. The Federals were rebuilding the bridge at Loudon and that all would be completed in a few days. He also gave the girls an account of the goods which had been brought into Knoxville and the great diminution of prices. He mentioned that the Feds had an army of about 20,000 with quite an accumulation of rolling stock upon the road. We have heard day after day so much of the power, magnificence and grandeur of the Federal Army that were we disposed to gloom we might be overwhelmed. But we are not cast down. We feel today as we did at first that our Father is sitting at the helm. We know that East Tennessee is now more in their hands than it has been at anytime but this is not all of the territory which Confederates claim. It does seem to me that I see the hand of my Father in it all. Our army is concentrating. Every place they take weakens them and gives us greater power to annoy and trouble.

Sept. 25, 1863

I felt so distressed last night and was enabled to pour forth my soul in fervent supplication. O that some might be raised in our Southern army to strike terror in the ranks of the Northern army.

Sept. 29, 1863

Alas, alas how unstable, how precarious are the riches and comforts of earth. Today in affluence and tomorrow in poverty. Such is earth and all things earthly. Last night after supper we had seated ourselves around our home fireside. Lizzie, Jennie McCarty, Fannie and the little ones Nannie, Ella, and little Silla were engaged in play. Dicky my only white guard, had gone over to his uncle Hirams to watch for some of our troops.

We were talking of what we could do for our own soldiers. That we could rise at the hour of midnight with cheerful hearts to provide something for them to eat when in rushed Nick and Dick saying guess who has come. We guessed two or three when Dick says Uncle Sam Powel and Mr. Wax. O the gladness of joy we had. The little ones jumped up and capered all around. Liz and Jennie gathered shawls and started to get the news. Dick had told us our Blountville friends were many of them in great distress. The town having been the scene of Yankee fury and pillage.[29] The courthouse and the dwellings on both sides of the street were destroyed to the bridge. I felt so troubled and awaited the return of the girls with an anxious heart.

Memory was active while they were gone. It pictured before me the peaceful home of my childhood where the Uncle, Mother, her four daughters and our dear darling brother[30] had gathered around the family altar had made a circle for Sabbath Evening catechizing from the Shorter Catechism. With the easy questions such as who was the first man to the little boy who sat by his fathers side. Tears came as I thought of the desolation which now marked that spot where my early life was passed.

The girls came. All was true, too true. Blountville was marked by its ruins as one of the many places which our Southern land presents of the desolating tread of a military force. The home of my childhood is in ruins, my loved aunt and her dear family have no home. Old uncle John Fain[31] with his silver locks is homeless. O how sad, how sad. The skirmishes took place on Tuesday the 22nd of Sept. The enemy planting their cannon on the old church hill and our forces I do not know exactly where. The first shell which struck was thought to be on aunt Martha's house and in a short space of a few hours that which had taken years to accumulate was in ashes. This is a sore calamity.

29. On September 22, 1863, Union army troops under the command of Colonel John W. Foster attacked Confederate forces at Blountville, under the command of Colonel J. E. Carter. This was the initial step in the Union's attempt to drive the Confederate armies out of East Tennessee. The Battle of Blountville resulted in about 150 Confederate casualties and about 50 Union casualties. Most of the town was destroyed during the battle. Taylor, *Historic Sullivan*, 211–13.

30. Eliza refers here to the Reverend Sam Rhea Jr., who was actually her first cousin. He was a missionary to Persia and died there in 1865.

31. Eliza grew up in Blountville, the recent scene of so much destruction. Uncle John R. Fain (a brother of Richard's father, Nicholas) was born in 1788 and lived in Blountville.

I had felt so anxious that my Father Uncle should live to see this struggle close but now how glad I am that he sleeps peacefully. The sound of cannon, the tramp of horse, the tread of the soldier, the firing of arms disturbs not the sweet repose of the grave. I fear that precious spot has been sadly desecrated. There sleeps my uncle, my mother and my loved sisters with many, many other dear friends. O my loved sister what anguish would have passed that heart couldst thou have known that in six months thy house where thy precious treasures were was to pass through such a trial.

Sept. 30, 1863

To me this has been a day of gloom and sadness. Troubles within and without. Today brother Hiram got home. He brought me several letters from my dear Husband and one from brother William Gammon. He gave me the confirmation with particulars of the sad destruction of my early, my loved childhood home. He writes, as he says, amidst the ruins of old Blountville. The courthouse and jail both destroyed. The third shot which the enemy fired struck Aunt Martha's house. The next the courthouse setting all in flames and was burnt he says intentionally as they could have avoided it if they wished. I have no doubt Blountville was one of the marked spots. There they gained ascendancy in East Tenn. The inhabitants were not able to save anything, the town was burned and sacked by the foul invader. They holding forth their fiendish revel over its ruins that night. My brother says in many cases nothing was left only what they had on. The fight was over the town. Our forces occupying the hill East and the enemy the West. He writes "many of the citizens sheltered themselves from the balls in my cellar. Mr. M. Haynes who is on the verge of the grave was carried to the cellar and remained there until the fight was over." He was then taken to Mr. Dulaneys a mile west of town and whilst I write, a report says he is dying. Brother Hiram told me his house and family were literally stripped of every comfort.

The enemy said they intended to come back and destroy the house but I hope the arm of omnipotence is already bared in our defense and that their fiendish purposes for the destruction of East Tennessee have been permitted to be executed as far as they shall ever be. The battle commenced between 1 and 2 o'clock on Tuesday, Sept. 22 and continued until sundown. In that short space of time the comforts of our two dear uncles which had been the toil and labor of many years were in ashes.

I alone am left of the original family (in this land) to look with regret on the destruction of my early home. True it had been changed and our little rooms were occupied as the counting room and sleeping room for the boys. I never entered it but with feelings so solemn, so sacred. Memory brought before me the place of each piece of our plain furniture. The cupboard, the half round table, as we termed it, the little stand on which lay the Bible and the hymnbook. The little bedroom where my mother and her four helpless little daughters had lain down to sleep. The children with childlike forgetfulness free from care, free from sorrow. The mother often bourn down with grief for him whom she had loved so devotedly. Did she lay with her who seemed to have been set as "an angel of light across her path in that stormy night" upon her arm fearing to move or speak lest she should disturb the peaceful sleeper. I have been told by some who loved her and knew her well that for six months after my loved but unknown father was taken from her that not a smile ever was seen on her face. O my sisters[32] with whom I lay so many nights like little nestlings you are spared the grief which I now feel. You are this evening enjoying the presence of all that was then so dear, but myself, in a home where Jesus dwells, home of peace, a home of security. The cruel scenes of war cannot make that home a desolation. O no you are all safely housed from the sorrows of life. I rejoice to know you are free. What is before me is known only to my Father yet I trust in him.

32. Eliza's father was Audley Anderson, and her mother was Elizabeth Rhea. Fanny McAlister was the oldest child and had thirteen children before dying in 1856. The second sister was Becky Gammon, who had eleven children before dying in 1863. Eliza's other sister was Nancy Gammon, who died in 1837 shortly after the birth of her first child.

My mother I have so often desired to hold communion with a spirit such as I knew thine to be since this terrible revolution began. So forbearing, so gentle, so lovely, I trust you have been near me. I trust thy influence has been exerted over me and that the spirit of God has taken they holy example and impressed it so deeply that nothing, nothing, no changes, no reverses, no prosperity, can ever efface its hallowed influence from my heart. O my Father let me feel ever thy presence, let me feel the wild fanaticism of man, the fury of the fiendish heart let loose in the earth is subject to thy control.

By brother Hiram I learned that my loved husband was very near being captured the second time at Bristol. His first escape was at Jonesboro. I feel God has delivered him. O how sad would my heart have been to know that they had in their possession my dearest earthly friend. I feel so distressed about those they now hold but they are young and I feel are better able to bear the harsh usage which the prisoner of war is often doomed to suffer.

By brother Hiram we learned without a doubt that the armies of Bragg and Rosencrans had met in deadly conflict and that Bragg by our Father in Heaven had been victorious.[33] That the divisions of Generals Hill, Polk and Buckner were called into the hottest part of the fight. If it is true can we, can we expect our friends are all safe. We do hope that God has been merciful and that our dear our loved ones are safe. We have asked him to shield them in the hour of battle, we believe he has.

Oct. 1, 1863

On Tuesday morning while engaged with household cares one of my little children came to me saying Mama a woman wants to see you. I went out to the front gate and there she stood. She began by saying I am out on a business which is painful to me that of begging help for my daughter who has a son down with white swelling and she is

---

33. The reference is to the Battle of Chickamauga, which occurred just below Chattanooga on September 18–20, 1863. The Confederates were victorious. For details of this campaign, see Foote, *The Civil War*, 2: 712–57.

obliged to suffer if the good people around do not help her. She told me she had the promise of 4 or 5 bushels of grain, that she wanted something to make the sufferers bed more comfortable and some clothing for her other children. I had not much to give but gave her a little tick, an old dress and an apron. She seemed grateful, said she would never have anything to give in return but that God would reward me. How rich the comfort when we have been able to relieve the distress of our fellow beings. Her name was Thacker, her daughter had married Daniel Bowman son of old Mr. Bowman who lived close to Mr. Harlans. He raised his sons in ignorance giving them advantages of no kind. He was industrious, sober and honest but seemed to feel all that life was made for was to work. He died leaving them a very comfortable living but it was soon squandered.

Lewis got home today between 9 and 10 o'clock leaving Bristol on Tuesday and walked the greater part of the way. Staid the first night at Mr. G. Rollins and last night at Mr. J. Lyons. We were all glad to see him; he was glad to get home. Fain Powel came out about 10 o'clock on his way to Bristol. He was anxious for Lizzie to go with him. She fixed up, he furnishing a horse and they left a little after 11. Fain has gone hoping we shall be able to hear from the loved in the army. Lewis has just sent me a note to Brother Hiram from Richard in which he says Capt. G. R. Millard had told him he had heard through a letter from one of the regiment that they were not in the fight. This is a relief. May they be secure is my prayer but I hope they have done their whole duty. They have shown they were willing to meet the enemy and brave the storm for their country defence. That regiment has been one for which many have prayed.

## October 4, 1863

On Friday the 2nd Peggy Martin[34] died about 2 o'clock having been a sufferer for several months. Mary sent for me on Friday but I was very busy with domestic cares and felt I had no time to spend

---

34. Peggy Martin was the mother of Mary and Amy Martin. Peggy appears to have been a free African American.

just then. I do pray that I may never feel so again. I had grown weary in well doing and now I have no peaceful reward. I went to see, but felt rather impatient and did not say one word to her that I now recollect of comfort or hope. She seemed to suffer much. I helped to fix her as well as we could in her bed and then left her. O how little did I think as I turned my back it is the last time I shall ever be permitted to speak with you.

Eliza Ruth, Naomi Fullen and myself prepared her for the grave. I sent for some of the neighbors. They came. Mr. Burton came and took the measure for coffin. Old Ahab the white headed and faithful servant was there, prepared the board for her. At night several came to set up. I went over and set awhile. We sang several hymns. The next morning the boys went to Mr. Merrimon who kindly consented for her to be laid in his burying ground. They went to work. Mr. Burton and Wood with Ahab and Lewis to dig the grave. Mr. Tilson made a plain, neat coffin. Mr. M. had it brought out. I went over to see how they were getting along, wondering as I went how I should get the coffin as it was reported a regiment of Federals were looked for in town. I was much relieved feeling it was from my Father when I found the coffin at Mr. M's. With the assistance of two black children and Wylie I started with it to bring it home. We met Hill coming and got along very well the children carrying it most of the way. We got her laid in it and moved her out in the yard. Then Mary and her little child took their seats beside it much distressed. We sang several hymns and after a while Ahab came saying they think the grave will be ready when we get there.

We had thought of having her hauled in a wagon or a slide to the grave but at length concluded she could be carried. After the needful preparation she was borne to the graves by blacks. There was no white man there. Old Ahab, Gus, Hill and old Ben Wylie were there and rested Hill. Mr. Burton and Lewis met us on the way. The top of the tiresome hill was reached and she was laid in her narrow house. The grave was soon filled up. We sang the hymn

*When I can read my title clear.* Mr. M. pronounced a benediction and we left the sleeping dust to the care of him who watcheth until he shall bid it rise.

Oct. 10, 1863
Fain and Lizzie had left home the 1st to go to Blountville to see the dear friends who had suffered so severely. They made the trip pleasantly until they were almost home. On their return they were halted, but not molested no more than to ask Fain his name, by a band of Col. R. C. Crawford's Yankee men this side of Mr. Carmacks. These men arrived in Rogersville on Sept. 29.

I found a distressed family, staid several hours and came home. While I was gone the Yankees had made their appearance at my home driving off my oxen. As I came along between home and Mr. Merrimons my soul was poured forth in supplication to my Father. I felt all was well although I knew not what had been done. The first news that reached me was mama our oxen is gone. But I was not moved, I felt the Lord would send them back. I came on to the house and found Lizzie had conducted herself very prudently and kindly. So much so that one of the men had promised to do all he could to save the oxen.

I had made up my mind to go to town and see Col. Crawford[35] and try to get them back. E. Ruth was here and Jennie McC and Mec was busy working with the molasses. Before we were ready to start some of the children came running in saying the oxen are coming, the oxen are coming. My soul raised to Heaven in gratitude. I felt my Father had sent them back and I felt like bursting forth in praise and thanksgiving. I went into the meadow attended

---

35. Colonel Robert Clay Crawford was from Rogersville. In March 1862, he was appointed a captain of Company B, Fifth Tennessee Infantry (U.S.A.), but in April 1863 he became a lieutenant colonel of Battery B, First Tennessee Light Artillery Battalion (U.S.A.). On November 9, 1864, a military court found him guilty of stealing a large amount of money from the bank in Rogersville, as well as horses and mules, on or about September 15, 1863. As a result, he was dismissed from the Union army. Johnston, *The Blue and Gray from Hawkins County: The Federals*, 71.

by Hill to welcome back our all for winters comfort. I told Hill to put his arms around their necks and kiss them. He was so rejoiced as he had taken a good cry about them.

After I got my oxen E. Ruth insisted on my going with her thinking I could assist her in getting back her horses. I went, we got in late next morning Friday. We set out tolerably early. I went to consult with Mr. Todd as to what I should do. He gave me his kind counsel to be prudent and firm saying he would do anything for me he could. After I got back from there Ruth and I set out to find Col. Crawford. It was sometime before we could get up with him. At length he was pointed out by some of the soldiers. He was going into Mr. A. Kyles. We followed fast as we could, found when we got there Mrs. Riley, Pace and Price. Mrs. R. was trying to get her negro boy back. We introduced ourselves to the Colonel. I felt how wonderful is the history of man but I do trust God in his infinite mercy has permitted this exaltation for his souls eternal good. May he become a Christian is my prayer.

After dinner I set out on Ruth's little mare which she succeeded in getting, but she got no others they had taken. I got from Col. C. a little paper giving me protection. I came on home and had given the girls an account of my interview with the distinguished Col. I was looking around to see about my things in the evening when someone came in saying two Yankees were coming. According to what I laid down should be my custom I met them at the fence. They told me they were a guard. At first I thought Col. C had thought it best in the plenitude of his tender mercy to send me a guard not knowing there was any more Federal troops nearer than Rogersville close to me. I had just gotten the words out of my mouth I have a protection from Col. C when I raised my eyes and the meadow seemed swarming with the blue coats. I was not frightened or excited but still self-possessed. The guard said to me that is the major of our regiment (65th Indiana) coming. Soon he came up, I said to him Major get down and come in. He told me he had not been well. I walked in with him and had a chair placed for him. I told him to take his seat in my house and keep it. I greatly preferred having him with us.

We then had a scene of confusion and had it not been for the efficiency of the two men who were my guards I should have been sorely tried. They told me to not let anyone come inside my yard, advised me to bring my things from the spring house. They asked me where my coops were. This made me think of my turkeys and chickens so I had my ducks, turkeys and chickens stored away under my kitchen.

As I was attending to my things one would say can you have me some bread baked. Another can you let me have a chicken, another milk. Some wanted something to cook in. I tried to be obliging as I could having the command of my Father ever before me to return "good for evil."

Some three or four white men approached me in the most humble manner with: Mistress will you let me have whatever it was they wished to get. I was horror stricken. No slave of the South had ever spoken with greater humility. After I came to the house I asked Major Brown if that was the usual salutation of the white man of the North to superiors. He replied there are a great many with us who are servants. He did not say positively whether they thus addressed ladies or not. I came to the conclusion the slavery of the North degrades the white whilst the slavery of the South elevates the black.

When supper was ready we sat down. Major B. asked a blessing. This was too much for my stricken heart to bear. I burst into tears and threw up my hands saying: O to think Christian is arrayed against Christian in this struggle almost breaks my heart. After supper (I having the Major, the quartermaster name Lt. Walter and the two guards names Brashers and Wells to feed) we seated ourselves around our fireside. Having besides my own family Annis Shaver (she and grandma Powel) having been driven from their home by a set of the lowest down) Sallie Powel, Ida and Pete Powel the major and grandma made themselves very happy with the children letting them say just what they pleased to them. Fannie and Annis had been pretty rapid in the evening and I was afraid lest they might get into trouble but all seemed to pass off well.

The major gave to Sallie and Ida his little boys but they would not accept the present saying they wouldn't have a Yankee. At length Sallie says to him you are too clever to be a Yankee. She afterwards found out he was originally from South Carolina and said to him I knew you were from the South.

I kept passing out very often to see if all was well. To me it was a grand but painful sight. The campfires were blazing all around extending from back of Sarah's and as far down the road as our eyes could see. I knew my rails that enclosed my fields which brought forth the sustenance of my family afforded the fuel of which the fires were made. The horses stood all around devouring the corn which had been made by my family for our years support. But not withstanding all I was enabled by my Heavenly Father to declare without fear that my husband was a Colonel in the Confederate service and my three sons were there too. I said that I also had one son and a nephew dear as a son prisoner.

I asked Major Brown if he thought the South had been treated right in regards to California and their slaves. He acknowledged the South had not been treated as she ought to have been but that he thought they should have sought a redress afterwards in the Union. I felt she had but was not well enough acquainted with our civil affairs to talk to him. The Crittenden compromise was brought forward as a ground of compromise sufficient to satisfy the South but as to this I could not talk. I had known what it was but had forgotten. I talked to Uncle Doctor later and he said the North would not accede. I felt so sorry that I had not remembered this.

My great consolation was our father is upon the throne and he will permit nothing more to befall us than is necessary for our good. I asked Major B to have family prayer that night. He did and prayed a feeling prayer asking the protection of God to rest on my family. He prayed for our distracted country so earnestly that some way should be opened up for peace to be made. He said nothing offensive.

I rose early the next morning, went out and told Lewis and Hill to get out of the way. Our breakfast over, while we were sitting around the table, there was an order for the major to appear at head-quarters immediately. We all thought they had orders to cross the country in the direction of Greeneville. We think they had their faces set towards the saltworks but were needed somewhere else at the moment. I went to milk (after they all got started) down to the lower meadow. Some of my cows were missing. I just felt they had killed them but after a little the venerable old Ahab came driving one. My heart went up in thanksgiving. Afterwards he found the other and I could not keep back the tears. I felt just like falling on my knees and pouring forth my soul in praise to my heavenly father. After I came to the house and got settled down I gave vent to my feeling for several minutes. I thanked my Father that he had still left my family in our comfortable home, that I still had something left to sustain life, that my poor Negroes were still unmolested. I have not experienced such a feeling of deep heartfelt gratitude to God in my life. I felt I could devote from that time my all to his service.

The major paid me for his breakfast. He asked me which I would prefer the Confederate or greenback. I told him if they were going to hold East Tennessee for any time I would take the greenback if not would rather take the Confederate. He paid me $1.00 for supper and breakfast which was enough. He had not eaten much but for my corn and hay the rebels guarded I felt I did not care. I was only a ten-fold stronger Southern woman than when they came.

As one of the guards rode off that morning he said to Liz goodbye Reb. She said goodbye Yank. He said if I get wounded I know where to go. She told him she would not love to turn off a wounded soldier but she wouldn't like much to wait on him. Lt. Walters bid us goodbye saying to me he wished me very well. I told him I could not wish him success but I did hope he might live to see his wife and children. And thus closed the scenes of Oct. 9 & 10, 1863. May I, if consistent with my Fathers will, never witness another such.

Oct. 14, 1863

Yesterday evening Powell got home after an absence of weeks. He came with one horse. I regretted the loss of the horse but feel it is nothing if my heavenly Father will only nerve the arm and hearts of our dear soldiers to never give up but to move forward trusting in him. Today about 11 o'clock Powell was arrested by the lowest element of society and taken to town but through the kindness of Mr. Netherland he was released without anything being done with him. Such men as Bill Williams composed the guard. He is claiming 150 acres of George Powel's land as part of remuneration for services rendered. This is a deplorable state of things, this is the result of Unionism.

Oct. 15, 1863

Through James Mitchell this morning a letter came for Cornelia Fulkerson. Mollie Ruth and Fannie took it up. It was from Dick Powel confirming the news of the death of our noble friend Joe Russell who fell at the battle of Chickamauga — I suppose on 21st of Sept as Richard's letter said he had fought almost through the battle.

Mollie fell in with Uncle Doctor who confirmed the news of the death of another good soldier from the 19th. Orville Looney[36] a neighbor boy. How much we lament the death of our brave soldiers but bow submissively saying it is the Lord's will. He is fighting our battles for us. We will trust in him.

October 19, 1863

This morning Mr. Merrimon came over to tell me he had heard that about 2000 Feds. had camped at Surgoinsville last night and would be on today. He told me he thought I had better not send the boys on the roads to work today. I felt it was kind in him to feel such an interest in one. He talked to me about hiding some of our wheat but I could think of no place where it would be secure, so I just committed all into

36. Orville B. Looney was a sergeant in Company K of the Nineteenth Tennessee (C.S.A.).

the hands of my Heavenly Father. About noon they passed along by Mr. Merrimons. Powell was there and thought they had about 300 men; they have several Negroes men and women. This evening we have news of the advance of Confederate forces.

October 20, 1863

The events of this day have been quite exciting. Before daylight this morning between 3 and 4 o'clock perhaps I was aroused from my sleep by a noise in the back part of my house. I thought at first that it was Lewis coming into the kitchen. I listened, then raised myself in my bed. In a short time I felt all was not right. I sprung from my bed, lit my candle and drew on my clothes, opened my door and hallooed to the top of my voice who is in my house. By this time they had made their way into my dining room through the old room opening the window from that room. I repeated the question who is in my house several times. When they came out they had a candle but blowed it out before they came on the porch. I spoke to them and asked if they had broken into my house. They replied no madam their pretext was hunting rebels. I told them as sure as there was a righteous God upon the throne of Heaven no rebels were hid about me. They told me they must search my house and I might go along. I talked to them a while telling them they might rely upon what I had said. After some few more words they concluded they would take my word for it. Told me not to be afraid. I told them I was not afraid of any of them. That the same Heavenly Father was watching over me which had ever been protecting me. I came to the conclusion after they left when I looked into my dining room that they were after the rebels' meat and bread. They took a large loaf of light bread, had broken open my spring house and taken my butter and some 4 for 5 chickens. They had intended, I think, to make a comfortable meal on the other small loaf of bread and apple butter but could not get along very well after I came on them rather suddenly.

They asked if I had a son. I told them yes I had a son but he was not at home and not of age for a soldier, that he was at his aunts across the way. After they left I felt uneasy least they should get him and take him on to town. My first thought was to follow on but was afraid they might hear me coming and think I was some one after them and shoot at me. I waited until day began to dawn when I threw my shawl around me and set off with Dick as my company leaving the children who by this time were all awake (I believe) to the care of my loved Mollie Ruth who had been staying with me for several days.

After I found out they had been in my house I went to the cabin and found from Caroline they had been in there to light the candle letting on to her they had roused me up and I had no fire. When I got to Sarahs I found they had been in her smokehouse and kitchen. They had taken some beef. I came back home and got things ready for breakfast when a Negro girl of Mr. Watterson's with her bundle of clothes came to the kitchen door. She had left her home to go to the Yanks. I told her she would miss leaving her old Master and Mistress as long as she lived. Caroline seemed troubled. I got her to stay today. She still says she will go in the morning to town.

Got through with this when two men from Fentress Co (name of one Brandon and the other forgotten) came up asking if they could get dinner about 10 o'clock. I told them I had nothing prepared hardly but would get them something if they desired it. I began to talk to them about being Christians. One of them seemed to listen attentively. As I talked I thought he seemed moved. I asked them would they read a tract. They seemed to not understand what I meant but at length got them to know. When they agreed to take one I gave to one *Are you prepared* to the other *Jesus the Soldiers Friend*. They left after getting a piece of bread and things moved on quietly until we were eating our dinner.

Jennie McCarty came saying I want aunt Eliza. I got up from the table and met her on the porch where she told me a number of men had been or were at Mr. Powels destroying everything. I left and went on to Sarahs. She and I took across the field and on the road caught up with Ann, Eliza Ruth and Jennie. We went on briskly but when we got there they were all gone. The poor Negroes were gathered around looking like some one was dead saying to her you are just ruined. We went into the house and a sad sight met our eyes. Her preserves, canned fruit, drawers, letters, beds were in utter confusion. Preserves eaten or destroyed. Cans of fruit taken, drawers pulled out and contents of some carried off. Others lay strewn over the floor. I felt sad to look at such destruction but every scene of this kind only makes me adhere more strongly to our Southern Cause feeling our Father who sitteth upon his throne is beholding with an eye of forbearance these deeds of darkness and letting them fill up their cup of iniquity. He who hath said vengeance is mine will repay and will avenge the wrongs we suffer.

While we were there two officers of the second Tennessee Regiment came having been spoken to by Ann as she came out. They seemed to feel mortified and spoke very kindly about aiding her in the search for her things. Her nice bed quilts were the work of her mother who has been dead for several years. She seemed to regret this loss so much. We went to work packing up what remained to send to town.

E. Ruth got Mr. Todd's wagon and driver. We got through and set out for home with E. Ruth riding in the wagon. The girls wanted me to ride but I felt the load was enough without my big body piled on.

We met several on the way. One was hunting a horse, another hay. I left them at the shop where we met several persons. Mr. Starnes, Looney, Mrs. Click and others I did not know. The whole world in East Tennessee is in a ferment. There is no rest with the Union folks more than with the Southern. The fearful thought of retribution is ever staring them in the face looking for the Confederates all the time.

October 21, 1863

The Lord has been our shield and guard during the night, no foe has been around that we knew of. At 2 I awoke from my sleep, turned the listening ear in every direction to know if all was right. I got up, struck a light, put on my clothes and looked out but all was quiet. The stars were shining brightly keeping as it were watch over the defenseless wives, mothers, children and sisters of southern soldiers who know not what our condition is.

I have given to three pickets their breakfast this morning although I know they are my enemies yet when they come to me and in a gentlemanly manner ask for something to eat I do not like to refuse. I tell them the Bible says "if thine enemy hunger feed him, if he thirst give him drink" and I fear not to obey its precepts. They belong to the 7th Ohio Regiment commanded by Col Garrard, Gen. Carter's brigade.[37] I gave each of them a tract, hope it may be seed sown for good to my masters kingdom. They tell me if they thought they were fighting to free the Negro they would lay down their guns and fight no more.

As dinner was almost ready two more of the same regiment came, wanted something to eat. I told them it was hard for me to feed them as the mills had been pressed and Southerners prohibited from getting any grinding done. They seemed to be very nice gentlemen and said they did not like to impose on good nature but did not go. I told them at length to get down and I would do for them as well as I could. They came in, washed and dinner soon being ready we set down and conversed pleasantly but pointedly all the while. I asked the names. One was Miller, the other Mitchell. Miller of New York parentage by father and by mother of old Federal Massachusetts. We would look for nothing but blue light Federalism from that source but I find he has a heart than can be reached by the kindness of the Southern heart. I feel he has Christian training, his notions are high toned, honorable. He says he is for equality of rights. We told him (Mollie, Mec and I) that was what we wanted and all that the South desires. He acknowledged the wrong of the North of intermeddling with the institution of slavery, says the Negro in a state of slavery is much better off than being free. Mitchell of Pennsylvania descent,

37. This cavalry unit, along with the Second East Tennessee Mounted Infantry and four guns of the Second Illinois Battery, was encamped four miles east of Rogersville under the command of Colonel Israel Garrard.

said very little but was pleasant. I gave to each a tract. I told them these tracts had been prepared for our Southern soldiers but they too had souls for which I felt very anxious.

October 25, 1863
It is the Sabbath and we are quiet and peaceful although our enemy is now around us yet we are still in circumstances of mercy. We know our corn, our fences and much of what is our earthly possessions are being destroyed and taken from us yet this thought moves us not. Our cause is as dear, yea dearer than ever before. It is the source of justice, truth and humanity. Every conversation I have with them tends to strengthen me and weaken them in my opinion. They have to acknowledge that slavery has been the inciting cause to this war. They all tell me if they thought they were fighting to free the Negro they would quit and go home. Yet every move they make seems to tends to this thing as the poor Negro thinks. He leaves a home of plenty and I may say peace and happiness. He goes to them, they take the deluded victims and in most cases put them in squads of 20 or 30 with an over-seer to work out a miserable existence in breast works or railroads with a ten fold severer infliction of punishment than he has ever known in his Southern Home if he fails to do his duty. This thing strengthens me in the deep seated conviction that a righteous God will not let such inconsistency go unpunished.

On last Thursday the 22nd Sarah and I went up the road. She to Mr. Carmacks and I to Mrs. Kinkeads. I did not stay long at Mrs. Kinkeads. As I road up the road I saw a youth approaching in soldiers rigging with a gun, cartridge box and haversack. As I drew nearer we began to talk. I found him to be a hired boy I suppose living with Mr. Thurmon by the name of Ben Willhelm. The name and the looks of the boy all enlisted my sympathy. I began to talk to him about what he had entered upon in the life of a soldier—its trials, its hardships its temptations. He seemed to listen attentively. I told him I wanted him to be a good boy and to pray every day to God to make him good and if he should never be permitted to see home again he would go a better home than earth can have. When we parted I bid him goodbye. Poor boy I do hope the little tract my father permitted me to give him may do him much good and bring forth the fruit.

I rode up to Mr. Carmacks. They were not willing to let us go until after dinner. We came home early. When I arrived I found Sallie Lynn and her little babe. I was so glad to see her. Here I found word from E. Ruth to me to come over to the farm that they had been there again. I mounted Susan with Dick and went over to Sarahs. She and I started but had just gotten under headway when lo and behold the blue coats in numbers began teeming off the hill. We turned and came back I into the meadow and Sarah into her lot back of the smokehouse. She counted 350. After they passed we came out and some 3 or 4 were behind. We came up close to them but did not pass any words. We went on to E. Ruths and Annis Powels. Everything a desolation so far as comforts were concerned.

After we had been there E. Ruth and I started to Mr. Armstrongs. Here we found another family in trouble. Their premises have been invaded. Such sorrow was never known in this land before. There I saw that old man whose life is wearing away piecemeal with that awful scourge cancer. He is much changed since I last saw him. His upper lip entirely gone. The upper jaw eaten so that you see the tongue as it moves. He talked but I could not understand him well. He is troubled. O how sad to think of one so near his eternal home being so annoyed.

Ruth got her cloth and set off riding as fast as possible until out of sight of those we felt might want our horses. We got out as quick as we could, Cousin Annis and I on foot, Sarah and Ruth riding. They overtook us when Annis got on behind Sarah and I before Ruth. We came on briskly but time moved more briskly and it was almost dark. Here we were with Ruth and Annis obliged to go home and no way to go the wagon being some distance behind. At length it was suggested that Sarah and I should face the storm. I felt I ought to come home as cousin Mollie and Jennie were here.

At length I suggested that Jennie should go and with that Ruth and I set off full tilt across the meadow. As we came along Ruth says make Susan go. I say yes we may as well kill her as for any one else to do it. I thought in all probability someone would take her that night. The words had not been out of my mouth when down we both went. She stumbled I think and my stirrup broke. I was hurt severely in my foot and ankle. Ruth escaped, I felt so glad she did as it would have been hard on her now. She has so much to try her having her things so much divided and little Stan so sick. My foot is much bruised and I have to keep it bandaged. I have not walked much since.

Saturday Sarah went to Col Garrard and petitioned for a guard. One was sent out from Co. H. I think of the 7th Ohio. He was a pleasant man of the Vallandigham stripe. We feel so thankful for such men being sent to guard rebel women and feel the Lord has done it.

While setting in my house my Sabbath days quiet was greatly disturbed by the entrance of 4 soldiers rough, ragged and of foreign tongue — Irish I suppose. I have never seen men so lost to decency in their appearance. They were so ragged that decency shuddered. I have never seen a Confederate soldier in such a fix no not even a Negro. They wanted dinner. I hesitated, one of them rather begged. I told them I would try but Powell coming in when they went out dissuaded me from it. I sent them some bread then they wanted some milk. I sent them a pitcher of buttermilk. They swore and seemed to want sweet milk. I had none scarcely. I sent for the guard and he was soon here and they were no trouble. I gave to two religious papers. The guards took dinner with us. I do feel the Lord has been my shield and backer.

Oct. 26, 1863

I felt this morning so troubled. The sight of those men yesterday made me feel terrible. I had never seen a Negro of the South in a more ragged condition. The guard sent us yesterday was Mr. Finley of the 7th Ohio. Co. F. He is a noble pleasant Vallandigham man and a true Democrat I suppose.[38]

Today Lt. Dryden and Sgt. Robbins took dinner; both seemed gentlemen.[39] Lt. Dryden lost his only brother at Chickamauga. What a war this is, no history of earth has ever recorded one of any similarity excepting the Bible which tells us of the falling out of the Jews. Father against son, brother against brother, son and father.

Oct. 27, 1863

No words will ever express the deep love of my heart to my Heavenly Father for his goodness and mercy to a worm. Last night I had Julia Lyons and Billy Armstrong. Julia is a noble woman; came down as she said on a work of mercy. Five of her black ones have left or been run from home. She thinks they were run off. She went to see Col. Garrard. She was not pleased with him. Julia is a true Southern woman—high strung but has had much to try her. Her house has been a scene of confusion from the liberty given the lowest element now in the Federal army to go round and destroy and steal the property of rebels who in days past and gone furnished to the families of some of those very men what has kept soul and body together since this war began. They took every horse of any value. What can the heart say when we think of the outrages which have been committed by this army since they crossed the Cumberland mountains. Nothing but vengeance is mine, I will repay saith the Lord. She left this morning and went to town with Mr. Todd going to assist her to try to get her Negroes.

---

38. Clement Vallandigham of Ohio was a so-called Copperhead Unionist who opposed President Lincoln's war policies. He was essentially in favor of peace at any price. (See Foote, *The Civil War*, 2: 631–33.) "Mr. Finley" was Joseph L. Finley, who served with the cavalry team for Company F of the Seventh Ohio, according to the *Roster of Union Soldiers, 1861–1865: Ohio*, vol. 1, ed. Janet Hewett (Wilmington, N.C.: Broadfoot Publishing Co., 1999), 480.

39. Samuel Dryden is listed as a first lieutenant in Companies F and H of the Seventh Ohio (U.S.A.), according to the *Roster of Union Soldiers: Ohio*, 1: 412. The same source (3: 309) lists Thomas J. Robbins as a sergeant in Company F, Seventh Ohio Cavalry (U.S.A.).

Last night was a clear beautiful moonlight. The dogs barked fiercely. I thought perhaps some one was about and I went out, was soon followed by Mollie Ruth. I set the dogs on by my voice and hands so loudly that Gus heard it across the way. Ruth and I concluded it was a dog they were after, came in, locked the door, took our seats. We were talking when a rap at the door drew forth the who is there. The reply a friend brought forth the question from me what do you want in rather a stern voice. He answered I came to see what was the matter. I knew then it was the guard. I opened the door, he came in and seated himself for a short time. He and Gus reconnoitered and returned with the answer all safe. He was in bed at Sarahs when roused, went back. The night was quiet here but at Sarahs someone took a towel and washpan. She heard the noise but thought it was the guard who had come down on the porch. His name is Aquilla Durham of the 7th Ohio, Co. B., a Vallandigham man. For these men I have a kind feeling. They love the South and I do believe would rather see her succeed than that abolitionism should gain any stronger hold in the North than it already has. It has been quiet today. The guard came over and we gave him a bath. I gave him a tract. Hope it is seed sown which will bear fruit for eternity. This evening Jacob Miller was arrested and taken to town by Bill Bass and Co.

Oct. 28, 1863
Still in mercy. I awoke early this morning and find meditation upon my bed, while all is quiet around, so sweet so pleasant. On Monday morning when I awoke the waves of trouble seemed about to overwhelm me when that beautiful part of my Bible was presented to my mind to console me.

The troops have been moved today higher up, perhaps as far as Mr. Eldridge Hords. I hope the day is not distant when the nineteenth and sixty-third Tenn. on the Confederate side will occupy this ground. Jacob Miller was released and sent home this morning. The charge is guilty of persuading Bill Bass to desert.

When facts were stated it seemed that Lizzie was the guilty person she having said to him after he telling her he was not mustered in that he had better just drop out into the woods and she would feed him.

The name of the guard last night was Fortner of the 7th Ohio.[40] He had good clothes and boots blackened. On Saturday the 24th I had two Tennesseeans; they came in to warm. Their names were Hickman from Sevier and Hart from Carter. Hickman was full of talk, all tired of the war and would like to get home to his family. I gave to each a tract. Poor deluded men I do feel so sorry for them. They think they are fighting for the perpetuation of American liberty when in truth it is to destroy the rights of American freemen.

Oct. 29, 1863

Yesterday Lizzie and Bug, after an absence of nearly two weeks, got home having gone up as far as Bristol. When they left (Friday the 16th) I did not know certainly whether they would go any further than Mr. Lyons. Mollie Ruth charged them to ask the advice of Mr. Lyons about the trip but they did not go by. They stayed all night at Nan Kinkeads and left early the next morning taking Nan with them expecting to go to cousin Newlands. They traveled very comfortably beyond Kingsport a short distance when they met a little boy saying to them if you do not want to meet the Yankees you had better go back. They were soon face about and got back to Uncle John Lynns as quick as the nature of the case would admit. Their horses were put away and they looked at the blue coats as they passed along.

On the Sabbath they went to Cousin Joseph Newlands and from there to Blountville on Monday. They found the friends all well; bustling with the evils of life with true Southern heroic fortitude. Whilst there my loved cousin Johnny Bachman took his

---

40. This, presumably, was Hiram Fortner, who served in Company A, Seventh Ohio Cavalry (U.S.A.). *Roster of Union Soldiers: Ohio*, 2: 11.

rib.[41] He was married on Tuesday the 20th of October to Miss Eva Dulaney daughter of Dr. Dulaney.

They went to Bristol one day but returned in the evening. They heard nothing of the loved ones who have long been confined in the Northern prisons. I did hope they were exchanged and that they would meet with them. What a burst of joy would have gone forth could they have met the trio. Sam, Mike and Nick—what tales they could have told. Poor Mike I fear has had a hard time but no one will bear all things better than he. He is a soldier indeed, ever ready for duty without a murmur. He has been confined at Fort Delaware said to be one of the worst prisons of the North.

They told us several amusing incidents of their trip. The evening they were coming from Bristol when near Blountville they met the Confederate pickets under full head way with the Yankees. In coming they met with Jimmy Rhea who told them Blountville was evacuated with the citizens going out with their bags on their backs. They asked him if they had not better go to Mr. Rutledges. He told them he thought they had as their horses would be in great danger in town. They accordingly made their way there. Nan & Liz were terribly troubled about their horses.

They had not been seated around the fire at night until they heard the approach of cavalry. In a short time the camp fires were blazing, the corn cracking and the joviality of the soldier was heard. Some two or three came riding up to the house and hallooed. Mrs. R. went out and they said can you give us anything to eat. No sirs, I am eaten out. I have a few small potatoes you can take and cook as we have no way to cook them. After a few more persuasive words on the part of the soldier she told them to get down. When they came to the light who should it be but some of our own noble soldiers. The girls gave the gray coats a most cordial welcome. Bug says to one little fellow are you right sure you are not a Yankee. He

---

41. This refers to the marriage of Jonathan Bachman, Eliza's first cousin. He had been paroled after his surrender at the Battle of Vicksburg. He then became a preacher and was Eliza's pastor in Rogersville for several years after the Civil War.

said yes I am, I have been fighting them for two years and expect to fight them as long as the war lasts.

They told of a quite an amusing circumstance which occurred when the Yanks were making their last raids about Blountville. They met an old Negro man and accosted him with where are you going. He replied to my wife's house. He had a little bundle under his arm. What is that you have in your bundle — my Bible — we want you to preach for us. I do not feel I can. O yes you must, after more persuasion he consented, opened his Bible and repeated this text. Go and live in peace with your brethren. The Yanks were confounded and galloped off as fast as possible.

Poor deluded, infatuated Negroes are flocking to the Northern army from the east, the west, the north and the south thinking they will free them. They are leaving homes of plenty; masters and mistresses within whose hearts are to be found the only true feelings of humanity for the African race to be found in the world (I suppose). They are cuffed, kicked and knocked by the self proclaimed philanthropists of the North. When I think of it I feel God is letting them fill up their cup of iniquity that his judgment may be more severe. I tremble for the North, the fiery indignation of the Lord of hosts seems to me to be gathering blackness every day. They know not what they do.

I have through the girls heard of the death of our noble and loved friend John Russell.[42] Poor fellow did he fall a Christian. He was brave, noble and generous. The first of our boys in this neighborhood to leave his home for the maintenance of constitutional liberty. Well do I remember the last time I parted from him. He had taken supper with us and soon after bade us farewell. I said to him John I want you to be a Christian and I do hope the Lord will bless you. O how little do we know where our next meeting shall be. Report says he was killed by a cannon ball and his body dreadfully torn to pieces with both legs shot off. My

42. John Russell served in the First Virginia Cavalry and was killed at the Battle of Brandy Station in Virginia on October 11, 1863.

heart feels for the aged father and affectionate mother. Their cup seems to be bitter; deprived of their darling boys in so short a time of each other.

## Oct. 30, 1863

Mollie Ruth and Liz came out. E. stopped with Sarah a short time when we set our for Mr. Russells. As we went along we met the forces under Col. Garrard returning. By the time we got to Mr. Russells we thought all had passed by pretty much but we were not long in finding this was a mistake. By the time dinner was over his premises around his barn and stables were under Yankee dominion.

Col. Garrard came to the house and ordered two rooms. I feel Northern officers are greatly lacking in politeness. He never noticed Mrs. Russell, Ruth nor I to give us even the military salute. Perhaps he felt we could not appreciate politeness amongst the Federals. Perhaps we could not but I for one felt no inconvenience from it. He was a man with the appearance of sinful man. Although finely dressed and well armed I felt his life was in the hands of God as well as the poorest private in the ranks.

We felt our work in the distressed family we had gone to visit was not done when Lewis came bringing the sad news that Nicky is dying.[43] We mounted as quick as possible and rode off. We came briskly home. Rode on over to Sarahs, went in and found the little spirit still lingering on the shores of the dark rolling Jordan. He had expressed such a strong desire to see us before he would go. He seemed so glad to see us and asked his aunt Eliza and me to pray for him. He repeated the Lords prayer to Mec and said he was not afraid to die—that he would go to Heaven. He had left a message for all the boys particularly Sam Fain to not drink any more liquor, to not swear nor chew tobacco. He said he had a good pap and tell him not to grieve for me. I

---

43. Nicky (Nicholas) Fain was the fifteen-year-old son of Hiram and Sarah Fain, who lived on an adjoining farm.

know he will meet me in Heaven. He asked his mother "will there be any Yanks in Heaven." I answered yes Nicky there will be Yanks in Heaven but they will be washed and made white in the blood of Jesus. You will never see a soldier with guns and swords but you will see the soldiers of the cross. Then his mother said you will see him with his crown of gold and palm of victory "I want you to wear a crown."

He seemed to be greatly oppressed for breath. Got up with some assistance out of bed, stood on his feet for a moment or two when his mother laid him down to die. He threw the clothes off. I told him not to do that I was afraid he would get cold. He said "I am going anyhow." He turned his lips to his mother to kiss and then to me and Lucy when he said all kiss me which were his last words I believe. Cousin Joe, Jacob Miller and Gus dressed him. He told Lewis goodbye when he came into the room after coming back with us. Poor Sarah her heart bleeds this night. None feels as she does. A mothers love is so pure, so unselfish.

Nov. 1, 1863

Tonight is the first night of our dear Nicky in the cold grave. I went over this morning between 8 & 9 and found from his appearance he had purged much through the night (blood from his nose) although they had watched him carefully yet this cannot be avoided. He retained his color very well but I suppose it was done by the presence of some brandy, bathing him frequently. He looked so calm and peaceful, like a little babe on its mothers bosom.

Mollie Ruth and the girls assisted in having everything made ready. They laid the white chrysanthemum with spruce pine all around. Mollie and I then took the covering of tartan and pressed it around as nicely as we would. Miss Mary McKinney and Lillie came out in the carriage. Miss Mary brought a nice basket of flowers to add to his decoration for the grave. Old Hannah and Polly came in to take a last look on the peaceful sleeper. Between 9 & 10 all was ready, Mr. Tolson having come out with his little wagon to convey the corpse. Miss. Mary so kindly offered Sarah, Lucie and I a seat in her carriage. Sallie, Lillie Rogan, little Sallie, Nealy and Nannie (Gus driving) went in the wagon. We met on the way Eliza Heiskell and Fain Powel leaving for Virginia. Eliza going to see her husband who is in Abingdon slightly wounded. We saw several soldiers passing and repassing.

Nick was taken to the old school church where Mr. Robinson was waiting. The corpse was placed on a table in front of the pulpit. Mr. R. opened the service with his short yet beautiful prayer. He then read some 10 or 11 verses of the 4th chapter of Job. We sang a hymn, prayed a prayer and sang another hymn. He took his text for the sermon from Job chapter 6 verses 7 & 8. He prayed again and pleaded for the bereaved family. The song of angels was then sung. This was a favorite song of Nick.

Nov. 2, 1863

We are still favored; our home has been so quiet and peaceful today. E. Ruth, Nancy and Mary Powel walked out this morning. E. went to the farm having heard through Jimmie Shay they intended coming after her milk cows today to kill them. I was so sorry I had no way to help Eliza to the farm. She is not able to walk.

While at Sarahs a lot of Col. Garrard's men came after forage, said they had been sent into this valley for forage. Sarah made a strong appeal not only for herself but for me. The young men seemed to have hearts not bereft of sympathy. They did not wish to strip women and children of that which would keep life in them. She told them we hadn't enough left to keep us up. They came in after the first set went away. A sgt. by the name of Brazart,[44] he seemed a very genteel young man—had been a printer I suppose of the Cincinnati Inquirer. He too is tired of war thinks the present Federal Congress which will soon convene will do something. Troubles such as I fear no country on earth has seen are now brewing for the North.

---

44. No soldier is listed with this last name in the *Roster of Union Soldiers: Ohio.*

Nov. 3, 1863

Another night of quiet has passed. We have not been molested in any way that I know of although they have found the way through here and are making it rather a thoroughfare. When I look around me and say O Lord why am I still the object of so much mercy and love, a poor worm so imperfect, so undeserving. I feel I have a Christian husband whose soul is poured forth now in such importunate prayer for his helpless family. Sarah has gone to Col Garrard this morning to see if she can get any protection for herself and me. I feel so sorry for her she mourns the loss of her little boy. We feel it is protection for us to have a guard. I do not know what the few ruffian looking men would have done last Sabbath had we had no guard.

Nov. 4, 1863

Another night past in peace and a beautiful day succeeded. How hard to realize our own loved mountain homes are now under Federal rule although every day we see blue coats more or less. Not a day passes without tidings of the terrible manner in which some of our noble Southern men and women are being treated. Some homes are almost a complete desolation. Mrs. Will Lyons has been so badly treated. I doubt whether she has enough left to keep her up. I do feel so sorry for her. She is afraid of them (so I hear) and they roam at large through everything. Sarah succeeded and we now have Mr. Finley to guard us again. I shall ever have a kind feeling for him.

Nan Kinkead, Liz and Bug went over to Mrs. Spears yesterday evening to set up. I suppose will return this evening. Yesterday we had news the Confederates were advancing. I do trust our day of deliverance draweth near.

A Confederate came within the lines. Sarah met with him and he gave her some papers and letters. He brought a Knoxville Register giving a list of the killed and wounded of the sixty-third Tenn. at the battle of Chickamauga the 19th and 20th of September a Saturday and Sunday.[45] Lt. Col. Abe Fulkerson commanding the regiment was severely wounded in the left arm. Co. A. Capt. [Wm] Fulkerson commanding, the Capt., 1st and 2nd Lts. wounded. Lt. Fugates arm amputated and 2 Sgts, 3 Corps and 20 privates wounded. Ab. Kesterson, Joe Russell and Rufus Wilbourn killed; all buried on the field and graves marked. Co. B. Lt. Saffell commanding with wounded: Lt. McClure, 2 Sgt., 1 Corp. and 17 privates.

Co. C with Capt. Powel commanding had wounded: 1st lt George H. Neill severely in the right side, Corp. James. H. Flora slightly in the leg and 28 privates. Wm. Earl was killed. In Co. D. Lt. McCallum commanding and the wounded were: 2 Sgts. and 20 privates. Co. E. with Lt. J. J. Aerce commanding with wounded: 1 Lt., 5 sgts., Corp. T. J. Glover and 20 privates. Henry Barnett was mortally wounded in hip (since died), as did Ben White wounded in the thigh. Sgt. T. Beidelman killed as well as R. King, J. Weaver, S. Smith and J. Bushong.

Co. F Lt. W. P. Rhea commanding had wounded 2 Lts., and 13 privates. In Co. G. with Capt. Wilkerson commanding the wounded included the captain slightly, Lt. Lane with an amputated arm. Sgt. M. D. L. Taylor and Corp. W. S. Alexander wounded dangerously in the lungs along with 11 privates. Private Henry Kidd was severely wounded in the leg and it was amputated but he died. John S. Alexander and Joel Rains were killed.

Co. H. was not with the regiment since it had been detached when at Strawberry Plains to take up the Rogersville and Jefferson Railroad. It was commanded by Lt. Rutledge and was cut off when the Yankees came in.

Co. I was commanded by Capt. J. T. Gillespie. Corp. Bayless and 13 privates were wounded. Capt. J. Gillespie and Lt. S. M. Deaderick were killed as were Sgt. Jno. F. Erby, Privates N. R. Capers and Wm. Barnhouse who since died. In Co. K commanding

45. Although Richard was the organizing colonel of the Sixty-third Tennessee, he was too ill with diarrhea and dysentery to be present at the battle. On November 9, 1863, his resignation from the army was accepted in Richmond.

was Lt. Byers. S Sgt. Bales and 16 privates were wounded. David Broyles was fatally wounded. Total wounded were 186 and killed 16 which are exactly one-half the number taken into the engagement.[46]

This same paper contains an anecdote of a Virginia Mother. A mother bereaved of three sons all that she had and all of whom had fallen in the war. She applied to the paymasters office the other day to receive their arrears of payments. It naturally excited the feeling of that excellent and humane gentleman and untiring friend of the soldier Major John Ambler.[47] She applied to him and he expressed his sympathy at her loss. With a nobility of soul which no matron either of Rome or of Revolutionary America ever surpassed she at once dried her tears and said with spirit that the chief grief of her heart was that she had no more sons to fight for their country. O it is such mothers as these that have sent such heroes to the field.

The Richmond Sentinel said: "This is the spirit of Southern mothers, they have laid freely yea gladly on their country altar their dear, their darling boys with the deep agonizing prayer to their Father upon the throne that he would use them as instruments in his hands for the uprearing of a purer form of Republican government. One whose cornerstone shall be his Holy Word. One which shall stand to the eyes of astonished nations as long as time shall last as the perfect system of civil government. One which shall ever acknowledge the triune God. One which our Father shall use for the Christianizing of all nations. One in which mothers shall never be found again withholding their treasured idols from the God who

46. According to Abraham Fulkerson, writing in Lindsley's *Military Annals of Tennessee* (588), 404 men of the regiment went into the battle and 202 were casualties—an account that agrees with Eliza's numbers. Fulkerson also wrote that 47 were killed on the battlefield and uncounted others died later of wounds from this battle. Another author, William F. Fox, listed 402 men in the regiment and casualties as 50 percent. Fox also noted that of documented regimental losses in the Civil War by Confederates, only fifty-three regiments suffered higher casualty percentages in any single battle. See Fox, *Regimental Losses in the American Civil War* (1898; reprint, Dayton, Ohio: Morningside Bookshop, 1974), 557.

47. John Ambler was a major in the general staff of the quartermaster department.

has done so much for them. O Mothers of the South awake, awake to the mighty work which is before you."

The more I see, the more I know of the movement of the Federal troops the more deeply seated becomes the glory. The work is his, let us all wait patiently on him and ere long he will show to us his mighty power in stilling this terrible revolution which has now been going on for nearly 3 years.

Nov. 5, 1863

Scenes today of no exciting nature. Went over to Sarahs this morning and borrowed 8 yards of cotton to add to my piece Mrs. Merrimon is going to weave. Mr. Finley the guard left not long after I got there to go to camp. I gave him a tract for Mr. Hardy and Myers *Jesus the Soldiers Friend*. Sent by him to get me a blacking brush and some paper. He returned before dinner bringing the brush and paper. Just having one dollar of greenback I could trade no more. I do not feel anxious to trade with them for any thing. He staid with us until after supper and we gave him some 4 or 5 more tracts for some of his friends. One to McNiall, Lytte, McCall and Jarvis of Co. F. Mollie Ruth sent to Lt. Dryden and I to Sgt. Robbins, all of the same tract. Lady of Virginia when writing that little tract for the Southern soldier perhaps the thought never crossed your mind, a Southern sister will make use of my little sheet to try to win the Federal soldier to the redeemer thou didst love so much. Precious messengers of truth they have formed an important part of my defensive armor since I came under the power of the enemy. I have given away several do hope my Father may impress the precious truth which they contain on the minds of those to whom given.

Mr. Finley related to us a circumstance which took place of thrilling interest to the believer and one which should impress the sinner deeply. Mr. F. felt it was a solemn warning. The evening before they went to Blountville the last time the men were cooking their suppers when one of them in a light careless manner for some slight offence said to another "Go to Hell." He replied "I don't want to go by myself." Next morning they were ordered to march when a call was made for a volunteer guard to advance. The young man who had uttered the last sentence above quoted and whose name Mr. F thought was Barnes came forward to go. They had not proceeded far when a ball struck him in the head. He reeled and fell from his horse a dead man. To the believer it is impressive showing the great importance of constant watchfulness and prayer. To the sinner it speaks in solemn tones "prepare to meet thy God." O Lord impress us deeply with the uncertainty of life and teach us to know thee.

Nov. 6, 1863
Glorious, glorious deliverance. The Lord hath been our helper. This morning I awoke before daylight. The rain was falling fast with the wind blowing hard and I thought of our poor thinly clad soldiers. My heart ached and I raised to God the prayer which has so often been sent up. O God deliver us and do not let it turn cold for we shall be stripped of all our bedding by the horse guard and the East Tennessee Regiments quartered in our midst.

Just after we had eaten breakfast some of the children and black ones stood looking to the road. I said Caroline what are you looking at. She said some soldiers are going along. I looked out and supposed they were home guards who have been doing so much mischief at Mrs. Kinkeads but of this a few moments soon told the tale. I again asked what do you see, when Caroline answered Miss. Liza the road is full of soldiers. We ran out and the shout we heard told us our deliverers in human form had been permitted by our Father to come. We had looked for them for so long. We had given them out. What a lesson has this taught us. Our Father is upon the throne, his watchful eye is ever upon us and when we least expect it his blessing is so often poured out upon us. We Mollie Ruth, Buena, Mollie, Fannie, C., Lil and I made for the road. The girls excepting Mollie crossed over where they with Lucy and Dick to help them gave the soldiers a cordial welcome. Mollie and I were glad yet our rejoicing was with moderation.

Cousin Eddie Gammon[48] rode back and spoke to me but I was so excited I did not know who he was until afterwards some of the girls having recognized him. Sarah brought out her bread and meat as long as it lasted to give to them. We felt so sorry we had no more to give. They went on to town capturing all the Federals there. The force on the old stage road moved on at the same time and two or three regiments came up the river by Mr. Rileys. Having them surrounded there was no possible chance of escape except through the river. Some few tried to make their escape there but were so hotly pursued they had to give in.

Sarah and I had a young man guarding us by the name of Finley. We had promised him to do all we could for him in the event our troops should catch him as a guard. He was at Sarahs and true to her word she hid him in the cellar. I went in to see him and found him in great perplexity as to what he should do. I told him we would help him. I came over home and got some old clothes then went back. I told him to put them on. I then took his gun under my dress and his cartridge box in a sack and came on with them. Put them all away and then went after him and got him safely home where I set my head to work to try to get him to his command. I went over to Mr. Merrimons to see if our troops had gone up the road. Found they had not but found out enough to know it was not a healthy region for our man to try to make his escape. I came back and told him he must sit still and I would plead for him.

I then concluded I would go up the hill and try to see what our men were doing. I took Mr. F., Lill, El and Nan with me. After we had climbed to a high point I said to them you stay here until I go further towards the road. I went on and on until I saw our men going out through the lane leading to Nancy McCartys. I supposed they had heard the enemy were making their escape down the river. I had turned around retracing my steps and slowly looking around to see what I could see and hear. I had not gone very far when I beheld a

48. Captain Edward Gammon served in Company M of the First Tennessee Cavalry. Eliza would mention his death in her diary entry of October 29, 1864.

scene terrible indeed. Some 75 or 80 Feds had made their way out and had come on down by Mr. Merrimons cutting across the field where I was. I stood for a moment paralyzed. I thought they were making for the hill to make a stand or to get through in some way to the Clinch road but of this I was soon appraised it was not so for our troops turned upon them and then what a yelling. I had often heard of panic stricken men but to have the faintest idea of their appearance you must see them galloping hats off. The look is terrible. Some of them as they passed would ask where are the Rebs. — how many Rebs and similar questions. I found a gap where I thought I could run the gauntlet. I did some nice running.

As I got through I saw a poor fellow whose foot had hung in the stirrup as he was jumping off his horse. Seemed to be unmanageable. I started to go to him thought I could perhaps help him but after a struggle he was disengaged and then what skedaddling. They ran in every direction. Up the hill, down the hill, across and some in the direction of Mr. Merrimons, some towards home.

All the while I was poling on in the direction where I had left my children. As I came up the hill guns popping in several directions I asked one of the blue coats did you see any little children on the hill. I began to feel my children are scared to death. I made my way to the house wringing my hands in agony and giving vent to a wail of woe when one of our soldiers said so kindly your children will not be hurt. I came on and the first sight that met my eyes was my darling Lil safe in Caroline's arms.

Mr. Finley had run thinking I suppose he could join with the men and make his escape with them. When I came into the house he was getting on his Yankee clothes having taken off the clothes which was another reason of his running not wanting to be caught with them on, face resting on his hand looked so sad. He said he would have to surrender but he would like to do it to an officer. I told him he should and struck across the meadow to where I could make inquiries of one. He asked me what I wanted. I told him I would tell him when I saw him. He replied I am an officer. I said to him well Sir

I have a federal soldier who wishes to surrender. He then called for a Lt. of the Virginia Calvary. I brought him on over, introduced him and asked him in behest of the pleading of a Rebel Colonel's wife to show mercy to the guard who had been so kind to us. He promised he would. They went to the stable and he got his horse, mounted and rode off. I gave him a parting blessing and do hope the Lord will be merciful to him and that he may receive favor from the hands of our Southern soldiers.

After he left I went over to take a look at the prisoners. I wanted to see if I could find any of the 7th Ohio who had shown us favor. I saw no familiar faces but one or two I passed back when one of the soldier prisoners asked me to light his pipe. Mollie Ruth took it and got a coal. We went back when some of them asked for a canteen of water. It was brought and then a bucket was brought and many came to the fence. When one asked Sarah if she had any apples she went and got some three or four dozen.

While standing and talking Sarah remarked that the back part of that gentleman's head was so much like Richard. I had noticed it before as it was grey and his whiskers grey. He was the commissary of the 7th Ohio I suppose. The prisoners were ordered to form a line which they did inside our meadow on the right hand side after which they were ordered in a short time to march. They came forward two by two. It is a solemn sight to see men surrender. I do believe it would almost kill me to see our own men panic stricken and have to surrender.

Mollie Ruth, Buena Miller, Powell and Fannie went to Mr. Merrimons where they had a fine view of the Feds as they tried to make their escape. They came along the ridge in front of the house, made their way down on the further side and then back up by Mr. Merrimons stable. Several of them surrendered in the yard and the lot by the Spring. Buena asked to some of them give me a gun. They answered her there are two down yonder by the fence. She said you will take them from me not understanding they were captured.

After the troops had nearly all left Mollie Ruth spoke to cousin Jimmy Rhea and pointed me out to him. He came across the road and spoke to me. I thought it was cousin Johnny Bachman and spoke to him saying I am so glad to see you cousin Johnny. But I soon discovered my mistake and felt ashamed of myself to think I was so lost by excitement. I brought him over home.

We had not been long at home when two gentlemen came riding up. Cousin J. went out and spoke to them saying to me Cousin Liza do you know who that is in speaking of the youngest one. I said no Sir. He told me it was cousin Jane Preston's son. This was enough, I told him to get down. He hesitated but nothing would do me but for him to get down. The other was Lt. Merriweather a very nice young man. I sent for Mollie Ruth. She came and we had a pleasant time. The girls, Mollie, Powell, Buena, Fannie and the good Southern woman Naomi Fullen whose heart was so rejoiced this day at the great success which had been granted to us that she came home from Mr. Merrimons and brought her flour. She went right to work to fix up something to eat for our hungry soldiers. I had been so annoyed about having grinding done that I had no flour scarcely. Some five or six came and took dinner. Several got a piece of bread and meat. Never in my life did I wish more heartily for something good to eat than I did this day but I could not cook. I was so glad, I felt I just wanted to talk to the soldiers all of the time thanking them that they had come to us and been enabled to do such great things for us.

After dinner cousin J., Lt. Preston, and Lt. Merriweather left going on to the encampment near Mrs. Millers which was just for a rest and to feed. They then went on but I do not know how far. We had a joyful time that evening as we all gathered around our home fireside. Liz and Bug had occupied a dangerous position one time in the morning. Nan Kinkead was with them. They were near to Mrs. Spears when two or three bombshells struck near. One came so close to Bug she fell down to the ground to avoid being struck by it. Another bursted within a few feet of Liz but neither was injured. They left this place and struck out up the river. They had staid all night with Mary Charles and next morning were soon acquainted with the fact that the Rebs had come. They left coming down towards Mrs. Spears where they met her and some of the black ones moving towards Mrs. Burems saying as they came by to the girls the Yanks are coming.

They got over a fence into a woodland. Here the girls were separated. Nan and Bug going one way and Liza and El going another. Nan and Bug came close to the fence where they could see them pass. They mounted a 10 rail fence when one who from some cause seemed to be in good cheer said, after giving the soldiers salute, ladies we are on a grand skedaddle. They thought the firing of the cannon began between 7 and 8 o'clock and continued until 11.

As they came home they came by Mrs. Lyons and then went to the battle ground having heard their were wounded who needed attention. There were only two lying near where they were. One was dead and the other mortally wounded. Bug went to the wounded one and asked him "if she could do anything for him. He said he would like to be moved. She said if you had some attention perhaps you would get well. He said "no kind lady I will die." She then asked him if he was willing to die and he replied yes. She then said do you think you will go to Heaven. To this he answered yes. She asked his name. It was Ellis son of Edward Ellis of Scott County, Tennessee. From there they made their way home. I felt so thankful that our Father had dealt so mercifully with us all. We had two soldiers killed and one was from the bursting of a gun in his hands.

Nov. 7, 1863

This morning I had my ox wagon geared up and took some wheat and corn for ourselves and some for Sarah. Mollie Ruth, Lucy and I set our for Mrs. Lyons by way of Mr. Ames' mill. When we left the mill we began to see some of the fruits of the Yankees surprise. Scattered papers lay along at different points. When we got to Mrs. Lyons they were preparing to remove the wounded. Mr. J. Annis was there with his little wagon and had taken in Mr. Petty plus one other. Mr. P. was severely wounded in the abdomen. Another wagon stood waiting. Doct. White the surgeon was very active. He was originally in Rome, Georgia but was in Cincinnati when the war broke out. J. D. Miller and several other were there. After the wounded were taken off we went to work to fix up our soldier as well as we could for the grave. Mrs. L. was very kind and furnished rags for binding up his head. Money had been left with Mrs. E. Fulkerson to have him decently buried.

Nov. 8, 1863

I went to church today in my ox wagon. For the two sabbaths past I was afraid to go in my wagon lest it would be taken away so I walked. I cannot stay from church if able to go. I could not but help feeling this holy Sabbath that God hath done great things for us. His hand seemed so manifest. The rain which fell on Thursday night softened the road so much that our soldiers moved along without any noise. Some of them who were along said it seemed like a funeral procession. We should all feel as Joseph did that it was God our Father who sent our soldiers to deliver us. We were troubled. We knew not how we were to be freed from the chain which seemed to bind us. Our oppressors had spoken boastingly of what they were going to do. One man had said to me "your sons will not get back home to stay again and they have given their last vote." I was not moved but felt my God in whom was all my trust was upon the throne. I told him that was as God pleased. I saw one who was with him but not the one who had said this walking along with the prisoners.

Eliza Ruth and I called this evening to see the wounded Federal soldiers. I found 5 in one room and two in another. In the room where 5 lay was Mrs. Merrimons nephew Mr. Petty. He was severely wounded in the abdomen. There was one lying to the right of Mr. P who was wounded severely above the knee. He seemed to be suffering much. I spoke to Mr. P asking him if he had ever been a professer of religion. He replied "yes at one time in my life I felt I enjoyed the comforts of religion." I urged upon him the importance of prayer, the great necessity of an interest in the great salvation of Christ. Told him the soul of man was the most important thing, the rest seemed to listen attentively. I left some tracts for a man by the name of Harman to read to the rest. One who lay near the door asked me to give him one. I bid them goodbye; they asked me to come again.

I have often thought of the moral destitution of our own army until my heart was pained within me but it is nothing compared with the destitution of the Federal army. They go not forth deeply imbued by precept nor example to try to do right. Rather they go forth to rob, plunder and destroy the people of the South.

Nov. 15, 1863

I was not permitted to attend church today for our Father came and took one of the little lambs of the flock which has so often gathered around us. Little Nealy[49] has been taken. Death came this morning about 8 minutes before nine and claimed his lovely victim. Sarah sent for me between 7 & 8. I started immediately. When I got there I found her sinking, she was pulseless, had a slight spasm. Her mother was trying to clean her mouth. Sarah told me she had a bad night; was so restless. Her little spirit was preparing to leave its clay tenement which it had inhabited for nearly 7 years. She was born June 2, 1857. She seems to be sleeping so sweetly on the bosom of him who said "Suffer the little children to come unto me and forbid them not for of such is the Kingdom of Heaven." I thought today as I gazed upon the dying child of the many friends who were in Heaven to welcome her. My mind dwelt upon that good grand-mother who has been for thirty years walking the golden streets of the New Jerusalem.

Poor Sarah her heart is sorely grieved but I trust she is bowing submissively. To Hiram it will be a severe blow. I wrote to him today by Alfred Owens. Mollie Ruth, Liz and Diana are setting up tonight. Sent for Diana on last Friday evening. I went to town in the wagon

49. Cornelia (Nealy) Fain, six years old, was the daughter of Hiram and Sarah Fain.

Richard Fain's resignation in November 1863 as an officer in the Confederate army. Ill health prompted Richard's resignation. From the John N. Fain Collection, East Tennessee History Center.

with Ann Powel, Mollie Ruth and Powell taking as we went along Buena and Jennie Mc who had been out trying to get in some wood.

I called to see Mrs. Heiskell and came back, went to the tavern (Maj. Edmonds) to see the dead soldier and make inquiry for those still living. I found Mr. Petty and a man by the name of Russell very bad but little hope of recovery. I then passed into the room where the dead lay. I found he was the same I had seen the Sabbath before laying near Mr. P's and who listened attentively to me. His leg was amputated sometime on Thursday. He was placed under the influence of chloroform from which he never roused. His name was Robinson from Fentress Co. I trust he did not die without hope. Poor deluded victim of a wild fanaticism that cares not how many bodies the juggernaut of war crushes if she can only ride triumphant through the land. From there I passed into the room where two lay. Mrs. Kneeland was busily engaged in dressing the wounds on both arms of one man. Another lay there with the thigh broken. From there I passed into another room where four were with three lying and one up. I spoke to them again of the great importance of being Christians.

I gave a short letter to a man from Scott Co. Tenn. enclosing a lock of hair in the little memorandum from Mollie Mc on the death of the soldier Ellis. I had found out on last Sabbath where he was from and was so glad. I do not know that I would have taken if off had it not been for Mrs. Lyons but now feel so glad and have thought perhaps they were praying Christians and that I a Southern woman was permitted to wash the face of their dead boy and take from his head a lock of hair and send it to them saying the heart of the believer in Jesus takes pleasure in doing all it can to relieve the sorrows of the hearts of the bereaved—friend or foe. I hope I may be permitted to know in this world whether they were Christians or not.

Nov 16, 1863

Monday night This is the first night of the sweet little sleeper in the cold grave. We laid her by her brother this evening about half after three. George Speck and Powell brought out the coffin. We laid her in when Mollie Ruth arranged the few flowers with spruce pine in a nice wreath. Mollie and Diana then carried the corpse into Sarahs room placing it near the window. Mr. Robinson, Miss Mary and Mrs. Hale came out in the carriage. I was so glad Mr. R. came. I have always felt services at home were more pleasant than anywhere else. Who feels like the bereaved, none and when at home all are permitted to be there.

Mr. R read a verse of the 4th chapter of II Kings then a few verses of the 107 Psalm and then a verse or two of the 23 Psalm gave the view which Bunyan takes of this verse "Yea tho I walk through the valley of the shadow of death I will fear no evil for thy and thy staff they comfort me." He thought was correct that it did not mean the valley of death but the tribulations through which the Christian passes in this world. We then sang that beautiful little song *What seraph like music steals over the sea.* Mr. R. then made one of his good prayers. He prayed so fervently that the affliction might be sanctified to the living. After which the last kiss was imprinted by mother, sisters

and other friends. Old Hannah came with feeble tottering step to take
a last look. I told her to kiss her that she had often kissed her in the
coffin. The coffin was then closed and borne to the grave in Mr.
Tilson's little wagon. Sarah went in the carriage with Miss Mary. The
rest of the family, Lucy, Ida, and Sallie going in the wagon. Sallie,
Mattie, Carmichael, Mannier and I going with them. Gus drove. We
buried her between three or four o'clock by her brother.

On yesterday there were it was said 100 Federal soldiers in
town. Alf Owens, Jacob Tilson and James Godsey went on into
town, came near being caught. They came out, went back after
they left. This evening Owens, Tilson and 3 others belonging it is
said to the 4th Kentucky started to go into town but saw the
Federal pickets coming. They came back and made a stand for a
short time on the hill beyond Sarah's house.

Nov. 17, 1863
Nothing of importance transpired today. The remains of Mr. Petty
were taken to the Gap, I suppose by Mrs. Walker's Henry. A scout
of about 20 of our men were in town today. No Feds but 3 being in
town but they did mischief taking an old horse from Mr. Tilson left
him by the rebels. He was just getting it so that he could have a
little wood. They having taken his mare on Sabbath and threatening to come back tomorrow to take him and his mule colt.

The sky cleared off today and the sun shone out so pleasantly.
We were cheered hoping some good news would reach us from
every quarter but we were doomed to some disappointment. The
papers we received did not bring us such tidings as we desired but
we still trust God is our Father and that he will bring deliverance
to the oppressed of the South before very long.

I went this evening to Jacob Millers to see about making some
arrangement for sending to the salt works. He was not there so I did
not tarry a great while. As I was coming home I met Rachel Saunders
who told me the Feds. were again in town. They had out a heavy
picket and a report that a regiment was going to start up the country

tomorrow. I do not believe this tho it may be the truth but we have heard a brigade was below town, that they were stretched along the road from Mrs. Blevins to Mr. Etters all of which was untrue. We believe now when we see and know. We do believe they were routed on the 6th in great confusion, we saw much of that.

Nov. 18, 1863

I have this day learned that our forces captured 800 prisoners, 1000 animals, 4 pieces of cannon, 60 wagons.[50] I have made this from the official dispatch of General Jones who commanded the forces on the Carter Valley road. The forces on the other road were commanded by Col. Carter and Col. Giltner. I have never learned certainly which was in charge.[51] Never was there a surprise which brought more gladness to the hearts of women and children than this did. Demonstrations of joy were seen along the road just as it was light enough to see and by

50. This was the Battle of Big Creek, in which Brigadier General William E. Jones, leading the Confederate forces, achieved a major victory, capturing 850 prisoners and 1,000 horses (OR, series 1, vol. 31, pt. 1: 550–66). After this battle the Union troops under Colonel Israel Garrard of the Seventh Ohio Cavalry retreated from the Rogersville area, which they had occupied since September 18.

51. On the night of November 5, in a cold and chilling rain, Colonel Henry L. Giltner of the Fourth Kentucky Cavalry (C.S.A.), who also commanded the Second East Tennessee Cavalry Brigade, left Kingsport with about twelve hundred men, heading towards Surgoinsville. Giltner's troops surprised the Union forces the next morning and routed them with no more than ten casualties on the Confederate side. Colonel Giltner reported that the Union casualties were about twenty-five or thirty, and of these, seven were wounded soldiers who were paroled and left in the care of a surgeon. Confederate troops under Colonel James E. Carter of the First Tennessee cut off the retreating Union cavalry as they attempted to cross Big Creek at Russell's Ford. The Confederate units involved in this battle included the Tenth Kentucky, Fourth Kentucky, Sixteenth Georgia, and Sixty-fourth Virginia. Also involved were fifteen hundred Confederate troops under Brigadier General W. E. Jones and Colonel James M. Corns, commanding the Eighth Virginia Cavalry, along with the Twenty-first, Twenty-seventh, Thirty-sixth, and Thirty-seventh Virginia Cavalries. They attacked at the rear to prevent the Union troops from crossing the Holston River at the ferry below Rogersville. Thus, a force of twenty-seven hundred men had attacked a much smaller force—twelve hundred Union cavalry—and captured most of them. Cavalry units under attack from a superior force would ordinarily have been able to retreat, but events conspired against the mounted Federals on this particular day. These circumstances included the effects of the bad weather and the fact that most of the Union officers were alleged to have spent the evening before at a dance in a public house in Rogersville. Clearly, the Yankee troops were taken by surprise, and their response was further complicated by command deficiencies: two of the three Union colonels were on approved leaves of absence. OR, series 1, vol. 31, pt. 1: 550–66; Johnston, Blue and Gray from Hawkins County: The Battles, 13–18.

the time they got to Rogersville it was unbounded. Cousin. J. Rhea told me he had never seen such a demonstration of joy in his life. He would not have missed it for a great deal. Even old lady Aunt Nancy Sensabaugh was so delighted. She would have done almost anything she could for the soldiers. Mrs. Simpson and Alexander were so rejoiced it is said they waived their hankys.

I feel when I think of it that the people of Rogersville and vicinity have so much reason to be thankful. Truly the Lord did a great and mighty work for us on the 6th. May his loving favor and tender mercy be made more and more manifest each day we live. There were some freed Negroes came in that day with the prisoners. Some of our men were greatly incensed at them. I heard one of them talking to one is a tone of great indignation. Poor deluded African — may the God of Heaven have mercy upon you is my prayer.

Nov. 19, 1863
The road has been kept well heated as the expression goes between here and Sarahs. Today we had intended killing our hogs but the appearance of blue coats deterred us fearing they might want a bait. None have gotten as far down as our house. The appearance of a few gray coats has struck terror to their hearts as I understand and they are retreating, forming lines of battle and falling back. Hope it is true and that the sight of another bluecoat may never be seen here only as prisoners.

I much fear Lewis has gone or been taken by them. I let him go to Mr. N's last night and he has not made his appearance today. I have ever said and still feel and say if one I have preferred Yankee rule to Southern let them go.

Nov. 20, 1863 Friday
Yanks all gone and we have determined to kill today.[52] Sarah has Jimmie Shay, Lew Davis, George Turk and I Powel, Ahab, Gus,

52. At this time hogs were commonly killed in the South when the weather turned cold, and hog fat was often utilized to make soap.

Hill and Jim—have 14 to kill. Eight for Sarah and six for self. We were through almost gathering up soap grease when to our great joy and gladness a company of Rebs came riding up. Our famous Capt. Owens with his little command went into town. Not long after they went by the home welkin began to ring with Papa, Papa has come. I left the hog region and broke for home. How gladly I welcomed by loved husband who has been absent so long.

Nov. 21, 1863

We feel so thankful that friends are being permitted to return to their homes after being separated under such trying circumstances. Our cavalry is moving today in the direction of Knoxville. Cols Giltner and Carter have passed beyond town tonight. We have grouped near us the 4th Kentucky under command of Col. May. Several have taken supper—cannot tell how many—hardy sons of Kentucky how deeply I sympathize with you. I fear the spirit of deep seated revenge which seems to work in the heart of every Kentucky soldier.

Nov. 22, 1863 (Sabbath)

All has been commotion this morning. So many of the soldiers calling wanting rations cooked. I set out in my ox wagon with Sallie and Fannie for church—got almost to the forks of the road when we met up with some artillery wagons. We had to halt until the wagons could pass. While waiting some of the men came to the wagon of whom I made inquiry what battery was passing. They told me Lowery's of Virginia. As one of the wagons was passing a young man riding on one of the horses swore. I told him it would not do for Southern soldiers to swear. He said "they could not help it sometimes when they got into a mud hole." I told him he must pray instead of swear—his name was Smith. The gentleman who talked with us was Mr. Broils Bond from Greenbriar Co. I think after a delay of several minutes we drove on to church. We were late but still I went in to hear a part of a most excellent sermon.

I went to see the Federal wounded. They were moving them from Major Edmond's to private homes. A man by the name of Hendrickson was taken to Mrs. Netherlands. He was the same one who was wounded at the forks of the road and taken to Frank Fulkersons. He was wounded in both arms. They had considerable trouble to move them. They ought to have been taken to private homes at first. Poor Mrs. Edmonds has had a trying time.

We came on home passing our soldiers going East and West. Some of the wagons have been turned back from here to get into a better foraging region. As we came out a wagoner overtook us. He was from Blount County knew Mr. Robinsons name and seemed to be a clever man. The brother of Col. Bean passed us on the way. I know he was a fast young man—was polite but did not know (I think) that it was the Sabbath.

Nov. 24, 1863

The evening of this day Robert Mitchell came asking to stay for he was very sick. We were moved with kindness and sympathy for him. He lay on the floor in the front room on account of fire. We then moved him upstairs. I borrowed Fain's lounge on Thursday. We from this time forward had more or less soldiers until our army pulled back. I feel so sorry that I have not put down the names of many who were here.

Dec. 27 1863

As I passed from the church today I heard the sound of the shoe-makers hammer and as I passed on the moving to and fro of our soldiers impressed me so deeply with the thought God is forgotten in our land. I shudder I tremble when this thought takes possession of my soul. After I came home my own son Isaac came with an order in his pocket to go this evening for the impressment of shoemakers tools. I felt he could, if he had only desired it, had been saved from this desecration of God's holy day. After he came Sam and Tom Powel came going on up the country to bring in soldiers belonging to their command. These things trouble me. I feel God will never bless a people who disregard his commands. Peace can never come until the fourth commandment is obeyed.

Our soldiers are dying and I do fear we are not doing all we might do to impress them with the value of the immortal soul. I understand from Mrs. Rogan that two had died in the hospital (Heiskell house) last night. I feel so sad when I think of them dying far from their homes in a land of strangers. On last Sabbath (20th) a young man by the name of Coffee from Maury Co. Tenn. who had been taken in by Eliza Ruth the Wednesday before died with no father, mother, sister or brother to shed a tear. No comrade soldier even to let anyone know anything particularly about him. When we got there Fain came down and told me he thought he was dying and asked me to go up. I went and what a sad sight met my eye. A young man first in the bloom of manhood in the jaws of death. I went up to his bedside and spoke but alas he was too far gone to give any satisfaction. 1 asked him if he had a mother. He answered Yes—she is just about your size. I asked him when he had seen her last—he replied just now as you came in. Eliza Ruth had come in with me. I knew the mind was wandering and felt it was too late to gather anything which could give much hope.

Dec. 31, 1863

The morning sun of the last day of 63 has risen, but not brightly in the natural world and the aspects of our political horizon is still dark and gloomy. May our Father cause light to rise out of the darkness and from a source least expected

# Chapter 4

## The Heart Bleeds from Every Pore: 1864

Rogersville was occupied by Longstreet's army until late in April 1864, when most of the troops departed for Virginia to fight with Lee. For most of the rest of the year, Rogersville was not really occupied by either army. In general, the Union forces came in from Knoxville on the south side of the Holston River, while the Confederate forces were based around Saltville, Virginia, and came down the north side of the river. Rogersville lay, in effect, on the border between the two armies. In August the Union general A. C. Gillem was ordered to East Tennessee to drive out the lawless groups that infested the region, but this drive culminated with his defeat near the end of September.

In June 1864 Eliza's husband, Richard, wrote to his son Nick and nephew Sam Gammon, who had been imprisoned at Johnson's Island for more than a year. He wished them good health and informed them that Kyle Blevins and James Merrimon had died. He continued: "We are passing through a fiery ordeal, may we come forth as gold from the refiners fire. God is upon the throne, he is holding in his own hands the destiny of nations. We know he will do right and that all things shall work for good to those who love and serve him. I do hope the effect of this war upon the hearts of the people North and South may be to make us better; may it be the means of the upbuilding of the Kingdom of God in both sections, and be for the maintenance of his holy word. The Bible must stand there is no power on earth can withstand or overthrow it."[1] The letter was received six weeks later, and Nick brought it back with him the following year, after he was released from prison. It is unclear how comforting this letter was to Nick and Sam, but it clearly indicates that both Richard and Eliza now considered the war a "fiery ordeal," as Richard described it, or a "sanctified trial," as Eliza wrote of it.

In early 1864, to her surprise, Eliza learned that the troops of General James Longstreet—who had been, in her mind, God's Holy Warriors—were as likely to steal her stock and food as Union soldiers or guerrilla forces. During the last nine months of 1864, conditions worsened for residents of Hawkins County as the successive waves of troops depleted the countryside of food for both animals and humans. The last straw for Eliza came on Christmas Day 1864 when Union troops, returning to Knoxville after destroying the Confederate saltworks at Saltville, Virginia, appropriated anything they could get their hands on, whether food or cooking implements.

Very few good mules or horses remained in the hands of civilians by the end of the year. During the period from April to the end of 1864, most of the troops traveled on horseback, and Eliza's home seemed to be almost a forward command force for Confederate cavalry. For most of this time, however, Eliza's husband and her sons Ike and Powell, now serving with local Confederate units, stayed

---

1. R. G. Fain to Nick Fain and Sam Gammon, June 7, 1864, Fain Collection.

away from home at night to avoid capture by Union cavalry or guerrilla units. Eliza even hid one Confederate soldier who had escaped his Union captors. The Yankees searched Eliza's house for him but were unable to find him. It is unclear from Eliza's diary where he was hiding during this search.

Eliza's daughters may have been part of the attraction of her home to the Confederate troops in 1864. Among these daughters were Lizzie, twenty-eight years old; Sallie, twenty-six years old; and Fannie, sixteen years old. It does not appear that Eliza's daughters contributed much to the war effort but instead helped their mother and the slave Caroline with the usual domestic duties of sewing and cooking. The girls and their friends seemed to move around constantly from Eliza's home to Rogersville or to the homes of their cousins and friends.

Jan. 1. 1864

A cold New Year, a sudden change took place last night which tries the feelings of man and beast to endure. Our poor soldiers will suffer this day. Just after we were done eating this morning two soldiers belonging to 37th Battery under Gen. W. Jones came in complaining of the cold. They had passed the night at the forks of the road where some wagons had been stopped. One of the soldiers was from Baltimore and the other was a Lt. from Eastern Va. On last Monday the 28th Mr. Robert Mitchell left us having been with us nearly five weeks. He had a spell of fever—was a pleasant young man. I hope he may be a Christian. The souls of our soldiers are so precious. On Tuesday Gen. Jones command moved up the road crossing the country towards the Clinch mountain expected to cross at the Little War Gap and the troops who crossed below at Big War Gap.

Caroline came home Tuesday having gone up Saturday to see her Father and Mother. My poor deluded Negro Lewis—I wonder how Christmas has passed with him. I think of him often and when a cold day comes I wonder how he is getting along. I was always so careful of him. Such a day as this makes me think of my loved boys who are prisoners on Johnson's Island.

On Monday night two soldiers from Gen. Gracie's command — names Robertson and Larmsden: came asking for supper saying we have plenty in camp but are so tired of camp fare and want to get something else. They belonged to 15th Div. I have felt deep interest ever since I read a little tract titled Major James Stewart Walker or the Christian soldier. I made inquiry of these men they told me he was one of the best men they ever knew and at first commanded their Co. — that the whole Co. was rather a religious organization. Christianity commends itself everywhere — truly those who honor the Lord shall be honored of him — we gave them their suppers. They set a few hours and bid us good night seeming much pleased with kindness shown to them. They mentioned while here that they had seen in some paper that the Federals were going to fix up a prison somewhere in the region of Norfolk for the prisoners of Johnson's Island. I do hope this may be true — our poor boys will be (if living) so rejoiced to come to the land of the South.

January 3, 1864
This is the first Sabbath of the New Year. My loved husband, Dicky and myself walked to town expecting to hear a sermon from our dear minister but were disappointed there was no wood. Since New Years morning the weather has been very cold indeed. Our soldiers have had a trying time. Sallie, Sam and Ike rode this morning. Sam and Tom have gone down towards Mooresburg in search of some missing men from their regiment. I feel so sorry such work has to be done on the Sabbath. War, cruel War loses sight of the Sabbath and all things which advance the interests of the never dying soul. We have heard cannon several time today are puzzled to know its direction — fear it is towards the mountains. Have as yet learned nothing as to the locality of the cannonading.

On yesterday 14 ambulances left Rogersville with the sick and wounded. What a terrible day to take men out. I do feel so distressed about these darling friends of somebody. One poor fellow, as he passed Mr. Merrimons, was pleading with the driver to go more slowly but his importunities were unheeded. They tried to get him in at Mr. Harris but could not. Such things distress me so much. I wish my home was ample enough in every way to take care of every one. I feel I have a heart to do it.

January 5, 1864

On yesterday we learned that the firing on the Sabbath was in the region of Blackwater and resulted in our capturing 4 pieces of artillery and a complete route of the Federals. I do hope the Lord will give us deliverance from a cruel foe—Ike left yesterday for the command, got to the river but the mush ice was running so much he could not cross—he came back told me a fine mule was drowned by jumping out. Got scared at the ice and could not swim out for the ice. Last night my heart was made glad by the presence of my first born so long since I had been with him any length of time.

Tom Powel was with us a short time last night. He and Sam had been out trying to get up some of their men. The boys all look greatly improved. Tonight our dear boys could not get over the river. So many wagons to ferry they returned to town and there tonight engaged as I feel sorry my children should be at a time like this. Our poor soldiers are dying far from home and friends—being buried in a land of strangers with no one to shed a tear over them and I do feel seasons of gaiety are so wrong now. My children love to dance. I feel so sorry to see them do it. I feel when the children of Christian parents do this what will the children of the ungodly say. What a stumbling block in the way of sinners. My Father, I plead that thine anger may not turn against us. O deal with us not as we deserve but according to thy tender mercy look upon us— into thy hands O my Father I commit every thing.

January 8, 1864

This day is still memorable as the annual return of the day of our deliverance from British tyranny. May the Lord make clear his aim and give us this day a fresh assurance of his love to the people of the South. Without his favor vain is our every effort. On the 6th our boys left home for Morristown where the Division is stationed. Col. Fulkerson (who left home on New Years day getting to Mrs. Russells on the 4th of Jan) went on the same morning. His health greatly improved and his arm healing up but still powerless.[2] I do hope his life may be spared and the use of his arm given again. He is a gallant officer and a noble man, O that he was a Christian. Dicky and Bob went with the boys to bring the horses back. He came this morning from town. Mollie Powell came out with them. Made the trip very well suffered from cold— snowed on them Wednesday. Last evening Cousin Sam Lynn came out from town.[3] His arm is useless—I fear he will never have good use of it again. I dressed it last night. He will carry the mark of the 21st of Sept. 1863 with him to his grave.

Ike and Cousin Sam left this morning. Cousin S. for home and Ike for hunting shoe making material. This morning two soldiers belonging to Col. Giltner[4] came for breakfast. Names Child and Etheridge from the western part of Kentucky upon the Ohio. They had been scouts as far down as Bean Station. Poor Kentucks I do feel so sorry for them shut out as they are and have been so long from home. Etheridge told me he had been a prisoner 10 months at Johnson's Island. Says the South has many warm sympathizers in the North and that the prison on Johnson's Island was one of the best the North had. Mr. Child told me his brother had

2. Colonel Abraham Fulkerson was wounded by a minié ball in the left arm above the elbow at the Battle of Chickamauga. He had also been wounded earlier in the Battle of Shiloh. In June 1864 he was wounded for the third time in Virginia, captured by the enemy, and held in prison for a year. He lived until 1902.

3. Samuel A. Lynn, a member of the Sixty-third Infantry (C.S.A.), was injured at the Battle of Chickamauga.

4. Colonel H. L. Giltner was a member of Company F, Fourth Kentucky Cavalry (C.S.A.).

been captured a few days ago in one of their skirmishes (below Rogersville perhaps near Bean station).

January 10 1864

Mr. R. in his sermon spoke of the desolations which we as a people are called upon to behold in our once fair and beautiful land. What desolation the onward move of a terrible army can make in a few short months. Our country is laid waste, our servants are decoyed from us, our stock driven off killed and taken, our whole country demoralized men forgetting there is a God; and woman shall I say woman losing sight of all that has ever given her any position in social life. Our schools all broken up for male education and but few, very few female schools still going on. The Sabbath has been desecrated. Murder, theft, falsehood and a black catalogue of crimes stalk unburdened as it were through the land since military law supplanted civil.

Mr. R spoke so feelingly of the desolated homes which this cruel war has made. The many hearts of wives, mother and sisters who were bowed with grief on account of its terrible demands. How many of those so loved have been gathered in the promiscuous heap and laid in trenches prepared by unfeeling soldier hands. Their bodies are then roughly handled and thrown in one upon another until one and another are forever hid from view, the dirt then lightly thrown upon them and they are left without a tear or a sigh unless some dear father, son or brother is there to weep and mourn for their loved dead.

January 12, 1864

On yesterday morning Ike left again for the camps. How anxious I feel about my children when they leave their home. We know not how, when or where the next meeting shall be. O my Father I do pray thee to watch over and shield them from the temptations and dangers of a soldiers life. I heard last week of the death of cousin Will Galbreath (son of Joseph). I felt so sorry he was a noble young man and I do believe he was a good boy. I never knew him much until last summer at the Plains. I saw him there so frequently his face is now so well remembered by me. He died at Marietta Ga. on the 16th of November at Ford's hospital. No friend to shed a tear over him. He sleeps in a land of strangers. He died the 4th day after leaving the regiment.

Another home broken up — On last Friday morning a very distressing accident occurred at the hospital. A young man, said to be from Mississippi, started home on furlough; got up very early before light and stepped out not knowing of any danger near, he fell into a well and killed himself.

Saturday evening, supper almost ready, two soldiers came to the door and asked just to stay in the house. Richard took them in — they had rations but went out to the dining room and took something warm. They were from Texas belonging to the first regiment commanded by Col. Robinson. Their first Col. was Senator Wigfall. Names Moore and Harris — very clever men I think. Mr. Moore was very ragged but very cheerful and happy. He would not sleep in a bed took it on the floor. Came down twice in the night for wood.

January 14, 1864

Last night we were seated fat the supper and someone came in saying two men were out at the gate. Richard got up and went out to meet them. They were loved friends — cousins Audley Anderson and Jimmy Rhea — felt glad to see them. They met on their way down about Mrs. Armstrongs. A batch of prisoners some 50 in number were brought to town on Monday or Tuesday evening. Some of the guards took one up to Mrs. Netherlands to get something to eat but she refused having been tricked before by some of our guards.

Today Liz & Sallie went to see Nan Kinkead. Lil[5] got her new shoes today after waiting on Mr. Biggs for several weeks. Her shoes were made by a Captain — who has been staying at G. B. Millers for some time — is a sufferer from rheumatism. She is very proud indeed of her shoes being the first ever made for her. She was 5 years old last

5. Lil (also known as Lillie) was Eliza's youngest child.

Oct. Ella[6] still barefooted—have felt more about my children being shod this winter than ever before—feel I am as I grow older becoming foolish about my little ones. It may be because they are little girls. El and Lil are going through a grand performance of play this evening. E. is acting soldier with a cap and Lil has made a visit to camp carrying some six or seven babies with her.

January 17, 1864

A lovely day—have to record the enjoying of another precious privilege—a quiet Sabbath with our church privileges still continued. Can we, O can we ever feel to our Father in Heaven as we should, when we hear and know of the closing of so many sanctuaries in the South. Ours still opened and our minister still with us. We feel this is a favor, great love shown to undeserving worms of the dust.

The remarks of our loved minister this day carried me back to those hours of mental anguish when I felt the hidings of my Father face and felt word upon words I would give it up if I could only enjoy the favor of my Father in Heaven. Well do I remember one night of anguish. I felt I would die and be lost eternally lost but my Father was leading me through the fiery furnace that I might never again despair of his mercy and love. This was in 1838 and I have never since had any doubts as to the truth of the Bible and the great doctrines therein taught. Since that time our churches have been shaken. The difficulty between Old Schoolism and New Schoolism[7] I have often thought was the starting point of this trouble of mind. I was shaken, I was bewildered and I was going into things which the finite mind has nothing to do with. The doctrines of Election and Reprobation were too much for my poor weak undeveloped intellect. I prayed, I fasted a

6. Ella, Eliza's twelfth child, was seven years old at this time.

7. There was a theological dispute among Presbyterians that reached Rogersville in 1838 and resulted in the formation of a new church by the New School Presbyterians. (See Ernest Trice Thompson, *Presbyterians in the South*, vol. 1 [Richmond, Va.: John Knox Press, 1973], 395–412.) Eliza joined this branch, which was more evangelical than the Old School. However, after the start of the Civil War, Eliza rejoined the Old School church in Rogersville because the majority of the New School Presbyterians supported the Union cause.

day every week for several weeks and God in infinite mercy to myself and family restored to me the light of his reconciled face. Since which time I have never sought to know what I feel is not my Fathers will.

## January 20, 1864

Monday morning I went to town not expecting to stay more than a few hours but did not get home until yesterday evening—as I rode through town Ella and Neppie told me to go back to the hospital and see the sick and wounded who were going to leave. In a short time I went to E. Ruths. She and I went—found them moving the wounded. An old gentleman by the name of Love was there attending to his son. They were bringing him down just as we went in. I spoke to the young man and then went into the room where the wounded one lay, his name was Carroll. He was from South Carolina—gave me some books (which Ella had loaned to him) to return. I asked him if he had read carefully one of them which was the series of Spurgeon's sermons. He told me he had read the greater part of the other—was a novel. I have no doubt he had read this more eagerly. Twas young— had never felt, I fear the great matter of life. I hope his sad loss may be the means which the Lord may make use of to draw him to the Saviour. His right leg had been amputated just above the knee. These two young men were kindly cared for by Mrs. Walker and Ella during their stay here. A warm breakfast was furnished them every morning from their table. I felt sorry that it was necessary they should have to leave. The morning was cloudy and damp but the accommodations at the hospital were so poor and nothing provided for them as rations.

Tuesday morning—Richard and I went over to Uncle Docs.—they were just ready to sit down to breakfast. They too have entertained many. They had that morning Col. McL and Lt. Sesom of the 50th Georgia Regiment.[8] Col. Mc was of highland Scotch

---

8. "Col. McL" was Peter Alexander Selkirk McGlashan, a native of Edinburgh, Scotland. He served as a colonel in the Fiftieth Georgia Regiment and lived until 1908. See the article on McGlashan on the website "Kyreb and Bootneck's Scots in the Civil War," http://www.scots-in -the-civil-war.net/mcglashan.htm.

parentage and Lt. S of French Huguenot extraction—both were gentlemen of politeness. Lt. S. had passed through the battles of Virginia—told the Doc. that the line of battle at Fredricksburg was one of terrible slaughter to our enemies. That in a space of two miles 1200 lay upon the ground—that they buried them in trenches which they dug of about 100 yards length and put 350 in one and 250 in another. This is the terrible thought—a mass of corruptible matter thrown in such a manner together. O how sad to think of being thus buried.

They left for Morristown that morning on foot. Some wagons were along carrying their baggage. My eye followed them and the prayer of my heart was O Lord preserve them and give to them thy spirit to enable them to do what is thy holy will. From here Ruth and I called to see Mrs. Heiskell—found her sitting up, though very feeble. Set with her awhile the time passing very pleasantly. We then went back home and called a short time to see Mrs. Simpson who was preparing to leave her home in Tennessee for one in North Carolina. Here we found other friends. After setting a short time I bade her goodbye—promising her that some of us would write. We meet, we part but none can tell when our next meeting shall be.

Monday night two soldier of Giltner's command staid at our home. Names Scott and Mayfield. Mr. Scott told them he had been here before and that I had taken down their names. In looking back I found 5 had eaten dinner with us in January of 62. The young man Morgan who was along that day died at Holston Springs. Another one had deserted. Mr. Scott lost his horse that night from overfeeding it on corn he had brought with him.

January 21, 1864

My husband left this morning for Morristown taking Dicky with him. Col. Walker and Powell went on with them from town. Richard had some bundle of provisions for the boys. Mrs. Merrimon sent some to Jim. Sarah to Pete and we to ours. We have tonight Capt. Carson of the 41st Alabama Regiment who lost his left arm at Bean

Station and a Mr. White. The Capt. dressed his little stump tonight in my room it being more comfortable than upstairs. His wound is almost well. His arm was taken off above the elbow. He came from Morristown today rode on horseback all the way. He has a family, to a father this must be a trying stroke.

January 22, 1864
The Capt. left this morning, dressed his arm again, he seems to have submitted with great resignation to his loss. His family a wife and two little boys will await his coming with great anxiety. I do hope he may be a devoted servant of Christ living ever in his fear. My spirit has been so restless this week. I cannot keep my mind staid on God therefore my spiritual peace is so broken. I look on my family their wants are so numerous. The means we have of supplying their wants so limited.

January 23, 1864
The Lord is still showing us great favor. We sleep in peace and arise feeling the Lord hath been keeping watch and preserving from all harms. Ike was permitted to get home last night. He came to the door with quite a noise and knocked. Powell went to open — when he jumped in so full of life and cheerfulness. I always feel so glad to see them coming in. I often wonder shall my children all be preserved through the great struggle of the South. When I hear of so many families who have been broken up, their loved ones dying far from home. Shall I, such a worm and one so unworthy, have my dear loved ones preserved.

My heart was so cheered yesterday evening by a short visit from our dear minister. He is so pleasant, I feel so delighted to have him come to our home. I had such a comforting conversation with him. I had been so worried about my children dancing. I had wanted to talk to him about it. I do feel it is wrong at all times, but now I regard it as so wrong and when the heart is once given up to this amusement it seems to be so dead to every thing that is right and good. My poor Liz seems to be bent on the indulgence of herself in this pleasure — cost what it may. She went yesterday over to Mr. Burems — returned today broken down.

January 25, 1864

All is still quiet with us. We hear rumors of success and reverse. Can give no credit to what we hear. Old Ahab tapped some of the sugar trees today. Hope we may have a suitable season for molasses making.

January 28, 1864

Little Jimmy Fulkerson overtook us coming home from Mr. David Lyons. He was coming from Virginia. He told us it was reported very currently that we had Chattanooga. We felt, we hope it is true but fear to be uplifted by the news.

    Richard went to town this morning. Brings us the news that Knoxville is certainly in our possession, that Tazewell is evacuated. Our troops had moved with the expectation of giving a surprise but the Feds were informed of it in time to get reinforcements sufficient to make them appear formidable. At least we do hope they are leaving East Tennessee and that we shall never see another Federal soldier.

January 31, 1864

The first month of 64 almost gone and yet we feel the enemy still lingers not willing to relinquish their hold on East Tennessee. O when shall the happy day come in which it shall be said they have gone back to their own land feeling there is a ruling Providence whose plans and purposes they cannot thwart with the combined powers of a universe. I feel today as I have ever felt, they cannot conquer unless God our Father permits them and the Christian of the South feels he will never permit the church to be destroyed.

February 4, 1864

Last evening Mr. Dickens of the 4th Kentucky from Campbell Co. Ky. Co. D his Captain Moore came in asking to stay the night. I cannot turn him out. Just before supper was ready soldiers came up begging to get lodgings for the night. One man seemed almost given out. Found he has been suffering from rheumatism for a great while. Has been but little with his command for 10 months. Name Watts belonging to the thirty-seventh Virginia Battalion of Cavalry commanded. by Col. Lewis. Mr. White was of the thirty-sixth Virginia Cav. commanded. by Col. Sweeney.[9] They were clever men—poor fellows I do feel so sorry for them—hope the day is not far distant when the soldier of the South will be permitted by our heavenly Father to go home in peace and independence. I am pleased with Mr. Dickens—he looks like Cousin Sam Rhea. Told me his grandfather was a revolutionary soldier—was at Yorktown when Cornwallis surrendered—had been barefoot 9 months. Told me he often thought of the hardships of his grandfather when riding alone at night cold, hungry and wet. He has been a courier for 3 or 4 months. He was moved by the conflict before him as he thought of the happy results of the revolution and what he felt would be the result of the present.

February 7, 1864
Went to church in my wagon today. Mollie Ruth and Lillie going with us. Richard called at Mr. Fulkersons to know if he had returned from Dandridge. Mrs. F. anxious to go to church but had no way. Richard told her to come and take a passage with me which she did. I was so glad she went for had such a rich repast. Row Kinkead and Fannie Fain came back with us. They having gone with the girls yesterday evening. Our church privileges continued. The means of going still granted to us.

February 9, 1864
The son of one of the men who left East Tennessee many years ago for a home in the West has just left us (Capt. John Groves of the

---

9. There was a Moses R. White in the Thirty-sixth Virginia Cavalry, commanded by Colonel James W. Sweeney. However, there was no person by the name of Watts or a colonel by the name of Lewis in that unit. J. L. Scott, *36th and 37th Battalions Virginia Cavalry* (Lynchburg, Va.: H. E. Howard, 1986).

ninth Tenn. Cavalry. Co.—his father John B. Groves was raised in this county and whose home was near where we are now living). He lived with Father Fain as a clerk for many years—went to Columbia and married a lady—lived several years in Columbia and for thence went to New Orleans where she and his 4 daughters died from that terrible scourge of the human family Yellow Fever. I love to meet with the children of my old friends and those of my husband.

February 10, 1864

Yesterday Gen. Vaughn & cousin Jimmy Rhea took dinner with us. They with other officers of the Brigade had taken a ride to look out a more pleasant place for an encampment, went and surveyed around the Ebbing & Flowing Spring, do not know what conclusion they came to. Gen. V. is a very pleasant man plain and unassuming. I think he is a good man. May he put his trust in that God who is able to deliver. Brother Hiram came over and took dinner with us—felt so glad to have him with us. I love so much to see brothers love each other—just as we were done dinner some of the children came in saying Kyle Blevins and Tom Powel had come. They came in and took some dinner—noble boys how my heart yearns over them. O that the Lord would make them feel the importance of giving their hearts to him. I know of no young officer in whose career I have felt deeper interest than Kyle. I look on him as a noble Southerner—he has labored under many trials. After dinner Kit Spears came—was on his way home—from the army at Dalton. He does not look well. I feel sorry when our poor soldiers look like they are wearing away.

Last night about 11 o'clock we were roused by a knock at our door. Richard called out who is there. The answer Major Randolph. Richard got up and let him in, he sat and warmed a short time when Powell took him up to bed. He had taken supper at Mr. Sensabaughs some 15 or 16 miles up the valley. This morning he left in company with my beloved husband. He going on to Dandridge my husband going out on the railroad on the hand car wishing to make some arrangements for the regular running on the road so that we may have a mail and some accommodation for those who wish to come and go on the road.

February 19, 1864

Cousin Nate Bachman and Uncle John Lynn came to our house in the evening. They tarried with us that night. I felt so glad to see them. They are friends I love so much. We spent a pleasant time that night in social conversation. Uncle John could not forego the pleasure of pranking with children. He took off his wig and offered it to Lil to comb. It was too much for her. She buried her face in her papa's bosom frightened greatly to us it was great sport. His bald head unwigged was a sight Lil had never seen before. Tom Powel and Sam Fain came in after we were through with supper, having been out on the road after some men they being here on detailed service getting up men who belonged to the service.

On the Sabbath evening I attended the services for the blacks. I felt great interest and we had a pleasant meeting and I trust a profitable one. I do hope some soul was brought to feel its need of the cleansing blood of Jesus. Mr. Robinson sang a verse or two of that beautiful hymn *Jesus I my Cross have taken*. After the sermon the communicants were invited to come forward. Some 12 or 15 came forward and took their seats. To me it was peculiarly solemn having been permitted that morning the refreshing of my own heart at the table of the Lord and I felt here are our servants whom God in his infinite wisdom and for purposes known alone to him as bond servants can come and know of the love of Jesus.

I think the blacks sung *Alas and did my Saviour bleed*. They sung that evening with great spirit *Jesus my all to Heaven is gone*. I love to hear them sing on earth and I know I shall love to hear them in Heaven when the spirit shall be disrobed of the clay tenements which they now inhabit and we shall all see Jesus upon the throne. Christ will then make all free. To me this is a delightful thought to meet with the members of my dear family—my husband, my children, my servants at the right hand of God.

On Monday Richard was intending to go to Lynchburg. When they got out to the river they learned there was a backward movement of our troops. This was passing strange but a few hours before, I might say, we felt all is well and was moving on so nicely. Pontoon bridges were built or in construction at Strawberry Plains. Our army all moving forward when lo all things stop, pontoons are removed and a retrograde movement takes place. Dicky comes back bringing us the unpleasant news. We feel this is trying. Major Lowe goes on to town, the young folks despite the news still continue to enjoy themselves. I go to my work carrying sugar water feeling our God in whom we have trusted will deliver.

Sallie, Mat & Sam took a seat on a log down towards the meadows. Liz as usual took the kitchen. Mollie Ruth upstairs working on a dress for Maggie Powel. Mollie Moore and Sam enjoying the company of each other. Fannie and Mollie Powel assistants about the kitchen. I believe Katy Moore and Nannie busy in the doll business. Thus we were all moving on, dinner came and after they still kept up their good cheer with each other until Major Lowe came out from town ordering Sam Fain to go some 15 or 20 miles after some men belonging to the detail. I came to the house found them all somewhat disconcerted. Kit Spears and Sam Spears came wanting the girls to go to a dance at J. Millers but of this I had no notion. Liz had gone up to Mrs. Kinkeads riding the horse which Sam had to take after supper. Before she got back Sam set out, I felt uneasy as it was dark and began to rain—blowed and rained very hard through the night. The girls Sam & Kit Spears with Tom and Powell took their seats in the front room. What they did I know not. Cousin Mollie and Tom came out on the back porch and promenaded for some time—there was no noise. Richard and I went to bed.

Next morning (Wednesday the 17th) between 2 and 4 o'clock we heard someone at the door. I called out who is there thinking at first it might be Sam returning. Would not let Richard speak lest it might prove a Yankee scout to arrest him. When to my joy and sorrow Ike let me know it was him. Joy to know he was safe and sorrow because I knew our army was certainly falling back. I got up opened the door and let him in. He went to bed, when we got up in the morning we found he was the bearer of a letter from cousin George Fain[10] urging the girls to go immediately to cousin Ben Earnests. All was now bustle. The pleasant visit we had contemplated with pleasure was at an end. Such prompt obedience I have never seen given so cheerfully before. They went right to work gathering up their clothes, some which I had washed for them but had not been able to iron. In a little while all was packed and they ready to go. Ike and Powell drove them down in Sarah's hack. In the evening cousin Mat came back bringing her clothes to iron. I was so glad she came; had felt so badly about them. Caroline, Fannie and cousin M soon had them done up nicely and now she must go back as they knew not how soon next day they might leave. Still no conveyance had been secured. Lizzie and Sallie went with her, Kyle McCarthy and Sam Fain walking. Ike drove the girls. Kyle came Thursday, he looks so well—is such a noble soldier. Next morning the girls Liz and Sallie came out, Fannie going down but still they could not get a conveyance. The boys went to see Lew Davis who agreed to take them on Saturday morning. Mat & Mollie came out and spent the day with Sarah.

February 26, 1864

Mr. John Armstrong was released from a suffering body and permitted to go, I trust, to Heaven. For years he felt the grasp of the terrible monster but with calmness and without murmuring submitted to the will of his heavenly Father. His was truly an awful foe being upon his face. He lived until it was I might say eaten up; when I first saw him 30 odd years ago upon one side of his nose you could see the appearance of the terrible scourge—a little harmless

10. George Fain was a distant cousin of Richard's who lived in Dandridge, Tennessee. His advice was misguided, and there is no evidence that any of Eliza's daughters were ever molested or in any real danger of bodily harm during the Civil War.

looking place of bluish appearance. Alas, alas who would have ever thought of its ravages. He was buried Friday evening at home.

On Saturday morning we were all commotion. Richard having determined to send the wagon with Sam. From an intolerably early hour until 10 o'clock it was hurly burly—having many things to do. Hill & Jim had to be fixed off but at last all was done. The wagon packed and farewells said the dear ones left again. Tom came by to say farewell. He and Sam have gone forth again to meet the stern realities of the soldiers life in the camp and on the field.[11] I do trust the spirit of God may go with them that they may think of the mercy and goodness God to them in sparing their lives and allowing them so many seasons of such good joy at home. That morning I bid my two sons Hiram & Ike farewell how my spirit yearns over my children. I want them to be Christians: humble, holy and devoted. Hiram[12] came on Wednesday went on to see his wife and child; returned on Friday morning with the intention of going across the country to Greeneville but found when he got to town the detail had gone. Major Lowe,[13] Ike & himself with Tom the black boy formed the company for crossing the country. They were rather afraid to go and determined to wait until next morning and go to the junction. Friday night all my family were at home but my two dear boys who live in one of the cold prisons of the North. I omitted to mention at the right place the joy I was made to feel on Sabbath morning the 12th when I got to town and learned that Sallie had a letter from my dear Nick telling us that he and Sam

11. What Eliza does not say is that while her son Sam and his first cousin Tom Powel went to Virginia with the Sixty-third Tennessee under the command of General James Longstreet, this was not the case with her sons Ike and Hiram, who were in the same regiment. They appear not to have gone to Virginia and were probably absent without leave until Colonel Abraham Fulkerson, probably as a favor to Richard, removed Ike from the roll. Hiram, however, was listed as absent with leave upon the authority of General P. G. T. Beauregard.

12. This Hiram was Eliza's oldest child. He married Bettie Lyons of Surgoinsville, Tennessee, in 1859. They had a daughter, Matilda, born in 1862.

13. This was Major J. G. Lowe of the Twenty-third Tennessee Infantry (C.S.A.). Lowe's unit was detached from the Army of Tennessee in November 1863 and went with General James Longstreet to East Tennessee.

were well and that they had been blessed with health ever since their imprisonment for which they were thankful.

On Thursday the 18th cousin James Rhea took his dinner with us being on his way to Kingsport whither the infantry of Gen. Vaughn's command had been ordered. From him I learned that another noble Southern soldier had gone to his rest. Cousin Audley Anderson who was wounded severely at Chickamauga—being shot in four places. He lingered long, we had hoped his life would be spared. He died on February 17, 1864.

On yesterday, the Sabbath we again assembled as a peaceful congregation to listen to the words of our divine master coming from the lips of a beloved minister—on love to our enemies. His text was Romans chapter 12 from verse 17 to last verse inclusive. I had a great desire to hear this sermon and have been gratified. I feel comforted, for to love our friends is no trouble but to love as we are required those whom we feel to be our bitter enemies is a hard struggle. He showed that the teachings of Christ to the Jews were intended to rid the mind of the errors into which they had fallen of indulging in a spirit of retaliation & revenge. The law "an eye for an eye and a tooth for a tooth" had been misapplied and instead of its belonging entirely to law for judicial procedure each one had taken into their own hand the avenging of their wrongs. Of this the Saviour wished to rid their minds. We cannot approve of the sins and wickedness of our enemies but we can feel for them as precious souls for whom Jesus died. We can pray for them and do them good whenever it is in our power. May this sermon do good is my prayer.

In the evening he preached to the soldiers from Deut. 34 6–9 verses. Mr. R. related an impressive anecdote of our own illustrious Jackson. One night having had a consultation with some of the officers he replied as they were about leaving that he would think on these things and return an answer at an early hour. Next morning as two of the officers were walking along one of them remarked: The old man wants to pray over this matter and having some business at general headquarters he returned not long after and found the iron man bowed in prayer, he was struck, he was awed, he felt in his heart he has something which I have not. That man was Gen. Ewell and it is hoped and believed that he became a Christian.

February 29, 1864
All alone the children sleeping, my husband gone. The rain falling without cessation. Kyle Blevins left town this morning to go to his command having recovered pretty well from his wound which he received in the last battle at Missionary Ridge.

March 1, 1864
We have had a gloomy day—raining pretty much all day. Powell went to town this evening, bring the news that the 3rd regiment of Yankees are somewhere between Rogersville and Rocky Springs. But we pay little attention to this as we have been hearing for several days of the advance of this regiment. Bob Powel came out with Powell. I do trust we may never see another Federal soldier only as prisoners.

March 2, 1864
Last night as we were all quietly seated by the fire some one hallowed. Powell went to the door when he recognized the voice of Fain Powel and Kyle. They came in and lodged, he and Kyle entertained us very much. Fain by a recital of his adventures with the Feds. when they were here. Kyle by telling us of several wonderful escapes he made when on detail between Cleveland and Knoxville—hunting bushwhackers who had been very troublesome on the railroad. 25 men were sent out—the most of them from the nineteenth (Co. K.) Kyle, Newt Richard (son of J. Williford), and Thomas Hogue. Williford was killed or captured; his fate unknown as yet. Of the 25 only 8 returned and they were in many perils. Kyle told us that 2 besides himself had gone to a Southern

ladies house to get something to eat; while there the house was surrounded but they made their escape and threw themselves in a gully under some little bushes. When the Yanks found they had made their escape they went to work taking everything from the woman (almost) that she had to eat. There was one old man along belonging to the neighborhood who had acted as an informant. They marked him well and after the Yanks separated from him took a near cut on him and caught him. They killed his horse and gave him a terrible whipping—leaving him tied to a tree. This to me looks horrible yet the necessities of war makes it necessary that a foe to his own country must be punished severely to intimidate the rest.

At another time they were run into a thicket of woods. Many were in pursuit—yet they were afraid to enter the retreat of the Rebs. It was almost dark and they determined to keep them there until morning when they expected to capture the whole. They fired many shots into the woods but without effect. About midnight they thought they had found an opening where they could get out accordingly they all made ready and with a terrible yell and firing of guns and pistols they charged and passed the nearest pickets fire throwing the whole into confusion. The Yanks running one way and the handful of Rebs another. The boys brought us news that two corps of Feds. were at Morristown. Whether true or not we cannot tell.

March 3, 1864

This morning we prepared Fain Powel for leaving with his uncle Hiram Fain, Ann, Mollie and little Maggie. They took black Ann. I felt so sorry to see Fain & Ann leaving. They intend to go to Georgia as their home. Poor Fain I fear he will be a great sufferer. His leg had been very painful to him. Some bones have been working out lately. Fain & Ann are friends we love so much. They have a sweet little child. I am so glad Mollie has gone with her brother & sister.

March 4, 1864

Three years today since the inauguration of the renowned President of the United States. What years they have been. May we as a people never be called to pass thru more such years is my prayer.

March 7, 1864

All are sleeping around me. I have just finished a short letter to a young Texan soldier named Robt. Camel who seemingly by accident was thrown into our family for a short time this winter. We all became much attached to him. He was very pleasant.

Yesterday evening after writing my thoughts suggested by Mr. R's sermon I took some religious papers, my Bible and went into Caroline's cabin. Fannie was there trying to learn her the tune of *Home to I would not live alway*. I joined in, we sang another hymn or two when Gus came in and not long after his sister Lucinda. After Lucinda left read several pieces in the papers. To me it was very pleasant. For the poor Negro I have a warm sympathy.

Ike came home unexpectedly—had been foraging on the road between Rogersville to Junction. Although he had been at home but a short time before, I felt so glad to see him. I love my children but O how deeply pained I do feel when I hear of their acting wrong. Today we were much gratified by the coming in of Cousin Jimmy Rhea. Had not heard of his return. He has now some staff appointment under Gen. Vaughn.[14] They are encamped at Ebbing & Flowing Spring and find it a pleasant locality.

March 8, 1864

Quite early this morning two soldiers belonging to Col. Slemp's regiment came up asking for breakfast. I at first thought I would refuse them but I could not. The thought of my own sons and the feeling I have for our soldiers always causes me to say come in. Breakfast over we went to work to get Ike started. Had bread, meat

14. James Alex Rhea had been a major in the Sixtieth Tennessee Infantry and later became a lieutenant colonel attached to General John C. Vaughn's brigade.

& molasses put up. At length all ready he bade us goodbye and mounted. As he was riding off I told him he must not say bad words when Gus called after him.

I then asked Gus if he had heard him swearing any lately. He told me he had and that Ike and Sam both swore so much and that when at home the last time they came near fighting each other. They would have fought had it not been for him (Gus). He said they swore so wickedly and that he never saw two brothers who disliked each other as they did. To me this was a powerful recital and I hope it may cause me to send up to Heaven many prayers in behalf of my wicked, my wayward sons. I have confidence in my servant that he told me the truth as I do believe he is trying to be a Christian. I know not what my loved ones will do when out of my sight and hearing.

March 9, 1864

This is the 28th birthday of my dear Lizzie. Her days are passing rapidly. I cannot realize that 28 years of her life is passed. My children are growing up so fast; for many years there was a little band going around me. During that time an old gentleman staid with us all night. He noticed my little ones and remarked to me you are now seeing your happiest hours in your family. They are now treading on your toes but after awhile they will tread on your heart. I could not realize that then but I have since and find his words so true.

This morning Hiram and Mr. Greer came by on their way up the country—did not tarry long. Sam and Sallie went to town. A short time afterwards Lt. Shields and Mr. Taylor came. Lt. wished to get a room to make out a payroll. Before they got underway Dick came saying: mama, they have taken our little grey mule. I asked Lt. to go if he pleased and see about it. He went immediately and followed them to camp where he found who had taken it. One of Col. Gillespie's men had found out from observation or report that the mule was captured and a branded one. Something I had not known before. I felt it was all right. I had no desire to retain anything which did not really belong to us. Having lost one of my best horses by the Yankees I felt it was not wrong for me to hold on to the mule. Lt. returned and told me Co. G. would hold onto him until an investigation of the affair was made. Ike came home this evening, went up to camp and returned with the mule. I hope he made a correct statement about the whole affair. I love to do right; the reward is one which yields much happiness. The days through which we are passing are testing the true character of everyone.

March 10, 1864

The clock striking ten and yet my children tarry, little thinking of a mother who sits alone. The 3 smaller ones are sleeping. Ella, Lil and Dicky. Nannie having gone yesterday evening with her cousin Jennie McAlister to Mrs. Kinkeads and not returned yet. Sallie and Fannie, of whom I was thinking when I began writing, are at their Aunt Sarahs. I feel sorry the girls went; it is so dark and the way so wet. We are passing through a severe ordeal at present. Gen. Vaughn's men are said to be so troublesome. There is more complaint of the bad conduct of these men than I have heard of our southern soldiers and I do feel so sorry. I have ever felt there was such a difference between ours and theirs, that I feel unwilling to believe they are acting so badly.

March 13, 1864

Have enjoyed a precious privilege today of going to the house of God and hearing from our loved minister precious truths. The North has departed from the Bible, she has set it aside for a higher law whenever she found it conflicting with her views on the subject of slavery. Their misguided zeal and sympathy for the poor African has entailed upon their country one of the most cruel, the most bloody, terrible wars that any people have ever known. While the South by her disregard for the commands of the high and holy one have provoked his wrath. The terrible sin of amalgamation has gone up before the great and holy one, until he has poured out upon us the fierceness of his wrath. This sin has for years been a great trouble to me. I have been so grieved at the thought of the white man enslaving his own flesh and blood—of changing the race of beings whom God in his providence and for reasons known to himself seems to have set apart as servants for the descendants of Shem and Japheth. We of the South have sinned in not speaking against this sin as we should have done. The Lord is now judging us for it.

March 14, 1864

I went to town today. My husband walked and I rode our noble old George in company with Mr. Robinson. Went to Mrs. Lou Simpsons to get some queensware having understood she was selling out with the intention of going to her fathers in Kentucky. Mrs. Piper has sold out and intends going as soon as she can get off. This evening we hear that some Yanks have again made their appearance at Morristown. We do not know whether this is reliable or not. This morning I bid my dear boys Hiram and Ike good bye—always feel sad to see them turn their backs on home.

March 22,1864

Nature has this day shown one of her wonderful freaks as she was about to commence the summer equinox. She attired herself in a full habit of white snow some 10 to 12 inches deep making men and beast feel insignificance and utter helplessness. We are all keeping close quarters. So thankful we have a home and a comfortable fire to sit by.

March 23, 1864

The snow this morning is rapidly disappearing. Our army will begin a backward movement in a short time. Dr. Toole here tonight having a chat with the girls. I learn from Sallie that he corroborated the information in regard to our army.

Easter Sunday, March 27, 1864

Beautiful calm bright day—have just gotten through with a great treat—the reading of quite a number of letters from my dear brother in Persia and his noble affectionate wife. O how cheering to the heart of the home Christian is the noble self sacrifice of the loved missionary for the poor benighted heathen for whom our precious Saviour died.

March 28, 1864

Things are wearing such a sad aspect this morning. Our armies have this day begun their backward movement. The wagon train and infantry belonging to Gen. Vaughn's command left us this morning. Rich and Powell left for the camp in search of a horse we call "old Red" and a mule which someone void of moral restraint took from our meadow on Friday night. The night was one of March's gloomy nights, raining, dark and somewhat windy. Naomi Fullen came through the rain and storm to communicate, as she thought and we all thought, an important message that four men were over at her and Mary's houses and from all she could gather she believed they were preparing to desert. We made arrangements that Sam and Tom Powel who was with us that night should go over in the course of an hour or two as though they were on the hunt of someone and take them.

I had this day gathered up the greatest quantity of sugar water that I had at any one time. Caroline had been working all day and old Ahab joined her in the evening to stay with her until through. While they were there one of the men from Naomi's came to the camp and tried to persuade Ahab to come to the house and get him some bread but he could not be persuaded. I feel he was the man who took our stock for between 11 & 12 o'clock they came from the camp and Powell with Bob Powel whom I had sent to the camp after hearing of the men being over at F's. Nick saw the horse and mule in the meadow. Before they came I had started supper but felt anxious about them and stood on the porch and listened for sometime. Not long after Powell came, Sam & Tom returned having arrested three of the men (the fourth missing) and taken them to camp. They belonged to the 3rd Tenn. Col. Lillard made inquiry who they were and just turned them loose and sent them to their quarters. This was considerable aggravation to the boys, but they bore it quite patiently after they got home.

On Saturday morning we learned the boys were not at home more than an hour before the three were back and lodged in Naomi's house all night. After we found the stock gone, Richard and Powell mounted and struck for camp but alas it was of no avail. The critters had gone with the critters. Powell remained in camp pretty much the remainder of the day hoping to make some discoveries but none could be made. We consulted on the right of going in search on Sabbath morning. I felt it was wrong and my husband, dear to my heart, concurred so readily with me. I told them it was a violation, I believed, of the command of God and it was better to lose than to transgress his law.

Saturday night, Will McKeldon and Capt. VanDyke, son of Judge VanDyke, came down and set a while—both so pleasant. Capt. V. informed me of the arrest and imprisonment of his aged father in the loathsome prison [Camp Chase]. The thought of the imprisonment so unjustly of a loved and revered father only make the already boiling blood of the brave Southerner from wrongs and oppressions heaped upon his loved land flow with electrical speed through every artery and vein of his body to strengthen his heart and nerve his arms for the redress of his wrongs. The mother of Capt. VanDyke was a dear and loved friend of my own loved sister Rebecca and for months after they left school they kept up a regular correspondence. I met with her in 61 and she spoke so affectionately of my sister.

In these pennings of thought intended in years to come to refreshen the memory of passing scenes I have neglected to mention the name of one whom I have always loved from a little boy. George Ross. When I hear that voice and the laugh which sounds so familiarly I am carried back to childhood days; never have I listened to a voice of a son so much like a father. The voice of his father was one which ever gave me pleasure when a young gay, light hearted girl and it was one which always fell upon the ear so solemnly. George has called several times, never tarried a great while.

This evening Cols. Bradford and Gillespie and my loved my noble cousin Jimmy took supper with us.[15] The Cols. are such nice pleasant gentlemen. For my dear cousin I do feel such great solicitude. He seems to be very steady. We have all formed such a strong attachment to him. Lillie thinks there is no one like cousin Jimmy. My loved son Samuel was not present at supper this evening. I have had some misgivings as to what he was doing; fear his heart is far from God. He is restive under parental restraint.

March 29, 1864

I feel so sorry to see my dear husband with his whitened locks leaving his home. I know he has many friends and that he will meet with kindness whilst with them but I know not where his refugee destination may cause him to go. When we are getting old there is "no place like home" although we may not have the comforts we may meet with in other places yet the thought of its being home and my own to do with as I please is such a sweet thought. This thought leads us to contemplate with feelings of such great delight the home which Jesus has prepared for those who love him. The reverses of war, the changing seasons of time affect not the beautiful the magnificent eternal home of the righteous.

Yesterday our poor self-destroyed but not uncared for brother [George Fain] left us. He thought he would go over the mountain and try to raise a company for home defense. He has not been well suffering from neuralgia or rheumatism. I never think of him seriously

---

15. "Jimmy" refers to James Rhea. James W. Gillespie was a colonel in the Forty-third Tennessee under General John C. Vaughn.

but I feel so sad. God has done by nature so much for him; he gave him a mind capable of such high cultivation and research, he made him lovely in disposition so that all could love him and gave him the advantages of good society, education, a Christian mother. All of which were such strong incentives to urge him forward in the right way but alas, alas in his case it fully verified the truth that "evil communications corrupt good men" this has been his ruin.

Yesterday morning brother Hiram and Ernest Fain left. Ernest got home Saturday evening having walked from the command at Lick Creek that day in a detachment of men (I think) 150 for the purpose of taking back the guns which the detail under Major Lowe had gathered up. Not having enough the Major armed as far as he could and sent them back across the country and sending the others up to Kingsport with orders to take muskets wherever found along the road. Ernest was permitted to remain until Monday. E. spoke so kindly of Ike. I love to see cousins love each other. Have heard nothing of my old horse.

March 31, 1864
This morning before I was out of bed 3 soldiers belonging to Capt. Lyon's Co. came asking for breakfast. They had been standing picket. I could not refuse although I felt I did not have much to give them. But such as I had they should have of it freely and cheerfully. Their names were Perry and Lloyd from Hawkins and Davidson from Virginia. Breakfast being over I determined I would take what force I could muster and went to making meadow fence. Nan, Dick and I, Old Ahab, Gus, Caroline and Nate did pretty good work considering our force. Got the worm all laid and the greater part of the fence put up. A man by the name of Ford came to get 2 chickens cooked. Old Polly did it for which he gave her 1 dollar so cheerfully. He was from Hawkins and had once belonged to the sixty-third.

Mollie, Fannie and Lucy walked to town. Mollie had been with us since Sunday. I love her and think she is so noble in heart.

After all was over in the evening and Sallie and I with our little ones had seated ourselves for our evenings work some one hallowed. I went to the door, so dark I could see no one; the voice was familiar. The question was asked have you stopped taking in rebel soldiers. I answered no but I do not know you. When he said Allen I knew then who it was and felt so good to see him. He seemed glad to get back. Sallie set him some bread, butter, milk and molasses. We had a long chat. I like him very much. He gave us the most minute details of the Vicksburg siege which I have ever heard. Our boys were captured on the 12th of May.[16] The description which the Capt. gave of their locality made me feel I could almost see the place. He told us of the incompetency and shameful conduct of many of the leading officers. Drunkenness seems to have been one of the grand feats which many of our commanding officers performed to the great chagrin and sorrow of our noble soldiers.

He seems to think Gen. Pemberton was utterly incompetent for such an important post. Spoke so highly of the gallantry and noble bearing of Gen. Loring who in disobedience to order marched his men in such a manner as to prevent their capture. This saved many a dear soldier from the hardships of imprisonment during the winter in the North.

April 1, 1864

Capt. Allen took leave of us pretty soon after breakfast. He expected to meet up with a squad of men whom he had asked for to go through the country infested with bushwhackers. Three of our men had been run by some 8 or 10 a day or two previous. This to me is a terrible mode of warfare. I have always disapproved of it;

16. Nick Fain and Sam Gammon were actually captured on May 17, not May 12, and Eliza uses the correct date later. The reference is to the surrender of the Sixtieth Tennessee at the Battle of Big Black River before the Union soldiers attacking them had even fired a shot. General John C. Pemberton was in overall command of Confederate forces at Vicksburg, but it is unclear which officers were responsible for waving the white flag of surrender. Primary responsibility probably rested with Colonel John H. Crawford, who was in charge of the regiment. After directing that the white flag be raised, he fled on his horse to Vicksburg.

the taking of the life of anyone without a warning is a dreadful thought. These are days of sore trial.

Not long after Capt. A left some 4 or 5 men forming a part of the scouts brought down the evening before by Col. Hume came out looking for the surplus stock of the country and that which was not surplus. One of the gentlemen came to the stable but there was nothing there. One was in the meadow driving off my yearling calves. I had 4. They were driven near the gate close to the house. I was there, a Lt. came up and I asked him if he were not going to give me a showing. He replied he had no orders as to that. Nan and El struck up such a yelling about their calves I forgot to ask the name of the Lt. or anyone else. There was a man along who formerly belonged to the sixty-third. They were very kind to me. I entreated for my cows and saved them. Would feel so sorry if the Yanks were to get them.

About an hour after I was cheered by the sight of my beloved husband. We felt so glad to see him. He brought us protection from Gen. Vaughn. I do hope I may not have to use it. One of my calves was left for which I felt very glad being a very pretty one. About 11 after two my dear husband left in company with Mr. Shields he having come out from town according to appointment. He parted from my husband at Mr. Merrimons. Just as we were sitting down to the table Sarah and Ida came over bringing us letters from Sam & Nick and cousin Sam in Persia. My heart was so rejoiced—date of Nicks Dec. 15, Sam G. Feb. 14 and Cousin Sam Oct. 14, 1863. The letters from Sam and Nick brings to us the cheering news of their good health but tells of the death of some of our loved brave ones amongst the number Jos. Yeonas.

April 2, 1864
This morning awoke quite early. The rain was falling quite fast. After getting through with my breakfast I determined to go and see Mr. and Mrs. Yeonas and bear them the sad intelligence; but they had heard the report before. I sat and talked a good while.

They bore the news with much fortitude. From there I wended my steps to Mr. Easteps. Had not been long in the house when the old lady let out on secessh generally giving Sam Fain a pretty severe rub for arresting her boy Samuel. I trust I was enabled to talk to her as a Christian pointing out her wrong feelings with Christian charity and forbearance. I always feel so happy when I am enabled to act right. I staid with them until after dinner and then bent my way homeward calling at Mary's and pushing Naomi's door but she was not there.

When I got home I found Dick had returned from town bringing word of the bad behavior of some of our men in town last night. They took E. Ruth's blind nag—demanded Mr. Todd's gray horse. With much authority and threatening but it was no avail. Mr. T. would not give him up. They placed Mr. Sevier under guard to his store and took I suppose what they wished. This morning 18 passed up the Carters Valley road; and they say quite a number on the other road. Sallie is suffering with her teeth.

April 3, 1864

Last night I lay down with a troubled heart. The bad conduct of our own men troubled me greatly. This morning as I was assisting to prepare my breakfast I was much impressed with the thought we may be reduced to great want for provisions, everything looks so dark and gloomy. The rain continues to fall, so that we cannot do anything about farming. Our horses have all been taken out of the country. The able bodied portion of most families, white and black are gone. Women and children with a few boys and a few stout black men are all that is left.

April 6, 1864

When will this cruel war be over, when will it be said families are again united not to be parted by its sad influences. My loved husband and son Powell (now 17) has just bid us good bye, left about half after 8 o'clock. I do trust they may soon be permitted to return. My dear husband intends going on to Blountville, hopes to be able there to observe the day of fasting and prayer set apart by our President which is Friday 8th of April. I trust it may be sacredly and solemnly observed by every Christian in the South. Who can do us any good if our Father in Heaven refuses his presence and blessing.

Last night two soldiers who were pickets at the shop came and got something to eat. I felt sorry I had no more to give them—names Richards of Hawkins Co and belonging to Capt. E. Lyon and Wolfe of Hancock belonging to Capt. Graham. He has been cut off from his Co; they are now in Georgia. Quite a number of rebels were permitted to see home yesterday. Cols. Walker, Heiskell & Powell and junior Sam came yesterday but did not tarry long. Richard and Powell got home about half after 3 or 4 o'clock. Powell went to town to get something for Ed and brought Fannie home. Cols. Walker and Heiskell came by for Richard. Col. H told us that a scout of 56 Yanks came up yesterday as high as Mr. Blevins. He asked Richard to send the key of the office to town to Col. McKinney to get some papers from the office in the suit of Bynum vs. Phipps—Some depositions. I sent Fannie to take the key—trust all things will work together for good to those who love our precious Saviour. Dear Cousin Ann is involved in this trouble.

April 8, 1864

O Lord may the labors of this day be productive of influences which shall be felt for all time to come. O Father in Heaven hear the prayers of the oppressed this day and if consistent with thy Holy Will give us peace; a peace which shall secure to the people of the South a position amongst the nations of the earth; a peace which shall in some way prepare the way for a great work to improve the moral condition of our poor servants. As my ear listened to the songs of Gus this morning as he set shelling corn in the crib for the use of my children and his my heart rises. I trust in humble and holy gratitude to my God that he has made him, I trust, a Christian. O when will the day come when Ethiopia shall stretch forth her hands to God, when every land shall acknowledge thee as their King and ruler.

Today has been set apart as a day of fasting, humiliation and prayer; desired by our representatives in congress and accordingly set apart by proclamation by our President. The allusion to it by our old and honored Christian brother Rev. A. Converse D.D.[17] in his paper dated 17th of March. In looking at the paper of date 3th of March I find the notice of the death of one our brave, youthful and gallant men. Col. R. F. Harvey—although personally unknown to me yet I shed tears freely whilst reading the eulogy of character passed on him by Mrs. Andrew Erwin and Gen. Gowan. I am always so gratified when I see or know the heroic deeds of a Christian officer for I feel this struggle is not only for civil but religious liberty. I do feel so anxious that every Christian of the South should maintain a firm and decided adherence to the cause which the large proportion of Christians of the South have espoused.

News comes to us again today in a paper of April 4 of the inauguration of a general exchange of prisoners. This to me is such cheering news. The thought of my boys with the sons of many of our neighbors being released from the dreary prison cheers me so much. They have had sore trials, but O how heroically they have borne these sufferings and trials. Some have forfeited their birthright and succumbed to the despots power. I feel so thankful so many have stood firm and unmoved. The prisoners of the winter of 63–64 deserve to have their names handed down to posterity for they have endured untold hardships.

---

17. The *Christian Observer* was an independent Presbyterian periodical published by the Reverend A. Converse in Richmond, Virginia. This periodical promoted the view that secession was ordained by God and that God would eventually bring victory to his people after testing them. Religious papers in the South sustained the morale of secessionists, as pointed out by James W. Silver in *Confederate Morale and Church Propaganda* (Tuscaloosa, Ala.: Confederate Publishing Co., 1957). Silver makes sixteen references to the *Christian Observer*, which is more than he makes to any other church paper.

I received this day a letter from W. C. Kyle[18] insisting on the return of my husband to his home, assuring him he has many friends on that side but O how powerless do these assurances fall upon my heart and ear. True he may have towards him the kindest of feelings and I have no doubt he is sincere. He may love him but there is no reliance to be placed in anything connected or associated with Yankee duplicity. They cannot be trusted therefore I want my husband beyond their power. How this war has demonstrated the character of man. The mask has been thrown off. The wickedness of the human heart has been so clearly shown. We have many, very many bad men and some bad officers in our army but we have many noble high toned moral men and noble Christians in our ranks.

Yesterday our men on this side of the river were fired on and returned fire across the river. Powell returned today; he and Eddie Powel having come down yesterday with the scouts. Poor boys they are passing through what is a very poor schooling to the eye and heart of a Christian mother. O that we may be enabled to pray in faith for their preservation. I do feel if my sons can only be permitted to return home without being a wreck in morals, I shall feel like living the remainder of my life entirely for Jesus.

That letter of W. C. Kyle troubles me. I would dislike so much to think that anything but the purest motives could influence him to any thing like this. My husband has been kind to everybody because he felt it was his duty to be so for suffering women and children. He has ever had a great sympathy; he is actuated by Christian principles and O that the Lord would be with him. We are living in constant suspense not knowing what an hour will bring forth; but it is not a painful one for we know our Father is upon the throne.

---

18. W. C. Kyle did not serve in the Civil War on either side. A man of wealth, he was a conservative Republican and mild Union supporter as well as one of Eliza and Richard's friends.

Sabbath Morning April 10, 1864

The cooing of the lone dove made me feel so sad this morning. I thought of the desolated sorrowful hearts, which are to be found in every part of our land, whose sorrowful wail so often rises from the lonely hearthstones of what was once called land of the free and the home of the brave. How many helpless widows and orphans this morning are sending forth to the hearer of prayer this sad complaint that war, cruel relentless war has bereft them of all that was so dear on earth. The aged father and careworn mother bow beneath the load of sorrow which oppresses the heart. They feel no more will that well known footstep, no more will that cheerful happy voice which has so often cheered the ear fall upon theirs again. Away, away far from home he sleeps in his soldiers grave, his blanket has been his winding sheet and his coffin.

I have this day been permitted to hear a sermon from our loved preacher (John Robinson) which I trust shall be thought upon much through the remaining days of my life. He made a selection of quite a number of passages. These passages selected as he said not by random but with a view to set forth in a clear and unmistakable light what he conceived to be the truth as taught in the Holy Bible in regards to the great doctrines of Covenant of Redemption embracing the doctrines of Atonement, Election and Final Perseverance of the Saints. These doctrines in the year 1838 came near dethroning my reason. The difficulties which had arisen in the Presbyterian Church caused much investigation, research and controversy. O how I wish I had a mind clear enough and an education sufficient to put down my thoughts on this sermon and to have been able to keep clearly and distinctly the different leading thoughts before me.

April 12, 1864

No Yankees yet, the boys are going back to town. E gave me a lift about cleaning out a patch of briers back of the garden. Yanks reported over the river. Our boys and they have been firing at each other without any damage. Trimmed the apple trees on the Hill; Nan assisting me. I feel so thankful to my Heavenly Father that he makes me able and willing to labor.

## April 13, 1864

All in circumstance of mercy. The Lord has been so kind to me; have been so busy today cleaning out the briers in the fence corners. Caroline helping me and my little satellite Nan ever revolving around me. This evening Nancy McCarty came; had been at the cabin and tells me our Southern Soldiers have made a complete wreck of her house almost. Poor Nancy her afflictions are great, may she be sustained from on High. O that she may learn afflictions are not in vain.

## April 14, 1864

While eating breakfast some of the children came in saying two soldiers are coming. When they came up one was Sam Powel and Capt. Bivens from Meigs Co. He brought a letter from Cousin James Rhea in which he said he had seen a very able address from the prisoners of Johnson's Island entreating the people of Tennessee to renewed devotions to our country's cause and to never, never agree to reconstruction. Signed by many of the officers amongst whose names were Col. Gregg, Lt. Potram and Nick. He looked for the name of our dear Samuel (Gammon) but in vain, I know he is with them in feeling.

## April 17, 1864

Left home tolerably early this morning for church hoping Sallie could get to Sunday School in time but we were too late. My ox wagon my only conveyance. I had felt so troubled this morning about how I was to get to church. Dicky having his feet sore from being rubbed by old boots ploughing. Gus not inclined to go but I feel the Lord will always provide when we do want to do our duty. Joe, Caroline's brother, came going to town so I asked him if he would help Nate to take care of the oxen. He answered so kindly and pleasantly he would.

I have been much impressed this morning with the thought of the wretchedness and misery which this cruel war has inflicted on the dark sons of Africa. They are many of them turned loose on a cold-hearted world with no friend to care whether they live or die. The duplicity of the white man has caused them to act with such deceitfulness that all the confidence which those who were once their protector had in them is gone and they feel they have none in those who were their masters and mistresses. I have felt very often of late that it does seem to me that God is going to destroy the amalgamated part of the race or place them in a different condition. May his will be done is my prayer.

April 29, 1864

Night before last a few minutes before one o'clock I was aroused I suppose by the barking of the dogs. I listened very attentively when one of the dogs made a noise like someone had struck it. I felt alarmed but did not get up—a few moments afterward the report of a gun fell upon my ear. My heart rose within me. My first thought was bushwhackers at Sarahs are killing some of our men or being killed. I was soon out of my bed and awakened my praying child. In a short time the report of another gun reached us; we went upstairs to look and see if we could what was going on. We then came back to my room. I dressed myself and with earnest prayer prepared to meet what I felt would soon be our terrible fate, subject to bushwhacking rule, every moment for at least half an hour was one of intense feeling and one of prayer that my Father would be a shield of fire by night round about us. Sallie lay down and so did I after awhile; but not to sleep. Sallie, Fannie and Nannie with myself were awake until after three.

This evening I learned the cause of our great alarm. Four bushwhackers went to Mr. Sensabaughs and demanded two rebel soldiers who had gone there to stay all night. Mr. Sensabaugh roused the men up, they came down and gave themselves up. They tied them and brought them down the road as far as the lane between Mr. Netherlands and brother Hiram, here they began their murderous work. They had left their horses there and walked to Mr. S's. The names of the two soldiers were Corriger and Southern. Corriger made his escape but Southern fell a victim to their wrath. Two of the bushwhackers left to go in search of a mule. Our men I suppose made some resistance and perhaps were gaining some advantage over the two when one of them knocked Corriger down with a gun. Southern started to run, they took after him and Corriger made his escape getting on his own horse. Southern would also have gotten away but the other two coming up at the time stopped him. They beat him with a pistol on the head bruising him so badly. They also stabbed him and then took him to Mr. Pryors and left him telling Mr. P., so I understand, that he must send for a doctor and have him taken care of. If he failed to do it they would come and serve him in the same way.

A scout of some 20 of our men came down on Thursday. Cousin Bay and Stevens came by and took some supper with us. They intending going over the river but did not I suppose, why I cannot tell. They took Mr. Southern with them on Friday. We were so rejoiced to see and know our men were coming back.

## May 1, 1864

A poor worm has been granted another precious privilege today—was permitted to hear another excellent sermon from our dear noble minister from Acts. 7:59 & 60. As I returned from church I was cheered by the news a letter from my dear prisoner boy. I felt so glad. I read and found he was well, that my dear Sam. G. had been sick but was much better and that a revival of religion had been going on and Lts. Gammon and Crouch of Jonesboro were amongst the converts. This to me was great tidings. I have so earnestly desired that my sons might in their prison find Jesus. A letter from my good soldier boy Sam tells me he is alone in the

Brigade. Hiram has gone with Gen. Gracie's brigade to Petersburg, Vir.[19] My poor wild but dear child Ike (age 19) has chosen a place in cavalry of Capt. Lyons, Co. A, Day's Battalion.[20]

May 3, 1864

I have been working hard today and scarcely know what I have done in my garden. Powell came home on Sabbath but was afraid to stay and went to town. He came out yesterday, got his dinner and helped me to stick my peas. He went away in the evening. I feel so sorry when I think of the condition we are in. My child cannot stay at home from fear of bushwhackers. How thankful I will be when we shall need no armed soldiery to pioneer the way to home for our loved ones.

May 8, 1864

Beautiful lovely Sabbath. All so quiet, so peaceful among the hills and green fields of this part of our loved East Tennessee. How hard it is for us to realize this day that the vast armies of Lee and Grant are confronting each other and for aught we know are in deadly conflict. We heard after we got to town that the battle began last Friday.[21] Whether true or not we cannot tell but believe it is. May the God of battles be with our brave officers and men upon whose shoulders rests this bloody battle, and may we who believe there is a God whose ear is ever open to the cries of his children—pray that they may be victorious.

19. The field and staff muster roll of the Sixty-third Tennessee, contained in the National Archives, lists Hiram Fain on April 18, 1864, as an officer who had been assigned to General Archibald Gracie's brigade on August 7, 1863. (See *Compiled Service Records of Confederate Soldiers . . . Tennessee*, Roll 347.) A typed memo by family historian Max Fain (see military papers of Richard Fain, Fain Collection) indicates that Hiram's name appeared on a list, dated April 18, 1864, of officers in Gracie's brigade who were absent without leave. The memo further states that on August 8, 1864, Hiram was listed as absent by authority of General P. G. T. Beauregard.

20. Ike had left the Sixty-third Tennessee, which was stationed in Virginia with Lee, and was now enrolled in a company serving in East Tennessee. He remained there for the duration of the war.

21. The reference is to the Battle of the Wilderness in Virginia between the armies of Grant and Lee.

We were permitted to go this day to the house of prayer. My loved husband was with us. We heard a most excellent sermon from our dear Minister. He said the North and the South have disregarded the commands of God. This day may be a day of sore trials to many of our brave and noble soldiers. I trust Christians of the South are praying. Charleston has been saved by prayer I believe. Richmond has thus far been saved by prayer. May they ever continue faithful.

## May 10, 1864

Have been enjoying such a delightful hour for two in the company of my dear daughters Sallie and Fannie. Sallie has been bringing up memories of days long past. These things are always so pleasant to me. My first born son and two oldest daughters with the many young friends of their schooldays were hearty participants in these scenes. I loved to see them enjoy themselves. Contrasting those days with the present the heart grows sad in the contemplation. Where are the loved ones of my family and the many youthful faces which there beamed with so much good cheer? Some are sleeping in the silent grave, other for aught I know are lying wounded and dying far from home and friends.

One year today since our lamented noble Jackson closed his eyes upon earth to open on Heaven. What a thought in an instant, in the twinkling of an eye "going from a world of sin, sorrow and hatred to one of purity, pleasure and love."

This morning my loved husband returned from town bringing the delightful and soul sustaining information that a dispatch was received by Mr. Todd that Lee has been victorious in capturing 12,000 prisoners, the greater part of the artillery of the enemy and had driven them over the rivers. We have no particulars of the casualties only that Gens. Jenkins and Jones[22] were killed

---

22. This information is correct. On May 5, 1864, during the Battle of the Wilderness, Confederate generals John M. Jones, Micah Jenkins, and Leroy A. Stafford were killed. On May 6 General James Longstreet was wounded by his own men as the battle continued.

and Gen. Longstreet severely wounded. Many no doubt of our brave, gallant soldiers have fallen and many more are rendered helpless for life.

Today about two o'clock my dear husband in company with Cousin Audley (Anderson) left home to go to Blountville. He may go on to Virginia. For the last few nights we have felt afraid for him to remain at home on account of bushwhackers. Last night he had determined to stay with us but between 8 and 9 o'clock the dogs gave the signal that someone was coming. Powell and Bob Powel went out in the yard. Richard went and heard them talking to Brother Hiram and in a short time heard them coming through the meadow. They crossed in the direction of Marys. We could not understand it felt excited. Thought it might be some of our soldiers in search of horses knowing that Capt. Bynum's scouts were to leave today. We sent Bob and Dick over to see Hiram. I walked down to the stable. When they returned they told us their uncle had asked the men. Do you belong to Bynum — No. Have you any news — No. Are you from town — did not understand reply. This created more uneasiness. Rich and Powell went over to Hirams and sent Gus over. We and the two little boys reconnoitered about the stable but all was quiet only the horses of the men enjoying their rich repast in the meadow. I could not go to bed, kept out of the house all the time but set down on the steps. Felt I was peaceful and not afraid. Raised my eyes to the Heavens. The stars were shining brightly; everything on high looked so beautiful. Was impressed with the thought in those regions all is peace — earth is convulsed but Heaven is calm.

Richard and George came over. R. seemed to be well satisfied it was no one intending to do great harm. Our picket came in when Dick heard his Papa say "I know it is some of our men." He was soon in bed. Gus went to his resting place. I came in and locked my door and was soon asleep. This morning we found out it was some of our own good soldiers who rested quietly under the beech trees while their horses regaled themselves pleasantly on the part of the meadow nearby.

## May 14, 1864

Last week was one of fearful anxiety and great foreboding of evil. I felt we must suffer for something to eat. Yesterday evening Fannie & Mollie Ruth went to town. Dicky went along to bring the horse back; brought back news of the confirmation of Lee's victory. Gen. Vaughn was at Kingsport and Buckner's division was not in the fight.

## May 15 1864

Attended church today in my wagon. Heard a sermon which I wish all could hear from Genesis 9th chapter verses 24–27. And Noah awoke from his wine and knew what his younger son had done unto him. And he said cursed be Canaan, a servant of servants shall he be unto his brethren. And he said blessed be the Lord God of Shem and Canaan shall be his servant. This is a subject I have had a great desire to hear our loved minister preach from. As Southern Christians the solemn question must be decided, is it right to hold in bondage a fellow being. The views advanced by Mr. R. on this subject I believe are in accordance with the Bible. God has in no part of his Holy Word said that it is a sin but instead of this he has given us rules to regulate the life of the Master and the Servant. The history of the races from the time the curse was pronounced on Canaan go to prove the fact that for reasons known to God alone they are a doomed race to servitude under the descendants of Shem and Japheth.

## May 16, 1864

O the blessings of this day. I cannot express my deep sense of thankfulness to my Father in Heaven for the favor he has this day shown to me. I have for sometime past seen and known that the meat which I had provided for my family must give out. This morning I fixed in my mind the determination to go and see one whom I have loved ever since I knew her as Alice Ripley. Having on last Saturday written a letter to W. C. Kyle in answer to his kind letter to me in regard to my husbands remaining at home. I had studied how shall I get this sent to him. I thought I would take it and read it to Alice. If she thought I had said anything calculated to wound him I would not send it. If not that would ask her to assist me in getting it to him. I asked God to put it into her heart to let me have a middling ham and some jowls. Directly after I got there she mentioned that Mrs. McKinney had passed going down to Mr. Blevins with Mr. M to stay all night. Mr. B and M expected to leave tomorrow for Knoxville to get or be remunerated for some Negroes which had gone off. I thought at once of my letter, took it and read it to her asking her advice. She told me she felt there was nothing in it to give offence. I wrote a line or two more asking him to write to my prisoner boys and enclosed it to him.

She had a note from Mr. R asking her to let old Uncle Sam (as he is termed) go along and he thought through his influence they might perhaps get back his daughter who had left Mr. Riley after he left home going into Virginia. I was deeply interested in the interest manifested by Malissa and her aunt A that he should have a comfortable outfit for his journey. He left haversack strapped on and a sack containing corn for his horse. I went out to look after him and thought O how good is the condition of the poor sons of Ham under Southern rule. We feel for them as no other people on earth do.

I mentioned to A. that I wanted her to let me have some meat that my family needed it. Without any objection she told me I should have a middling and that if her black family whom Mr. R. had taken away did not return she would spare me more. My heart rose in thankfulness. I then asked her if she could spare me any joints and some jowls. She replied "I will let you have a ham. We have used all of our jowls." My heart was full.

May 17, 1864
One year today since our dear boys fell into the hands of the foe.[23]
What a long year it has been to them and to us. But it has been a

23. The reference is to Eliza's son Nick and nephew Sam Gammon, who were captured during the Vicksburg campaign and were now imprisoned on Johnson's Island, located in Lake Erie's Sandusky Bay. This camp was exclusively for Confederate officers. Captain William A. Wash of the Sixtieth Tennessee wrote an account entitled *Camp, Field and Prison Life: Containing Sketches of Service in the South, and the Experience, Incidents and Observations Connected with Almost Two Years Imprisonment at Johnson's Island, Ohio* (St Louis: Southwestern Book Publishing Co., 1870). According to Wash, it was left to the regiment's lieutenant colonel and the captains to make the controversial decision to surrender without putting up a fight, resulting in the capture of twenty-five hundred men by a force of only four thousand. Wash placed the ultimate blame on General John Pemberton, but for him to do otherwise would have forced him to admit his probable role in the decision not to make a defensive stand.

In *The Civil War* (2: 377), Shelby Foote defends Pemberton by noting that he had chosen a defensive position that was impregnable to a frontal attack. The general had placed the troops behind parapets of baled cotton and supported them with high-sited batteries to the rear. Foote notes that General John A. McClernand, acting on his own, sent in Brigadier General Michael Lawler's four regiments, which made a surprise attack after wading through a bayou, while the Sixtieth Tennessee fled without firing a shot.

James M. McPherson (*Battle Cry of Freedom: The Civil War Era* [New York: Oxford Univ. Press, 1988], 630) states that the main body of the Confederates, the Sixtieth Tennessee, fell back in demoralized fashion when attacked by Grant's cocky Midwesterners: "The rebel position at the Big Black was strong, but an impetuous brigade in McClernand's corps, chafing at its lack of a share in the previous day's glory, swept forward without orders." It appears that Colonel John H. Crawford of the Sixtieth Tennessee had panicked and abandoned his troops to the enemy. The Confederates' failure to put up a fight tarnished the reputation of the Sixtieth as well as that of East Tennesseans in general.

Concerning Johnson's Island, Wash's book contains an appendix in which a Confederate medical officer among the prisoners stated that only forty-five deaths occurred at the prison between November 1863 and March 1865. However, the chronically ill men were released and probably died later. This was especially true of those with incurable diarrhea, which was likely the result of tuberculosis of the intestinal tract. Overall, Wash's book paints a rather more favorable view of the prison than the brief account by Henry E. Shepherd of his imprisonment at Johnson's island. (Shepherd's narrative is available online at a Web site maintained by the University of North Carolina Libraries. See http://docsouth.unc.edu/shepherd/shepherd.html.) The major problem seemed to be the lack of sufficient food and the occurrence of scurvy among prisoners who were fed a meal of hardtack and salt pork once a day. However, these soldiers were readily cured when they were given onions or potatoes to eat. Despite the camp's exposure to the winter storms that periodically swept over Lake Erie, the medical officer stated that this did not seem to affect the physical health of the prisoners.

On page 150 of his book, Captain Wash includes an account originally written in August 1863 that stated: "Capt. Gammon and Lieut. Fain, of my command, have each just got a full suit of Confederate gray from a cousin in Louisville, Kentucky." On page 260, referring to events that occurred on September 5, 1864, Wash wrote: "at that time my friend, Lieutenant Nick Fain, of the 60th Tennessee, was sick in the hospital and sickness was on the increase."

year of great mercy. They have had good health and kinder treatment I suppose, than they anticipated. I do feel the Lord has been their great protector and friend. Many of the brave and noble soldiers who surrendered on that day have found graves far from home and friends. This to me is such a sad thought, but this is one of the many sorrows which war brings.

We thought we surely would have had some news today from Virginia but none came. We feel great suspense. I sent Dicky down to town with Buena. He brought back word that 50 of our men had made their escape from Knoxville. They report we have whipped them at Dalton and that they are rapidly leaving East Tennessee.

May 19, 1864

On yesterday morning I left home, went to town and there awaited the coming of Mrs. Riley. She and I having made an arrangement to make Alice Kyle a visit. She came in a short time and we were soon on our way. When we got there we found Alice sitting in her room alone, she seemed so glad to see us. I love her and have for many years. She too is passing through the deep waters, her husband and sons away from home all the time. Not long after we got there Mrs. Kneeland returned from Mrs. Blevins telling us that Mr. McKinney and Blevins had left for Knoxville taking old uncle Samuel. Awhile after dinner one of the black women came to the house saying the Rebs have Anthony a prisoner (this was the boy who had run away some time ago taking Billy's horse). Mrs. Kyle seemed to be excited; said she did not want him there. Poor Negroes how my heart pities them decoyed from peaceful happy homes where a kind mistress or master felt for them as no other person does. Now to be thrown out on a cold hearted world.

We had some conversation with the soldiers passing and soon found out they belonged to the third Tennessee, Col. Morelock commanding. Major Toole[24] and some two or three others passed first

24. Eliza apparently reversed their titles since the roster of the Third Tennessee Mounted Infantry has Samuel Toole listed as lieutenant colonel and William C. Morelock as major.

told us they had taken no Negroes but they had seen two or three who had made their escape from Knoxville and were winding their way to old Sullivan. Our troops had a little brush with some of Fay's men who it is said were making their ways to Rogersville for plundering purposes. After awhile quite a company, perhaps 44 or 45 passed along having 8 or 10 prisoners. I was looking for a familiar face when Capt. Allen came up to the gate. I was so glad to see him. The news from Virginia and the West is, as we think, all favorable to our cause. Some Yankee dispatches give us a little uneasiness.

After our men had passed awhile Mrs. Robert Kyle and Mrs. George McCauley came to Mrs. Kyles. They seemed to be much troubled about one of the prisoners—Mr. Jesse Berry who had been acting as chaplain. Just as we were leaving Alice Kyle gave me a piece off of a beautiful little bush—a species of honeysuckle. I spoke to her about some meat and she gave me such a kind assurance, that if she had any to spare I should have it. I felt so thankful to our Father in Heaven. Just as we were about ready to mount our horses the brave and gallant George Ross came up; he got off to fix my bridle. Old Baly having slipped it. I do not think I ever thanked him; I feel ashamed. We rode on together talking to him about the news from Virginia. He seemed to think all things were working right there although he had Yankee papers giving a different view of things. But he said their reports were so conflicting that it was difficult to gather anything from them. As we passed Mrs. L. Mitchells we stopped after a few moments to talk with the girls. We rode on, as we were coming along not far from Mr. Kenners we were overtaken by Mr. T. Amis who had started to go to see Mr. and Mrs. Lee. As I parted from him I asked him if he could let me have some meal. He replied I cannot, I do not get a peck at a time.

Alice and I stopped in town, went a few moments to see Aunt Fannie. Had sent for Mr. Todd we wished to ask him some questions about the signs of the times and to speak to him to use his influence to have this poor old man Berry released if he could and felt he was not a dangerous man to the interests of our Government. After getting the views of Uncle Doc. and Mr. Todd we felt pretty comfortable and set out for home. Just as we were about to part A. said to me in a rather low voice; are you scarce of breadstuffs. I thought she wished to get some wheat knowing hers had been a failure last year. I replied I am tolerable. She said to me send over your boy when you send for the oats (I had asked her for oats) and I will send you a turn.

May 26, 1864

The Lord still merciful to us, we have lain down and slept no evil coming upon us. On Monday morning I set down early and wrote quite a long letter to W. C. Kyle asking him to exert his influence, if he had any, with Federal authorities to secure the parole, exchange or release from prison of my dear noble boy Samuel Gammon.

A letter from my dear husband and several papers still giving us cheering news in regard to our country's affairs. One of them contained an account of the death and burial of our noble gallant but lamented Gen. J. E. B. Stuart. I feel he is one of the martyrs to the cause of Southern liberty. Brother George got home that evening. Hiram and my dear Richard had determined to stay a day or two longer to see whether anything could be known or heard about our dear boys in Virginia. I have been looking so anxiously for the last two days to their coming.

On Tuesday morning as I went about my domestic concern "a woman wanted to see me." I came and found Mrs. Willis, she told me that my dear Bet was sick with diphtheria and wished me to send for her that evening. I had Sallie to assist in hurrying dinner so that I might make ready to go. I had Dicky to yoke up my oxen and get the wagon ready. We were soon off—returned that evening. Bet's throat was very sore. As we were coming down the first hill this side of the house the wheel caught against a stump with such force it threw me out of the wagon with Maxie in my arms. We escaped without being hurt.

On Wednesday morning Mr. Hacker came out and tuned a piano which Mr. T. had loaned to F to practice on. Cousin Mollie &

Joe Walker came out. Cousin J. cauterized Bet's throat. On Thursday evening Mr. Flora came from Bristol bringing us the first news of the casualties in the sixty-third regiment on May 16 in a fight which took place at Drewry's Bluff. He passed by Mr. Merrimons telling him of the death of his dear boy Jim. I heard it that evening.

On Friday morning I went over to see them. Found a troubled family—William's wife[25] in great distress on account of the news from him which was that he had taken the oath and joined the Federal Army. I do not believe he has gone into the northern army. I staid until after dinner. As dinner was nearly ready my dear husband came riding up. He got off and came in—confirming the news about poor Jim. We tried to comfort the bereaved and distressed family.

### June 8, 1864

Sad, sad news has come to us this evening. Our loved, our noble high souled Jimmy Rhea has fallen. We all feel so sad. He was loved by all who knew him. My soul is moved so deeply as I think of him. He was killed last Sabbath near Staunton, Virginia where the commands of Gen. Vaughn and Gen. Jones met a greatly superior force of the enemy. Our men were repulsed. Gen. W. E. Jones and Lt. Crawford are mentioned by Richard as killed.

### June 9, 1864

News this evening gives us a hope that our loved friend still lives, but a wounded prisoner. Mr. Mitchell came home bringing a note from Col. Bradford to Sallie in which he says that James Burem, is killed and out of 160 of his men in the fight 45 are wounded, killed or missing. Mr. M. wrote upon it that Mr. Brewer had received a

25. William Merrimon, the oldest son of George and Orleana Merrimon, was born in 1839 and married Kitty Bates in February 1861. He died on March 5, 1865, while serving in the Union army, whereas his brother Jim died while serving the Confederacy. The source of this information, the Merrimon family papers, are archived at the public library in Rogersville.

dispatch which stated that cousin Jimmy was not killed as reported but wounded and in the hands of the enemy.

June 12, 1864

Attended church this day and heard a sermon of great interest from Luke 6th chapter, verse 31. This sermon taught as I believe Bible truth in regard to the great social relations of life. He dwelt particularly on the relation of master to slave. This has always been a relation of great responsibility and one which I have ever found so difficult to fill as I felt I should fill it. May we be enabled to know and discharge with fidelity to God our duties in this great and important relation.

June 14, 1864

Today we were favored by Capt. Bynum with a letter from my dear husband and some papers. Lou Kinkead and R. came down this morning. They staid a short time here and then went on to Mr. Ms. Lou had a letter from her husband in which he gave her to understand that Will Merrimon was not right. Which makes us believe the reports we have heard about him. I feel so sorry for his wife. She is a true Southern woman who feels her whole heart is in the cause of Southern freedom. She feels degraded by the conduct of her husband.

As F. was returning from town this morning she met up with Capt. Allen. He told F. he was coming here tomorrow. Alas how short sighted is man, a few brief hours brings a different tale. News came the Yanks were at Mooresburg. A few men started down the road and went as far as Mr. Bs when they had to beat a hasty retreat. Capt. A with 5 others including Powell were sent out to picket the Clinch road. After dark a messenger was sent for them to go to town and all get together and make a stand against them. Col. Heiskell and Wyly Miller passed through by our house after dark going to Mr. M's. They reported the Yanks advancing. Capt. A. and Powell came over and they went immediately to town.

June 15, 1864

This has been a day of much excitement, but night is upon us and all have gone to bed or are preparing but Lil and myself. The Lord has been merciful. The Yanks camped last night upon Mr. Price and took nearly everything. Three men by the name of Mitchell, Cleaveland and Cowan of our men were upon picket there. I suppose they behaved it is said so bravely in defying the advance of the destroyers of our once happy homes. Capt. Allen with his squad, Capt. Bynum and others commanding their little squads left town this morning before daylight and went quite rapidly as far as Mr. Blevins where they were met by the enemy at the bridge. Our men were driven back, but from all that I can learn without confusion or terror. They would halt and shoot and then get forward as fast as possible. Two of our noble soldiers were very badly wounded; one left at Mr. McClures and the other at old Mr. Mc's. I trust they may live. Whether we have lost more or not we cannot tell. About 7 this morning one of the men who was with Capt. A. last night came back to get his clothes which he left at Sarahs. He gave us the first news we had of our men falling back. I thought of them as soon as I waked.

About half after 7 Capt. A. came by Sarahs. I was on the lookout and went over to see him. He told us of the casualties above mentioned, he looked so sorry to turn his back on us. We felt we wanted him to get out of their way and we would battle as well as we could. Just after he left or a few minutes later Ike came home. I started as fast as I could but before I got there he was starting. He had no time to talk but came by to get Ed's colt and his clothes. I wanted to talk to him but could not. Sallie told me he looked very much worn down. I followed on in the sight of him until he turned the meadow fence and began to go up the hill. I still pressed on after him determining to know whether he got away safely or not. When I got to Mr. Ms no trace of any could be seen.

While there we heard the reports of guns several times and after a short time discovered two soldiers riding for their life and a loose horse following. We watched with great anxiety their onward move. When they got within 4 or 500 yards of Mr. Ms they called a halt. We thought one of them had lost his hat and they seemed to deliberate for a moment for two when one went back—in a short time came back leading the loose horse. Mother Eve was too much roused not to speak so I stepped to the fence and asked if the soldier who had been riding that horse was killed. He replied no that the horse had given out and the man had taken to the woods. I then asked if they were pursuing and he replied yes. They are coming as thick as H-ll back there. I was shocked at his wickedness to see a man in the very jaws of death as it were giving vent to such language. In a short time the other man came up whom we took to be a Mr. Hicks but it was not him. He rode up to the fence and asked for a drink. He had his pistol all ready for firing. I begged him to not shoot as there were so many women and children. He spoke of the cowardice of his pursuers—he swore. I felt I must reprove him and did. He asked about the roads and left.

I then wended my way homeward—met Liz coming after me although she had sent an escort of Ida and Nannie. I tarried too long so she had to come. We came on back. She and Fannie and I set out to find if possible our soldier who had gotten off his horse. We went along to my flax patch. F. struck up Dixie thinking if he could hear it he would come to us. We heard nothing until we crossed the fence into the furtherest field when we heard Dick and Pete Powel. They with old Ahab had gone to take a look. We called, they came to us. They told us the Yanks had passed up. Dick thought there was quite a number. We came back to the house.

I began to think of preparing something for dinner. As I was passing my cellar two men came riding up. One of them said to me we have been captured by the Yanks and are making our escape. I asked are you soldiers; one replied no citizens. He told me his name was Wright and that he lived in Long Valley. They were in a great hurry. After I came back on the porch Fannie says to me do you think those men are right. I thought they might be but the only thing which caused any doubt—they were most too well mounted to be captured Southern citizens. Sarah halted them and Liz went to hear their tale. She and L. came back directly then they with F. went to Mr. M's. When they returned they told me those men were renegades. After dinner Liz, Lucie and Fan. went to town to get all the particulars they could.

After getting through with my sewing I thought I would go into the garden to hoe a little and replant cucumbers. I had hardly begun when El came running saying mama a southern soldier is in the house. My heart beat for joy thinking that our men were perhaps getting back but when I came and saw him my heart was all anxiety to get him something to eat so that he might get away. Sallie and I soon had it ready. Just before he sat down the girls returned from town bringing the unpleasant news that Rogersville was subject to bushwhacking rule and that they had taken James Hale[26] a prisoner. William Sizemore seemed to be the ruling spirit. The girls met them going down and said James looked frightened.

The soldier who came proved to be the man who had jumped from his horse. He said his horse seemed to give out and he felt they would get him if he staid on him. His name was Rhineheart and the two men with him this morning were Lt. Blevins and Callaway. It was Callaway who went back and got the horse. Mr. Rhineheart left not long after he got his supper. He said he thought he could keep out of their way. I was afraid for him to stay here on account of bushwhackers. I would feel so troubled if they were to get him as I know they would deal so hard with him. Thus has ended the 15th of June.

June 16, 1864

We have slept in peace and no foe has been permitted to come near our dwelling for which my soul rises with gratitude. We have had

---

26. James Hale enlisted in Company K of the Nineteenth Tennessee in May 1861. The next year he joined Company C of the Sixty-third Tennessee but apparently did not accompany the regiment to Virginia in the spring of 1864. James was a tanner by trade and never married. He died in 1896.

the pleasure of feeding 3 rebels for dinner: Mr. Rhineheart from Meigs, Mr. Henry from Rhea and Mr. Miller from McMinn. All 3 of them dismounted by the fight of yesterday. Mr. M and H had to jump from their mule and horse between Mr. Kings and McClures. Mr. H. made his way up last night. He and Mr. G got together at J. Millers and I suppose Mr. M. went there too.

Our soldiers left this evening between 4 & 5 intending to go up Carters Valley as far perhaps as Mr. J. Youngs. Last night Gus and Ben brought home a bee stand which Mr. Sensabaugh loaned to me until I can get a start.

June 17, 1864

Still in merciful hands! My family have slept in peace while neighbors and friends have been visited by the cruel, bloodthirsty and cowardly bushwhackers. They visited Mrs. Harlan, Mrs. Miller and Sarah Fain. This is the second time they have been to see Mrs. Harlan. They robbed Mrs. M and Sarah of some meat and other things.

This evening a loaded wagon drove up to Sarahs. We were anxious to know what it meant. I went over and found it to be Mag. Huffmaster with a wagon load of Lavinia Phillips plunder and 3 of her children. They had gotten Mrs. Smith, one of the most resolute women I have seen, to come over with them. She furnished wagon and oxen and she came along herself on horseback. I felt so sorry for Mag. She looked completely worn down with care and trouble. The things were left at Sarahs with Mrs. S. returning from there home.

June 18, 1864

The Yanks crossed the river at Kingsport going along the road taking the Negroes, horses and mules. They took two Negroes from the farm belonging to uncle J. Bachman. I do feel so sorry about one of them as he was such a faithful servant and Fannie got him when a boy but this is Northern philanthropy to the poor outcasts of Canaan. These boys, it is said, were taken off tied from a home where they had lived so peacefully and bountifully.

June 19, 1864

We still live unmolested. It rained some during the night and I hope I shall be able to attend church. The privilege has been granted but alas nature was too powerful for the spirit this day in me and with shame I acknowledge I was sleepy at church, to me this is deep mortification. Many soldiers at church today. Mr. R prayed so fervently for them today.

June 21, 1864

Mr. M and Ike came back and took dinner today. This evening my loved husband got home bringing Tom with him. He brought my flax cloth from Mrs. Lyons. We were so glad to see him. He brought me a letter from my soldier boy Sam. The best letter I have received from him. Sam seemed to lament the death of Jim Merrimon so much. He was a noble soldier ever at his post and always ready to do his duty.

We all felt so comfortable this evening little thinking that a few hours would see home in great confusion. Just as all were nearly ready for bed the voice of someone was heard at the front part of the house. We did not know who it was and felt timid but Ike soon recognized the voice of his comrade Galloway who was the same gallant but wicked soldier who passed Mr. M. that day of the retreat leading the horse. He got up and talked to him. We learned the Yanks were coming across the river to town and a force coming across at Chism's ford. He also said that Capt. Owens and his men had been fired on and two were killed — Daniel Hord[27] and Mr. Louderback.

All went to work to get off. Brother Hiram and George were soon ready. Richard, Ike, Powel and Mr. Mitchell came by and all were soon off. They left about half after 10 and went up to Mrs. Harlans (R.H. & S.) while the others went to Jesse Courtneys. All was then quiet and we prepared to sleep.

27. In *Blue and Gray from Hawkins County: The Confederates* (111), Sheila Johnston lists a Daniel C. Hord from Hawkins County who enlisted in the Nineteenth Tennessee on May 20, 1861 but had been at home on leave because of illness since October 1862.

June 22, 1864

We rose early and found that all was quiet. No enemy had been near us excepting bushwhackers who had done the foul work of murder on the two above mentioned. Sam Powel and Billy Carmichael came early having been on picket at the ford. Not long after breakfast Ike, Mr. Mitchell and Rhineheart came and in a short time Richard and George. Fannie, Sallie Hasson and Buena came out and they had a merry day.

June 27, 1864

O what sad news does this morning bring to us. Jesse Courtney is dead—murdered yesterday evening by bushwhackers. He, wife and a little boy whom he had adopted had eaten their suppers and Mrs. C. asked him if he had brought in the axes. He replied he had not and started to go after them. He went to the kitchen door and opened it partly. A man stepped forward saying surrender and before he had time to say a word he was shot in the right side. The bullet not coming out but supposed to have lodged in the region of the heart. He walked across the kitchen into their room then turned and went back into the kitchen. He made an effort to step into a little room on their porch when he fell.

His wife had a candle in her hand but in some way perhaps by Jesse falling against it was put out. She then had to light it whilst doing this Jesse had turned himself around with his head on the doorsill. What moments of horror these must have been to that poor suffering woman. When she got to him he breathed two or three times and all was over. What horror, what anguish seized the soul of this woman with no one near her but that little boy of 6 or 7 years.

A husband dead lying in his blood which had flowed profusely. The murderer still lurking for ought she knew around her dwelling. She told me she tried to hallo but could not. She then tried to blow the horn but could not. At length she started the little boy to go to Mr. Lawsons who lived some two or three hundred yards or so from them. After the little fellow started his heart failed him and he hallooed back to her "Mama I am afraid." She talked to him a little while and told him to go. He then went on.

Mr. L. had heard the report of the pistol organ but could not leave his wife as she was sick and very much alarmed but when the little boy told him his papa was killed and his mama wanted him to come and blow the horn for her—he came and blew it. Mrs. Biggs heard it and she and Mr. Biggs started (I think). When they got there they heard the wail of woe from the distressed—were afraid to go in at first but Mr. Biggs at length went in and what a sight met the eye. There sat the stricken wife and the little boy over the dead body of her beloved husband gory from the work of the dark hearted assassin.

Two of Mr. Biggs little boys went up to Mrs. Harlans. Rachel went about 1 to Mrs. Cs. There she and Mrs. B and C. exerted themselves and succeeded in getting him laid upon a bed and straitened out. They then had to wait until 3 before any men could come to them. Neal Harlan and Mr. Hedrick came down to J. Millers and got him and Mr. Hicks (a soldier) to go with them and just here let me say I do think the men who were with Capt. Gibbs acted cowardly. There were about 20 of them that night at Sensabaughs when the alarm was given. They sent out to the 2 little boys mentioned before and asked them what was the matter. They told him Mr. Courtney was killed. They asked what he was and the children said a rebel. They put spurs to their horses and were at Mr. Sensabaughs in a short time. But not one of them was willing to go back and stand as a guard until Neal and the others could wash and dress him. I feel this is a lasting shame on the name of those men.

I intended going up early but had nothing to ride and felt it was so warm I could not walk well. Between 10 and 11 Lizzie Miller came after me. I made ready and we were soon off. L. stopped at home. I went on and got there just as they were finishing their dinners. I found Mr. I and his daughter Rachel Saunders, Matilda Wells and some three or four others. I went into the room where the corpse lay and raised the covering but the face was covered with cotton there being quite a discharge from the mouth and nostrils. I did not remove this cotton.

June 28, 1864
Attended the burial of Jesse today at Mrs. Harlans. We sang *Why do we mourn departing friends*. Truly these are days of sadness and distress when quiet peaceable citizens are killed in their own houses.

July 3, 1864
Peaceful and quiet. The Lord has been our shield and protector and I do trust his arm is being made bare for our deliverance. It is said that our enemies admit Sherman is defeated with heavy loss.[28] Rumor also says that Kirby Smith has had an engagement near Memphis defeating the enemy and capturing over 200 wagons.

July 4, 1864
Memorable day, still will the recollection of 76 make a thrill of delight pass through my heart. We cannot forget the struggle of the noble and brave for independence in our first revolution. The descendants of many who then stood shoulder to shoulder with the Fathers of southern freedom are now in the ranks against us in this second and more terrible revolution.

My heart is so sad this day. I fear my dear, my loved soldier boy Sam is a prisoner.[29] We heard on Saturday that the greater part of the sixty-third was captured and that Col. Fulkerson was wounded twice. This came through Wm. Gammon. I still had a hope that it might not be true, but I fear it is too true. Mr. Mitchell

28. This was a false rumor based on hope rather than fact.

29. This proved to be incorrect. Sam Fain returned to East Tennessee in January 1865, apparently one of the large number of Southern soldiers who became weary of the war in Virginia and returned to their homes to defend their families. According to Sheila Johnston in *Blue and Gray from Hawkins County: The Confederates* (223–63), 38 percent of the two hundred men from Hawkins and Hancock Counties who served in the Sixty-third Tennessee were listed as deserters. However, Ike, Sam, Hiram, and Ernest Fain were not so designated.

came back today and he says the news had reached Bristol that they were nearly all captured. A superior force was sent against that portion of the army to which they belonged and succeeded in surrounding them. I feel I would rather they were captured than killed. The time for probation is still lengthened out.

## July 5, 1864

Our men captured on yesterday the horses and guns belonging to the Sizemore[30] clan and came very near getting them. Ella Walker, Buena McCarty, Mrs. Mitchell Calloway and Mrs. Dunwiddy took dinner with us. This evening Sarah, Eliza Ruth and Mrs. Powel came over to us. They and children and Jennie Walker came out and took dinner with Sarah. Mr. Mitchell bid us goodbye this evening expecting to leave in the morning on a secret mission as far down as New Market. News this evening by two men of Gibbs scouts is that Gen. Morgan and his men would be in our neighborhood tonight.

## July 10, 1864

Attended church today and had the great pleasure of my dear husband for company. We heard a great sermon on Salvation. This morning by Capt Bynum we received letters from dear friends. I had one from my dear boy S. in which he speaks of the fight near Petersburg in which at least two-thirds of their brigade was captured. Amongst the number was our dear friend Dick Powel. We feel so sorry to hear of any of our dear friends being made prisoners but feel it is better than to hear they were killed. Major Lowe was captured also. I hope the trying scenes through which my dear S. is passing may lead him to adore his Heavenly Father.

## July 18, 1864

Last evening about dark three soldiers came riding up. They were just getting back from a scout to Claiborne County where they live and

30. The most lawless band of Union sympathizers operating in and around Rogersville was the group led by William Sizemore.

were greatly worn down. They report no Yanks troubling the citizens there but on Friday or Saturday night about 40 came up as high as Bean Station. Callaway says 27 ate breakfast the next morning. They also say they came up with an old man by the name of [left blank] who had acted as a spy for Gen. Longstreet. The Yanks had taken him (not knowing I suppose what he had been doing) as a prisoner and put him to work on the fortifications at Knoxville. He made his escape with 27 others by overpowering the guard. He was under a Negro overseer. He reported to them that there was in Knoxville about 500 white soldiers and three regiments of blacks.

July 19, 1864
On yesterday Capt. Owens with his brave and daring band were fired upon near Kirkpatricks Mill. I fear there is a bad spirit with Mr. K. which may lead to serious results. Capt. O. will not long be trifled with. He and his men had been going round all the night before over there. About 40 men were stationed upon two hills (20 on each) commanding the road and when they got there they had good aim. However there were no serious casualties that we know of now. They scattered and he made for the river. He succeeded in making his escape but he was alone and greatly troubled about his men. Yesterday evening he was at Mr. Rileys when one of his men came galloping up having captured two horses. From him he learned all was safe.

Yesterday Capt. Frank Fulkerson took dinner with us. Last night Sarah came over and gave us some music. The young folks gathered in. Lucy, Tilla Carmack and Mr. Rogers with our own struck up a dance. I do disapprove of these thing so much now. I feel how can sisters and brothers dance when they think of the condition of dear brothers and friends.

July 20, 1864.
Last night just as we were about going to bed Mr. Rogers came over from Sarahs and called to Capt. Bynum who had gone to bed

that Capt. Gibbs had moved his men up to J. C. Millers having heard that 2 of Kirks men were on the hill back of brother Hirams. Capt. was soon up and ready for riding. He went to Capt. Gibbs and sent Ike, Mr. Rogers and Callaway to town after the men who were there. After getting to town they determined to go down the road to Cooks after some men who went out yesterday on a scout. They went as far as Mr. Blevins (left town 12 after 11). The men had returned and they came back with Ike and Mr. Mitchell coming here about 3 A.M. Richard took his gun and went over to brother Hirams the first thing next morning and when he returned he told me the whole thing had started from poor simple Jack of Powel. Jack told them he had seen and talked with these men and they were well armed. Thus another incident is over without any damage but it is better to run 20 times than to be caught by such men as Kirks. The bushwhackers of Capt. Owens the other day proved to be a false alarm. Instead of 40 there were 3 and it was some of his own men running after them and firing which was mistaken for Bushmen. I do not wonder at Capt. Owens being easily excited when he feels superior numbers are against him. There is a large reward for his head.

July 21, 1864
Yesterday was the 18th birthday of my dear Powell. I hope the Lord will have mercy upon him. He is young, thoughtless and restive under parental restraint. He feels such a great desire to be a soldier. His Papa has been anxious about him and has kept him back fearing he would not be able to stand the soldiers life. He feels there is great glee in being a soldier. But could he have one such siege as our brave boys in Virginia have had its novelty and gleesome appearance would be gone. It is said they lay in the trenches at Petersburg for 62 days.

   This evening just a short time after dinner an ambulance drove up to Sarahs and they sent word over for the boys, Mr. Mitchell, Ike and Powell to come over and help to take a wounded man out. They went, came back and told me he was Mr. Tefftallow who was left at Mr. McClures when our men were driven back on the 15th of June. I went over to see him. I fear he is a disabled soldier for life. He was shot 3 times after he fell from his horse from a wound. He told me they must have fired some 18 or 16 shots at him after he was down. This would not be believed by the lovers of Lincoln freedom.

Just before I got over there Mr. Cleveland passed up. He had been staying with E. Ruth for two weeks or more. He was on horseback. I learned from Mr. T. that they had left him there to go after one of the wounded at George Powels farm. I talked to him a short time and strove to impress him with the importance of being a Christian. The men returned in a short time bringing the wounded man. His name was Smith a son of Jos. Smith of Ky. who lives in Barboursville. They were soon laid side by side and driven off.

Another rumor this evening of the advance of the Yankees. I hope it is false. Some of our men have gone over the river amongst the number our noble little Callaway. I have formed a strong attachment to him. I find him a brave, noble boy and hope his stay amongst us may lead him to be a better boy. I heard he and Mr. Rogers have made their home with Sarah. Mr. Mitchell and Dunwoodie with us until Mr. D. was ordered back to the command. He staid with us on Wednesday night. He seemed glad to get back.

Today Mr. Rhineheart was here having made the trip safely through. He says he could take 200 men and go to Chattanooga. He, Mr. Henry and Lt. Blevins went together. They are good soldiers and this Lt. B. is the same who was with Callaway in the rear the 15th of June. Sam Powel is with us tonight and not well.

July 22, 1864

Callaway returned this morning saying they went over as far as St. Clair but could make no definite discoveries concerning the Yanks. He, Mr. Relton and Sam. P took breakfast with us and then went to town. Richard went down, returned a short time before dinner bringing a letter from our dear Hiram to him. He says up to the time he had heard from the boys Tom, Pete and Sam were safe but they had lost another good soldier from their rank by the name of Robert Earl. Elisha Wright had been wounded severely in the head. I felt so glad to hear from my first born. I find I love him so tenderly.

Just after dinner today Ike came bringing the news that the Yanks had been seen over the river this morning and they were perhaps moving up the river with a view of flanking our forces here. Not long after he came Mr. Rogers and Callaway came. They got their dinner and then made ready to leave. They were going to Chism's Ford. Richard went intending to go to Mr. D. Lyons with him George and Mr. West. Not long after they passed Lts. Blevins and Ivy passed through. A negro riding in great state was close behind them. I wondered if he could belong to them but Caroline knew him and said it was Billy Bynum. She felt he was one of the darkies of the Confederacy.

July 23, 1864

This has been a day of great trial. To me this morning quite early Mary sent for me saying Amy[31] was very sick. I went over, found her just as had been told me; I felt every particle of human sympathy leave my breast. I could not keep my tongue. I staid a few minutes and came back home to make some arrangement for sending for cousin Joe.

When I got to the gate I was suddenly arrested by the report of guns. I listened for a moment when some 15 to 20 guns as I supposed were fired. I thought I heard them hallooing as though one or the other were making a charge. I was soon at the house and told the boys to get ready and be off. I sent word to those at Sarahs and

31. Mary and Amy were sisters. Amy was a pregnant free woman of color who receives no mention in Eliza's diaries until 1864. Eliza disapproved of what, in her mind, was Amy's immoral conduct and lack of industry. However, Eliza allowed Amy to live in one of the cabins on the Fain property until the birth of her child.

in a short time the boys from here were all ready. Just before they got off Sgt. White and Mr. R. from Surgoinsville came along without their breakfasts. The boys from here had eaten. Callaway and Massengill next came over. We made them get off and get something to eat. I was sorry I had not stopped Sgt. M. and Mr. R. but was afraid I did not have enough for them having fed Sam and Ed Powel, Mr. Mitchell, Mr. Atchley, Ike and Powell. Ike had taken his gun and made for the knob to see if he could hear or see anything. In a short time he learned it was Morgans men firing off their guns.

I went back to Amy's having sent for the doctor. In a short time she was a mother. My heart ached as I looked on the scene before me. A wretched, degraded woman and a helpless child born for eternity.

July 24, 1864
The Lord still merciful. Nothing of interest today. Mr. Mitchell, Cowan and Ike sent out this evening on picket somewhere on the river. Rumors come to us of fights East and West. Hood has taken the place of Joe Johnson—said that he has had a considerable fight repulsing the foe. Early and Hill met and repulsed those sent to recapture the stores which they had brought out of Maryland.

July 26, 1864
This evening I was so delighted. Just after dinner a while I started to go over to Marys, had passed through the gate when I saw a lady coming. I supposed it was Melissa but soon found it was my dear Bet. She said to me Hiram is just behind. I was so glad for the thought had often been on my mind shall I ever see my dear boys again. I was so thankful and grateful. He brought a long letter from our tried soldier boy Sam dated 11th of July to his papa.

Hiram went down to town yesterday evening and brought out Bettie and her dear little babe. This morning between 10 and 11 Mr. Mayab came out from town where he had been staying a few days with E. Ruth. He was in the fight at Drewry's Bluff and was wounded severely in the leg which had to be amputated. He is upon crutches. How many, O how many disabled will be seen through our country when this cruel war is over. He was wounded on the 16th of May between 8 & 9 o'clock just as Major Aiken was killed. He was a brave man but he was not a Christian.

### July 28, 1864

Fannie returned this morning from town having staid all night with Buena. Bug came with her. Mr. Mitchell, Ed Powel, Powell Fain, Mr. M. and Ed went up to Mr. Carmacks. Ike and Mr. Cowan went up to pasture to look at a horse. Ike traded for it for Hiram. It is a nice little animal.

Ike told me last evening that Johnny Halloran[32] was dead. He was a noble soldier wounded in the army at Drewry's Bluff. He returned home in June and had almost recovered as all thought. He was talking of starting back to his command next week. O how uncertain is the life of man and upon what a little thing does it seem to hang. He was walking along the road or path with some one and seeing several birds remarked I will kill one of those. He stooped took up a little rock and threw but at the sacrifice of his life. His arm gave way and was broken again at the same place where he had been wounded. Gangrene ensued and in a few days closed his earthly career. Another great soldier gone to try the realities of an unknown world.

### July 29, 1864

Still peaceful, still secure trusting in God. Mrs. Fulkerson, little Mary and Hamilton Hale came out to see us and staid a short time with us until after supper. They seem to enjoy our milk and bread as much as we used to dinner coffee or tea. The Lord is teaching us a great lesson by this cruel heartless war. It is that we can do on far

---

32. Johnny was a sergeant in Company C of the Sixty-third Tennessee.

less than we once did and be happy. The things of this world do not give peace. We have heard today that Lt. Kipshear and men met up with bushwhackers at little War Gap. Rumor says 3 of our men wounded and some of theirs killed.

### July 30, 1864

With deep regret I learn the rumor true that a good soldier has fallen by the name of Hays. Another I fear mortally wounded and left at Mr. Mallorys. Two others were wounded but not badly as I understand. It is said that Mr. Hays killed two notoriously bad characters named Hi Winstead and C. Buttery and that another one was supposed to be killed. O what a terrible state of things. Man is becoming so bloodthirsty.

### Aug. 2, 1864

On last Saturday morning about 9 Mr. Robinson and I set out for Mr. Lyons. He having the previous Sabbath made an appointment to preach at New Providence. My dear husband felt he could not go just at that time. Waiting to hear that everything was more quiet before he would leave. Mr. R. and I travelled slowly but surely and we overtook on the way a batch of prisoners. Seven I think, most of them taken in Greene County. They had the notorious Collins and another accused of bushwhacking tied together. Capt. Buckner and Lt. Night had command. I suppose there was a guard of some l0 or 12 (I think). We arrived at Mr. Jesse Lyons just about dinner time. To our great satisfaction here we met Ella Walker and Neppie Neill. They having gone before us.

Not long after we arrived here the guard and prisoners came up, threw themselves on the ground under the shade trees in the yard. Dinner was soon ready and we all enjoyed it very much. Just as we were through Major Toole came up having been ordered (I believe) with the members of the 3th Tenn. to report at headquarters. How little sympathy is in the heart of the Southern soldier for men who are living the life of some of the prisoners. They seem to feel there is little hope of reform in such characters. Mr. Lyons gave the guard and the prisoners something to eat and sent it out to them by waiters. After resting a while they left. Poor wretched deluded men may the Lord have mercy on them.

When I got in sight the first one I saw was my sweet baby standing on the style as though she was looking for us. We found Mr. Lyons quite unwell and much swollen. After supper we had our prayers and the next morning we made preparation pretty soon for church. We had our breakfasts, put up dinner and were soon ready. My loved, my darling boy was there (Hiram). He had the horses made ready. Mr. R. preached his sermon on slavery from Genesis chapter 9 from the 24 to 27th verses. This is a subject of the greatest importance to us as a people. After the first service there was an intermission of 15 to 20 minutes. We took our dinner and were called together by the singing of a hymn. Mr. Sawyer a refugee from Knox. Co. leading in the singing. Mr. R. then preached from Job chapter 23 the 8th, 9th and 10th verses. This to me is a delightful sermon. We had a large congregation at both services.

The exercises over we prepared to leave, came on to Mr. Millers and here we halted. Richard sent my horse to the shop for some new shoes having one put on his. A short time after Ella and Neppie came up, had not time to tarry. As we mounted a threatening cloud stood before us and in a short time began to discharge its contents but still we moved on. At length we found we were going to have a heavy rain—we called a halt at the home of Mr. Chase here we had to stay for more than an hour. The rain fell beautifully, refreshing the vegetable world. Richard thought we had better go back to Mr. Ms but the majority being against he succumbed. We then had no alternative but to go forward. We were tolerably well supplied with protection against the rain. I was riding on some shawls which Bet had taken up with her. I gave one to Neppie the other to me. Ella had a gents shawl and Mr. R. his overcoat. I gave Richard the blanket which I was riding on. I had an umbrella and a shawl. Neppie drew hers over her head covering hat and all. Ella took off her hat and drew the shawl over her. Richard had his blanket and our servant Tom mounted bareback on his mule with a pair of boots thrown over his neck composed the traveling caravan. I know we presented a novel spectacle to beholders. When I fell behind I took a look and laughed heartily. On we passed splash, splash but the rain was moderate and at length ceased. On we came night closing in around us. Neppie kept the lead all the way. When we got to Mr. Russells she turned her horse for the gate. Richard and I followed but felt I would rather go home. It was such an imposing but the dark hill and the rickety bridge stood before. My heart failed and I bent my course with the rest. We were received kindly by Miss. Mag. Patterson. Mr. Craig, and Frank Fulkerson were there. Several soldiers had called for supper—they were waiting on them. Richard told Mrs. R. to put herself to no trouble but to just give us what was convenient. Neal soon had everything fixed so nicely for us—took our suppers then went into the parlor. Miss. Mag Patterson played several pieces amongst the number *Who Will Care for Mother.* Now I was so pleased with it. I think the words are beautiful.

We retired soon after prayers. I felt tired but everything was so nice and so comfortable. At an early hour we heard the bell ring calling up the servants. Everything seemed to move so orderly. Breakfast was prepared for some soldiers by the time we were up. We came down and found Mr. R., Miss Mag. P and Mr. Fulkerson already seated by a snug fire. The girls not long after made their appearance. We then had prayers and breakfast soon came on which was so plentiful and so nice. After that I sat and talked some time to Mrs. R. and Neal. We then began to think of home but had some more music. We heard again the piece spoken of before. It is so sad but not greater than the reality. How many mothers weep in loneliness for the brave and noble son who has fallen far from home.

Richard and I got home before the little ones knew. They were so glad to see us and we were so glad to get home. I felt I had been gone a long time. After dinner Richard went to town and returned bringing the news that the Yanks were at Morristown and had a skirmish with some men under Capt. Arnold. Our men driven back with the loss I fear of a very valuable soldier by the name of Lt. Johnny Goodwin. I was so sorry to hear of his misfortune. I hope he may live but he has fallen into hands I fear where little sympathy will be felt for him.

Ike and Zack came by from Mr. Rileys and got their supper. Mr. Rhineheart called by for them and had his supper. They went on to town. Sarah came over and gave us some music. The little children took a dance with the larger ones instructing. I feel so opposed to dancing, feel I will not again give my consent for the little ones to do it. They left soon after and then we had prayer and all sought that sweet invigorator of mind and body—sleep, sleep.

August 3, 1864

The Lord still merciful. Report after report comes to us that the Yanks are coming yet we are secure. News today is that they have come up the railroad to the Gap. A scout of about 100 men left Rogersville this morning, went up and crossed at Chism's Ford with a view of getting in behind them. They are said to be Michigan men. Our men were Gen. Morgan's men under Col. Alston who had been ordered to Rogersville. Capt. Bynum and Lt. Gibbs are I suppose under the command of Col. Alston. I hope they may be successful and that they may all be preserved.

We had today Major Will Fulkerson[33] and Mr. Charles for dinner with several little girls. Mr. Charles was telling us of the scare he got last Sabbath. The great bushwhacker story was more or less some of our own soldiers firing for their own amusement. Lt. Smith as he calls himself was so scared he never stopped running until he got near brother Hirams as I understand.

---

33. Will Fulkerson was a captain in the Sixty-third Tennessee and commanded Company A. He was wounded in the foot during the Battle of Chickamauga and permanently disabled. He was promoted to major in 1863 and to lieutenant colonel in May 1864. He retired in October 1864 because of ill health.

August 5, 1864

This day has been set apart as I understand by the President Lincoln as a day of fasting, humiliation and prayer. May Christians of the South not forget it. O may they importune the God of Heaven to put a right spirit into our enemies that they may see the folly of their ways and undertaking. Prayer for measures of peace may prove a blessing to both sections of the country.

Yesterday evening the boys returned having seen nothing but the taking of a few bushwhackers. The Kentucks burnt the house of Mr. George Kinney who is reputed to be a very bad man. The offence it seems was they fired on some of the men from the door and Mrs. K. being asked where those shots came from replied right out of my door. Whether this is true or not I cannot say. Such things trouble me. I have ever been opposed to the destroying of the homes of women and children.

August 7, 1864

As Richard and I went to church today we overtook a soldier and a lady carrying a little babe. We spoke to them asking the soldier if he was one of them which had been wounded at War Gap. We asked if he was going home to which he replied he was going a part of the way with the lady who was the wife of a soldier who was mortally wounded at War Gap then brought to Mr. Mallorys and from there removed to Mrs. Harlans where he died. O how sorry I felt for her and asked her how many children she had. She told me 3 and spoke of the great trial which she was called to bear. That life was so dark and dreary that she never could be happy again. I tried to comfort her but felt inadequate unless divine grace was sustaining the bereaved one. I bid her goodbye and told her I hoped that God would sustain her in her deep affliction. She seemed to feel and answered she hoped he would. The name was Kingsolver.

We heard today that Gen. Early had burned Chambersburg. I regret to hear this. It may perhaps be necessary but I have always felt I did not want us to do anything which we felt would not yield the peaceable parts of righteousness. Whether this is part of God's mighty plan to bring our enemies to see what they have done to us remains to be seen. Can we ask Gods blessing on such work. If not I feel it is all wrong, wrong. O that God would give wisdom, grace and strength to our generals to enable them to act as a Christian people should.

August 14, 1864

Did not attend church today as had no saddle without depriving my dear daughter E. and I felt I would on this deny myself sometimes to give her the privilege. We had a report yesterday that Col. F. M. Walker was killed.[34] He leaves a widow and 3 orphans. She has lost a truly noble and lovely husband.

August 21, 1864

O how the peace and quiet of this Holy Sabbath has been disturbed. This is the first Sabbath we have not been permitted to assemble at the house of God since this war began on account of disturbance from the foe. This morning about 6 Mr. Cowan came riding up saying the Yankees are in town.[35] We had Lt. Duvall, Mr. Mitchell, Callaway, Ike and Powell sleeping so sweetly under our roof. The news was soon told them and five were quickly dressed and their horses made ready to mount. Before they got off the men encamped at Big Creek belonging to Gen. Morgan were moving down Alf Owens having been sent as a courier to them. They went as I understand to the forks of the road and there gave back going by Mr. Merrimons. They saw the enemy in front and sending a force through Mr. Fulkersons field

34. Frank M. Walker, the colonel in charge of the Nineteenth Tennessee, was killed on July 22, 1864, at the Battle of Peachtree Creek in Atlanta. His commission as a brigadier general reached the army the day after his death. He had been in charge of the Nineteenth ever since its reorganization following the Battle of Shiloh in 1862. Heiskell, "Nineteenth Tennessee Infantry," in *Military Annals of Tennessee*, ed. Lindsley, 377

35. General A. C. Gillem and troops of the Ninth, Tenth, and Thirteenth Tennessee Cavalries (U.S.A.) attacked Rogersville but retreated from the town on the same day. *Tennesseans in the Civil War*, 1: 343, 365.

out back of Brother Hirams with a view if possible to flank them. But their plans were thwarted and our men were not allowed by our Father to be taken. Our men did not seem to be alarmed. Some fifteen or twenty mostly Kentucks passed through here saying as they went by "ladies the Yankees are coming you had better go into the house." I could not go in but felt like standing and talking to them all the time. I told them to do their duty as good soldiers for I felt the Lord would deliver them out of their hands. By this time a force of the Yanks were seen moving back of Brother Hirams fields. A part coming through the field north of the house and on through the gate by the house into the road. They traveled as though fear troubled them.

I went over first after I got through with breakfast (which was hurriedly swallowed) to see a wounded man who had been brought to Sarahs on Tuesday or Wednesday. I had not been to see him for want of time there being so many soldiers about wishing to have something done for them. His name was Green Parkey. I was fearful the excitement might be too much for him but found him as comfortable as could be expected. Looked at his wound which was a flesh wound through the hip caused him much suffering.

I came back home and went over to Mr. Merrimons while the Yanks were on the hill east of Sarahs to see if I could find out anything about our men but all were gone. I did not tarry long; came back and went over to Sarahs again. By this time our men began to make their appearance. Callaway and others, some of Lt. Gibbs' men, I think, went on in the direction of town.[36] I was so much in hope our men would follow them. Not long after they passed two men came in back of Sarahs belonging to Gibbs' scouts who had made their escape from the academy across the knobs, leaving their horses concealed in the woods after hobbling their feet. Names Lt. McKeehan and Schergter and were much fatigued.[37] I gave them something to eat

36. Lieutenant William W. Gibbs served in Company C of the Fourth Tennessee Cavalry Battalion, which defended Saltville in October 1864.

37. R. R. McKeehan was a second lieutenant in the First Tennessee Cavalry, Company L, but there is no known Confederate soldier with a last name of Schergter.

after which they began to think of getting to their horses. I told them I thought the best plan would be for them to take to the hill which commanded both roads. They did so. After all things had quieted down I took my book of Psalms and started upon the hill thinking I would go alone to read and meditate on the kindness of the Father in sparing me from the enemy power.

Just as I passed the fence I heard a voice saying Mrs. Fain. I supposed it was one of the men who I had told to go up there, I quickened my steps and soon reached the top of the hill when a voice said come this way. I went to the fence and there I beheld a sight which I cannot soon forget through the fence. I looked upon a face which I scarcely recognized it was so worn and wearied. I said is this you Capt. He replied "yes, what is left of me." I said are you wounded "no, but completely worn down." He was in his sock feet and shirt sleeves. This was about 11 o'clock I suppose. He asked me if there was any Yanks about. I told him no and to get over the fence and come to the house. We had him water to wash, clothes, to change and something to eat. He lay down and slept awhile after which he felt he would go to town if he had a horse. Sallie started to the pasture on Mr. M's farm taking Jim with her to get a nag which belonged to him. She met Mr. Cleveland on the way, he went back got it, came on and he and Capt. Bynum were soon off. I told Capt. to come back and stay all night with us. He told me he was fearful that every person who were in the houses had been captured. We felt so much solicitude that Liz went to town taking Dicky to look for Capt. B's coat and boots. We learned through Mr. Bob West who had been saved by Mrs. Kenner from capture that they had taken Col Heiskell[38] and Col. Walker. We felt so troubled to think these men were taken. We knew Col. H. was a prisoner for the war and our sympathy for Col. Walker was so great. He had returned but a few

---

38. John W. Walker and Joseph B. Heiskell were captured on August 21, 1864, by Lieutenant Colonel William H. Ingerton of the Thirteenth Tennessee Cavalry (U.S.A.) and taken to prison (*OR*, series 1, vol. 39, pt. 1: 485). John Walker was the father of Colonel F. M. Walker, who was killed at the Battle of Peachtree Creek in Atlanta.

days before to the embrace of his loved family to enjoy the sweets of home which were so necessary to sooth his troubled heart as he mourned for his brave and noble son.

Mr. W. also said they had in cold blood murdered 3 of our brave soldiers: Mr. Hewy, Leach and Wilson. Mr. H. was shot 15 minutes after he surrendered. This is so sad. Last night we lay down in peace, tonight 3 of our brave soldiers are lying in death. O the horrors of such a scene.

Fannie has returned having been in town last night. She tells us she saw Mr. Hewy at Mr. Hassons where he boarded that he seemed to be such a nice gentleman and spoke of the business of today. He said that the prisoners would be started quite early that he would be at church and see them there. O how little we know what a day or an hour will bring forth.

I fear the murder of these men has been provoked by the murder of some 6 or 7 men under Bill Sizemore near Mossy Creek. I have always felt our men ought not to murder after they had surrendered. I know there is much excuse for them. They have taken so many who were reported as bushwhackers to Bristol and our authorities turned them loose. They have grown weary and feel their own lives are in jeopardy all the time. Yet when men are taken I do not think it right to shoot or murder them. The boys have all been at home this evening. Ike, Lt. Duvall and Mitchell were much exposed today but mercifully preserved. They galloped out towards the Gap of Knob just as the forces were rounding the fence. The cry of halt was given but not a shot fired upon them. Ike and Mitchell have been sent on picket to Charles Gap by Captain B. with a promise another man will be sent. We have had such a hard rain this evening; the whole land is deluged with water.

Captain Bynum is here and I have had a solemn conversation with him urging on him the great importance of being a Christian. He has been so wonderfully delivered this day. He told me sometime ago he had a Christian Mother. He says his wife is a Christian. I do hope the solemn impressions which this day has made may never wear off. He feels had they taken him he would have been in Eternity before this. Many, many of our men have escaped this day by hiding in different places. Some in cellars, in peach trees, in weeds, in corn and other places. Truly this has been a day of deliverance to our people.

This evening a very nice genteel man by the name of Matthews belong to a mess composed of 6 including Mr. Jacoway, Ballard, Capt. Wall and two others of names unknown, called for some bread which I had baked for them of yesterday. I came very near distributing it this morning; feel so glad now I did not do it. I have formed the acquaintance of the above named gentlemen and find they are real noble men from Mississippi. I do hope their lives may be spared. Captain Wall looks to be in bad health.

Powell and Callaway have come very wet indeed. The girls Jennie McCarty, Jennie Spears and Lizzie with A. Owens have come. They too are very wet and changing their clothes. The two Jennies lost their horses in town this morning. A. Owens came out and got them something to ride. Our soldiers are very dear to me. I look upon them as the pillar of cloud by day and the pillar of fire by night which God our Father has raised to preserve helpless women and children from the insults, cruelties and degradation which a cruel unprincipled foe led on by the wild fanaticism of the North would impose were it not for them.

Aug. 22, 1864

Last night after I had penned the events of the most wretched Sabbath of my life and we felt all was quiet, that the day of confusion and trouble had given way to a night of rest for the weary and worn all retired to rest. Alas, alas in this we were mistaken for between 1 & 2 o'clock Mr. Rogers (Hugh as the boys call him) came over saying our pickets have been fired on. I ran upstairs and awakened Capt. B and the boys. Lt. D., H. Owens, Callaway and Powell were soon ready and all off but Lt. D. He kept his nag saddled and ready at the stable. I made him a pallet on the floor of the parlor where the aching head of a noble soldier found repose. Next morning we could make no definite discovery in regard to the firing of last night. We had to come in this morning 4 of Gen. Vaughn's men belonging to the thirty-first Tn. Col. Bradford came across the mountain as a scout of some 75 men having been over there in search of bushwhackers. Not long after they came Powell, Callaway and Cleveland came. I forgot to mention that just as I was dressing I heard footsteps on the porch and found our esteemed friend Mr. Cantwell and a soldier by the name of Gluck from the thirty-first. They had made a narrow escape of capture on Sabbath and lost horse, saddle and all. They had on no socks and asked me for a pair but I had nothing that was much to give him but an old pair of cotton ones. I felt so sorry I had no yarn socks.

Several soldiers were at Sarahs for breakfast amongst the number Mr. Poats; he too having escaped capture on Sabbath by the self possession of his wife. She hid him in a cellar with some four or five others amongst the number Frank Allison of the sixty-third. Her house was searched by Bill Owens she requesting that he should do it. She talked to him without fear and Bug who is not afraid of any of them stamped her foot and told him to dry up right off as he could not talk that way in her presence and he did dry it up.

Soon after breakfast Mr. Cantwell and Gluck left, felt so sorry I had no horses for them. Soon after they left Mr. Poats came over on his way to Virginia. I had a letter written to my dear boy Sam but could send him nothing else. He soon left taking Tom Woods some 10 or 12 miles to bring back the horse. For supper I had Mr. Moss and Key of Morgan's command and very nice gentlemen.

August 23, 1864
Last night was one of great quiet. I forgot to mention in yesterday records that Mitchell and Ike were ordered by Capt. Bynum on picket at Charles Gap with the promise another man should be sent to them. He failing to come the boys did not go which I think was wrong in these days of peril but for aught we know the neglect of

the man to come may have saved three lives from bushwhackers. Capt. B., was I understand, much offended with the boys (not Ike and Mitchell) but Powell and Callaway and think he ought to have felt so. They were on last night, I think. Cowan was the other man.

Having undertaken some washing for a soldier with the promise that he should have his clothes this morning (which promise was foiled by the rain of the Sabbath night making my spring so muddy) I determined to help wash myself. I went at it with great resolution; washed but a little while when Mr. Robinson came. I soon came to the house for I am always so glad to see our dear minister. Soon after I came he told me he was on his way to the United Synod at Lynchburg. He said that he had been praying to the Lord that he would open up a way for him if it was his holy will that he should leave his people for a season to avoid the wrath which Brownlow's articles[39] might excite in the minds of the Federal troops. On the evening before he had visited our uncle Doc.—told him of the notice in the Observer in regard to the synod. He felt this is the very thing I have been praying for and determined to go. We had him a cold meal of bread, butter and milk. His faith is strong and my soul is ever refreshed when with him. He remarked while here we do not know what an day or hour will bring. The sad results of Sabbath had impressed him deeply.

We had today for dinner Mr. Moss, McDowel and Prince of Gen. Morgan's as well as Capt. Bynum, Callaway and Ike. Ike traded his grey mule to Mr. Prince. After dinner he and Callaway mounted, with Ike on the black mule and Callaway on a captured pony of 13th Tn. They set out for town intending to trade them off but why or what they were after I cannot tell. They went out to Mrs. Rileys and all seemed to be peace but alas we knew not what a storm was gathering. Liz was preparing to iron and I was busily engaged putting a back in Lt. Duvalls vest and Sallie was darning. Between 3 and 4 o'clock Powell came galloping up saying the

39. Eliza was referring to articles appearing in the Unionist newspaper *Brownlow's Knoxville Whig and Rebel Ventilator.*

Yanks are in town. Some 15 or 20 minutes after our ears were pained by the sound of shot after shot. Our men running and the Yanks in close pursuit. They were Lt. Skillman's scouts which they had run from Mr. Ricks. When they got to the second hill beyond Hirams they called a halt, wheeled and came back as fast as they could saying as they passed they had killed a man upon the hill. After all passed Liz and Sallie went over to look for him but found none. They did not stay long.

Morgan's men under the command of Capt. Cantwell passed down; they found the Yanks in heavy force in line of battle on the hill beyond Mr. Fulkersons. The Yanks then moved forward, formed a line just east of the house. Our men were noticing their movements and did not I suppose form a line of battle until they came to our meadow where they dismounted and formed a line along the dividing fence. Here they remained some half or three-quarters of a hour then they moved off in column through our meadow and wheatfield and on through Mr. Netherland's fields. They did not seem alarmed but went off quietly and calmly. After they had been gone perhaps an hour the Yanks came forward with great caution. The Col. halted at Sarahs and made inquiry but could get no information. He then sent over to our house but we were ignorant here to the question "how many Rebs; which way have they gone," et cetera were put to us but we did not know. They moved the advance into the meadow throwing down fences without compunction. Divided their forces into the right, left and center. They moved forward part going on through the field to the right out through Gus' sugarcane patch and through our lower meadow. I do not know when, where or how they got back after they had left; perhaps half an hour later the main body of the forces moved forward; came into the meadow halted. They waited a short time for the Rebs when the order was given to move back.

Before they left Caroline, Gus & Ahab commenced putting up fences for our cornfield and every place that was exposed; cows and calves getting together; hogs out, everything in utter confusion. I and

Cary went to the cornfield fence and went to work to get it up. When they came pouring through the meadow we succeeded in getting it stock proof, whirled and was coming on the house. Just as I came through the gate one of them called to me saying old lady give me some meat and bread. I told him I had no meat, he then asked for milk. I told him I had it and would give him some. He then asked me what I was and I told him a southerner. Your family in the Southern army? Yes. Have you any sons with the troops this evening? Yes two. I told him I thought the South was right he then said "you don't think so now" I told him yes I did. He then said "you think they will whip us?" I told him that was with God. He then began to hurry for his milk. I asked him if he would take it from a Southern woman. He said "yes you won't poison one will you?" I told him no. Got him a canteen full of buttermilk; gave some to another in his canteen and then they were soon off. Thanked me. I was so thankful when I saw them going. Hoped I should see no more. The Lord was our preserver and the great benefactor of our dear soldiers. No one was killed or wounded this side of town. O what a deliverance. Shot after shot and yet with no effect.

Aug. 24, 1864

Had a peaceful night; no enemy came near. All our boys gone; will any of them get back today cannot tell? This morning a man came from the direction of the stable, I did not know him but as he drew nearer Liz said that is George Etter (Sallie, Ell and Sarah went down this morning to get the news and found no Yanks in town). I was very glad to see him. He had a hard time the evening before. The Yanks caught him in town with several others. There were 12 or 15 of Skillman's men and Frank Allison. Got him as they came by his home I suppose. George told us he had made his escape at the river by jumping the fence and running for life to the woods. Told one not long after he was taken a Negro rode up, demanded his old pocketbook but he handed it to a white man who examined it and returned it saying nothing there but Confederate. As they passed Mrs. Speak's door he handed it to one of the girls. They behaved so badly in town on yesterday shooting through Mrs. Speak's house. They threatening to burn Cousin Ann's house down telling her she had Rebs hid there on Sabbath. They intended to search for them and made her disclose her hiding place. They went in but with great cautiousness. There was a cavalry saddle hid which they did not see or would not take. I imagine the former was the reason.

I have felt so thankful this day that no foe is permitted to remain near us. O that our Father would drive them to the land congenial for them. They made a general sweep of everything in the shape of horseflesh that could travel. Took cousin Joe Walker's nag; left him on foot to practice.

One of our men rode from Mr. Rices wounded in the bowels. When he got to town he stopped at Mrs. Heiskells, so much exhausted he sank on the floor. His name was James Smith from Lebanon Tenn. I fear from what I can hear he will not live. How dreadful is this cruel war wresting from the loved embrace of a widowed mother her darling boy upon whom perhaps she was leaning as the stay of her declining years. Sallie has gone to town to set up with him tonight.

August 25, 1864

Last night as we were eating our supper a rap on the door made us look wild. Liz opened the door, someone spoke but she did not recognize him. He said "you don't know me" and she answered no. He replied Jimmie Cooley. We were so glad to see him. He told us he came near being captured Tuesday evening. He had made his escape back of the institute and had been from that time until then making his way here. It so happened that I had two soldiers horses which they had loaned to Leah Young and Sallie Hasson. Buena had rode the one Leah had out that day with George Etter's clothes. She and Lissa Kidd came, Lissa bringing Ed Powel's. Not finding them here they went on to Mrs. Spears but could not meet up with them. They came back. While they were gone Bug came riding the other horse. So I mounted Jimmie on one of them that night and told him to get out. If he met up with the owner of the horse to hand him over; if not to keep him until it was safe for him to come back and then bring it back as I supposed the men would call for them here.

I always feel so comfortable when I get a Reb started; I feel they will not be caught for I never see one leave but I pray that God will take care of them and shield them from the power of the enemy. This day our hearts were made glad and sorry too by the return of our boys. I had gone over to Sarahs, was returning when I got near home and who should come galloping up but Lt. Duvall. I felt so glad to see him yet with trembling. Ike, Callaway and Capt. Bynum came this morning, went on to town and came back for dinner. We felt so glad to see them. They took themselves into the third hollow below the meadow until we could know something more of the Yanks. We had reports they were coming from Kingsport and in every direction. Almost directly after Lt. Duvall came Sam and Ed. Powel and Mitchell. We soon had some bread, milk and butter for them. They then took to the hollow with the others. After awhile E. Ruth and old Henry came. I was not at the house and they rode on through and down to the hollow. My very heart sank within me for I have gotten so I do not have much confidence in Negro flesh. I just felt our boys may all be betrayed.

Lizzie was not at home having gone to town with the intention of attending the burial of Mr. Smith who died this morning between 6 & 7 o'clock. Sallie gave me quite an affecting account of his deathbed scene. Several of his comrades had called to see him the evening before. Lt. Skillman and some two or three others called this morning but the conflict was almost over with him. He was too far gone to notice them. He asked the girls on the evening before to sing for him. Sallie thinks he asked for *Amazing Grace.* They sang *Rock of ages cleft for me.* He asked them to sing *Kiss him for his mother;* when they were through E. Ruth leaned over him and asked him if she must kiss him for his mother. He replied yes.

Lt. Skillman called a few moments to see about Mr. Baker another noble one who had fallen from a wound near Mrs. McCares. He told us he had lost 75 men from his company since its formation but no death troubled him as the death of Mr. Smith. We were hurrying for our supper intending for the boys to take to the hollow and spend the night.

Aug. 28, 1864
The sun has again risen in splendor upon our homes. Our Sabbath has been one of quiet. A passing soldier occasionally bringing in some news but our enemies, it is said, are travelling in the direction of Cumberland Gap. God grant that it may be true and that we may never more see another. I feel it is impossible in thought to crowd the events of the past week into 7 days. It seems as if we had lived months. Our God has been for us, he has delivered our men from death and captivity. To me it is a miraculous deliverance so few of our men taken, such plans thwarted, so few have fallen but those who have are the noble and the brave.

We as yet have heard of only six killed. Three last Sabbath: names already mentioned — Mr. Smith of Lebanon, Tenn. who died at Mrs. Heiskells on Thursday morning at 6 o'clock trusting we hope in Jesus. He delivered many messages for his mother, brothers, sister, aunt and comrades saying "tell my mother her son died praying" tell my comrades to "not put off preparation to a dying hour" and many, many others all bearing on the great interests of the soul. He seems to have fallen in the strength of manhood and promise. Mr. Bailey and Sergeant Daily who was killed as before spoken of.

Eliza Ruth and I called to see Uncle Doc and Aunt Fannie; both in bed. Aunt F. with flux and uncle Doc. with a chill. I hope that their lives will be spared and many days given to them. Dear Mag with her little loved ones needs so much to have their counsel and prayers. We came back to E's and took dinner. While there heard my dear Husband was at home was so delighted, left in a short time. Came to Mrs. Rogans to see Jimmie and found him on his lounge comfortable but a very bad wound, not regarded as out of danger yet—do hope the Lord will spare his life. I came on to Cousin Ann's where Bob had brought his mothers old nag for me to ride—got home safely and found my dear husband at home with the loved ones. Jimmie Rogan had been shot on that morning a week after he surrendered. He was taken to the jail by Bill Sizemore in cold blood without any charge against him. Mrs. R. is bearing it with true Christian fortitude.

I was on my way home last evening when E. Ruth hailed me and urged me so strongly to stay. I consented. I had been down as far as Mr. McClures to see a wounded man by the name of Baker belonging to Lt. Skillman's scouts. The Lt. was anxious he should be removed above town feeling he would be more secure but he was not able to be moved. I much fear he will not get well. I feel he has a good praying nurse in Mollie Ruth. I do hope the Lord will spare him. Mollie told me he had a chill Thursday evening. She felt he would die but she staid upon her knees an hour and a half with him working with praying. I have no doubt for him. He was wounded on Tuesday and was a dear friend of Mr. Smith.

## August 29, 1864

Nothing of great interest today except that 34 Yanks were in Mooresburg this morning. I hardly think it true yet it may be. Mitchell and one or two others went down the road hoping to be able to cross the river but it was too high. All returned here tonight feeling it was not very safe. They then left and went up the road. My loved husband with them. He seems to be unwell. I feel so sorry that he cannot stay. My dear boy Hiram came down today before dinner.

## August 30, 1864

Ike and Mitchell returned for breakfast this morning. They all staid at Mr. Sensabaughs. Not long after breakfast Powell and Ed came.

In a short time they and Mitchell went to town. Shortly after they left my dear husband came. The boys tarried in town awhile and came back saying the news was that the Yanks camped at Mooresburg last night. They left not long after, Ike, Callaway, Powell and Ed to go up the road to get the horses shod. My Hiram and others went up Carter's Valley. He did not come to see his mother this morning. I do not like for him to do that.

After they left George Fain came over. Sallie fixed something for him and Rie to eat. They too have left and now we have no dear male friends to feel anxious about. I do hope they may not be gone long. Report after report this day has come to us that the Yanks were coming but this evening we hear none are nearer than Mooresburg. Our boys still linger around.

August 31, 1864

We feel lonely this night. Sallie and I are sitting opposite each other. She writing to Sam and I penning the events of the day—have been quite busy—trying to dry fruit, make cheese and gather vegetables. After dinner I told Sallie I would go right off to see the Yeonas family who have been much afflicted for several weeks past. One of their loved ones has been taken from time to eternity. But a short time since a son by the name of Wesley died Friday the 19th of August about 10 o'clock. He had fever was greatly deranged the greater part of the time while sick—was a good boy to his parents. I found Mrs. Yeonas in one bed, Dick in another, Eliza in another. How sad is affliction at all times but peculiarly so now. Mrs. Russell had been to see them. She is such a kind neighbor.

Our boys were making preparations to leave. Mitchell and Ed went up with Lucy and Tilla Carmack, Powell, Ike and Callaway went to town, returned got their suppers and cut out. They seemed to feel all things were not working exactly right. They told me Wilber Carter had been run from the Gap today, heard tonight that the immortal Capt. W. S. [Bill Sizemore] had offered a reward of $3000 apiece for two of our men.

Sept. 1, 1864

How rapidly is time passing bearing us onward to great eternity. Almost a year since the Yanks first gained any permanent foothold in East Tennessee and since we were first made to feel the galling yoke in the upper counties of East Tennessee. We have seen and known comparatively little of them. They were not permitted by God our Father to remain long driven back until we feel they are afraid to come amongst us much.

Sept. 2, 1864

Had a quiet night no alarm from foes. In the evening Sallie Hasson and Buena came out. Jimmie Mitchell, Ed & Powell at home; thought this would be their last night at home for some time. I suppose the girls thought they would come and be with them. They bid us goodbye this morning. I felt sad to part with them feeling they had never known anything of soldiers life.

As we were eating dinner some of the children said there is a soldier at the door. Dick went first and said it is Mr. Forbes. I went and found as D had said. Mr. F. a youthful but noble looking soldier. In a short time Sallie came in. We had him to come out and take dinner. I had just remarked to Sallie we are lonely without our boys and how often we will look in vain for them not knowing there was one of them near us. Mr. F told us they had a scout of 20 whose duty was to watch the two roads. I do hope our father will give us his blessing. Before the dinner things were put away I saw someone coming by the stable. I looked and who should it be but our three dear boys who left this morning. We were glad to see them. The scout they expected to go with had left about an hour before they got across the river under Sam Spears. I trust it is all for the best.

Lizzie and Fannie returned this evening. Fannie having been gone a week last Tuesday to stay with the Miss Guthries and Liz left home Tuesday to go to Mr. McClures to assist in nursing a wounded soldier who belongs to Skillman's scouts and was wounded on the 23 of August near Mrs. Rices through the shoulder, rode without a bridle to Mrs. Mc; his horse falling in the mud hole beyond the house. He was thrown off, got over the fence into a thicket but his pain was so severe he could not remain concealed. Came out and called for help, the inhuman wretches wanted to kill him but one whose name was Smith Powel said "he loved to kill Rebs as good as any one but not when they were in this fix." Through the interests of this man and Annis Fry with a Negro of Barsha named Lizza they prevailed on them to let him live. He was taken into the house, his wounds bleeding profusely all the time. When he was laid on the floor the blood ran across the floor and his suffering was intense but his work was over. He died last night about 12 o'clock; his name was Baker lived about 12 miles from Nashville. Another noble life sacrificed to the demon of war. Liz says he called so often for his mother. Alas, alas that mother could not hear the cry of her darling boy. He will be buried in town near to Mr. Smith a dear comrade for whom he often called. Death occasioned from Typhoid Fever. Thus has fallen another one of our dear soldiers far from his home surrounded by strangers but tenderly cared for by dear stranger friends. Had he had medical aid sooner perhaps it might have been different. Cousin Joe thinks the system was under the influence of the disease when he was wounded. His wound was not dressed until Thursday.

Sept. 3, 1864
The Lord still showing mercy—our 3 dear boys rested quietly last night in Ahab's house, he standing picket for them. The old man says he had an uneasy night. The thought of any of them being caught seems to trouble him greatly. It has been raining this morning. We were greatly cheered this morning by the news that ten of prisoners taken last Tuesday week had made their escape. Jack Harry came over to see the boys. We were so glad to see him. Frank Allison, Mr. Dismukes and Mr. Ramsey are among the number. I do feel so thankful they have gotten away. They had marched them from one place to another until they were completely worn down; their feet very sore. They made their escape Thursday night having cut a hole

through the weatherboarding. They lay in about 112 miles of the Gap until last night when they made quick time I suppose. Some bare-headed and all without boots or shoes. They produced quite a sensation in town this morning. Many ladies called on them to congratulate them in their successful escape. They say they have had but 1 ration of flour in 11 days and that their living has been on corn mostly. The ladies of Rogersville as usual set themselves to work for as good an outfit as they could get them. Mrs. H. gave to one the boots of Mr. Smith. E. Ruth gave to Mr. Allison the knapsack of Mr. Coffee. To another Sallie gave a pair of Dick's shoes. Mec an old hat of Sam's and others gave until the 10 were shod.

Sept 4, 1864

Have had another peaceful night. No enemy came near. There was quite a storm of rain, thunder and lightning. The girls are making ready to go to town. The girls have told me since they came out that they believe Mr. Hewy was a Christian that he was sitting in his room that morning reading in his Bible. That after he was taken the inhuman monster Bill Sizemore came up to him—he was asked if he belonged to any of the scouts. He replied "no." How do you like being a prisoner? Very well when I cannot help myself. He then asked him one or two questions more and then deliberately put his pistol to his head and shot him. Mr. H. made a leap up exclaiming "O God have mercy, have mercy" when he fell to the ground. Mrs. Rogan told me when she saw him, as I understood her, "that life was nearly gone, that the whole body was in anguish." Two weeks to a day since that horrible scene occurred. I feel the foul perpetrators of such inhuman acts cannot escape the judgement of a righteous God. The innocent blood of Mr. Hewy is crying to Heaven for vengeance. Can a man who does this ever have one moment of peace? I say he cannot.

Sept. 6, 1864

We are still unmolested. Have been so busily engaged today; took the children Nan, Ella, Sil, Ida, Sallie, Cin, Nate and Jim in the wagon. Went over to the orchard today to get some apples to make cider. I had sent Dick to town to tell his Aunt E to send Bob on. After awhile he and Stan came. We got the apples and came back. The girls with Ahab had been busy with the fruit.

Dick brought us back Yankee news that Atlanta had fallen into the hands of the Yanks. I do not believe it. It may be true but I must have it from another source before I give credence. We were cheered by the sight of two Rebs today, not nearer to us than the road and yet we were pleased to know that any were so near. They were Mr. Rogers and Cowan. They left last Saturday week with Capt. Bynum.

Sept. 7, 1864

I feel this night so oppressed with the cares of life. Have been working so hard to try to get along. Have been making cider; took the hands and went to Mr. Netherland's press. Made about 15 gallons. I suppose I have undertaken to do too much. Why my dear friends expect more of me than they seem to of others I cannot tell. My family is large, they have to live and yet they seem to feel I can do all. I feel I am to blame. Sarah seems to have no such trouble without a full recompense. I love my friends and feel I am willing to do for them all I can; more than I ought in justice to my family. The news of this evening effects me more seriously than all things else and I do suppose it is one reason why I feel so oppressed. Labor does not often make me feel as I do tonight no matter who I am laboring for. O when will this strife cease, when O Lord when shall the joyful tiding be borne on every breeze that our God is reconciled with us and that peace is granted to our distracted land.

I had this morning a letter from my soldier boy Sam; felt so thankful to hear from him. He seems to feel grateful to God for the great deliverance which has been given to him since this war began. The letter came by Mr. Harris who is on furlough but cannot go home on account of bushwhackers. I met his wife this morning as I went up; did not know her she looks so badly. He expects to stay

but a short time here. He has been at Mrs. Harlans. I do feel so
sorry to see our men coming home when they have not one moment
of enjoyment after enduring what they have done for such a long
time. It is so hard to be denied the few days of furlough in peace.

The boys had sent by Mr. Harris for some provisions. If we
could only send it to them. I feel I have so little to send my poor
boy; I feel almost sick at the thought. No nice ham or anything else
that I feel worth sending. I did not say that I would do anything.
Would love to and feel so badly but O there are many poor mothers
in our Southern land who cannot now afford any luxuries to those
who are so dear. I must acknowledge something to my own heart
which I do not often do and this is it is pleasant to me not to be
alone in that.

While at Sarahs, Neal Harlan, Lizzie Miller, Maj. Runnels
and Haynes Carmack came. Major seems to have great fears that
Atlanta has fallen. When I began writing this felt much as he does
but I have listened to my little children praying at my house, have
prayed and wept bitter tears myself and now feel so greatly comforted. Still believe that if she has fallen God our Father will not
permit them to gain any ascendancy by it and that it may prove the
overthrow of Sherman's forces.

Sept. 8, 1864

I awoke this morning at 2 o'clock. Slept but very little after my
thoughts troubled one. The cares of my family, the troubles of war,
the unfaithfulness of those around me made me sick at heart. I rose
early, dressed and went to the spring. I looked at a cheese in press,
fixed my milk for breakfast and then assisted about the milking.
After breakfast I determined to perform a duty which had been
troubling one for several weeks. That of going to see poor Amy to
tell her she must hunt her another home. O how sad I felt as I
crossed the field. When I got there she was in the yard, turned and
went in without seeing me. I went in and in a short time told her
what I had come for that was to tell her she must hunt her another

home. That it had cost me many bitter tears and much trouble of heart. That when she came to me I felt I had given to a poor lone friendless woman a home for her life if I had one. But I felt she had by her own bad conduct deprived herself of it; that I felt I could not keep such a person on my place if I knew it. That I wanted her to be a Christian and train her poor little child for heaven. She at first seemed stouthearted and said she thought she could get another home and that there were other places. I told her she might find it harder than she thought for. But before I got through with her she shed tears and so did I—poor wretched wanderer.

As I was going back I saw two of the boys as we call them come to the kiln (Mr. Rogers and Cowan). When I got there I found E. Ruth had come while I was gone. The rain was falling, we had on our kettles for making apple butter. E. had brought out her smaller kettle. I had borrowed a larger one from Mrs. Miller. The apples and cider were in one, the balance of the cider in the other. We asked our boys the news. They told us they thought Atlanta had fallen. That Gen. John Morgan was killed and his staff captured.

Just as dinner was ready who should come up but my dear son Ike and Jack Harry. We felt so glad to see them. They brought news confirming the above and that Gen. Morgan had been killed on Sabbath morning at Greeneville. He had been betrayed by Mrs. Williams[40] who had sent word to the Yanks after our men left for Blue Springs that there were no forces in G. but Gen. Morgan and his staff. They came upon him and demanded his surrender but he

---

40. Eliza's attribution of the betrayal to Mrs. Lucy Williams gives credence to Williams's own claim to have been the woman who betrayed General John Hunt Morgan. Her story had reached Rogersville within five days of the time Morgan was killed. In *War at Every Door* (186–87), Noel Fisher doubts the veracity of the later claim by Sarah Thompson that she was the one who betrayed Morgan. (For details of the Thompson claim, see A. A. Hoehling, *Women Who Spied* [New York: Dodd, Mead & Co., 1967], and the Sarah Thompson papers in the Duke University Special Collections Library). There is also the claim that James Leahy, a twelve-year-old boy, betrayed Morgan. It is possible that all three actually attempted to notify Union troops or that it was just a lucky break that allowed the troops under General A. C. Gillem to catch Morgan. However, a report by the Union officer William Ingerton simply states that he had learned that General Morgan was at Mrs. Williams's home without indicating who told him. See *OR*, series 1, vol. 39, pt. 1: 489.

fought it is said to the last discharging 12 shots at them. Thus has fallen another of the defenders of the South. His blood will cry for vengeance on her who was his betrayer. Ike and Jack went to town, did not tarry long, came back and left in a short time going back up the country. O Lord I do pray thee to watch over my poor wayward son. I fear he has lost sight of his duty to his God and to Man. My heart is so grieved. I hear so much that he has done which I feel and know is so wrong.

Sept. 9, 1864

This evening I had a short call from friends I love — Nellie Fulkerson and Mag Patterson who had been spending the day with Sarah (Fain). O how much I love them, how thankful I feel to them for the many kindnesses shown to my family since this war began. Mr. Patterson's family have shown such marked kindness I never can forget it. They have suffered sorely. Few have been more completely broken up than they and no persons I have ever met with seem to bear it as they do so submissively and cheerfully. Mag told me this evening her mother had been sent word privately by the commanding officer at the Gap to come and take possession and he would send the family away who were occupying. The property of Mr. P. had been advertised for sale as deserted, confiscated property. I felt so glad Mrs. P had been permitted to return to her home.

Sept. 10, 1864

Nothing of great interest transpired today; have been quite busy with fruits. Made over 5 gallons of peach butter. I sent Dick today to see his aunt Eliza about some beef. He returned bringing the news that the Yanks had Bristol. They had men in on our men whilst burying Gen. Morgan. I do not believe one word of it but still such news is so worrying. It seems to have come from a Mr. Wilkinson who was down the road at Mr. Blevins. He says they got their information from the Gap. Sent Ahab and Gus to assist Mr. Merrimon about killing a beef. They bring the same news from the same sources.

Sept. 11, 1864

Sabbath Peace and quiet have been granted to us today (nearly 1 o'clock). I have been reading a little Sunday school book to Nan and Dick. After I was through reading I took the 2nd volume of the union quarterly and went over the first lesson with my dear Nan. I feel so anxious that my younger children shall be taught the scriptures. I feel I sorely neglected the older ones. My sons know nothing of the Bible.

Zack Lyons came down today after the doctor. His father not so well; had a chill last Thursday night. I much fear he is never to be well. He and Dick have gone on to town. The girls have returned with news of the escape of Sergeant Black from Knoxville. He was one of Major Lowe's men who disappeared rather mysteriously during their stay here. He and a Mr. Terry went to Choptack and that was the last was heard of them until today that I know of. He was wounded. He thinks Mr. T was sent to Camp Chase. He understood Mr. Heiskell was in prison. I do feel so sorry for Col. Walker; his trial is a very sore one. I trust we shall all be delivered from the tyrants yoke.

I visited this evening the Yeonas family. They are in a bad fix. I do feel so sorry for them. Eliza is very sick had a sore on her neck (left side) which had run a great deal. Mr. Yeonas looks so badly. He seems to be in such deep distress. I spoke to her about striving to be submissive to the will of God.

Sept. 12, 1864

Heard yesterday that the bushmen were troubling some of the citizens again. They were at Mr. John Charles and one or two more places on Saturday night. These men are a sore trial to the people. I understand Lizzie Miller came down for Brother George to go last night and join with others in trying to get them. E. Ruth came out today and told me she had a letter from Tom by Mr. Russell. The boys in tolerable health. She also told me that Mr. R. thought our troops were moving down and the Yanks falling back. Hope all may be true. He also said that E. Heiskell had a letter from Carrick dated 27th saying Atlanta impregnable.

September 13. 1864
Still in Peace. O teach us and enable us to feel as David did when penning that beautiful Psalm of all consolation to the righteous (91st). This has given me a comfort which I felt was more to be desired than the wealth, praise or any thing which earth could give. Often when my heart has been troubled and particularly at night when I have thought that before the morning should dawn upon us we might be subjected to the search of the bushmen or our dwelling might be laid in ashes. O how precious is the Bible.

I felt so comforted this morning reading the 79th Psalm. The prayer in that Psalm for deliverance is one which we feel every Southern heart can offer in sincerity and truth. O Lord we feel we can plead that the sighing of the prisoner come before thee. Many, many dear friends are this night in loathsome prisons under the oppressive yoke of the most terrible tyrant God our Father ever permitted a people to be placed under that of a wild fanaticism. Our sons, our dear relations and our dear friends are all sufferers tonight. When we hear of such men as Cols. Heiskell and Walker being confined in a place so loathsome as a Knoxville Jail with charges against both as we hear of which they are innocent how earnestly can every Christian friend pray that the sighing of the prisoner may come before thee. This morning quite early Zack and Dick started to go to Mr. Lyons. At Mr. Millers they heard the sad news of the death of Mr. L.

Sept. 14, 1864
Mr. Lyons was buried today at New Providence. He is laid in his narrow resting place where war can disturb him no more. He died unexpectedly; had during the day on Monday several spells but got better. In the evening Cousin Joe left him sitting up but that night about 11 Julia gave him some medicine. She was sitting reading,

got up not long after went to him and found him getting cold and almost pulseless. Mr. James Phipps was there, had staid all night with them. Mr. L died about one o'clock without a struggle, eyes and mouth closed, hands crossed upon his breast. There was quite a quantity of blood discharged from the body after death.

September 15, 1864
Liz is quite busy today preparing something to send to my soldier boy Sam. I have not felt that anxiety in getting this up that I often have done but hope he may get it.

September 16, 1864
Last night we got our box prepared. I took over to Sarahs what we had, got it all packed. She will nail it up. No news of importance. We hear many reports but pay little attention.

Sept 18, 1864
We feel our peace and quiet disturbed this morning but not as it was before. Instead of enemies we are today feeding our Southern soldiers. We have had several: a Mr. Blanton from Jackson, Mr. Cothran, Mr. James, Mr. Martin, Lt. Short and Mr. Clark have called to see us. I do feel so much solicitude for our dear soldiers. While Mr. James was here he told me that when he was at home the last time he found an interesting revival of religion in progress. That he and Mr. Martin had both joined the Methodist. I gave him all the good advice I could, told him to be faithful for he had nothing to fear. I do love to meet with one of our dear young soldiers who have come out and professed Christ. When it is said of the Southern army they are coming up to the help of the Lord against the mighty then may we look for a permanent peace God will give us.

I awoke early this morning before I knew there were Rebs of any number near us. Was so deeply impressed with the words of the psalmist "trust in the Lord for in the Lord Jehovah is everlasting strength." I have been so unwell today and yesterday. Hope I shall soon be well if it is my Father will to that. I bow without a murmur. This is the standpoint from which I have viewed every thing which has come upon me for many years past. Nothing can harm me without my Father's will. No foes can molest, no disease can invade, no misfortune come without his Holy Will.

Sept 19, 1864

Have given breakfast to 7 of our soldiers belonging to Wheelers command: J. S. Patterson, P. B. Anderson, L. M. Strickler, W. J. Hacker, T. S. Edwards, G. M. McWilliams, F. Olive belonging to fifth Georgia, Anderson's brigade, Col. Byrd. We had today for dinner Lt. Short, Mr. Cothran, Lt. Somerville, Mr. Tigret and Taylor of 8th company Andersons brigade and Robinson's command. For supper J. Stewart from Beauville Parish in La., Nat Simmons from Talladega, Al., tenth Conf. Regiment commanded now by Capt. Holt.

One poor lone soldier rode up this evening. His appearance aroused my sympathy. He asked if we could give him something to eat. I told him I did not know whether we had any bread or not. Liz with her kind heart for the poor soldier thought she could give him something. She went to work and got him some bread, butter and milk. When he got off his horse he looked as though he could hardly walk. When he came up on the steps he told me he was suffering from erysipelas in his feet and legs. I told him to come through. He was black ragged and dirty but I felt he is a dear boy of some mother or sister. I knew as soon as I talked to him he had seen better days than these. On the back porch I had some water and soap prepared for him, to wash his feet. Poor fellow his socks dirty as you can imagine and had stuck to his sores so that the scabs came off as they came. I gave him some beef foot oil to grease, then bound them in some clean nice rags. I gave him a pair of old socks, hunted an old shirt for him. Thus made him as comfortable as my limited means would allow. His name was Brantley from near

Macon Georgia.[41] He seemed so grateful and told me he would ever remember me with emotions of the warmest gratitude.

Tonight for supper Mr. Clark, Mr. Cothran and Lt. Short. It is now almost 11 and they are just leaving. Lucy has been here, Sarah came over and entertained them for a short time with good music. We have had a very pleasant time. Lt. S. and Mr. Cothran telling us of what is said to Georgia soldiers as they pass hey you guber grabber, which way—here goes the guber grabbers. They came up with remarks of their great natural facilities for grinding cane. The thought by their foolish remarks of getting them to grind up ours was suggested to my mind as artificial means—machines or mills are hard to get hold of. The thought was so funny I could not keep it back so I gave vent to it. We all had much hearty laughing. Poor soldiers I love for them to have what happy cheerful hours they can while with us.

Sept. 20, 1864

Have had this morning for breakfast 4 soldiers belonging to 10th company. J. H. Moore of Heard Co. Ga, J. R. Russell of Chambers Ala, Tom Linson of Chambers Co. Ala, J. M. Jones of Chambers Co. Ala. This has been a day of excitement. Soldiers passing and repassing. C. B. McKnight of Chambers Co. Ala, came to get bread baked. Lizzie having agreed to bake for Mr. Taylors mess while he remained. I felt she could not do it. Mary Martin being here Liz got her to do it.

E. Ruth came quite early this morning for me to go with her to camp to see about two small beeves the soldiers had killed. I went with her and we were directed to Capt. Holt's headquarters. Found him a gentleman of very pleasant address. Spoke very kindly indeed to E. in regard to her beeves and told her it was with much regret he

41. This was possibly George W. A. Brantley, who enlisted in the Second Battalion, Company D, Fifth Georgia Cavalry, but was reportedly discharged on August 9, 1862, by order by the Confederate States District Court. However, because Eliza mentions him just after referring to several soldiers serving in Colonel Robert H. Anderson's Fifth Georgia Calvary Regiment—a unit into which the Second Battalion had been incorporated in 1863—it is possible that George Brantley either returned to service or in fact never left it.

had been put to the necessity of killing her stock but they came here as strangers without rations. The men were worn down and very hungry and that they were compelled to have something to eat. He has suffered more severely for something to eat on this raid than he had ever done at any time in the war. I asked him if he had any flour and he replied he had not. I then gave him an invitation to dinner if he could leave. He spoke of the fall of Atlanta. He felt it could not be occupied a great while as he felt it was untenable. When they left the women and children were hunting places of security, that it was not safe for any one to be going around. This to me was rather cheering as he made me feel it was to strongly fortified for Yankee ingenuity to manage but with their accustomed rage and malignity they have made it crumble beneath the ball, shell and shot.

Eliza and I returned home from camp taking the hide of her beef to the farm. Here we tarried until I felt it was growing late and began to feel anxious to get back. Soldiers coming and going all the while. While there a young soldier came for a pair of pants which they had made. I had Ike's woolen gloves with me and he was much struck with them. He asked me to look at them, took one and tried it on said he would love so much to get a pair of that kind. E. Ruth told him of Mrs. Hyter. He said he had a pair but they were too small. He drew them from his saddle pockets, had rolled up in them an ink stand and remarked "my mother put this up for me when I was leaving." The manner and voice when he said my mother impressed me so pleasantly.

We came on home and found Mr. Taylor, Mr. Knight and Stevenson; had not been long here. When Capt. came bringing with him Dr. Beard of m[iddle] Ten[nessee] I was glad for them to come and in a short time my highly esteemed young friend George Brantley came. He looked so greatly improved from yesterday. He had on his boots. We soon had dinner; they seemed to enjoy it much. Capt. and Dr. did not tarry long after dinner. An order had been sent after the Captain left for the regiment encamped on Mr. Netherlands to move — they were the fifth and tenth Confederate. They passed on with Mr. B. T. and S. remaining to get some clothes which we had washed and were mending. While they were here Mr. Brantley was telling me of Gen. Walker. He had an escort composed of some of the sons of the best families around Macon. That he had left his home the last time to go on this escort feeling he would have a place where he could not be exposed and have comparatively speaking an easy time but in this he was disappointed. They had been assigned to the tenth infantry and been in active service ever since the death of Gen. W. He spoke of the undaunted bravery and great wickedness of Gen. Walker. I asked him if he was an intemperate man and he replied he was. I felt this accounted for the reckless bravery with which he seemed to rush to the jaws of death. He told me that just before he went into his last fight he gave utterance to a roll of oaths which made the hair of his men almost stand on end and that just as he entered on that field from whence he was never to return alive he swore one of the most terribly wicked of his life. The closing part of which was as sure as my soul will go to h-ll. The first part I cannot remember but O how horrible was the last. In a few moments or hours from that his frail bark was launched on the great ocean of eternity.

Mr. Taylor recited another instance when God had given up the bold blasphemer. That of a man whose brother was killed by his side. For a moment or two after his brother was killed he seemed to be overpowered with grief but the demon of darkness and revenge seemed all at once to take their place in his heart. He rose from his grief posture and with one oath after another declared he would avenge for his brother. He commenced loading and firing; had fired 3 shots when a ball struck him just about the same place in the head that his brother had been struck, and sent him unprepared into Eternity. O these are instances where God seems to have given up the bold blasphemer to the punishment which he in his command had said should come upon them. He would not hold him guiltless that taketh his name in vain. How can a soldier swear has been a question which has often arisen in my mind.

After we had the clothes of our men made ready; they took their leave of us with feelings of deep regret. May these passing friends be cared for and shielded from danger by that God who is able and willing to save all who will call upon him. After all left we gathered together to talk over the scenes which had passed. Bug had made a purchase from Mr. Taylor of a nice ladies tweed cloak and swapped a pair of pants and a shirt. Mr. T. told us he had taken it from a home in middle Tenn. where a Southern man had to leave and his premises had been occupied by a Yankee Capt. and his lady not far from Murfreesboro. They came on them just at supper time. They left a smoking supper on the table and broke for town. The house was soon rifled. The lady had so much nice wearing apparel. He gave Liz one of her nice hooked embroidery.

Sept 21, 1864

Soldiers all gone. What a contrast between today and yesterday. We were cheered by the coming home of my dear husband and brother Hiram. We are always so glad to see the dear loved ones come home — they determined to spend the night with us. Mr. Cothran and Mabin have come from camp. Mr. C. seems to be so glad to get back here. He spent a long time in this neighborhood in 62 when Col. Starnes regiment was here. This morning Mr. Rogers and Mr. Cowan came; they had been riding all night before to bring the dispatches to Gen. Williams.

Sept. 22, 1864

Last night we had Rogers, Cowan, Wilber, Carter, Cothran and Mabin. Mr. Cothran and Mr. Mabin went up to Mr. Sensabaughs for breakfast. The other gents left soon after breakfast. Cothran and Mabin came back and set an hour or so and then bid us goodbye. We were so hopeful that Gen. Williams[42] would be induced to do

---

42. Brigadier General John S. Williams commanded the First Tennessee Cavalry Brigade, and his troops were involved in the successful defense of the saltworks at the Battle of Saltville, Virginia, in October 1864.

something for us but we hear he has moved on up. I do think he ought to have sent his men as Gen. Vaughn desired him to do. We feel had he done it they could have captured the Yanks at the Gap. My husband tarried at home last night but could not rest pleasantly as he felt uneasy.

Sept 23, 1864

My husband tarried until after dinner yesterday when he and brother H. set out. They went to Mr. Millers and staid all night there. What days of trial we are now having; our dear friends cannot come home and have one pleasant hour. We feel assured days of this kind will not always continue.

My husband at home today for dinner. Mr. Louderback came with him. Poor old man he is suffering sorely. He has heard that the Yanks brought wagons to his house and have taken off all his Negroes some 25 in number. He says he will have remuneration, if no other way he will take it from Union men for they are the cause of our troubles.

Sept 25, 1864

Beautiful lovely morning; nature wearing the calm lovely serene look of autumns delightful days. This morning the coolest we have had but no frost. I hope we may have no frosts to nip for sometime. Beans, much corn and pumpkins are still many and much so green. Peace and quiet is still our portion. We know there is war in our land. Our dear, our loved families are broken up; corroding care and anxiety for our dear loved ones who are daily yea hourly exposed to the uncertainty of life which war brings tells our saddened hearts. We are under the galling yoke. We do not have many of the luxuries of life we once felt so essential to happiness. Neither do we have the martialed forces, the bloody battlefield, the agonizing cry of the dying, the plaintive moan of the wounded to tell us you are living amid the scenes of war.

We have now a sore trial upon us that of being deprived of church privileges. Our dear minister is still absent. Since he heard of Mr. Eagletons ill treatment he feels afraid to come back and we do not wish for him to come if such as that awaits him. Mr. E. was at New Market, was taken and ordered to lay off his coat then his shirt which he refused. They then tore his shirt from him and two began whipping him. He was struck several times over the head.

Mr. Damewood left this morning to go to town and if possible to make his way across the knobs to know what is going on. Fannie and Dick have returned from Sabbath School bringing news very unpleasant that Gen. Early has been defeated in the valley of Virginia. I had hoped there might be news more particular.

I went over to Hirams. George was setting on the log by the block, I set down and had a few words of conversation but he knew nothing particular. Old Mr. Epps had brought the news from Bristol. Early defeated by two army corps of Grants. Gen. Rhodes was killed and Fitzhugh Lee wounded. I do trust that our Father is not going to give us into the hands of our enemies.

September 26, 1864
Last night Gus and Caroline (who had been to Mr. Wattersons to see Carries sister) came home saying they understood Gen. Williams men were moving down but of this we know nothing certainly.

September 27, 1964
The news of Gus and Caroline all a mistake, understand Col. McCallisters battalion of about 100 men is on the roads above. Brother Hiram came home Monday between 11 & 12. Not long after dinner Richard and Samuel Powel came. Liz gave them their dinner. We then sent Fannie down for Mec. She and E. Ruth came out. Ruth went back. We feel so glad to have our dear and loved friends come home although we have much anxiety about them yet we love to have them to come home. Mr. Damewood is still here, has gone to work. He and Ahab made a furnace yesterday for boiling our molasses.

Last night brother Hiram, Sarah and Lucy came over. Sarah gave us some good music. They did not stay very long. Hiram thought he would wish to stay at home; but he found it was not pleasant and set up the greater part of the night. Richard awoke about 1, could not sleep got up dressed had Liz to awake Sam Powel. They left the house and went to Ahab's cabin. I felt greater uneasiness about them after they left the house than I did before lest they should take cold. Richard has determined he will not spend another night at home unless he know more of the where-abouts of our troops. This morning Miss. Mary Mc and Mrs. Rogan came out. Mrs. Rogan was anxious to see Mr. Rogan and wanted Richard to see him and tell him to send her word and she would go and see him did not wish him to come home unless it was perfectly safe. They did not stay long. While they were here E. Ruth and Annis came, they were on their way to Mrs. Armstrongs. Ruth had letters from the loved ones in Georgia amongst the number was one from dear Fain Powel in which he pleaded so earnestly for the prayers of Christians in his behalf.

September 28, 1864

We have lain down and slept sweetly. Mr. Damewood still with us and has been coughing. The news of this day has made us feel rather sad. We learn our troops have fallen back to Greeneville and do hope that it is only for a short time. I sent Dick to mill today to get me some meal. He returned bringing with him one of our poor wounded soldiers. Mr. Mason who belonged to Co. K 19th Tenn. regiment.[43] He was wounded the 22nd; the same day that Col. F. M. Walker fell. Mr. Mason is wounded in the hip; on crutch walks pretty well. I hope he may soon be well. Seems so anxious to get home but I feel afraid for him to go. He has concluded to wait a day or two. Mr. Damewood has gone to see about his clothes and family. I hope the bushmen may not overhaul him.

43. Lieutenant John Mason had previously been wounded in the thigh at the Battle of Chickamauga. He was the color bearer of the regiment for two years and was promoted from sergeant to lieutenant in 1864. According to Worsham (*The Old Nineteenth Tennessee*, 71, 129) Mason displayed remarkable bravery at both the Battle of Murfreesboro and the Battle of Atlanta, where he was wounded.

September 29, 1864

What will this day bring forth? We have slept in peace. The Lord has been our guard. Mr. Mason seems to be more unwell this morning and feels apprehensive; his wound is not doing so well. I fear he has been going on it too much and have sent for the Doctor. Poor soldiers how my heart feels for them. Old Ahab has gone to get some red oak bark. I will boil it and make a strong ooze so that the wound can be bathed in it. Have sent Caroline to town for the Doctor and E. Ruth's kettle as Liz plans to make more jam today. Fannie and Buena are going up to Mr. Carmacks. Lucy and Eliza H. went up yesterday. This day the news is that Gen. Vaughn has fallen back to Bristol. The Yanks are attempting to come through at Pound Gap. Generals Williams and Giltner are going to meet them. Major Reynolds has been at Sarah's today and talks of leaving this evening. We feel so sad to think of being given up but still have hope that God our father who is ever watching over us will save and shield us from our enemies.

Cousin Joe has been here and directed me to poultice with flaxseed Mr. Mason's wound. He says he is fearful it is going to slough again. Tonight Fannie and Buena have returned. They bring news that the copperheads of the North are opening the prisons, arming our men and turning them loose. That they have opened the prison of Camp Chase. They say that our men have had another fight in Georgia whipping Sherman and retaken Atlanta.[44]

September 30, 1864

Mr. Mason rested tolerably well last night. His wound seems to be very tender. We had him moved upstairs this morning. I do hope he may do well. I have washed and dressed his wound nicely and it is very tender. Sarah has come this morning and brought much good news. The news which F & B brought in regard to the releasing of our prisoners by the copperheads is corroborated. That they had been released at Camp Chase and were marching toward Camp

44. None of these rumors were correct.

Denison.[45] The news was that Gen. Hood had given Sherman a terrible whipping and that Early had turned on Grant repulsing him with heavy loss to Grant that Gen. Vaughn had moved up on the railroad as a feint to draw out the Feds from the Gap had torn up a mile or two of the track and cut the wires. This to me sounds strangely yet they often do much to deceive. Gen. Williams was going to cooperate with Gen. V. and they felt sure of success. We are now elated. What will be the news by this time tomorrow? All is change here nothing certain, nothing stable on our little star.

## October 1, 1864

Last evening just as we were done supper one of the children came to me saying: Mama the stable is lined with Rebs. I looked out and to my great surprise saw some 10 or 12 seated and lying on the ground. I left all and went to see who it could be. It was our faithful Capt. Owens and his men.[46] They had set out of foot to meet up I suppose with bushmen. I asked no questions as to where or what was their business feeling it is best for women to know but little unless they can be of service. They waited about half of 3/4 of an hour for Alfred Owens to come. We gave them some bread and apple butter. To Captain J. Charles we gave milk, bread and butter. Mr. Mason sent for Capt and seemed so glad to see him. After which they soon left, had been gone but a short time when Alf came. He left his horse and followed on but could not meet up with them. He came back we supposed about 12 we all being wrapped in sleep.

45. This rumor was untrue. Camp Chase held as many as ten thousand Confederate prisoners by the end of the war. Conditions there were overcrowded and unsanitary, and the food was poor. (See "Camp Chase," in *Historical Times Illustrated Encyclopedia of the Civil War*, ed. Patricia L. Faust [New York: Harper & Row, 1986], 109–10.) Camp Denison was another Union prison, and like Camp Chase it was located in Ohio.

In *Battle Cry of Freedom* (765), James McPherson notes that the copperheads, working through the Sons of Liberty organization, had planned an attack in August on another prison, Camp Douglas in Chicago, in order to free the prisoners. This attack was to take place during the Democratic political convention, but the plot collapsed.

46. Captain Bill Owens was the leader of a group of Confederate guerrillas, not a regular army unit. His title was honorary, as it does not appear in official Confederate records.

October 2, 1864

This has been so far a quiet Sabbath. Mr. Mason quite comfortable. His wound seems to be doing much better than I thought it would when I first looked at it. Lizzie, Fannie, Ellie and Dick went to church today at Ebbing Spring. I have spent the day reading to Nannie who seems to be much interested—read to her the account of the Crucifixion of Christ as recorded by St. John. After I was through reading for Nan I asked my little black ones their questions. How anxious I feel for their salvation. I do trust the Lord will work for the moral good of Hams abject sons. Truly they are the greatest sufferers in this terrible war.

October 4, 1864

We are still in circumstances of mercy. The Lord has kept watch while we slept. Mr. Mason improving very fast. His wound is doing well but has not as yet sloughed as anticipated, is running a great deal. The place which looked so dark is almost a natural color.

October 5, 1864

Still in much suspense and trouble. News so calculated one hour to elevate, the next to depress. As Dick went to mill yesterday he met up with Capt. Owens who told him that Gen. V. had a fight with the Yanks at Carter's Station. He had captured several and killed some. That all was well, that he (Owens) had a fight with some bushmen on Saturday night killing 3 and was then on his way down the country.

We were enjoying this little oasis of news when E. Ruth, Mollie Ruth and Buena came out after dinner telling us that Bristol was evacuated. Mr. Todd was just from there and Gen. Burbridge with 16th regiment mounted was coming in at Pound Gap and that Gen. V. had been ordered up immediately. My heart just sank within me, when to my great relief they said we have some good news which was that a courier had been captured bearing a dispatch from Gen. Schofield to Gen. Burbridge. Gen. Schofield having had one from Gen. Sherman ordering the troops to come immediately to his aid. Furthermore Gen. Forrest was in middle Tennessee doing there much harm and that his army was in great peril. The troops may be called to retreat at any moment and we know not which way they may go but we do know desolation will mark every footstep. Our Southern friends are those doomed to the greatest suffering. We have heard through the girls that Col. Heiskell has been removed from Knoxville, it is thought to Nashville.

My dear daughters Liz and Ellie have gone today to see about getting some leather. My dear daughter E & F so kind to me. I have felt so feeble for some weeks past and can do no hard labor. They have taken all the care of the house off of my hands. I sew and knit. Mollie Ruth is with me now talking to Mr. Mason. She is one of the dear ones to me.

Oct. 6, 1864

Liz and Ellie returned late yesterday evening bringing a letter addressed to W. Kyle from my dear Nick dated Aug. 15. I felt so glad to hear from him. I feel sorry he is compelled to ask so many favors from those who are not with us in feeling. I trust all will work out well.

Liz brought us news that the cry was raised in town the Yanks are coming. Mr. Hicky was here and Mrs. Speck told him he had better get away and he did so coming out by Sarahs. We felt no uneasiness, went to bed and slept so sweetly. This morning we heard the Yanks had been in town last night. Fannie sent to Lucy for a note which she received stating that there were some 15 or 20 who had passed through town bearing dispatches to the Gap. They went to Mr. Netherlands as stated by Jordan and entered the house with pistol in hand. They asked Mrs. Heiskell if there were any Rebs there and she replied none but her. They then told her they had fired on Owen's scouts killing 3 of his men but this we find is not true. They got Capt. horse which he had left at Mr. Annis. Dick saw the Capt. himself, he told him of the loss of his horse but said nothing of men and I know he would have mentioned it had he lost any.

Sarah came by just now on her way to Mr. Russells to see if she can get his machine to grind for them. She told us they had heard today that Grant's army was deserting in great numbers and that Gen. Lee had given order for them to be passed through our lines so that they might the more easily make their way home. These are the items of news we have this day.[47] I have felt such deep concern this day about Col Heiskell. Liz understood yesterday he had been removed from Knoxville and that Mr. Netherland could not find where he had been sent. He had been sent off, as I understand, secretly.

October 7, 1864

This has been another day of joy to us although this morning the news was depressing. We had it that 12,000 Yanks were coming down the road. We felt if that force was coming our men had been driven back. I had dressed my soldiers wound and was seated quietly enjoying a conversation with dear Mollie when I raised my eyes and who should I see but my dear boy Ike. I was soon at the gate. He was quite hungry. Mollie and I soon had him some bread, butter and preserves. He told us Major Day and Capt. Watkins had gone on to town and that another portion of our men were pursuing the Yanks towards the river. This was pleasant news to us. We knew they were running and therefore would do us no harm.

This evening Mitchell, Rogers and Ike came telling us of the work of the day. They were not successful as we had anticipated on account of our own men failing to be at the right place. Too many came to town. The Yanks all escaped capturing some four or five of our boys. Rogers came very near being captured. We feel thankful none were killed as we know of. The boys said Mr. Cluck was missing. I hope he may yet come up.

47. There was no truth to this rumor.

October 8, 1864

This morning not long after I was up I went out to get something for my fire when who should come riding up but our dear young soldiers of the new issue as they are called: Powell, Ed & Billy. They had lain down on the roadside above Mr. Russells somewhere feeling they could not come through the picket while daylight.

October 9, 1864

Satan has been pursuing me all this morning with anxious cares concerning my worldly business. I have felt so badly. O Lord help me to throw off this never ceasing anxiety. All is still quiet. Liz and I are seated in my room by a comfortable fire. Quite cool today, had a little frost last night. Mr. Mason still doing well. We had this morning for breakfast our three boys: Ed, Billy and Powell, Mr. Hicks and Pinkerton who came in yesterday and staid all night with the boys. Mr. Pinkerton is an Irishman who came to the United States in 48. I asked him many questions about the auld country. What their houses are built of? Mostly he told me brick and rock but the rock work was different from here. His home was in or near Belfast. He told me of the great processions which the Protestants have. The 12th of July is their great day and that often at such times the Romanists prey upon them, but that they give them fight and whip them back. Poor down trodden Ireland, when will the time come that the foot of the oppressor shall be removed. What a people they might have been had it not been for Romanism. For them I have ever had such a deep sympathy.

About 12 today my loved husband was again permitted to hear the kindly welcome to home and we to hear and know that he was again permitted to be with us. Not long after we had eaten dinner other loved ones were permitted to come. Brother Hiram, Tom, Powell and Ike. We felt so glad to see them. Poor Tom was chilling; is now lying on a pallet in the corner suffering with his head. How sad I feel when I look at our poor boys returning worn down and constitutions all shattered. Never again, I fear, will they be the stout robust sons we once looked on.

By my dear husband is confirmation of the news of the death of our dear, dear Bob[48] and in Sallie's letter she mentions that he died on the 17th of Sept. in Forsyth, Georgia. Tom has just been giving me an account of the terrible condition of our dear, dear Sam Lynn. How much more desirable is death where hope is given. But I do trust the Lord is leading him and he may yet be one of his loved followers.

Girls return from Dunkard meeting—Eliza and Sallie Hanson, Florence Alexander, Buena and Fannie. Not long after they came Colonel Heiskell came but before him E. Ruth and Stan came. Col. told us he had it from a reliable Union source that Sizemore would be in town and desired that Sam Powel and Capt. Sevier should be sent for. We started Dick and Pete after them. Sarah came over and took Buena and E. Hasson home with her. We got all fixed for the night.

Ike, Ed, Billy, Sam P. and Powell went to the stable. All were almost wrapped in the sound slumber for the night when a rap at the door broke in upon us. Richard roused from his drowsy sleep and asked without a moments thought who is there. When a voice replied me. Who are you was the next question. Bob Powel was the reply and with him Hugh Heiskell. What do you want? Let me in and I will tell you. When in he told us that Sizemore with nine men had been in town and had searched for Sam at Mrs. Walkers and for Col. H. This was quite enough, a scene of disquiet ensued. The boys were sent on to Jake Williams to know what force was there and for arms. Mollie, Ruth and Liz set out for their Uncle Hiram

48. This is probably Robert J. Rhea of Sullivan County, who was born on December 18, 1837. A son of Robert P. Rhea, he was one of Eliza's first cousins, and he died of wounds from the battle of Atlanta on July 22. (See Edward F. Foley, *The Descendants of Matthew "The Rebel" Rhea of Scotland and Ireland* [Bowie, Md.: Heritage Books, 2000], p 131.) Robert Rhea was in Company G of the Nineteenth Tennessee. (See Worsham, *Old Nineteenth Tennessee*, 130.) Sam Lynn was another of Eliza's first cousins; he survived the war, married, and had a family before his death in 1884.

and George. They were soon all here when a regular military business was instituted. Pickets were put out, a countersign given which was Rogersville. Horses were prepared and Col. H. was so anxious to get to town. He felt could they only capture the disturber of our peace it would be so nice. But the plan to remain and give them as good a fight as they could here was agreed on. The little boys soon returned and with them Jake and Mr. Cockram. They all were on the alert and should Mr. Sizemore come then they would have been some work done. Sam not being well lay down on my bed. E. Ruth lay down there too. I crept in with Lil in the bedroom. Mollie and Liz after sometime went upstairs. I look upon the feat of Bob & Hugh as brave and noble. Can a people be conquered where there is such an indomitable will in our little boys. They left town after Sizemore went out and walked out here. We went to bed soon after they came back from Mr. Millers.

October 10, 1864.
Arose early this morning and the boys were lying in my room taking their rest. Mr. Cockram and Jake got up pretty soon and left for home. After breakfast the girls left for town. Col. H., Sam Powel, Tom, Ed, Ike and Powell here for dinner. In the evening the boys went off and fed somewhere but returned before supper having an addition to their number of several: Sam Spears, Pony Chesnut, Alf Owens and Lt. Webster. After supper Alf and Lt. Webster went to town to reconnoiter leaving their horses. When they left the boys thought they would go to the hollow but after some talk we concluded it was best for us to send for Mary Martin and Amy and they take possession of her house. Richard and Tom staid in the house, the other boys would come in and warm and then stand picket an hour or some minutes I think assigned to each.

October 28, 1864
We are once again in great trouble. Our friends are again compelled to leave their homes. Our soldiers were occupying the

country as far down as Bean Station on this road and to Morristown on the other. I fear we were feeling too secure. We were losing sight of the omnipotent arm of Jehovah and trusting in man. What a lesson this disaster has taught us.

This evening news came that Gen. Vaughn was fighting; that both he and Major Day's battalion had been ordered about daylight to Morristown. Fannie and Dick went to town. Dick soon returned bringing the sad intelligence of the defeat of Vaughn. His artillery captured and half of his wagons; that Major Day had been ordered to Kingsport. Richard was not disposed to give much belief to the account supposing the men who brought the information were stragglers who had left before they knew anything of the result. We rested quietly on this until after supper. Lt. Duvall and Kyle McC with us. K. came out this morning and after dinner took a horse and went up to Mr. Carmacks. After supper brother Hiram came over to see what they intended to do. Just as we were through supper, as I stepped on the porch I heard Sam Powels voice. I had just remarked to Liz that I thought Carrick would come out here. I asked Sam who was with him. No one he replied. He came in and confirmed the news by Dick excepting the capturing of the wagons. I must confess a gloom came over me, but my trust is in my God.

He also told us that Sizemore and clan were reported in the neighborhood. After some consultation it was agreed on that Kyle should go to town, get his things, return and they would go up the road tonight. We felt there might be a risk in it and persuaded him not go but for them to leave immediately. Just as they were ready brother Hiram came over saying Joseph Huffmaster and two other soldiers were at his house and felt they might make a stand there. But after some consultation concluded it was best for them to leave. About 8 o'clock they left us. We felt so sorry to say goodbye. May we be enabled to plead fervently in the name of Jesus that we may not be long separated and that we may not be given into the hands of our enemies.

I had closed my book for the night and turned around to take a smoke.[49] Liz my dear companion in these hours of trial was fixing for bed when footsteps on the porch raised us from our enjoyment. The first thought I had was that it was some or our boys but in an instant almost my heart began to beat fast from the thought it might be bushmen. A rap at the door with who is there from Liz in a determined voice brought the reply: Wiley Merrimon and Mr. Hamlin. She soon opened the door and they came in and set awhile.

## October 29, 1864

Last night after Mr. H & W went to their rest and Liz and I were preparing for bed footsteps on the porch again made us feel someone else is coming. In a moment the well known voice of my young soldier boy made us start with a feeling of gladness. The door was soon opened and in walked the dear young soldier boys Powell and Ed with Mr. Haly. We were so rejoiced to see them; had expressed our anxiety to each other about them. They were sent with a verbal dispatch to Major Day. They had much to tell us of the disastrous scenes of the day to Gen. Vaughn's troops. The pickets began firing at daylight and about 9 o'clock the Yanks made a charge breaking the ranks of our men and putting them to flight. Some of the men it is said acted very bravely. We lost, they think, about 150 mostly prisoners but amongst the killed is numbered the noble and gallant Eddie Gammon. We do feel so sad as we think of his early and untimely fall. Another home broken up.

They think Col Lillard[50] is also killed. He too was a gallant officer. We mourn bravery. The fight commenced beyond Morristown, fought through the town and were driven back to Russellville

49. While Eliza was much opposed to the use of alcohol, she did not object to the use of tobacco. Her diaries contain innumerable references to the purchase of snuff and chewing tobacco.

50. Colonel Newton J. Lillard, who commanded the Third Tennessee Infantry (C.S.A.), was not killed. He was pardoned by President Andrew Johnson on January 6, 1866, and lived into the next century, when he replied to the Tennessee Civil War Veterans questionnaire.

where the infantry were. As I understand Major Day came to their assistance. They were not pursued much beyond this point. We were made to feel quite anxious about Ike. He was sent alone to Bean Station to tell pickets to come to B.S. and there await further orders. He did what he was commanded to do but the waiting was not pleasant to him so he left about 12 at night and started in the direction of home. He came up about 12 today. His mule had fallen with him and lamed him considerably. Have for dinner all of our dear boys and feel so thankful.

October 30, 1864
Another beautiful morning. The boys returned quite early this morning having lodged last night in Mr. Sensabaugh's barn. Have had breakfast over. All have left for town. By Gus we hear that some persons passed on the Carters Valley road last night. There were 7 horses belonging to soldiers taken from J. C. Millers last night. Buena and Fannie have gone to town. We feel so anxious. Mr. Hamlin passed by this morning on his way home. He asked me if I knew what forces had passed up last night. I told him I did not. He then told me a regiment had passed Mr. M before they went to bed. The boys went to town ascertained that they were rebel soldiers.

October 31, 1864
Richard, Sam Powel, Mr. Mason and Mr. Stiffle left Saturday evening. Richard intending to go as far as Mrs. Lyons. The boys left yesterday after dinner and went up country. Saturday evening after Richard left (telling me to not let the boys stay here that night) Will Watterson came. He was anxious for them to go to town and so they all fixed up to escort him down. Kyle, Ed, Mr. Haly, Ike and Powell. They returned almost dark bringing Jake Tilson with them. I was glad to see Jake had heard he had left us and gone to Knoxville. But I think he had no notion of that. Mr. Haly sang several pieces for us. Saturday night they left and lodged in Mr. Sensabaugh's barn.

I set out this morning to see about shoemaking. Went to Mr. Amis to see about sole leather; took my dinner there. They were so kind to me. While at Mr. A. Powell came along. I hailed him and he came to the house. Told me his papa had sent him down for Jim to take a horse for Sallie. I left very soon coming by Mr. Yeonas to get him to make the shoes.

Came on home and found Lou, Kyle, Capt. Mc Camie and J. Tilson here. They left not long after I came going to Mr. Rileys. Powell spoke of going but gave out. Got Liz to go to town and get the news and see where A. Owens was. Not long after she left E. Ruth came on her way up the country. We told her to get down and stay all night. Powell remained until after dark when he took a notion to spend the night at Mr. Merrimons. As he started off he heard the sound of many horses. In a short time Pete Powel came in great haste from his aunt Sarahs to inform him that there were quite a number of men coming out from the Gap of the Knob. I went to the stable in search and found him mounted on Julianna. At the gate told him to stay until I could go and find out who they were. Pete and I went. Our own men and Dr. Mitchell with them who said they were absentees mostly from Longstreet's command.

Nov. 1, 1864

Still in peace but was troubled about what to do about sending Jim.[51] Concluded at length to not let him go but to let Fannie take the horse. She and E. Ruth set out about 8. Just before they left A. Owens came telling us there was no Yank at the Gap unless they came yesterday. Bug and Buena came out today. The girls tell us that they heard the 13th Tenn. regiment [U.S.A.] and one other are to be sent this side of the river but I do trust our Heavenly Father will shield us from so great a calamity.

---

51. Jim was an eleven-year-old slave belonging to Eliza. His father was Gus.

November 2, 1864

Nothing has been heard this day in regard to our troops. We know nothing of their position. The day is of comparative peace but not without anxious thoughts for the loved ones far away. My spirit yearns for a meeting with my prisoner boys and my soldier boy in Virginia. I was thinking of him last night. The children were making some candy. Liz called it taffy. The rich story they had on Sam occurred to me and I could not help longing. This has been a gloomy day raining most of the time. I have been busily engaged making preserves and preparing apples for jam. Liz has been spinning. Jennie McC quite unwell from jaundice and looks very yellow. Sent Gus and Dick for a beef to Mr. Kleppers. They brought two but one was for Mr. Sevier. Nannie helped Carrie to iron. I find my dear little children can be so much help when they try.

November 4, 1864

No enemy as yet permitted to come near. Although day after day we hear report after report of their approach yet they come not. Have been engaged killing beef. Ike at Mrs. Seviers came out intending to drive theirs to town but concluded to kill. Sent Johnny back for the wagon. He assisted us and the boys helped him. He cut mine so nicely. I felt glad of his help. Old Ahab's[52] shoulder being so weak he was not able to lift.

As we were eating dinner our boys came up, Kyle, Ed and Powell. They had eaten at Mr. Merrimons but soldierlike took another bait at our home. They then went to town and brought out Eliza & Sallie Hasson, Buena & Lucy, Capts. Kyle and McCamie and A. Owens. Jennie McC. went home in the wagon. Nannie going with her and Liz riding Mr. Merrimons nag. She and H returned with the others. A short time after dark, Ed and Alf came over. Alf asking if any one had been here. We replied no. They then harnessed up and were off. About 12 o'clock I was aroused by Powell at the door. He

52. A slave belonging to Eliza, Ahab was approximately sixty-four at this time.

told me to open. I got up and let him in. He had with him Capts. Kyle and Mc Camie, Ed and Kyle. They had been to town, all quiet.

I started Dick over the river this morning after Mr. Wright's shoemaking tools. Bug went with him have some fears about them. Mr. W. has promised tools to any one who will go after them for the making of our shoes. As I look on the little sore feet about me I felt I would be willing to risk a good deal to accomplish this.

November 5, 1864

Got up late. Awoke before daylight; the wind was whistling around our dwelling. My ill clad family filled me with care and trouble. My prayer went up to my Father to show us mercy and temper the winds and cold of this winter so that we may be able to bear it. O for our dear soldiers how earnestly I do feel as many of them are poorly clad.

We gave breakfast to the boys — Lon & Powell then went after the girls. Eliza, Sallie, Buena, & Lucy came and after enjoying themselves for a while the boys began to say goodbye. Ed first going to get his boots mended. Kyle and Jake Tilson who came this morning went to Mr. Carmacks. We prepared Powell, Lon and Capt. M. a little dinner then Powell bade us goodbye expecting to go to his command. He and Lon went up Carters Valley and Capt. M. across to the main road thinking he would make his way to Bristol.

He told me this morning of his capture. He Lon and Jake went down the road on Tuesday evening to Mr. Blevins. Sizemore and some of his men were on the road and saw them pass. They followed (or at least some while others were sent after the rest of the men) to ascertain where they were going. Not a great while as I understand after they got there they determined to leave lest something should come upon them, learning from some of the black ones that Sizemore had crossed the river to this side that evening. Lon and Jake were out of the house just thinking on leaving. Capt. M was still inside when they were suddenly made aware of the presence of the Sizemore band. They had left their horses some distance from the house and came through the graveyard and down back of the houses. Quite a scene ensued. Lon and Jake made their escape with Jake losing his horse, saddle, bridle, blanket and clothes. Lon lost his fine shawl. Capt. M. was captured but succeeded in giving his papers and pistol to Ance. He was taken first to Mr. Marions which seems to be the rendezvous of Sizemore and his clan. From there he was taken across the river to Mr. Bradshaw's house where he made his escape. He lost all excepting what he had on. He had a fine over-coat which he left hanging in the house. He seems to regret this loss more than any other.

This is the first day we have done without dinner. After we had gotten almost ready to eat A. Owens with 7 or 8 men came. The evening was dark and dreary with rain falling at intervals the greater part of the day. I do not know what the boys intended doing but think their notion was to harass Sizemore.

November 6, 1864

This is the 12th Sabbath since we were permitted to go to the house of God and hear the pleasant and cheering words of our dear and loved minister. His last sermon was the 14th of August. O how appropriate was his last text for the days unseen then by us but which have since been upon us. How little he knew of what was before us. That the dawn of another Sabbath morning would be witness to high Heaven of such scenes of horror and wickedness.

This day one year was a day of great deliverance. We had been under the juggernaut of despotism for more than a month. Our homes had been one continued scene of anxiety and care to keep what we felt would be so necessary for the life of those whom God had given to us. Many, many were the indignities and insults which many wives, mothers and daughters were called to endure in this short period. They were cussed, their houses searched, long treasured relics taken, the last mouthful of provision almost swept from them. Order to cook for such a number which if denied would only be made more rigid by redoubling or trebling the number. Husbands cursed and abused by the very offscouring of humanity. The sacred hours of the holy

Sabbath broken in upon by the intrusion of ruffian looking men (some of them so ragged as to be not fit to appear in the presence of men much less women) demanding something to eat. An aged mother of Israel cursed by some. Our houses entered at night under a pretext to search for rebels while it was to steal something to eat and above every other insult was that of a portion of Satan's emissaries going to the house of God to entrap if possible our dear minister. But God was with him and his words were "wise as serpents and harmless as doves" so that they were not able to carry back any evil report.

On the 6th of November 1863, God our Father sent us a noble band of men (shall I say noble, I fear that is wrong for amongst the number were those who feared not to break God's commandments by taking his name in vain and taking what did not belong to them) but they appeared so to us that bright and lovely morning. With what joy and enthusiasm did we look upon them as they moved forward. Since that time we have never had a locality of Yankees for more than 24 or 30 hours. I do trust God will never let us have again the tread of one Yankee upon our premises. We have had them in sight since then 3 or 4 times, once in our house but I have never been treated insolently but by a few at any time.

We have heard today that Gen. Bushrod Johnson's brigade is at Jonesboro but of the truth of this we know nothing. After hearing this Mollie Ruth and Bug came. They told us that the Yanks attempted a flank movement on Gen. Vaughn that he had fallen back to Carter's Station, that they were expecting them in town today and that a force had gone up between them and the mountain on the other side.

November 7, 1864

As breakfast was almost ready this morning Amy came over saying Amy's baby is dead. I felt shocked for I did not know that she had been sick. I could not help exclaiming. I feel thankful the Lord has taken it in mercy to himself. Poor little thing I have often thought of it. What a dark prospect seemed before her. A mother lost to virtue. Not smart, no thought of management or industry but above all one incapable of training for Eternity. God is so kind in removing it to himself.

Last night was one of peaceful quiet. I awoke quite early and found it was raining. I felt troubled for I had hoped we should be able to get our wheat finished sowing. Sent Dick for Mr. Wright this morning but he could not come until Wednesday. Dick tells us 51 Yanks passed down the road last night. They will I have no doubt make a great effort to hold the country until after the election which takes place tomorrow.

## November 8, 1864

O God may this be the day of our deliverance as I understand it is the day of the U. S. Presidential election. This morning I took my smaller children and Gus with a few precious flowers and went over to Amys, looked at her babe and put the flowers around her. I spoke to the poor wretched mother on the great importance of being a Christian and told her that God was again calling on her to follow him. Would she bow or would she still continue her sinful course. She must now make a decision. She was much distressed. I let Gus and Ahab take the wagon with Mary, Amy and Awood to the grave. The grave had been dug at Mr. C. Sensabaughs by the side of her mothers.[53] Mr. R. Huffmaster made the coffin and Dick brought it out. Sent him down this morning for some leather he had gotten the day before at Mr. McClures.

Dick brought us back news that the Yanks are falling back and that Gen. Vaughn has been reinforced with 4000 men. General Hood has fallen on Sherman, whipping him and capturing between 4 and 5,000. This is pleasant if true but no news elates me (by rumor) these days. We have been too often deceived[54] yet I trust it may be so. I feel there is good news in store for us.

---

53. This grave was for Amy's baby. The infant was buried next to the grave of Amy's mother, Peggy Martin, who died on October 2, 1863.

54. This was a false rumor.

November 10, 1864

Yesterday Mr. Wright came to make shoes for us. The children were greatly pleased. I sent Dick and Jim today to haul some more tops for his aunt Nancy. Bug came out on the wagon, she brings us no news. What suspense—how trying to us. I have often thought of my dear prisoner boys in the last few days. O that the events which have been transpiring in the North may give our prisoners relief.

November 11, 1864

Ann returned last evening without meeting up with Lon and Capt. M on the way to Mr. Millers. She brings us the news that Major Day had been ordered to Jonesboro. I hope our foes may be driven back and East Tennessee delivered. These hours of trial are difficult. Ann told us that her father and mother had gone to Knoxville.

November 12, 1864

We have expected to hear the sound of cannon this morning as our boys told us yesterday that Gen. Breckenridge was advancing upon them.[55] Gus thinks he heard it but none of our white family have. Bug went home yesterday evening. We have received news this evening that our troops have been repulsed at the Gap. The news it is said is from a Union source. We do not believe yet we cannot help feeling anxious to know a true statement. Our men having of late met with repulses on the railroad.

November 13, 1864

We are still in circumstance of mercy but hear nothing in regard to our troops on the railroad. I feel they are not moving with much rapidity or some of the loved ones would have cheered us with their presence before this. We hear today by some soldiers passing that our troops have been repulsed at the Gap. This is Union rumor

55. This was the so-called Battle of Bulls Gap. On November 12, 1864, General John C. Breckenridge attacked Union troops under General A. C. Gillem, who retreated on November 13. Gillem lost six artillery guns and some 150 prisoners. Johnston, *Blue and Gray from Hawkins County: The Battles,* 47–50.

whether true or not we cannot know but have very little confidence in it. The report says Gen. Breckenridge was repulsed six times.[56]

Sam Powel left today intending to go to the sixty-third regiment and take his place as a soldier. I feel he cannot stand a soldiers life.[57] He will let the world see that he is willing but not able. I do trust the Lord will be his shield and preserver. I feel sorry to say good bye to any of our loved ones but always feel I would rather they would go than be branded in after life with being a coward or not wanting to aid their country in her mighty struggle. I always feel like saying go my son, be faithful to God and your Country. I have ever had but one feeling since this war began. I believed the South was right and that she was struggling not only for civil but religious liberty. Every day but fastens on my mind more deeply this solemn truth. When I look around on our country and see the demoralizing influence which an adherence to Unionism has produced—lost to sense of humanity, holiness or truth.

When I hear of the suffering and wretchedness of our poor slaves and think of the prospect which seems to be before them I often think with what anger and indignation will they look back upon the destroyer of their peace. Under the pretext of giving liberty they have fasted upon them a bondage more cruel, more exacting than Egyptian. Our sin if a sin was not national, theirs is. May the God of Heaven open their eyes and let them see the fearfulness of blind unrestrained fanaticism.

Sam and George Speck were together, George is carrying the mail. Sam brought me a few lines from Richard by mail, Kyle McC came out with them. He brought me a letter which he says he got at Mrs. Rileys from Sam Gammon dated June 13, 1863.

56. The Union rumor was incorrect. The Confederate forces won this battle.

57. The Sixty-third Regiment was stationed in Virginia. Sam had joined the Nineteenth Tennessee Infantry in 1861 as a lieutenant and then joined the Sixty-third Tennessee when it was organized in 1862. He was thrown from a train and seriously injured in the spring of 1863 but returned to active duty on November 18, 1864. Sam was captured at Hatcher's Run, Virginia, on April 2, 1865, and sent to prison, from which he was released in June. Sam lived until 1890.

The first I suppose that he wrote after his imprisonment. Where it has been travelling for a year and 5 months is a mystery. It was sent forward from Knoxville by John Clinton Johnson I suppose.

Kyle has been telling us how they set out Friday night to hunt Sizemore and they traversed Choptack from one part to another. Left their horses on his fathers old farm upon the river and moved round in the direction of Mr. Blevins leaving a guard with the horses and at the Bridge. Between the bridge and Mr. Blevins they saw some dark figures approaching. Kyle being in advance halted them. They proved to be old Elijah Russell and his two daughters returning from Russellville. They were much frightened. Our men set them to Mr. Blevins to spend the night. They gave a call at every union house and captured one man by the name of Clemmins, three or four guns, 10 horses and a pistol or two. I have always been so anxious that we might have no such trouble as this but it seems to be absolutely necessary for the peace of our country and to preserve the lives of good citizens that such things must be done. I do hope our men will be brought to feel the eye of God is upon me and fear to do what is inconsistent with his holy commands. This is my greatest trouble as men become so demoralized by such proceedings.

November 14, 1864

Mr. Wright returned this morning and tell me there was heavy firing at the Gap the greater part of the day Saturday. It commenced before daylight. He also tells me that Branch Tucker and his son have been killed by bushwhackers.[58] They had gotten home in the day and that night were attacked. O how sad are such things. No southern soldier or citizen can remain at home now in much security. Will there be one family when this cruel war shall end found in the South who have not tasted the bitter fruits.

58. According to Johnston in *Blue and Gray from Hawkins County: The Confederates* (168, 187), Jacob Tucker, a sergeant in Company D of the Thirty-ninth Tennessee Mounted Infantry, was killed on November 11, 1864. However, Branch Tucker, Jacob's father, was a lieutenant in Company G of the Thirty-ninth Tennessee Mounted Infantry and lived until 1900.

We were made to feel glad this evening by the arrival of George Powel and E. Ruth.[59] She is just getting back from Sullivan to visit George and Mollie. George has been absent ever since February since he now has a home in the southwestern part of Georgia. He looks very well shows signs of old age coming on his beard which is long and very grey. There were 4 soldiers with them: Mr. Pickle, Johns, Jake Tilson and Kyle. They tell our men have been successful at the Gap. We had heard this before but did not know certainty of its truth. The Yanks were hemmed in by a force sent below. The Yanks left last night. We captured a wagon train, a railroad train and 51 prisoners. We lost it is said 30 men killed at the Gap who were thought to be mostly Kentuckians. My heart grows more and more sad at such announcements as this. I feel so pained to hear of the loss of one of our dear soldiers.

November 15, 1864

I awoke quite early this morning. My heart was so troubled—I tried to pray—but the news which came to me from Johnson's Island[60] was so heart rending I could think of nothing else. E. told me she had seen a long letter from Melville Gammon to his mother which was sent out secretly. In it he told her of their sufferings and remarked that were they near her slop tub he feared she would have little left for her cow. They often went to bed hungry sighing for the crumbs from the table at home. This has been to me a day of much grief. I have shed many tears. She heard that my dear S. R. G. had been paroled and would come home; that his health was very bad. My thoughts have been turned so often today on the wretched condition of our prisoners at other places. Johnson's Island has been represented as one of the best. What must be the worst, what tale of horror shall go forth to the world of Yankee inhumanity. They have it in their power to stop this suffering by granting an exchange which the South is ever ready to receive.

59. George Powel was fifty-seven years of age and married to Eliza Ruth Fain, the sister of Richard Fain.

60. Eliza's son Nick and her nephew Sam Gammon were prisoners at Johnson's Island.

November 16, 1864

We have soul cheering news this day that Gen. Lee has had a great victory capturing 10,000 prisoners and that Gen Hood was at Murfreesboro. Gen. Breckenridge is said to have been very successful capturing from 500 to 1000 prisoners, all of their artillery, wagon train, ambulance, horses, mules and commissary stores. This is so delightful.[61]

November 17, 1864

A while before dinner was ready three soldiers of the second Tennessee cavalry called for dinner. Their names were Johnson, Wilkins and Gallegher. Not long after they came in we were cheered by the return of my loved husband. He had taken Hiram's horse, putting Hiram[62] to drive the wagon. We were so glad to see him.

November 20, 1864

A Sabbath of sweet rest. We have enjoyed undisturbed this day the pleasure of my own loved home. My husband, seven of my children and the daughter of my lamented sister R. I have no words to express my gratitude to my Father for giving me a home where I have remained so undisturbed during the mighty struggle which shakes our land from center to circumference. So many have been driven from their home without a comfort. Many, very many of them to go into a land of strangers to find a resting place for the wornout body until Christ shall bid it rise. O that our father would give us rest from our enemies. We hear today that our troops are around Knoxville. I have thought often of my dear boys who are there with the troops. My poor wicked, wayward Ike causes me such deep anguish of soul. I have thought so often of my dear Hiram this day. O that he would come to me and tell me his sorrows. I love him as no earthly being loves him. All his frailties of

---

61. These were false rumors, as the Civil War was going badly for the South at this time.

62. Hiram was on leave from the Sixty-third Tennessee, then stationed in Virginia, and he may have developed tuberculosis at this time. He died from the disease on January 5, 1869.

character can be borne by no one as they are by me. Although when I know he is wrong my heart is sorely pained yet I love him. My heart is drawn by tenderest ties to my firstborn.

November 29, 1864

At home in peace. My loved husband permitted to stay day after day unmolested. Our family altar again reared morning and night— delightful seasons. We received today letters from our soldier boy in Virginia[63] and the Hon. G. A. Henry. God has been so kind to my dear boy in giving him health and strength to perform his duty as a soldier the greater part of the time since his stay in Virginia. The other letter which I mentioned is from Hon. G. A. Henry[64] in regard to the possibility of a special exchange being granted to our dear boy who has so been long a prisoner. He says special exchanges have been granted only at the will and option of the Federal Government. They bring forth a man for such an exchange and we select one to return for him. He seems to think the Yanks make it a money making business; that our men can buy their liberty. This shows the corruption and depravity of that government and more.

December 4, 1864

This has been an unquiet Sabbath. The mind is ever anxious and it unfits us for the solemn duties of this day. Yesterday just as we were

---

63. This letter is apparently one dated September 28, 1864, from Sam Fain to his father. It was sent from Signal Hill, Virginia, where Sam was serving with the Sixty-third Tennessee. Discovered in Eliza's diary, it has since been reproduced in Johnston's *Blue and Gray from Hawkins County: The Confederates* (229, 280). Sam Fain wrote that Sam Lynn, a distant cousin, had lost his mind. Sam also said that he was in rather low spirits and that "more than half of our brigade is unfit for duty. They are chilling. I have had two slight chills but I feel pretty well now. Hope I may be able to stay with the Co. We are all very anxious to go to East Tennessee but fear we will have to remain here. I would love so much to get back to E. Tenn." The original letter is now archived in the Fain Collection.

64. Gustavus A. Henry was one of the two senators from Tennessee serving in the Confederate Congress. His explanation about the problems of prisoner exchange was self-serving and incorrect. The real problem involved the South's refusal to include ex-slave soldiers in the prisoner exchange. In January 1865 the South finally agreed to exchange "all" prisoners, and Sam and Nick were in fact exchanged shortly thereafter. For details on the prisoner-exchange issue, see McPherson, *Battle Cry of Freedom*, 566–67, 798–800.

eating our dinner and supper together Mollie Speck came with Dick. He having gone after Mr. Mason to change Kyles horse for the mule taking it with him as far as Mr. Russells for Andy Johnson. Andy having on account of his wound to ride sideways.

Sarah brought us news that the Yanks were reported at Mr. Rices and that Major Day with some of his men had come into town last night, were 50 in number. We felt the enemy were coming near but could not tell what an hour would bring forth. Some of the children then came running in saying Brother Ike is coming. I was soon out at the gate and gave him a hearty welcome. Lt. Rogan was with him. They brought us information that on Friday night they came to Cobbs Ford, crossed over and ascertained that the Yanks were moving down. Not knowing their force and bearing orders from Gen. V. to not risk any engagement they retreated. The part of Major Day's command who were on this side of the river were firing. Lt. R. having command of those on the Southside brought them up and crossed this morning at McKinney mill. The main body of the men under Lt. R. went up to Mr. Russells. He after getting something to eat went to town to report to Major Day. Not long after Ike came Andy returned to get his clothes intending to go to Mr. Millers. After him Kyle and J. F. came. The day passed in a scene of confusion. Kyle and Ike have been telling over before the girls, Dick and myself many of the scenes through which they have passed.

December 5, 1864

On Friday night we had quite a scene of confusion. After making all as comfortable as we could (I having to see Andy dress his wound which is rather a serious one having gangrene again). He was using caustic. We retired to rest about 11. Kyle McCarthy came from his aunt Sarahs saying get up Uncle Dick the Yanks are in town. We were soon out and Dick was up. I aroused Mr. Mason and Andy. They were soon up. By the time I got on my clothes quite a number had collected. They were soon all in moving order excepting our wounded men. We prepared for Mr. Mason Dicks mule but for Andy we could make no provision in the way of a saddle. I told the boys some of them would have to let him have theirs but as no one seemed willing we concluded it was best for him to stay. The others were soon off. Mr. R., Richard and Mr. Rogan went to Mrs. Sensabaughs. The rest to Mr. Carmacks but would we have only known the quiet which was in store for us that night they all could have rested comfortably in their beds. I said they had all left but did not think at the time that Kyle and J. Tilson remained and went to town. They returned about 4 A.M. I got up and let them in and gave them something to eat.

## December 11, 1864

The Lord is still our helper; no enemy has been permitted as yet to molest us. We hear they are at Bean Station. A captain Messick who was taken prisoner at Mooresburg a few days ago reported them as 6,000 strong. We cannot ascertain whether his information was by observation or Yankee say so.[65]

## December 12, 1864

Last night we were quietly seated around our fireside feeling so thankful we had a home and a comfortable place to shelter us from the severe cold which came so suddenly upon us. Col. Sam Powel[66] came and was very cold having rode from Mrs. Armstrongs without warming. In a short time after he came some one rapped at the front door. The door was soon opened and our friend Mr. Jacoway was brought through. He seemed to be suffering very much from neuralgia in his face and head, had a very sore foot and threatened with chills. We made him as comfortable

---

65. General George Stoneman left Knoxville on December 10, 1864, with six thousand Union cavalry on a 461-mile raid into Virginia. Those troops returned to Knoxville on December 29, 1864. *Tennesseans in the Civil War,* 1: 352; Foote, *The Civil War,* 3: 721.

66. Sam Powel was a colonel in the Twenty-ninth Tennessee Infantry (C.S.A.) but was severely wounded and resigned his commission in 1862. After the war he moved to Hernando, Mississippi, where he lived until 1902 and became a prominent lawyer and farmer. He was a brother of Richard Fain's sister's husband. See Mary G. Draper, "The Powel Family," *Distant Crossroads,* October 2000, 122–23; this periodical is a quarterly publication of the Hawkins County Genealogical and Historical Society.

as we could. He asked me to have some pepper tea made which I soon had ready. After him Ike came in very cold having gone over to Mr. Rileys and after him Lt. Carson and Kyle McC. We soon had a fire in the front room and all were soon comfortable. We had a quiet nights rest little thinking what the next few hours would bring forth. We were up quite early hurrying to get Ike and Lt. C off, Major L. having ordered Ike to be at camp by daylight. All was bustle until they got off. Col. S. and Richard left for town.

Between 1 and 2 Richard came telling us they were fighting at Mr. Blevins. News came they were firing in town. We began to prepare for them to leave immediately. Richard had determined to take his wagon out taking Jim to drive. All were soon off. Mr. Mason who had been with us a week going in the wagon. I had lost sight of Mr. Jacoway who had loaned to Fannie his horse this morning to ride to Mr. Rices. He took off to the woods. We felt so uneasy about him that Sallie and Dick went on the hunt of him. They found he had climbed to the top of one of the knobs commanding a view of the road. She brought him back.

There were many guns fired. What has been done we cannot tell. Sarah and Lucy have been very kind giving us all the information they could get. Mr. J. lay down before the fire. Lizzie made some more pepper tea for him. Sallie and Lucy Fain went over to Mr. Merrimon's and brought us the news that the Yanks were still moving up, that 4 pieces of artillery had gone up and that they were going to cross at Chism's Ford.

The girls fixed a bed on the lounge in the front room tonight for Mr. J. After he had lain down Lucy came over to tell us of the capture of two Yanks at their house. They came riding up and made inquiry about the Rebs. They knew nothing about them. The men dismounted, came in and were warming and preparing to eat some apples when lo, two rebs made their appearance at the back door of the house. Lucy was going after the apples and saw them. They asked the number of Yanks. She replied two. They answered we will take them in and were going right in to take them but she, as I understand, told them to not do it. They went out and took their horses off. Lucy told the Yanks she thought she heard a pistol fire. They went out to mount and be off when to their utter dismay their horses were missing. They were giving vent to wicked expression when the words halt and surrender brought them to their senses. They were soon disarmed and the prisoners of Capt. K. McCarty and his aide decamp Jacob Tilson.

We have had a night of suspense but it is now 11 and no one has come to our dwelling. Fannie Gammon and I went out once thinking we heard some persons talking, passed round to the cabins and saw two forms moving off. From Aunt Polly we learned it was Gus and Caroline. G. had been to Mr. In. and came back to get Caroline to go over and see the finely mounted darkies.[67] The girls have been out and learned from Caroline they had nearly all passed before she got there.

---

67. These were probably members of the Fifth United States Colored Cavalry from Kentucky. They were part of General George Stoneman's army, which proceeded to defeat Confederate forces at Marion on December 17–18 and at Saltville on December 20–21. The destruction of the saltworks in the latter engagement was no doubt comforting for the African American troops, who had been involved in an unsuccessful attack on Saltville in October 1864. That earlier attack was led by General Stephen Burbridge, who had attempted to revive his military career by recruiting and training white and black soldiers in Kentucky. He raised a force of almost five thousand men and on October 2 attacked a Confederate force of about half that number defending Saltville. However, Burbridge appears to have been a lackluster tactician, and the Confederates routed his troops. The Union troops retreated to Kentucky, leaving their dead and wounded to the enemy. The subsequent murder of black soldiers by the Confederates has been a source of controversy. In a 1991 magazine article, William Marvel estimated that probably no more than 12 black Union troops were murdered after the battle. However, a local legend in Saltville claims that 118 men of the 600-member black force were killed or wounded in the battle and that the wounded were executed the next morning and their bodies dumped in a nearby sinkhole. Another author, Thomas D. Mays, has suggested in his book on the incident that 46 members of the Fifth U.S. Colored Cavalry were killed. Estimating the numbers is complicated by the fact that in September, the unit was composed of untrained and even unregistered former slaves riding green mounts. Thus, it is difficult to know whether the individuals listed as missing even accompanied the unit to the battle or whether they may have deserted after the debacle at Saltville. By December, however, the unit was outfitted in fine uniforms and riding trained horses. See William Marvel, "The Battle of Saltville: Massacre or Myth?" *Blue and Gray,* August 1991, 10–19, 46–60; and Thomas D. Mays, *The Saltville Massacre* (Fort Worth: Ryan Place Publishers, 1995). In addition, David E. Brown, a descendant of one of the members of the Fifth U.S. Colored Cavalry, summarizes the historical controversy on a Web site devoted to the regiment; that site includes a letter, dated August 21, 2000, from Marvel, in which he revises his figure for murdered black soldiers from 12 to 19. See http://www.mywebpages.comcast.net/5thuscc.

The infantry was coming up tomorrow and they were now on their way to Saltville again. I do hope and trust the Lord will thwart them again in their expectations.

December 15, 1864
On Tuesday E. Ruth, Mollie, Powell and Buena came out and staid until after dinner. We heard nothing of interest only that they were looking for the infantry to pass through. Lou Carmack came down and told us that the boys Kyle and Jake were at their house the night before with their prisoners but did not stay all night.

Wednesday came but still we heard nothing of the movements of our men. Mr. Jacoway left that evening and went up the road with brother George. George came back this morning bringing our horse. I felt uneasy about my loved husband. G. says he found the horse coming home. Suppose R. left his wagon and the horse somewhere on the road and that the horse had gotten out. We heard this morning that some soldiers and wagons passed down on the stage road. We could not know what it meant. I sent Dick down to see about some blacksmithing. He returned bringing us the sad new that Gen. Duke's men had been stampeded and some 60 or 70 of our men captured. Amongst that number was my dear cousin Samuel Lynn. I felt so troubled. Sent Fannie and Buena to town to see and hear the particulars. I then went over to Sarahs to see George and find out if possible something more about my own loved Richard.

There was a man sitting on the porch which I took to be a soldier. He never looked up nor spoke. His jaws were bound up. I thought he was a soldier who had been wounded but I soon learned from Sarah who he was—a Yankee soldier from Grant's Army deserting said there were many leaving as he had. We talked to him for sometime. I asked him several questions but was not pleased altogether with what he said. He thought that Grant would take Richmond and that the South would be subjugated. This was not palatable to us from a deserter. He was from Michigan. He had stopped hoping to get some employment so as to be able to get some clothes. He was not able to do the work G. wished to have done. George told him he thought Mr. Riley would like to get some help. He came on with me. We gave him some bread and milk. He said that when he left he was beaten by some of his comrades who left the army with him and robbed him of what he had. I feel rather suspicious of him but trust our Father in Heaven will let all things work together for our good.

While at Sarahs it was reported that Gen. Magruder was at Loudon. How earnestly we hope this may be true. Fannie and Buena came back this evening having with them Sallie Hasson, Mollie Powel and Annis Shaver who got to Rogersville yesterday. They tell us the prisoners were taken on this morning.

A report comes to us that Gen. Vaughn has been cut off. We do not believe it yet we do not know. The girls also tell us that Sizemore with 15 men all drunk were in town yesterday threatening the Fains with great destruction. We hear that more of the poor deluded blacks have gone off with them. Poor creatures may they have their eyes opened.

December 16, 1864

Night has again closed in upon us with our anxious hearts still unrelieved. We heard nothing today calculated to cheer. A report has come to us that firing was heard in the direction of Jonesboro. I cannot think Gen. Vaughn would be there unless the couriers who were sent to him failed to get there. Mollie and Bug came out today and gave us particulars about our prisoners. They told us they had shot some of them for having on Yankee clothes after they surrendered. This to me is such a terrible thought. The prisoners were furnished by our folk with something to eat but they were not permitted to give it to them. Cousin Mollie Walker had been pushed out of the room where her brother was by a soldier with his gun. Mr. Jacoway returned today but would not sleep in the house tonight.

December 17, 1864

This night 31 years ago I was a bride. O how little I thought of the vast responsibilities I had assumed. How little I thought of the duties which lay before me. I had married one who was not a Christian. I had made when about 14 years of age a profession of religion but had not lived the life of the Christian. Mine was a formal religion then but O the goodness and mercy which has followed me. God has given me to see myself a lost sinner without the love of Jesus. He has been pleased to convert my dear husband, he has given to me many precious children some of whom I humbly trust are his children. He has enabled us thus far to raise our family well supplied with the necessaries of life. He has given health in a remarkable degree. He has given many religious advantages. To look back on 31 years how short they appear. Mine has been marked with great happiness. My husbands love has been so true, so noble. We have rarely ever had one unkind word. May the remaining years of our pilgrimage be marked with a purer love than what has passed. No news today as to the movement of our troops. Kyle and Jake came back today and said the prisoners were released by taking the oath.

December 18, 1864

A footstep on the porch started me but I was quickly relieved by Kyle saying Aunt Eliza. I got up opened the door and he told me they had a reinforcement of two men who were pickets on the river below Mooresburg and were cut off. Mr. Irvin of North Carolina and Mr. Morton from Kentucky near Lexington. I felt thankful to know they had been preserved. They took their horses to the stable, fed them and then came to the house. Not long after breakfast Kyle and Dick were about the stable when they heard guns firing. They came to the house, all took their guns and were soon off upon the hill. They went near enough to ascertain that some troops were moving down. Kyle came back, gave us the information and told us to send for George. Bug and Liz went over to Mr. Moores and returned soon bringing us the sad intelligence that it was Yanks taking down prisoners. This cast a damper over our joyous anticipation. We had hoped they were falling back. The girls could learn nothing of the particulars but saw 11 prisoners moving along on parole. They asked them several questions and learned they were taken at Bristol. Said it was reported they had the saltworks but he did not believe it. The girls now began to think of going to town. The rain falling at intervals and the muddiness of the way caused some hesitation. At length Fannie Gammon, Sallie Hasson and Fannie Fain determined to go. I felt some misgiving lest Mr. Jacoway who has lain in bed the greater part of the time for two days should be endangered. They set off with rather sorrowful hearts fearing some of our dear boys were taken. After an absence of three or four hours they returned with news which relieved our troubled hearts.

The prisoners about 200 in number they say were mostly citizens taken to the academy hill. The ladies followed on with their baskets of provision through rain, mud and mire to feed the prisoners and amongst the number was our dear Brainard who gave the girls several items of pleasant news. Breckenridge was in front and Vaughn in the rear pressing the Yanks and that they were going out through Pound Gap. He felt all would be right in a few days. He thinks the disaster was caused by Col. Morgan failing to do his duty.

A short time before dinner was ready Dick came running telling Kyle a Yankee was coming from town with a prisoner. The boys were soon off (Kyle, Morton and J. Tilson) on their horses, went to the road and found Dick was mistaken about a prisoner. There they found one fortunate Reb who had made his escape by stopping at E. Ruths until the rear guard passed by. She then sent Pete out with him to join his command. His name is McNabe and he had been a prisoner taken at the same time with our boys, had been paroled and they had taken him.

December 21, 1864
Wiley Merrimon came over to ask to put in our meadow a young nag which had been left the day before by some Yanks. He told us

that there were about 200 that had passed down having some Negroes and prisoners. They said the rest of the force would be on yesterday and today but none have come. We dread to see them coming back as desolation and destruction of fences and provision marked their path as they went up. We fear it will be much greater as they return. It rained most of the day Monday, turned much cooler that night. The next morning the girls Mollie, Bug and Lissa set out on foot for town. The boys, Kyle, Jake, Mr. Morton and Irvin went up to Mr. Carmacks on Monday. They returned this morning. Mr. Jacoway assisted in killing our beef.

Saturday E. Ruth came out bringing a letter from my dear Sam Gammon addressed to Mr. Blevins asking assistance and saying that necessity had impelled him to ask aid. He requested him to tell me to send them flour, bacon and fruit. O how gladly would I have done for their comfort but alas I have no means to help.

December 25, 1864

A Christmas never to be forgotten. The second Sabbath since this war began that the Yanks were permitted to destroy its peace and happiness. What a scene has past before us today. We had hoped to give to our dear boys Kyle, Mr. Jacoway, Irvin Morton and J. Tilson a plain dinner, but alas how often are our pleasant hopes blasted. The boys came down the road this morning having staid at Mrs. Kinkeads last night. They stopped at Sarahs and Kyle came over here and talked to us a short time. He told us they were going to town. Jennie McC tried to persuade him not to go but he was so determined. I thought it no use for me to say anything. I now regret so much I did not use my powers of entreaty. They were at Sarahs waiting to get a lunch (excepting J. Tilson who rode forward as a picket towards town) resting in perfect assurance. We had all our misgivings about them lest Sizemore and his men might run in upon them little knowing that a large Union force was moving down our valley. The advance guard came in sight moving down the hill; our boys attempted to escape by running to the woods but they were soon surrounded by some in front with others in the rear coming through the fields east of the house. They had them and they had to surrender.

Fannie Gammon and I were left at home trembling with grief and terror thinking Sizemore's men had them but of this we were soon relieved. Two of their horses broke loose and made over here to the stable where they were accustomed. A little wicked Michigan man took after them and as he drew near his oaths and threats at old Polly to head and catch the horse made us feel we have a wicked foe to deal with. Sallie, Lizzie and Fannie gave orders for him to catch them himself. Old Polly true to the instincts of her nature made for the house and he had to follow on to the stable and get them. After they with the prisoner boys left who should come heaving up but our poor little Jake. I tried my best to persuade him to go back but on he went and got a short distance inside the meadow and fired upon them. They started back from the shop hill in full pursuit. He turned came on to the corner of the yard where he fired again. This filled them with desperation and they came charging and cursing. They followed on towards the hollow where he evaded them by taking to the right and they to the left. They soon found their pursuit unavailing and they turned and came on back. Upon riding up the house they gave vent to some of the most wicked oaths and threats I had ever listened to. The Major or Col. came and told me if I did not tell where he had gone he would burn my house over my head. I told him I could not for I did not know no more than he did. He then demanded his name. His terrible looks and threats, I must confess intimidated me and I told him his name was Jake Tilson. He then asked we where his father lived and I told him about 6 miles below Rogersville. This is all that I regretted saying this day. I so much feared they would wreak vengeance on his poor father. The officer turned to another saying mark that name. We then had a scene for several minutes.

The same little fellow who captured the horses dismounted and came to the front door porch pounding with great vehemence saying open this door. We told him to come round the house. He came swearing the shot had been fired from the house. He was ordered by the officer (whose name was Major Keco) to search the house alone but Liz followed. He went to work opening drawers, presses and desk. Another one came in and he went to work opening the children's drawers. I came in after the Major left and followed them too. I told them I had neither men nor arms secreted about my house. I then began to talk to them about their wicked conduct and told them we would meet again at the Judgement seat of Christ; that the deeds of this day would be recorded and that I had told them the truth. They concluded they would take my word and did not go upstairs. After they left I went over to Sarah's and there heard that some of them had remarked we regarded them as a rough set. They said that Gillem's men were coming and they were nothing compared to them. I told Gus to come on home and we would try to put away some of our meat. I came on back thinking what shall I do. I planned to move it into the cabin loft. Gus came and we went to the stable to take care of a government saddle which had attracted some attention belonging to McNabe. Having that secured we came to the house and were just about to commence the work when Gus told me they were coming down the hill.

I felt we can do nothing and I just felt all I can do is to trust in him who hath ever taken care of us. In a few moments some of them were making their way across. Something to eat was all their cry. We tried to feed them giving a piece of bread and meat. Some were easily served; at length some 6 or 8 with two Negroes came. We told them we would give them some bread and meat. One man got off saying he wanted raw meat and ham at that. When he dismounted they all got down. Sallie took the dining room. I took the ham man to one side saying to him I will give you a piece of meat if you will only keep the rest out. I told him to stay there and I would bring it to him. I then began a search for my smokehouse key but could find it nowhere. In the meantime Sallie had been feeding him.

One man went into the kitchen and got hold of my coffee pot. He came marching along with quite an air of triumph. I said to him you are not going to take my coffee pot. I told him I would not take anything belonging to him. With this he said give me some milk. Fannie remarked I will if you will give up the coffee pot. He relaxed his hold and I took hold on it and he let me have it. My ham man kept following me saying can't you find your key. I told him no.

Old aunt Polly came to the door of the kitchen where she was battling all she could to save my cooking vessels saying they will take all. I then ran in there and stuck some behind a big box. While doing this one of the Negroes went into the room where my meal and flour are kept and whipped off my bag of shorts being everything in the flour line I had. As I was starting to head him off here comes the coffee pot man again saying I want something to make up bread in when we stop tonight. I told him I did not have anything and that some of my pans had been taken from, which was last Fall and of which I thought when I spoke. He then said "I want my coffee pot." I said to him "are you an honorable man." He replied "yes I am" and I then told him he would not take it for he had said he would not. He turned about saying I will not trouble women and children. I told him I thought he was too clever to do that.

As I came from there I met up with the ham man saying can't you find your key. I would like to have a piece of meat. I told him I would have given it to him if I could have found the key and that I did not want him to break open my door for they would take all I had and I had but little for my family.

I should have mentioned that before this set came Mr. Merrimon, Polly and some of the children came over. Mr. M. was very kind and tried to engage them in conversation as much as he could by giving vent to such expressions as have you had a fatiguing trip. You must have suffered a great deal. You have destroyed much. I asked the ham man if his hunger was not appeased I would give him some milk if he could carry it. With words of kindness through my Fathers care I prevailed. As he left I thanked him for not breaking open my door.

After they left we were not troubled much more. Some four or five more came at different times but I had nothing left to give them. I made out to give some cold hash and a crust or two of bread to a young fellow from this county named Bellamy. Some hash was still left when another came and I scraped it in his tin cup telling him I had no bread left. Three more came after that but I had nothing for them. They conducted themselves gentlemanly. After they left being the rear my heart was lightened and I felt I could shout with loud praise and adoration to that God who had watched over me and my dear family through such hours of trial with a care and power surpassing all the care of an earthly Father.

After all had quieted down Liz and I went over to Sarahs. She had a trying day being on the road and her house, smokehouse and kitchen were all at their mercy. Jennie, Lizzie, Nannie, Dick, Ellie and Caroline were all there and each one tried to do what they could to save her things. They took all her hams. She succeeded in locking her cellar and keeping them from there. I feel she escaped wonderful as her house was not entered. Some of her cooking utensils were taken and a good deal of her poultry. Just as we went in our dear brother George who had been remarkably preserved by hiding in the kitchen loft in the morning while they captured the other boys and taking to the woods during the interval which elapsed came in. I felt so glad to see him safe. While we were relating the terrible scenes through which we had passed Dick came running in saying uncle George more Yanks are coming. We were afraid for him to go out and told him to fall down behind the bed. He did so and they soon passed. Sarah asked them if there were any more behind. They replied you will think so before morning. About 6000 men are coming. We knew this was untrue.

Liz and I came back and had our supper over our chickens which had been prepared for our Christmas dinner. After supper was over we all set down talking over the day and our trials and began wondering if any of the prisoners would make their escape. Fannie Gammon gave vent to her feeling of indignation in such a way as to cause us to laugh. She and Lizzie have made a vow if the little speckled faced Michigan man who was so smart with his white leggings ever gets into their power to give him one good beating with a horse whip. Between 9 and 10 we all retired to rest, worn down with the scenes of Christmas Day 1864.

December 26, 1864

A short time after I lay down last night a footstep on the porch startled me. I had been laying praying for our deliverance, thinking of my dear boys whose life was wearing out on Johnson's Island—of the boys who were captured on Sabbath—lay praying for their escape feeling that the God of Heaven was saving them by sending rain and a dark night. I lay there and listened attentively to see whether I could hear more than one. A slight rap at the door, still I lay, another rap and I said who is there. A voice I did not recognize said Mrs. Fain. I again said who is there and he replied Jacoway. I was soon out of my bed. The door opened and I gave him a hearty welcome thanking God for his deliverance. He was very wet and had walked from McClures, made his escape when the relief guards took charge of them and ordered them to march out of the camp into a house nearby. Just as he came out, an ambulance standing close, he stood behind it and shied around. All was so dark he was soon beyond observation and detection. We had quite a time over him and the children all but Liz got up to welcome him back. Sallie got dry clothes and something to bind his sore ankle. He seemed so glad to get back. We were awake then until after one. None of the rest have yet come up but we hope they may escape. I fear Kyle will be closely watched. Lucy came over and Ida and Sallie to welcome Mr. J. back. I hope and trust he may escape without further trouble. I feel at times rather uneasy as we have had two horses taken lately from the stable. Last Thursday night Yankee Bull as he was called was taken. Last night Kyle McCarthy's little mare as well. We were at a loss to know who had taken the first but ascertained from Mr. Sizemore on last Saturday when he made his appearance just after daylight with a squad of men under the command of Lt. Weatherford that one of his men had taken Yankee Bull.[68]

68. This was neither the first nor last time that Eliza was visited by Bill Sizemore and his lawless band of Union sympathizers.

Dick was making the fire and the door was partly opened. He came dashing back into the house saying Mama the Yanks are here. The clanking of sabres—the words surround the house close up soon told the tale. I sprang from my bed and broke into the bedroom arousing the girls. I took no time to put on my clothes but appeared in my gown and bare feet at the door. They were still on their horses. Lt. W told me not to be alarmed that nothing should be disturbed but that orders had been given by Gen. Gillem that the two houses should be searched from garret to cellar for the boys. I told them I would give them my word as a Christian woman none were here but Mr. Sizemore could not be satisfied. Lt. W. told me that nothing should be molested. The girls Fannie and Lizzie Fain had put on some of their clothes. Fannie G. had dressed herself. Lt. asked me to go with them to see that nothing was disturbed, not being dressed and it being very cold the girls proposed they should go. I could not stay back but followed on. The search being completed they made preparations to leave. Lt. W. told me he knew Hiram very well but I do not know whether he told me the truth or not. I know that about Gen. Gillem's order was false for he was not there but he treated me kindly. All of which I feel is from my Fathers hand. Nothing was molested and the boys not found. This is the first time my house has been searched since the war began. The day is past and all are again quietly resting but myself. George[69] is in Ahab's house. Mr. J. upstairs and it is nearly 11 o'clock. I trust the Lord will watch over us this night and shield us from danger.

December 27, 1864

Learned from J. Tilson he had taken Kyle's little mare himself. Poor Jake feels lonely without Kyle. I do hope he may be permitted to return but fear he will be closely watched.

---

69. This was forty-eight-year-old George G. Fain, the brother of Eliza's husband.

December 28, 1864

This would have been my mothers 88th birthday had she lived. O how often do I find myself looking back on my young life with its warm associations. My early home not elegance or costly but lovely, lovely. My father uncle, my mother, sisters and dear little brother cousin awaken within me so many tender and joyous recollections. My schoolgirl days on the old hill west of Blountville. Although the old log schoolhouse has given place to a better and the old church walls have crumbled down yet memory paints all as vividly as though it were but yesterday. The scenes of our departure from the home of my childhood to our new home in Rogersville, the kind reception which was there given to us. The events of succeeding years crowd upon me and I find myself today the only representative in America of the little group who gathered around the hearthstone of my childhood. My brother cousin I trust still lives but the mighty oceans and the seas roll between us. I often feel sad and my spirit is often so weary of earth. I long for Heaven, I long to meet my Saviour and other dear friends who have gone before me to that bright world. Earth is so unstable, our dearest hopes and warmest anticipations of earthly happiness seemed to be formed now as targets for this cruel war.

Last night sometime after we lay down I was aroused by someone on the porch, a rap at the door made me call out who is there. A voice which was familiar replied Ryan. I sprang from my bed, opened the door and to my great joy found Serg. Ryan who had made his escape about 12 miles below Bean Station. He came in and told me how that night they were put in an old corn crib but he noticed as soon as he entered a place where he thought he could come out. Being near the ground he threw himself across it. After all was quieted down, having before spoken to Morton, Kyle, Capt. Fort and Lt. Bachman he crept out and made his escape.

The editor found Eliza Fain's diaries in this trunk while searching for stamps in an upstairs closet of his parents' home, which they had inherited from Eliza's granddaughter. Most of the diary volumes were recycled account books or ledgers. Photograph by John Fain.

The springhouse for Eliza's home, with the brick house belonging to Hiram Fain (Richard's brother) visible in the background. The house was built by Hiram and Richard's father, Nicholas Fain, in 1829 and faces the old stage road that later became Highway 11W, before a new bypass was constructed north of the property. The commercial building between the springhouse and Hiram's home represents recent suburban sprawl extending from the center of Rogersville, two miles to the west. Photograph by John Fain.

The small creek that runs through what was once Eliza and Richard Fain's farm. In 1897 fire destroyed the original frame house in which Eliza and Richard lived. Photograph by John Fain.

Portrait of Nicholas Fain, Richard's father, by Samuel Shaver. Nicholas was the first mayor of Rogersville and a successful businessman. From the collection of George Fain. Used by permission.

Portrait of Elizabeth Anderson, Eliza's mother, by Samuel Shaver. Elizabeth had been a widow for fourteen years until she married Nicholas Fain in 1832, after the death of his first wife in 1831. From the collection of George Fain. Used by permission.

Daguerreotype (three by four inches) of Richard Fain. It was probably made in about 1850, when he would have been thirty-nine. From the private collection of John and Ann Fain.

Carte-de-visite photograph of Lizzie Fain, Eliza's oldest daughter. This photograph was given to Sam Fain in 1866. Sam married Lizzie's sister Sallie in 1867. From the private collection of John and Ann Fain.

Cabinet photograph (4.25 by 6.5 inches) of Ike Fain, one of Eliza's sons. It was taken in Chariton, Iowa, in 1890 with his son Richard Rhea Fain. From the private collection of John and Ann Fain.

Cabinet photograph of Powell Fain, one of Eliza's sons, with his wife, Sallie, and their seven children, taken in about 1896. The children are (front row, left to right) Julia, Dick, Hiram, and Nelle, and (back row, left to right) Will, Robert, and Sam. From the private collection of John and Ann Fain.

A formal photograph of (left to right) Dick Fain, Sallie Fain, and Powell Fain, three of Eliza's children. This was made in 1904 in Knoxville, Tennessee, by Knaffl & Brother. From the private collection of John and Ann Fain.

An informal photograph of (left to right) Powell Fain, Dick Fain, and Sallie Fain. This was taken in 1909 on the porch of Sallie's home, located beside Mossy Creek near Jefferson City, Tennessee. From the private collection of John and Ann Fain.

Carte-de-visite photograph of Andrew Johnson, distributed by E. & H. T. Anthony of New York and based on a negative in Brady's National Portrait Gallery. This photograph was discovered among Eliza Fain's family papers. From the private collection of John and Ann Fain.

The editor, standing by the front grave marker for Hiram Fain, Eliza's oldest son, who died in 1869. Hiram was buried in the cemetery beside the New Providence Presbyterian Church (visible in the background) near Surgoinsville, Tennessee. Photograph by Ann Fain.

The grave marker for Hiram Fain. The black iron cross near the stone is of the sort typically placed at the graves of former Confederate soldiers. The flag is probably a Memorial Day remnant. The Maltese-cross marker measures twelve inches across and is mounted on an eighteen-inch stake. The reverse side bears a garlanded Confederate flag and the letters C.S.A. The visible inscription says, "1861 deo vindice 1865"; translated, it reads, "With God as my Avenger." Photograph by John Fain.

**In Loving Remembrance of**

### Mrs. Eliza R. Fain.

Died Jan. 19, 1892.
Aged 75 Yrs., 5 Mos., 18 Days.

A precious one from us has gone
A voice we loved is stilled;
A place is vacant in our home,
Which never can be filled.
God in His wisdom has recalled,
The boon His love has given
And though the body slumbers here
The soul is safe in heaven.

Eliza Fain's death notice, a broadside measuring approximately 4.25 by 6.5 inches and printed in gold ink on black card stock. From the private collection of John and Ann Fain.

This monument for Richard and Eliza Fain and their two youngest daughters stands in the graveyard beside the Rogersville Presbyterian Church. Photograph by John Fain.

The Rogersville Presbyterian Church, which was erected in the 1840s and stands within a few yards of Eliza's grave. Photograph by John Fain.

Photograph of an unknown Union soldier who belonged to Company F of the Second Tennessee Cavalry, a unit that was organized in and around Maryville, Tennessee, in 1862. The soldier wears a Hardee hat and a cavalry shell jacket and holds an 1860 cavalry saber. This tintype photograph (2.25 by 3.25 inches) is in a so-called Union case with a pinchbeck mount marked "Waterbury, Conn." From the private collection of John and Ann Fain.

An illustration from *Harper's Weekly* magazine (March 12, 1864) shows the bridge at Knoxville over what was then known as the Holston River but is now considered part of the Tennessee River. The ruins of the prewar bridge are depicted, and beyond those is the pontoon bridge erected by General Ambrose E. Burnside in November 1863 near First Creek. The illustration shows troops crossing the pontoon bridge and camped along the riverbanks. From the private collection of John and Ann Fain.

# Chapter 5

## Overpowered but Not Defeated: 1865

This was a terrible year for Eliza as she had to face the defeat of the South only weeks after her home was ransacked by guerrillas. While there is no evidence from the diaries that Eliza ever wavered in her support for the Confederacy, the same was probably not true for her sons. Sam had been in Virginia with Lee in the Sixty-third Tennessee at the start of the year but had apparently returned home sometime in January. Many soldiers serving with units around Richmond had grown weary of war and had possibly realized that the cause was hopeless. This was especially true of those from divided areas such as East Tennessee, where the threat from Union troops and Unionist guerrillas to their families was of more compelling concern than the situation in Virginia.[1] Although Eliza did not specifically condemn Sam for deserting, she was clearly upset that he had returned home. Sheila Johnston, in scouring the military records for two hundred men from Hawkins and Hancock Counties who served in the Sixty-third Tennessee, found that only 13 percent of the men died during military service but that a

---

1. Groce, *Mountain Rebels*, 106.

staggering 38 percent were listed as deserters by the end of the war.[2] In contrast, the desertion rate for Hawkins County residents enrolled in the Nineteenth Tennessee was only 15 percent, while 25 percent of the soldiers in this unit died or were killed during the war. The Nineteenth Tennessee was organized just after war was declared, but the Sixty-third was organized the next year, when the options for able-bodied males were either to volunteer or be drafted.

Sam joined Ike, Powell, and Hiram in local Confederate defense units that acted more like guerrilla forces. Neither Hiram nor Ike had gone to Richmond with the Sixty-third when it left East Tennessee the previous summer. Ike was serving in George W. Day's Confederate cavalry unit. Powell, whose parents had finally permitted him to join the army, was a private in the Sixtieth Tennessee Mounted Infantry. What Hiram did after he was assigned to General Archibald Gracie's brigade is unclear, but none of the Fain boys were ever officially listed as deserters.[3] Nick and his first cousin Sam Gammon were released from a Union prison and returned home in late February. The whole family had a glorious reunion in which they celebrated the safe return of all the Fain males from the war. However, their jubilation did not last long. The Confederate army retreated towards Virginia, leaving the Rogersville area as a no-man's-land with the Union forces located on the south side of the Holston River. During the time between the retreat of the Confederate forces and the arrival of Union troops, William Sizemore and his band of guerrillas made life miserable for Confederate sympathizers around Rogersville. Both Richard and his sons were away from home most of the time between the end of March and the arrival of Union troops in Rogersville.

2. Johnston, *The Blue and Gray from Hawkins County: The Confederates*, 223–63.

3. Johnston, *The Blue and Gray from Hawkins County: The Confederates*, 228–68.

Eliza, along with her younger children, daughters, and a few slaves, remained at home; otherwise, the Fains' house and barns would probably have been burned to the ground by the guerrillas. Some rules of civilization still seemed to apply, however, and Eliza must have realized that even the evil Sizemore would not murder or rape either her or her daughters. Even so, Eliza lost her old horse, as well as the last of her food and many possessions of value, to Sizemore's band of bushwhackers in early April when they threatened to burn down her home. Shortly thereafter the war ended and the last of her slaves left. Eliza's husband and sons returned to the family farm after the Union army occupied Rogersville, but her husband was robbed of his coat on the way home. On April 25, 1865, Colonel Joseph H. Parsons of the Union army was ordered to move his unit to Rogersville, and that ended the reign of terror by bushwhackers. Richard's coat was returned to him, and two years later Eliza got her horse back by going to court. Horses were the best means of transportation at that time, and in the chaos that followed the end of the war, many horses were stolen from Union sympathizers by Confederate guerrillas and vice versa. Eliza's son Ike was involved in some of this activity and accused of horse theft. In the end, it appears that regaining one's horse was a relatively sure thing, provided that one could find the animal and prove ownership.

In May 1865 Eliza's husband went to Knoxville to take the oath of allegiance and, since he was a West Point graduate, to apply for a pardon from President Andrew Johnson. The pardon application, which was submitted on June 15, 1865, by Richard's attorney, A. A. Kyle, stated that Richard Fain "humbly represents to your Excellency that he, like thousands of other in the Southern States, was so far forgetful of himself and his duty & his allegiance to a great and good govt. as to lift his hand against it. He was a Col. of a Tennessee Regt. & in many ways committed treason to the United States Govt. He confesses to the delusion and deeply regrets what he has done & has for some time past desired to see the national Authority restored & never again to attempt another rebellion."[4] The application was accompanied by a statement signed by A. Caldwell, Hezekiah Davis, Thomas A. R. Nelson, F. S. Heiskell, A. A. Kyle, John R. Branner, and C. H. Mitchell. All of these men were, in all likelihood, Unionists; they claimed that there had been no special complaint against Richard by loyal citizens and that they knew of no evidence that he had arrested or annoyed Union citizens. On September 21 Richard had W. C. Kyle carry a letter to Washington that requested action on his request. In that letter, Richard stated that he had always been a warm personal and political friend of Andrew Johnson and that he did not feel disposed to engage in any business until restored to his rights of citizenship. However, once the pardon was granted in October, it did little to alter Richard's status, except to exempt him from lawsuits that might have confiscated his property. Not only had Richard and his sons fought on the losing side but they also discovered that any jobs around Rogersville that might utilize their skills had been taken by white Unionists. Thus, they found it impossible to obtain work. Some of Richard and Eliza's sons left the area to seek work elsewhere, and Richard had to commute to Mossy Creek, where he became a clerk working for his wealthy relative, Sam Fain. Although Richard and Eliza still had their farm, they had lost everything else, and Richard was no farmer. Furthermore, he appears to have been in ill health ever since resigning his commission in the army.

4. Pardon application of Richard. G. Fain, *Case Files of Applications from Former Confederates for Presidential Pardons, 1865–1867* (Washington, D.C.: National Archives and Records Administration, Microfilm Publications), RG094, M1003, Roll 49 (Tennessee, Ea–Jo).

Eliza had some difficulty accepting defeat, but her distress was eased somewhat by the genteel behavior of the conquering Union troops, who allowed secessionists to maintain honor in defeat. When her husband traveled to Knoxville to take the oath of allegiance, a family friend convinced her that this action involved no renunciation of principles, except with regard to freeing the slaves. Eliza clearly understood that slavery was the underlying cause of the war, and in May 1865 she still thought that slavery was ordained by God. In September she expressed the belief that the Christian of the South had no hope. By November, however, she accepted the idea that God no longer supported slavery, and she saw the South's resigned submission to its defeat as evidence of this. Eliza believed that divine ordination of slavery had been withdrawn because of certain evil practices that had become associated with it—specifically, the sexual exploitation of female slaves by white males. As an evangelical Christian, Eliza believed that African American slaves were as human and as worthy of salvation as European Americans. She slowly came to realize that they were entitled to the same rights as whites.

Eliza struggled during 1865 to accept the defeat of the Confederacy, which suggested that God had deserted their cause. Eventually, like many supporters of secession, she attributed that defeat to the North's superior power. Eliza's faith clearly helped to sustain her through this difficult time. The words of her diary provide unique insights into how Southerners reacted to defeat. The value of personal journals such as Eliza's is that they reveal what their authors thought and believed at the time they wrote them and not how they would feel years later, after their memories had shifted and the stories they told had changed.

January 1, 1865

The first day of 65 is upon us. Today has been a quiet, peaceful day but my heart is so cold and my love for him who had done so much for me so faint, so poor. The snow is still lying thick upon the grounds but it is not so cold as it was this day three weeks ago but was cold enough to make me enjoy my corner with heartfelt gratitude to him who is the giver of every comfort.

We are tonight alone. Brother George has gone to his resting place in old Ahab's cabin. The boys have gone somewhere on the other road not feeling safe to stay here on account of Sizemore. Poor fellow he disturbs us so greatly. I feel he is filling up the cup of his iniquity. O that the Lord would convince him of his sin and wickedness and cause him to stop in his wild career to seek pardon before it be forever too late.

January 8, 1865

Two weeks today was one of intense excitement. Our boys captured, our home threatened, our spirits humbled before the outlaws and barbarians of Lincoln despotism. I had been favored by God with a self possession and calmness ever before but at this time I was unnerved and shaken. As I thought on this the question arose in my mind will the evacuation of Rogersville throw us into the Federal lines. The more I thought upon it the more awful it became until I felt myself shudder with horror at such a probability. The few days or weeks we have been under the yoke have been too much for us.

January 15, 1865.

Day of anxiety, day of trouble but no evil has come upon my loved family or near our dwelling. Last night as we were quietly seated around our fireside with family present: Richard, Sallie, Fannie, Nannie, Lillie and Fannie Gammon. Dick having gone to the cabin to assist in blacking. Powell, Ed Powel and Jake Tilson came. Powell remarked to his papa that "he had better fix to get away from here as Sizemore with 39 men had come and captured Mr. Clint Charles knocking him down three times after he surrendered." This was sad news to us all. We had hoped that citizens would be permitted to remain at home in peace. The boys went over to Mr. Charles after he was taken away. We were all anxiety and bustle until we got them all off. Brothers Hiram and George were sent for. They were soon here and all were off. Hiram, George, Richard and Powell going to Mr. Russells. Ed & Jake to Mr. Rileys. We then quieted down with some fear that before a rising sun would again beam upon us we might be visited by the vandal foe.

We arose this morning in peace. Not long after breakfast brother G. came telling us of the fearful calamity which had come on dear friends across the river. The vandals visited Mrs. Spears and found, it was said, Lazarus Spears and a young man by the name of Manis. The boys it is said made resistance and drove off 26. They thought they had driven them away and then the boys went to the barn. A company returned, surrounded the barn and killed Spears & Manis. The reports say they killed Newt, Charles and Theo Schrivner but of this we will hear more. George had only heard that they were there and captured the boys wounding one of them. I had to send Dick and Jim up to Mr. Russells to take two colts which could not be taken away. Last night when they came back Dick gave us the information that they had killed Spears and Louis Manis. We felt there might be some mistake in it and after the boys came out (Powell and Jake) we started Fannie and Dick to Mr. Russells to bring back Ike's colt and hear a true statement. Upon the way they met Ike, Mr. Pinkerton and another soldier who was an Ohio man who had been drafted to serve 7 months in the Federal Army then came to ours and had been with us 12 months. They turned and came back to the house. He gave us the news of Newt and Schrivners untimely fall. O how terrible, how awful do these things appear to us.[5]

5. Sheila Johnston, in *Blue and Gray from Hawkins County: The Battles* (61), described this raid as the work of Union bushwhackers from Greene County. It resulted in the death of Louis Manis and Lazarus Spears. Other than his name, the sole inscription on Lazarus Spears's tombstone is the word MURDERED. Newt Dyer and Theo Schrivner were captured at the same time but escaped on the way to Knoxville.

My Ike swapped horses with the Ohioan for one he had taken from Mr. Russell. O Lord do not let thy wrath burn against him but look in tender mercy and send thy Holy Spirit to woo him from the paths of sin and wickedness. The Ohio man left soon after dinner for town. George, Ike, Ed, Jake and Powell went up the road. Mr. Pinkerton staid until dark and then went to town. Caroline and her father (Uncle Joe) returned quite late from town.

After Mr. P left Sallie, cousin Fannie, Fannie and Dick took their Bibles and read some. After they were through reading I went into the cabin and invited Old Uncle Joe to come into the house and pray with us. I came back and arranged all seating the blacks on the left of the fireplace and my white family on the right. I then opened the Bible and read John 14, sung *When I can read my title clear.* Gus raising the tune and we all kneeled while the poor sable son of Africa breathed forth in solemn broken accents his prayer to his Father upon the throne—truly to me it was a solemn scene and my soul was refreshed. Religion was so beautiful so lovely.

January 16, 1865

All still. No enemy has yet disturbed us this morning. Just as we were through eating breakfast 7 men rode up asking for breakfast. They belonged to Gibb's scouts. They have started to go down to the plains. I had Amy moved today to a house of Neal Harlans near the mill. While gone I learned that Capt. Gibbs had taken charge of a flag of truce and his men had returned up the country. I do not know what the object is. Some say they have in view an exchange of prisoners captured on Stoneman's last raid on Tuesday the 17th. The boys still at home.

Thursday cousin Fannie Gammon with Richard and Fannie Fain left about 2. Just as they were starting Powell and Billy Carmichael came riding up not long after with Ike and John Sevier. We gave them dinner. Ed and John not eating. They soon after left and we felt so sorry to see them leave not knowing what was to come. Ike and Ed had gone down that morning as far as

Mr. Blevins. We felt it was wrong for them to go but they were perverse and would not listen.

January 22, 1865

After getting through with breakfast I set down and had some pleasant conversation with cousin John Earnest. Soon after he left Jake Tilson came. I felt glad to see him as he had not been here since the boys left. I talked to him impressing him with the importance of doing right. I asked him if Zack his brother had taken Mr. Davis's horses. He replied no. I then told him of their being here on Friday in search and that I had promised to do all I could to get Zack, should I see him with the horses, to return them. As I talked to him I thought his countenance unusually sad. I said to Jake "you are lonesome since the boys left." He replied "yes but I am going to my command as soon as I can get ready." I asked him where and he replied to the scouts. I asked whose, his reply "Capt. Foy's of Greene Co." I said nothing more only told him if he got any news today in town to come by and tell me. He then left the house and started on. When he got over to Sarahs he halted for a moment or two talking to Major Rannels and then set off. Major R. saying to him Jake I will not go to town as you are going. If you get any news come up and let us hear.

And now I come to the tale of horror. After passing the hollow of the first hill beyond the shop he was fired upon, surrounded as we suppose, and cruelly murdered. Whether he made resistance or not we cannot tell. We were much excited. Cousin J. Earnest came running across the meadow. I had his horse sent for, he told me a bullet whistled near him in the meadow and he was soon off safely. We then began to think of the fate of our poor Jake. Sallie, who had been watching their movement told us she thought they had taken him to the woods across the field. Hearing two shots afterwards we supposed it was true and that he lay dead in the woods. I went over to Sarahs. The girls (Lucy and Lizzie) talked of going to Mr. Car-macks. I met Liz in the meadow and told her I did not feel they were safe, that I was fearful they were still watching our movements and should they attempt to go they might be intercepted. After some deliberation Lucy concluded she would come over here and go through by Mary Martins taking Dick with her. Liz then set out on foot with Cin for company for town. After she left Sallie and I concluded we must try to find the body of poor unfortunate Jake, as we left we saw a man riding up to Sarahs. Nannie met us and told us it was Mr. Tilson, that Jake was killed and lying by the road. We moved on briskly and found Sarah and Mr. Tilson just leaving. He came and asked Sarah if that was Jake not being able to recognize him for the blood which had smeared his whole face. We all then set out. Mr. Tilson, Sarah, Sallie, Nannie and I, as we came near we discovered Liz and Cin. were there and soon saw poor Jake lying on the ground near a corner of the fence on the left hand side. What a sight met our eye there in deaths icy embrace with his face so disfigured from blood we could scarcely have known who he was. Quite a quantity of clotted blood near by.

A wail of woe went up. I thought of the immortal soul of my poor Jake for whom I had so long had such tender yearning. I had so often spoken to him of the importance of being a Christian, of the importance of conducting himself in such a way that no stigma should be upon his character. He listened attentively and I thought he felt like doing it but was ever quiet and never much to talk. He made no answer. He never swore an oath in my presence. I had never listened to harsh opprobrious language from his lips concerning any human being.

Poor Jake he never had the religious training and advantages of a home where the Bible was revered and its sacred truths held up as worthy of the most earnest investigation of the tallest intellect. I loved Jake. Last fall was a year under the yoke when he and Jimmie Cooley were our couriers. Often have they come by here leaving their horses, and going on to town on foot and then coming back giving us all the information they could get.

I had him brought to our house in our ox wagon. Mr. Fulkerson's boy (Barr) coming to our assistance. We got him in without much trouble. Sallie came back—prepared the lounge. When the boys came they brought it down and placed it in the parlor. We then brought him in—placed him on it drawing off his boots and straightening out his soldier jacket. I had washed the blood off before he was taken from the wagon but as we moved him the blood began to drip from his ears and head. We had not discovered until then that he was shot through the head. A ball had pierced him just below the right cheekbone going through and coming out on the left part of the back of the head. Another ball had entered the left side about the heart.

I felt so much sympathy for his poor father. His heart seemed almost crushed beneath the terrible stroke. After looking at him for a few moments he said "I cannot stand this and will you take care of my poor boy." I told him I would do everything I could and Sarah made the same remark. He bowed so thankfully and rode off. As he went he threw himself forward upon the saddle to give way to his grief. I trust the Lord will give him comfort. He is living, I think, in great fear, was robbed yesterday of some of his meat. We have no male friend tonight to set with us to watch over the lifeless body. But woman, woman is here with all her deep felt sympathy. Jennie Walker, Buena McCarthy and Harriet Hill came out soon after they heard it. Late in the evening Polly Hamlin and Nannie Merrimon came over and Lucy.

January 23, 1865

The night has passed without interruption. Poor Jake is lying cold as marble. His face is pleasant, no distortion of feature. I do hope a precious Saviour has had mercy upon him in his dying moments and given him a home in Heaven. This hair [sewn in the diary] is a lock of poor Jake's taken off by some of the girls.[6] His sister Cynthia and his two little brothers (Charles and Rufus) came with her. She seems to be so distressed. I have sent Gus after the coffin. The girls going

---

6. The lock of hair still remains in the diary, where it is sewn to the page.

down with him. Mr. Fulkerson has been out this morning showing us kindly sympathy. They left about 4 with Jake's remains. Frank Fulkerson and James Hale having walked out to assist us in laying him in the coffin. Cousin John Earnest and Alf Owens came in today about 1—we were so glad to see they still lived. Their presence was timely. I do feel the Lord is so kind to me, he gives me friends in every hour of deep distress. Jake rode a very nice little bay mare which he called Queen of the West. The bushmen got all he had that was any account. I sat up until 2 last night.

January 28, 1865

This day week was the last our poor lamented Jake was to spend on earth. Could we have known this solemn truth how gloomy, how sad would have been our feelings. Well for as the future is hid from us helpless dependents upon the great, the eternal God how watchfully should we live. This has been to me a sorer trial than any I have passed since this unholy, this terrible war began. Never in my life have I been so harrowed by any thing as the murder of our brave, noble Jake. If I could only have known that he was permitted in his last moment to call in faith upon Jesus how consoling it would have been to me.

Yesterday Eliza Ruth, Jennie McC and little Stan came out bringing the pleasant yet I must say painful news that my dear soldier boy was in the country above here. We have no pleasure to see one of our loved ones coming home. The atrocious deeds of bushmen fill us with horror but we do hope our God will give us deliverance. She also told me that I was threatened by the bushmen to be robbed of all my meat and lard. Eliza Ruth and Sallie went today to see the Miss Armstrongs and ascertain, if possible, the place of the murderers and robbers. They have been quietly reposing in that region all week. Had our men been here they might have had them all dislodged. The weather has been very cold since Monday and perhaps it is this which hath saved us from their depredations.

January 29, 1865

At home now and all has been quiet thus far. Never, never shall the sad occurrence of last Sabbath pass from memory. Jake's upturned bloody face with the large quantity of blood he had lost on the ground. The manner in which it was done and the number who came to take the life of one Confederate youth are things which are indelibly fixed. Brother George came an hour or two ago; he brings us news that the report is white flags float along the lines of both armies near Richmond, that peace commissioners have met there. One of the darkest features to me in the Federal Government is their unwillingness to make an exchange of prisoners. They have at all times this business entirely at their control. O how many lives have been lost in their cold, uncomfortable prisons. How many widows and orphans are now crying to Heaven for the great avenger of all to avenge this inhuman cruelty.

January 30, 1865

The day had almost passed yesterday without any exciting scenes. George after eating his dinner set out for some place where he might be more secure than at home. He had not gone far when he met up with two soldiers. In a short time they commenced coming in numbers. Very soon my dear boys Sam and Ike came along with cousin Willie Tuck Gammon with them. We were so rejoiced and so thankful to see the loved ones particularly Sam.[7] He had been gone so long. He looks rather poor but seems to be in good health. The girls returned with him bringing Bug. Our house was quite a scene of confusion for an hour or more.

Major Day having with him 75 or 80 men had come to ferret out Mr. Sizemore but he was not to be found. If he had been at home their manner of procedure gave him every opportunity to make his escape. I fear many of them have acted badly. Mr. Alvis came over while we were eating breakfast to complain against those who

7. Sam had apparently left the Sixty-third Regiment in Virginia and returned home.

stopped at his house for taking things of no value to them but much to him, took several old horses not fit for the service but excellent work nags. They also took his hat and left him without. These things are such a great mortification to me. I do dislike anything of this kind so much with our Confederate soldiers. We expect our enemies to act in this manner but men who fight for the high and noble cause for which Southern soldiers fight we do feel such acts so degrade their character. May the God of Heaven forgive them for such deeds of wickedness.

January 31, 1865

We had with us last night several soldiers belonging to the 12th battery as well as Sam, Ike, George and Tuck Gammon (son of James), Bug, Buena, Sallie and Dick. We made out quite well as the soldiers slept on the floor in the front room. Ella Walker, Mollie Powel and E. Heiskell came out this morning. We had hoped they would spend a pleasant day with Sam but the peace of one day now is too uncertain for a hope.

Ike had intended going to the command but was not ready to leave as the others left and James Sevier was coming up. He did not hurry himself off. We were so anxious he should get away as we heard so many reports of what Sizemore said in regard to him. At length he and J. set out and went across to Mr. Merrimons and soon returned saying they heard the report of 12 guns. This put us in a scene of excitement and hurry to get them off. Sam and George were soon ready but before they left a man in Yankee uniform was seen going up the road. Ike stopped off to see who he was and found out he was a Federal soldier by the name of Shelton coming home under Gen. B's protection.

They all were soon out of sight. About half or three-quarters of an hour after they left who should come up from the other road but my little soldier boy. He said his papa and uncle H. were just behind. We felt so uneasy but hoped all would be right. Dick and H. soon came; we were so glad to see them. Not long after they came

Brother George and Sam came and we found the reported guns were Mr. Merrimon's hands breaking ice out of the sugar troughs. A good joke on the boys but yet I felt such a mistake is far better than a reality attended with disaster. Rich, Powell and Sam left this evening and went by the road as far as Richard Sensabaughs. Powell went to Mr. Charles.

February 5, 1865

This morning sometime after we had eaten breakfast Ida came almost breathless with excitement saying we have good news. They have caught Jesse Burton. Tom Miller had given the information. He was brought by Sarahs wounded through the body. He had been caught after daylight this morning at home. Our men ran in upon him; he had a little girl as sentinel but our men were too vigilant and when she discovered them and went to communicate they were near and rushed forward. He got out of the house and made resistance but of no avail.

I would like much to know whether he had anything to do with the dark deed which was committed this day two weeks near our home. I felt God will bring such men to swift recompense. Never did I feel until that day that Christians should make it a subject of special prayer that God would deliver such men into our hands. I had felt they were very bad men but felt we should pray that God would make them good men, that their hearts might be brought under the influence of the Holy Spirit. But I now feel O God deliver us from the power of such men by removing them from our midst if it is thy Holy Will.

The scenes of trouble which every Sabbath are occurring fill me with horror. Our men have this day killed Jesse Burton.[8] They took him up the road, turned towards the Ebbing Spring, took him up towards Mr. Amis's sawmill. They told him to pray, he got down as though he was when he made a bound and made for the woods.

8. There was a Jesse Burton from Hawkins County who was a member of the Sixty-first Tennessee Mounted Infantry (C.S.A.). He went absent without leave in April 1863.

They ran it is said 1/4th of a mile and he came near getting away but he tonight is numbered with the dead. Another widow and fatherless children mourn this night for the husband and father. O that the Lord would shorten these days of calamity.

I received by Jake Miller this evening a paper from my dear cousin J. Bachman containing an article headed *Day of Fasting and Prayer* in which our Congress has set aside the 22nd of February and recommended the President to proclaim it throughout our Southern Land.

### February 7, 1865

All are gone of our male family tonight but brother George. Richard, Sam, and Powell left this evening. Richard going to Mr. Russells, Sam to Mr. Millers and Powell to Mr. Wm. Lyons. Brother Hiram left an hour or two before. They thought best not to stay in town lest Sizemore with his heartless associates might come. The ground is covered this evening with snow that fell last night. Ike came home yesterday evening, did not tarry long. Major Day with about 60 men came down yesterday evening and left this morning intending to go on to Thorn Hill. I felt reluctant for Ike to go being badly mounted.

News came to us that a peace movement is on hand. When we think of almost 4 years of horrible carnage from war, our land laid waste, our dear friends slaughtered and disabled for life, the cries of widows and orphans and of the desolations of Zion the heart bleeds from every pore. We cry out O Lord how long until we shall see thy face reconciled. I have ever felt the Lord would give us an honorable peace and I feel so tonight.

### February 11, 1865

This has been to me a week of considerable anxiety. My dear boy Ike has been absent all week with Major Day. I know nothing tonight of him. Cousin Joe Galbraith came up today. He reports from rumor that 10,000 Federal troops are at Knoxville. We heard through Brother Hiram and he through Capt. F. Fulkerson that

Burbridge[9] was at Cumberland Gap. Whether these things are true or not we cannot tell. Cousin Joe told me today that the Yankees would hold all of Tennessee by the last of March. I told him I do not think so and that I felt God would not give us into their hands.

No bushmen have ever visited my home to rob or plunder. I have been most signally blessed. My dear husband and sons have not spent many nights for the last month away from home but thou has provided for them kind friends in the neighborhood where they rest quietly at night returning every day. Mr. Russell, Mr. Lyons, Mr. Sensabaugh and Charles and Mrs. Harlans.

February 12, 1865

Have had a more peaceful day than we have spent for several Sabbaths. O how pleasant. My dear son Ike returned this morning. We were all so glad to see him. I awoke this morning about 3, felt so troubled about him. I slept no more but spent the time in prayers to God for his protection and care over my dear son.

Major Day with his men camped last night at Mr. Wm. Clippers and were fired upon about 1 o'clock by bushmen. They were enabled to give them a short chase but do not know that they killed any of them but thought they had wounded some as there were signs of blood. Our men were unhurt. We feel so thankful to God when they escape. They all left this evening going out on the other road.

February 16, 1865

On Monday evening flags of truce met in Rogersville. The Federals bringing up some 15 or 16 prisoners amongst the number Major Clarkson. The Rebels bringing down two Southern ladies who wish to pass to their home. I have not ascertained why Federal prisoners were not brought but suppose they had been sent forward perhaps

9. General Stephen Burbridge was in charge of Union forces in the district of Kentucky at this time. However, because of his incompetence as an administrator and his poor record as a general, he was removed from command in February 1865. Mays, *The Saltville Massacre*, 70–71.

on the railroad but of this I know nothing. Both sides I understand were much disappointed at meeting in Rogersville. The Rebs were very anxious to go as far down as they could and the Feds were anxious to go up as far as they could. Our men proposed to them they might go up until they came to the first picket if they would allow them the privilege of going to theirs first but the Yanks declined. That night the young folks met at Cousin Annis and had a dance. Two Yanks were there. Ike says they were Copperheads, that they had been drafted. Some of our men it is said stole pistols and I suppose tried to get hold of some of their horses but they were closely guarded. I understand Zack Tilson got one and made for the Rebel lines upon it. Poor Zack I fear no good will come of him. He is not like Jake. Ike tried to swap horses with them and while riding round trying horses some of them helped themselves to one of his spurs.

Tuesday morning when Richard returned from Mr. Russells he told us of the flags of truce. We had known nothing of it until then. He also told us that Major Clarkson would pass up that morning. Lizzie and Fannie went across to Mr. Merrimons. We felt so anxious to hear from our dear prisoner boys with whom he had been confined on Johnson's Island. After staying some time they returned and he came along soon after.

While they were absent I went to the barn to see about some flaxseed and flax which had been laid out there. Just as I was leaving for home Ike came along having with him Eliza and Sallie Hanson and Buena. When I got home I found Lizzie and F. Lizzie told me that Major Clarkson gave them a very pleasant account of our dear boys and spoke of my loved N. as one of the best boys he ever saw. He said he had made a profession of religion. My heart was so deeply touched. I felt that my Father has been giving to me the great desire of my heart concerning my dear child when I was lamenting his sad condition. I do trust he is leading them both to that fountain opened in the house of King David and that their imprisonment may be a sanctified affliction. Major Clarkson spoke of their quarters as being as comfortable as a prisoners life could be expected. The room which they occupied was I suppose 10 by 12. They had bought paper and had a stove. Their greatest privation was something to eat.

We had a call last night from Captain George Ross. He is so pleasant and I love to meet up with him. He told us he had heard that Judge Vandyke had fallen a victim of Northern brutality, had died in prison. How sad we feel to hear of the death of our noble brave men. That family has been sorely visited since this unholy struggle began, lost 3 sons and now I fear the Father. May that bereaved wife and mother draw consolation from the unfailing fountain. I trust she mourns her loved ones as not lost but only gone before. I knew none of her sons but John and he was a lovely rep-resentative—so noble, so good. George told us that he had heard his father had been sent South again. I trust it is true for I feel he is too old to brave the hardships of prison life. Sam returned just as George was leaving having gone across to Mr. Paynes in company with J. Miller and Capt. Phillips to learn something in regard to the movements of the bushmen if possible. George came back and staid a half hour or more. He and Sam went to brother Hirams and staid all night. George was telling us of his close proximity to Sizemore when at Morristown. He said he supposed that he had lost the nicest chance of his capture of any man since he had become an object of notice. He went into the house of a Mrs. Dickinson, a warm Southern woman, but she and her daughters either from excitement or fear or a feeling that he had made his escape failed to let them know, not knowing the prominent position of the great man Sizemore, that he would be quite notable game should he be caught—made his escape. This morning Sam and his papa left intending to go to Major Day's headquarters to see if anything could be done to secure Sam a place in cavalry service.[10]

10. As did many other soldiers that winter, Sam probably left Lee's forces in Virginia without permission. His father was trying to help him enroll in a local Confederate unit to prevent him from being listed as a deserter. We do know that Sam never appeared on the roll of his regiment as a deserter, but the clear inference is that he, like many others, had grown weary of trench life and concluded that the war would soon be over.

February 17, 1865
Sam has a promise from Major Day that a man will be sent in his place. I trust he may be permitted to go into the cavalry service if O my Father thou seeth it best for him. He seems to have grown weary of infantry and more tired of a soldiers life than I love to see the patriots of the South be. O when I think of what we fight for, when I think of the injustice of our enemy towards us, when I think of the dark malignant designs formed against us, when I think of the noble who have fallen, when I think of my blessed Bible which I feel recognizes the existence of slavery, when I think of the wretched condition of our poor deluded servants my heart is nerved to its greatest determination to never give up and to urge every soldier to not be weary but to go forward trusting in our God for he will deliver. I feel our Father will not give us up to be trodden down by the oppressor.

February 19, 1865
God is good. This has been a most lovely day, the air is cool but the sun has shone so brightly it looks like spring is coming. We have had rather a quiet day. The reports of yesterday have made us uneasy. Richard left this evening, thought he would go on up the country. I dislike for him to leave on the Sabbath but we feel it is best to not stay when such repeated reports come. O that we might have peace once more so that our Sabbaths would be free from disturbance, our church opened and our minister permitted to return. Major Day and Capt. left soon after breakfast. I do hope we may never again be subjected to Yankee rule—the thought is so painful.

I heard yesterday something connected with the prison life of my dear boys which impressed me so deeply with a sense of God's goodness to sinful fallen beings. There was a storm passed over the island sometime in the Fall which blew down much timber and owing to this they have been supplied with wood and made more comfortable this winter than last. This winter here has been much colder than last but whether it has been there so or not I do not know. I feel the hand of God supplied my prisoner boys with fuel and many others. Some of them in all probability would have sunk under the rigors of a Northern winter in prison had it not been for his providential dealings.

The news of the past week has been to me so pleasant. A letter from Samuel Powel to his mother breathes forth the ardent longings of a soul desiring salvation through the merits of Jesus. News also from Nick McCarty that he is reading his Bible, has become a very steady man and the news from my dear boys at Johnson's island gives me more real pleasure, more hope in the final success of our cause than to know we had million upon millions of men to bring into the field.

Kit Spears came this evening to see us. He left the army at Tupelo on the 27th of January. He has been telling us of the fall of our noble high souled Arthur F.[11] He was killed on the 30th of November near Franklin. He was pierced by eight balls, 7 through his body and one through the head. His body was carefully cared for, he was laid in a nice coffin purchased by Jake Williford at a cost of $50.00. He was interred in a deep grave. At that point the enemy was driven back with the dead and wounded of both sides falling into our hands. Kit also told us that the enemy burnt up the possessions of cousin Sallie Dillahunty leaving her entirely destitute of clothing and every home comfort.

March 4, 1865

This day witnesses the inauguration of President Lincoln and the Vice-President Andrew Johnson (traitor, traitor). O Lord defeat the plans of these wicked men and bring all their expectations to naught. The cause of Southern Freedom seems to be thought by many in a most perilous condition. South Carolina is now the seat of war with our Western Army. The enemy at last accounts had possession of Columbia and Charleston which had been evacuated by

11. "Arthur F" was Sergeant Major Arthur Fulkerson from Hawkins County. He was killed at the Battle of Franklin.

our men. Savannah has fallen but this is not a triumphant victory to the foe.

Mike McCarty arrived at home on Monday the 27th of February and on the 1st of March Nick McCarty arrived. Nick had been in Blountville several days waiting on Mike thinking he would come that way but Mike made a very direct course for home having been a prisoner from the 16th of May 1863 until sometime in February of 65.

Nick had been absent longer than Mike but then he was not in prison. Mike looks so well and has grown rather taller and his skin looks so clear and well, had many hardships to endure from cold and hunger part of the time during the winter season. He was bareheaded, barefooted and without pants but the Lord was with him sustaining and preserving him.

March 5, 1865

This is the first Sabbath I have been in town for a great while, went down with the expectation of hearing a sermon from Mr. Flora but after getting to Eliza Ruths learned with great pleasure that my dear cousin Jonathan Bachman would preach. We attended— Sallie, Ike, Ella and Powell—and heard a very good sermon from these words "the pleasures of sin for a season." I was much pleased with his views. He spoke pleasantly and kindly to the young in regard to the fascinating amusements of dancing and card play. He said he had often been asked if he thought a social dance among friends or a game of cards was wrong. He said he was not prepared to answer that question but the command of God was to abstain from very appearance of evil and that there were no amusements which had been so soul destroying as the two named above, none have been sought after so eagerly, none have led so many astray. Therefore we should abstain from every appearance of evil. He also spoke of the power of prayer. No influence for evil could prevail over us so long as the heart was kept right by a constant application to the living and true God for help to do our duty.

March 16, 1865

This day has been set apart by our President as a day of fasting, humiliation and prayer. We have been much blessed in being permitted to attend at the sanctuary and hear a very excellent sermon from cousin J. Bachman.

March 17, 1865

Last night I was permitted to welcome my dear, my beloved Nick home, just returned from his long life of imprisonment on Johnson's Island. He had left Samuel Gammon behind on account of a horse. He met Powell who had left on Tuesday to go after them a few miles this side of Blountville. How the heart rejoices to see those who are so dear separated as we have been under such trying circumstances. My dear child looks much better than I expected. He has lost one of his front teeth. This day we have been made to rejoice again by the coming of our dear Samuel Gammon.

Hiram has been with us for several days; has been suffering much from boils. I have not had a visit from him since he left his home to go to Baltimore to seek employment when he seemed to feel so happy and love us all so much. O the anguish of Soul I have had for my first born. He does not love my dear Saviour and I know should the Master call for him his spirit would be found wanting in its preparation to meet him who died that he might live. O to see my children turning to Christ as their only friend would give me more pleasure than anything else I could know concerning him.

March 18, 1865

I am this night enjoying a privilege which has long been denied me; that of having my 12 children under our roof for their suppers. I may say 13 for my dear Samuel Gammon is as one of them; could I only have had Bet[12] and little Max I feel my family would have been complete. O what reason have we to bless our God for his kind preserving

12. Bet was Hiram's wife, and little Max was Eliza's only grandchild at this time.

care over our dear loved ones. When I look around and see the many families whose loved ones return not I feel so thankful. I feel God my Father has dealt so kindly with us worms of the dust—unthankful and ungrateful as we may have been yet he has shown us favor. We have had the pleasure of meeting many friends during the past two weeks. Gen. Carter's company being located in this region of country and his headquarters a house on the road belonging to Mr. Amis. On Sabbath the 5th of March we had several dear, dear friends to dinner: Cousin Johnny Bachman, Jimmy Rhea, Joe Crawford, Cornelius Lucky, Tate and John Earnest. Cousin Will Rankin has been with us for several days. We love our friends and feel so proud of them; they are to us clever and good.

March 19, 1865

I arose this morning with my heart filled with the pleasing hope of attending church with more members of my family than I had been permitted for many, many long months. My beloved cousin Johnny had told us on Friday when he called a short time to tell the boys that he would preach today. I feel so thankful this evening. There were present at church today Nancy's 3 boys, E. Ruth's one soldier boy (Ed), my six including my dear Samuel Gammon. There were 34 present related to all the families besides many others related to our different families as well as my dear cousins Johnny Bachman and Cornelius Lucky. We had a noble, an excellent sermon from cousin J.

March 20, 1865

We have some fears from what we can hear that our troops will not be permitted to remain long with some thinking they are to go to Virginia, others to North Carolina. I hope they will be permitted to move forward instead of backward. Cousins Bob Anderson and Bob Bachman came down this evening. Mrs. Alexander and cousin Cornelia came out to see Sarah today and they with Sarah called over a short time this evening—gave us some music. They left before supper. With some persuasion I prevailed on cousin Bob to stay with

us and take supper. They are two noble soldiers. I feel very proud of
my kin who are in the service. They all seem to be soldiers from a
sense of duty. I love such soldiers, they feel their country's cause dear
to their hearts. This evening Fannie brings us word from reliable
authority that Stoneman is in Knoxville and that reinforcements are
coming in through the night and are set to cross the river. I do hope
our Heavenly Father may thwart their plans. Send us help O God.

March 21, 1865
Today we had several of loved ones with us. Hiram still with us and
we have had no such pleasant time with my dear boy since he first
left home to make a living. I do love my children and I cannot bear
to think of them living sinful and wicked lives. I feel my dear boy
with Nick Mc and J. Miller has been spending several hours in a
way I do not love playing cards. I do hope they may see the wrong
of such a precious waste of time.

This evening the boys brought out some of the girls. Lizzie
Mitchell, Lillie Rogan, Buena, Mollie Powel and Eliza Heiskell.
The last three stopped off at Sarahs; they had thought to have a
great time but quite a storm of hail, wind and rain rather thwarted
their plans but the boys contrived to get them over at a rather late
hour. They have had music, dancing and great enjoyment. I do not
enjoy their dancing. I feel now is no time to dance—are right on the
frontier our enemies are preparing to move somewhere—we do not
know how soon all the loved ones of our families are to be scattered
-perhaps never return. Cousin Tate came back today. I looked upon
our dear boys tonight as they set at the supper table and thought it
may be and is more than probable the same group will never surround my table again. Nick Fain, Sam Gammon, Sam Fain and Ike
had much good humor over days and scenes gone bye.

March 22, 1865
The girls spent the day with us and are tonight at Sarahs having
another round of enjoyment. Lizzie Mitchell seems to have such

heartfelt pleasure in the society of Rebs. She dreads the hour that puts a close to these hours of enjoyment and has taken a good cry this morning as we have news the troops are falling back. The wagons were sent back as far as Kingsport on Monday. I have been much engaged patching and darning trying to get all ready. The girls have been helping me. Mollie Ruth came out today bringing the boys clothes. I do not think that Nick and Kyle will leave unless driven out by a superior force. I feel I would be glad for some of our boys to stay here if it is safe and unless a force more than we at present anticipate should come. I think they can stay as the move of the Yanks is on the railroad.

Hiram, Tate, Ernest and Eddie Ryan left this evening to join the command which is at New Providence having left Ebbing Spring yesterday at noon. A gloom gathers over us whenever we think for one moment that we are to fall under Yankee rule and I must say it is truly delightful to me that such thoughts do not often harass me. I do feel God will be our shield and protector. I do not believe we are to be much troubled by them.

March 23, 1865

We have had a sad parting this morning. The girls all came over to say goodbye. Seven of the dear ones have just left; Nick, Sam, Ike, Powell, Fain Powel, Ed Powel, Samuel Gammon and Will Rankin. They have again turned their backs on home. Dick went up to the mill and from there to Mr. Lyons while there he saw a man who said he had been run out of Greeneville by the Yanks was wounded slightly—he came back and told Papa. Richard determined to leave that evening. We had dinner and he left soon after. He and I had been very much engaged in doctoring Sibbie[13] but she died and I felt it is all right for I never felt satisfied about having her. I wanted her to go back to her rightful owner. Ike had traded for her and she was his but not the soldiers who first took her.

13. Sibbie is the horse that Ike obtained in the "swap" mentioned in Eliza's entry of January 15, 1865. The horse that Ike traded for Sibbie was probably stolen as well.

So we are again a family of women and children while tonight we have Nick, Mike McC and Bob Powell. Nick and Mike are still unmounted. Kyle and Rhineheart with the two men belonging to the sixtieth made a trip through Poor Valley—Rhineheart has secured a beautiful animal. Kyle swapped and has him a very passable horse. They are here tonight inclining to make a search for Bill Owens. I have been giving the boys a talk tonight. Poor Rhineheart is, I fear, too reckless in regard to human life. I dread to see this spirit fasten on the heart of any of our dear soldiers.

March 25, 1865

All is still peace rumor after rumor come but we do not feel alarmed. Some say there is quite a host of Yanks between here and Knoxville on the railroad but we do not believe all we hear. Some say 70,000 but numbers trouble not so long as we feel the God of Israel keepeth watch. Ike and Billy Boyd came by and got dinner. I gave them something before ours was ready. Billy talks very jovially about the Yanks and especially the Union folks. He says he would love for us to take Knoxville more than any other place for these people who go there think it is their heavenly home. Sam Gammon and Nick left this evening. This life is not very palatable to them. I hope all things will be well with them. They have no idea of being prisoners again if they can help it. I hope they may not be taken again.

March 26, 1865

This morning the sun arose so clear and beautiful. Sallie and Dicky went to town to go to Sunday School. After they left we felt anxious to know what our boys who left us this morning had done. In a short time some returned and said they had made a trip through a portion of Choptack—had taken two horses and captured two men: Mr. Slagle and Clemmons. The horses were taken from Mr. Rice and Harvey Young. The two men were taken on to J. Millers and from there they were sent on up to headquarters. I hope they have not murdered them and we begged for the life of Mr. S. Before this war began I knew, I then thought he was an honest man and felt so much solicitude about him and felt he surely had not begun to do acts of wickedness at which every feeling of the Christian heart revolted. I do hope his life has been spared. I have urged our men to do right and to never do anything which would call down the wrath of God upon them.

After they left I took my Bible and gathered my little family around me. I read some asking some questions. I then went out and read to old Ahab the book of Esther—was so deeply impressed with God's special care over his peculiar people. After reading I came in and assisted in preparing dinner for my dear family.

A short time after we were through Nick Fain came back with Kyle Mc and Ed Powel with him. They wanted dinner—we gave it. After talking a short time they left going out to Mr. Cheathams. An hour or two after they left Mrs. Pinkerton and Bug came out in search of our boys bringing the news that a scout of 75 Yanks were out towards the nose last night. They saw our boys but not knowing their force they were afraid to attack them. They also report that 500 Yanks had gone over the mountain.

March 31, 1865

This has been a week of some trial yet it has almost passed away, I may say quietly and peaceably. Rumor after rumor has come to us yet all things are quiet around us. We do not know whether our enemies have gone towards Bristol or returned to Knoxville. On Monday morn I took Gus with the wagon and El and Nate and set out for Mr. Rogans after some corn and lard. I walked over to Sarahs and there found Capt. W. Armstrong and 3 men who had been down on the railroad making reconnaissance. He reports the Yanks moving up in a force as he supposes from all he learns of about 800—said Sizemore with 25 men was at Cobbs Ford on the opposite side of the river Sabbath evening. I felt a little uneasy to make the trip lest Sizemore and clan should have made their way up; but I felt I must go. We had rather a rough road but got along very well. Soon made known my business—found there a Mrs. Wright and daughter (Union) who were on their way to Knoxville. I felt deeply impressed while there of the demoralizing influences of Unionism—women could use profane language without a thought of Eternity. Mrs. W told me her husband and son had been killed by our men. She made his case out as a very cruel murder. We have to know both sides before we say anything. I know he fell into the hands of a very bad man—Mr. Williams the son-in-law of Mr. Carmack. I have ever felt disturbed when I thought our men acted without mercy. From Mrs. W. I learned of the death of Lt. Moore—he was caught at Starnes on Saturday by J. Willis. They were brought across the mountain quite early on Sabbath morning and murdered in a most cruel manner. Five white men and 2 Negroes being the murderers. A man by the name of Wolfenbarger was also killed. With him two good soldiers have fallen. I fear they were not prepared for death. This is the solemn thought.

On Tuesday I make horse garden in the evening. We were made to feel glad by the return of some of our dear boys. Sam Fain, Johnny Earnest having come on through from Bristol. Nick and Kyle Mc, Mr. Rhineheart and Pinkerton. Sam and John brought us news, if true exceedingly cheering, that Sherman's army is almost used up. A dispatch from Gen. Lee reports 22,000 prisoners taken.

The boys went on to town, returned then got supper and then left. Sam and Johnny going to their command. They went up to Mr. Carmacks and passed the night. On Wednesday night between 11 and 12 I was aroused by the noble soldier Kyle saying we have been on a scout and want to stay all night. He, Nick Mc and George Ross were together and had been out on the river. J. Miller, D. Miller, T. Miller, Rhineheart and Pinkerton with them—heard that Sizemore had not come into the neighborhood. They also heard there were no Yanks at the Gap. The boys were quite wet having been out in quite a rain. George and Kyle went on down below town and returned this evening. I fear George was drinking—my heart feels so troubled when I think of one like him becoming a victim of the terrible scourge of mankind. How fallen, how fallen could the mother see her son drifting on the billowing waves of intemperance to the certain destruction of the undying soul unless stopped in its downward career.

## April 1, 1865

The boys came down today. Kyle, Nick Mc, Sam Fain and Mr. Pinkerton. They were out on a scout Friday night in Caney Valley—were fired on by bushmen. All escaped unhurt. I feel so thankful when a kind Providence directs the balls aimed at them in another direction. These bushmen have been troubling the Southern citizens very much. I fear they may be permitted to go on by the Federal Government until our men shall become desperate and turn upon the Union folks with a feeling of desperation. They have been restrained by our Government and female influence. Women of the South have generally urged our Soldiers to do right but they are beginning to feel entreaty will be useless.

## April 3, 1865

Sam came home today and tells us they had a fight on Sabbath with the bushmen killing 4 of them. Kit Sizemore and Nelson Johnson being two of them. The others he did not know and says that it was with great persuasion that the lives of Mr. Sizemore and James Courtney were saved. The men of the 2nd Tenn. who are now here are perfectly desperate on account of the killing of Lt. Moore. I do feel it is a terrible state of things and I do feel the Union people could do something to suppress this robbing, plundering and murdering by the ambush of our citizens and men. This evening with the assistance of Gus made some garden—put in tomatoes and bean—hope I may have a good garden. The little children started to school this morning—Dick, Nannie, Ellie and little Sallie. The first day of Nan & Ellie at school.

## April 4, 1865

Have been busy all morning and cannot see what at. So many jobs to attend to. Lizzie started this evening to go to Mr. Harris in search of sweet potato seed. She stopped at Mr. Merrimons and he told her Mr. H. had none. She bring back to me the sad news that Wilber Carter has been caught, severely wounded and his leg amputated above the knee. There is not much hope of his living. He with two others were inside the lines taking horses it is supposed. The other two men escaped. This is too hazardous a business. The fate of a spy should that be fastened upon them is fearful.

## April 5, 1865

We still live thanks to our Heavenly Father. This has been a day of intense feeling with us all. This morning about 5 o'clock we were again visited by a set of outlaws such as I have never seen and hope it is the will of my God I shall never look upon such another. I had awakened Dicky to make his fire, heard them coming and said to Lizzie they are upon us get up. I was soon dressed excepting shoes and stockings. They demanded the opening of the door. I opened and Mr. William Sizemore stood before. He said "Good Morning Mrs. Fain, I am here and I intend to tear you up and burn your house down." After saying this he gave orders for them to go ahead. I told him to wait until I could say something to him. I then told him if he began this work retribution would take place. He replied "My family are out from here now and I do not care a d— —m" and such a scene ensued for about half or three-quarters of an hour I have never witnessed. Doors bursted open, my house literally full of robbers. They took my silver spoons: 7 large, five plated teaspoons, 12 small silver teaspoons and a silver dessert spoon—all the meat in my smokehouse and many other things and last but not least my old horse George with Dick's saddle.[14]

14. Fannie Rhea Fain of Blountville also kept a diary during the Civil War, and in her April 9, 1865, entry, she wrote, "Bushwhackers robbed cousin Eliza Fain extensively." Fannie was a daughter of Sam Rhea by his second wife. Eliza thought of Sam as her father-uncle. A Northern sympathizer, Fannie called the Civil War a "wicked, sinful, and most unholy war" that kept her from her husband, John Hammer Fain. In 1865 John was forty years old and had to leave Blountville to keep from being conscripted into the Confederate forces. Fannie's diary is held in the Archives and Special Collections of East Tennessee State University in Johnson City, Tennessee.

They then left for Mrs. Millers. I thought not of the loss of property but of my dear darling boys and just felt and prayed to my Father to preserve them and all would be well with me. As they came back Sizemore with some 6 or 8 men went into my cellar carrying off my fruits in cans 7 or 8 in number. This finished their work of plunder. Sizemore as he rode off at first told me to prepare breakfast for 28 but I told him I could not do it. They had broken open my springhouse and destroyed everything of milk, butter and no breakfast was prepared, but I this night in the language of Job say "what shall we receive good from the hand of the Lord and not receive evil" I do not fear for what man can do unto me as long as I have an abiding trust in the God of Heaven. I feel he will preserve our lives and that is all that I ask. Truly God is a shield. He is our protector. I feel his great power over me tonight. I feel this night there has been a work begun today the consequences of which I feel will fall on guilty heads. The Lord has said "Vengeance is mine, I will repay saith the Lord." This is sufficient for me to know.

From here they went on to town. The only family that seems to have been the object of great spite is Nancy McCartys. They ordered breakfast from the different Southern families I suppose. I understand that Sizemore with 5 others by invitation took breakfast with Mrs. Netherland. They arrested all the Southern men but released all excepting Mr. Norman and James Gouldy. Both of whom it is said went with them through choice.

Sarah was also a sufferer in their route. O how closely knit are the hearts of our dear Southern people. We sympathize so deeply with each other. Lou Carmack came down this evening. She tells me the boys are all safe. Bug McCarty and Mollie Powel came out from town. Buena and Malissa came over from Mrs. Rileys. We had much conversation. I hope we may all be enabled to feel and do right.

47 years this night my loved Father lay a corpse leaving a widow and 4 little daughters. I trust all of his family excepting myself this night are in Heaven free from all the strife and cares of

earthly life. How sweet to have a home where "thieves do not break through and steal"—such a home is Heaven.

April 6, 1865

This morning Bug and Liz went up as far as Mr. Harlans to send word to the boys that these men were on the lookout—would waylay them to take their lives. A short time before dinner Mollie Ruth and Sallie Dick came out. They were anxious the boys should be warned saying they understood that a scout of bushmen had passed through town the night before. While we were setting out to table Mollie Ruth saw two men galloping down the fence into the woodland. All got up from the table in haste and came out to the door when another was seen riding up the lane. Our anxiety was soon relieved by the appearance of my dear boy Sam and Mr. Rhineheart. As they came through here the rest came down the road numbering in all 11. They were on their way to town intending to arrest Union men and hold them for the Southern men arrested by Sizemore but we were able to tell them they were all released. This caused some delay in their movements but they at length all left for town. I felt somewhat afraid lest a wrong spirit seize the hearts of our dear boys and they would do something which God could not approve of. I want them to tell Union citizens they left their home at the start of the war for the protection of home and all that was dear to their hearts. They were now thrown in here as a guerrilla party for that business and they felt Union folks could if they would protect them against bushmen and that they intended if it was not done that they should feel the hand of oppression on them—that they knew them and they knew that. Such work was not pleasant to them but if nothing else would do they had determined to prosecute with vigor the work of destruction.

April 7, 1865

I woke this morning before 3. As I lay on my bed communicating with my God my soul was so overwhelmed with a sense of the goodness of God. I feel the visitation from the bushmen is one of the greatest blessings I have had since the war began. I do feel it is a sanctified trial. I feel I have made progress in the divine life. The spirit of God is poured out upon me—I feel I can approach my Father in such love, such fervor of heart and such deep humility. I feel so thankful there is nothing meritorious in man. I feel I was enabled to pray this morning with stronger faith for the success of our country's cause than I ever felt before and I do feel God has heard me. I feel he will not give us up to our enemies. He has said "ask and ye shall receive, seek and ye shall find." He is sincere, he is true and I now await with feelings of pleasure the news which shall come to me of the success of our armies from the 5th to the 10th of April 1865. The news of the evening has had a tendency to depress the spirit. We have heard that the Yanks were crossing the river at McKinney's Mill. Whether true or not we cannot tell. We also hear from Union sources that Johnston's army has been defeated by Sherman. But of this we know not the truth.

April 8, 1865

This is the 28th birthday of my dear boy Nick. O how glad I would have been could he have spent it with us, but this cruel war has broken up all the sweet enjoyments of home. I have been engaged this day as I am every Saturday patching up old rags but it is with such a thankful heart I do this work. Liz went to town today to get her shoes mended.

April 10, 1865

I could not sleep last night. As I lay upon my bed my Soul was so full of "what will my Master have me to do." I revolved in my mind as I believe under the guidance of the Spirit many things. At length it seemed to me as if it fastened on the deep importance of a female prayer meeting. I just felt if I lived to see the light of another day I would go to town and see the Christian women of Rogersville as to whether it met their approbation. I thought I would go in the spirit of a Christian and see Mrs. Netherland and

Mr. White.[15] I had much of what I wanted to say talked over on my bed with self to see whether I wished to use any harsh epithets or anything unbecoming the followers of Jesus. I could not see or know that I had one word which the Bible did not sustain. In the morning when I got up it was raining and I felt my Father did not approve of my plans but of this I was soon relieved.

I felt I should have to contrive some way for my dear Sallie to get to her school and I had none but my ox wagon. I doubt whether any aristocrat of England or France is as proud of their gilded carriages and prancing horses than I am of my old shabby wagon and two nice white oxen. I told Jim to gear up and we were soon on the way.[16] When I got over to Sarahs she said she would go if I would wait. I told her I would. She was soon ready and the two Sallies, Sarah and I with Jim composed our company. Sarah loaned me an umbrella and she had one which added much to our comfort. When I got to Eliza Ruths I found Mrs. Harry and Laura Alexander there. After much pleasant conversation I told them what was the principal object of my coming to town—it was to see if we could start a female prayer meeting. Mrs. Harry spoke up and said she had been thinking of it. I felt the spirit is at work and we can do it. I spoke to Laura Alexander first on the subject as she had asked me to go into a room for a private interviews. She seemed to concur in my views. I left the matter with her and E. Ruth and

15. Tucked into the front of the volume of Eliza's diaries covering this period (now in the Fain Collection), there is a draft or a copy of an undated letter to a Mr. White. Whether the letter was actually sent is not known. In the letter Eliza wrote: "I write you this note asking of you if you have there some knives and forks as the men who visited me the other morning left one without enough to set my table with the promise, if not taken by bushwhackers, I will pay for them, but if they are you need not expect one to pay you as I feel from the depths of my heart that you Union sympathizers can suppress this house plundering if you will. From a sense of duty to my family I write this note to say to you that Southern people will no longer submit and for your own safety and the safety of other citizens I beg of you to have this business suppressed. I have no desire to see evil befall any of you but on the contrary rejoice when you all live in peace and quiet. I feel God is upon the throne. We are passing through a terrible revolution. God has some great purpose to accomplish in his government and I do feel the church of the South is secure. Your friend with feeling of kindness, E. R. Fain"

16. Jim was a twelve-year-old slave and apparently the only male in residence.

came on upstreet in my wagon. When we came near Mrs. Rogans, Margaret gave me the sign through the window she wished to speak with me. I made Jim halt. Upon the steps sat two rather blue looking men. Mr. Sevier and Mr. Rogan. My heart felt sad to think of the high souled spirit which was bowing in fear (as I thought) before such a power as a Lincoln dynasty.

While here Meg presented me with two knives and forks. I thanked her and felt I did not wish to take them telling her Mrs. Carmichael had sent me some. She rather pressed me and I took them feeling they come from the hand of God. I spoke to her of our plan for a prayer meeting. She seemed to approve. I then came on to Annies and here goodness and mercy again met me. She sent me out 3 tumblers. I felt all is from my Father's hand. From here I drove directly home. Sweet home on earth where my Father has fitted up such a beautiful home on earth for the sinner—what must be the home of his redeemed child in Heaven.

I had like to have forgotten the news which Lincoln sources had going through the town. It was that Richmond was given up— Lee's whole army surrendered and that Lee himself had made his escape and that the Confederacy was played out. It never moved me one particle. If Gen. Lee is the man I think he is he will share the fate of the brave and noble who have stood shoulder to shoulder in defence of right. I believe he is a Christian and would as soon think he would renounce his life as willingly as his Christian principle. I know he reads his Bible and feel if he does he feels this war is to establish the true doctrine of God's Holy Word in regard to slavery.

April 11, 1865

I was awakened this morning by the barking of dogs. I listened and thought I heard the tramp of horses. I sprang from my bed saying to Lizzie they are here again. I was so much frightened for a moment or two but no sooner was my hands and heart stretched out to God than fear departed and I felt I could meet any number of my enemies. I listened, I heard nothing more and I lay down upon my bed. Dear little

Lil was frightened so much. She too thought she heard the tramp of horses; this was a little before 4 A.M. I lay not sleeping any more but praying and what a delightful hour of prayer that was. I was nerved by it for anything. I felt God's sustaining grace and my soul rejoiced in the Lord. I had such exalted views of God, his character, his greatness and majesty. I thought too upon the causes of this war and the tendency of everything which had been brought forward by the Federal Government, all all seems to be for evil. There is no good, there is nothing connected with it which has any tendency to elevate the soul of man and bring him to Heaven.

I rose about 5 and urged on my dear daughter E the importance of rising early, being energetic that she might be a useful laborer in the vineyard of the Lord. As soon as I was dressed I went into the kitchen and found without much surprise that Caroline[17] a servant girl belonging to Mr. Watterson had left. I made an examination about her clothing. She had taken all belonging to her and her bed clothes which were her own. Mine she had left. I had felt for some weeks she was not the same servant she had always been before. She had been discontented, complaining of her labor — seemed to take no interest in anything she had to do which was quite a trouble to me. I had borne all in great patience thinking she was sick working often myself much harder than she did to shield her. I have no doubt now this is what awoke me at four and had I opened the door I might have seen and known all about it but I never feel like opening my door unless it is demanded or necessary. I felt sorry for the poor Negro feeling she had started upon a life of trial such as she had never known before. I thought of the poor creatures wants and would so gladly had she made known to me her intentions given her something for her journey. I feel no feelings of unkindness towards our poor deluded servants. The sin of their discontent is resting upon

17. It is surprising that the slave Caroline stayed this long. She appears not to have gone very far, since the Fains made numerous payments to Caroline and her husband, Frank McCarty, during the postwar years. Caroline was actually hired help, having been rented from the Wattersons for fifty-two dollars a year.

the heads of those who would drag God from his throne, if they could, to carry out their great principles of false philanthropy. I was unmoved as to any inconvenience to which I might be put about my work. I knew I could get along. I know how to milk, to cook and get along with all the labor I was in the habit of carrying on. None of the others knew anything about it: Old Polly, Jim, Gen and Nate. Three children were sleeping in the same cabin and old Ahab in his but they heard it not. From all we could discover from the tracks they had a horse and oxen. No news today.

Captain Armstrong[18] with a scout of men passed down; heard this evening that our boys have been over the river and that they have killed 3 bushwhackers. I trust God will take care of them and preserve them from every danger. We feel they are in his hands and I never have felt so perfectly easy about one of my sons when in the lines as I do about my dear Sam. I believe it is a feeling implanted in my soul by the spirit of God in answer to prayer. I know not a hair of the head of one of them can be hurt unless it is my Father's will and to that I bow in resignation. I feel he put it into the hearts of our soldiers to not leave us to the power and merciless brutality of such a man as Sizemore — and that he too will not suffer a hair of the head of one of them to be injured unless they by acts of cruelty and a disregard of his holy commandments call it down upon them.

April 12, 1865

This has been a day of constant rain. The water is flowing plentifully all around — how pleasant to feel our Father does all things. Sallie sent Dick out this evening with a note from Mollie Ruth urging us to send word to the boys to get out of here saying that Mat Speck had returned from the Gap bringing news that Grant's official dispatch was that Richmond was given up — that Lee's army

18. William Lyons Armstrong enlisted in Company G of the Thirty-first Tennessee (C.S.A.) as a private but was soon elected a captain. From 1862 until he returned to his home in the spring of 1865, he was on the staff of General John C. Vaughn. He was a Presbyterian and lived until 1908. He is buried in the cemetery beside the New Providence Presbyterian Church outside Surgoinsville.

had surrendered retaining their side arms. She also told that they had the wires and were dispatching to Vaughn that reinforcements would be sent with a view to entrap him—that they had the names of all the soldiers in here and if taken they would be killed—but not one uneasy feeling has this exerted in my heart. My trust is stayed upon my God, my prayers to him.

April 13. 1865

This morning I arose early—made preparations for washing. I had a fire kindled—the water on. Soon after breakfast I gathered my clothes and was off to the wash house taking Gen[19] with me leaving El and Nate to assist Lizzie about house cleaning, churning and dinner. Old Polly came into the kitchen today, she has suffered for several weeks from rheumatism and some days can do nothing and others creeps around a little. After I began washing old Ahab came to help. I got along wonderfully thinking God helps his creatures whenever they help themselves. We finished about 3 o'clock. After getting through I came to the house and found Lucy here with a Chattanooga paper containing the account of Gen. Lee's surrender with his army. It may be true but I do not believe and even were I to believe this it does not for one moment shake my confidence in my God as to the position which the South shall occupy amongst the nations of earth when this struggle shall cease.

Just as we were through and making our comments who should come riding up but my soldier boy Sam. We felt so glad to see him. He wanted clean clothes and his pants mended. I made inquiry of him about the reports of his plundering Mrs. Kyle's house.[20] He told me he had not been in on it. Thus it is with Lincoln adherents with regard to truth.

19. Gen (also known as Cindy) was a ten-year-old slave. Gus, her father, left the Fains in August 1865.

20. Alice Kyle, the wife of W. C. Kyle, was one of Eliza's longtime friends, but the Kyles were old-line Whigs who opposed secession. Sam had apparently joined a Confederate unit that was involved in harassing Unionists, perhaps in retaliation for the attacks of Sizemore's band on Confederates. It is interesting that Eliza accepts without question the word of her son.

April 14, 1865

I went to town today and made several calls. I found dear friends many of them in sore trouble because of the news we are receiving in regard to Lee's army. The saddest sight to me is the Christian heart giving way under it. I feel if it is God's will the North shall have our Southern country. We will open up another home for the Christians of the South in other lands but I never believe for one moment we will be given up.

April 17, 1865

Arose early this morning—I went out to my kitchen saw Gus and talked to him of his wrong conduct in leaving Saturday evening without letting me know where he was going. He having gone into the Brice Settlement. I told him I did not want him to go away and that I had confidence in him and I did not want the last remnant of confidence which I had in the African race destroyed by his leaving us. I felt this was not designed to make their condition better but worse and that whenever the plans of the Federals were served by them in this war they would care nothing more for them—said the Southern heart was the only place where any true feeling of humanity and kindness existed towards that race, that the North never had been willing nor would she be willing to be taxed to buy them a home anywhere or furnish means for their transportation to their own land. He listened attentively but said nothing.

Our hearts have been sorely pained this day. About 10 o'clock while washing Liz sent me word to come to the house that Sam was here. I came, he told me that a large portion of Gen. Lee's army had surrendered and that Gen. Lee with 200 men had escaped, that they had been flanked by Sheridan somewhere in the region of Lynchburg. He also said we had lost 15,000 men killed and the Yanks 60,000. What a loss of souls. O my God this is the horror of war, the loss of the soul. They fought 11 days when overpowered they were without ammunition or food.[21] From

21. This rumor was incorrect. Lee surrendered to Grant with his entire army.

Sam we learn that Gen. Echols[22] had disbanded his army telling those who wished to go home to their families, those who wished to surrender to go to Lynchburg and those who would follow him to come on to the trans Mississippi. Major Day also made a speech to his men. It is said but few went with him.

April 18, 1865

Nothing of interest has occurred today but the heart is sorrowful but not in despair. This morning Rachel Saunders and Dorcas Harris came by going on to town. D. Harris was in trouble having heard they had been robbing them again a night or two ago. The face of every Rebel woman is a good index of their hearts.

R. Saunders and Mrs. Wells came by this evening as they returned home. They brought us the news that President Lincoln was dead and Seward had been mortally wounded and died.[23] We feel the hand of God is in everything. It is said they were returning from the theatre that night after a day of great rejoicing over the downfall of Richmond and were assassinated. What this will do for us is known only to our Father.

I said at the outset nothing of interest had occurred but I had forgotten about brother Hiram. He returned today and seemed to feel so sad. He could not refrain from shedding tears. He tells us that Gen. Lee's army killed and wounded more Yankees than we had men to fight them. He told us he heard our dear boys belonging to Gen. Vaughn's command were at Wytheville.

April 19, 1865

Another night of peace and quiet has passed over us for which we do feel so thankful. I heard yesterday by the children that my loved

22. General John Echols was in charge of Confederate troops in southwest Virginia and, upon learning of Lee's surrender, dissolved his command, of which the Sixtieth Tennessee was part. Some of General John C. Vaughn's brigade crossed into North Carolina to serve as part of the escort for President Jefferson Davis as he fled from Charlotte, North Carolina, to Washington, Georgia. *Tennesseans in the Civil War,* 1: 302.

23. The news about Seward was untrue. He survived the attack.

husband, brothers William and Abram Gammon were coming down and going on to Knoxville to take the oath.[24] I feel never would I do this, rather would I lose all possessions—yea life itself than take an oath which perjures me before God and man. They may kill the body but they cannot the Soul. I do not believe they will do it.

Mollie left us this morning. I love those girls of Nancy's so much. They are all such good girls. Lucy went down today, returned at dinner time bringing the news that Mr. Kyle was on his way to the saltworks, that Sizemore would be in town this evening and that Mr. Netherland would be home this evening with quite a Yankee guard.

## April 20, 1865

We had quite a rain last night, too wet this morning to do anything with farming—feel but little like working but know it is my duty to labor trusting in my Father but the hours are so dark. The news has just reached me that they have murdered Henry Wax—came in last night and took his life, do not have the particulars. Last night was rather a wakeful night as the dogs barked so fiercely I could not help thinking that someone was about.

## April 21, 1865

We have had a very quiet peaceful day. No news from our army. My heart is sore this evening. By Fannie I learn than Sam Fain was wounded in the leg and unable to walk. They were trying to take a

---

24. Secessionists were told that if they did not take the oath, they would lose their property and all rights. Richard had to apply for a presidential pardon since he was a graduate of West Point who served as an officer in the Confederate army. In a letter dated June 15, 1865, Richard asked President Johnson for a pardon, stating, "Your petitioner Richard G. Fain humbly represents to your excellency that he, like thousands of others in the Southern States, was so far forgetful of himself and his duty & his allegiance to the great and good govt. as to lift his hand against it. He was a Col. of a Tennessee Regt and in many ways committed treason to the U. States Govt. He confesses to the delusion and deeply regrets what he has done and has for some time past desired to see the National Authority restored." On September 21, 1865, Richard wrote a second letter to Johnson, stating, "If you can show clemency to any person it would be to one who had always been your warm personal and political friend" (*Pardon Petitions*, Roll 49). The president signed the order to issue the pardon on September 29.

horse I understand from one of our soldiers who I suppose was going to take the oath. I am very sorry they do these things. I feel men have a right to take the oath if they please; but it is with deep regret I hear of them going. I would rather have shared the fate of the brave and noble to the last moment than to have left now.

I cannot bear to see the Christian heart of the South give way. My dear daughter S. whom I love so much as a Christian seems to be at times so prone to doubt and look with a feeling of distrust on the dealings of God with his children.

April 22, 1865

Last night I was awakened about 12 o'clock by the barking of dogs. As I lay listening I thought I heard a voice saying halloo. I listened, again it came. I sprang from my bed, went in and awoke Liz and Sallie. I then spoke and asked who is there. The answer came George Etter.[25] I was so soon at the door, opened it saying "Lord have mercy on you." He asked if there was any Bushmen around that I knew of. I told him no. I asked him many questions in regard to our dear boys. He told me he thought Hiram was coming for Mrs. Lyons as the others he knew nothing of them. He had not heard from Sam, had heard that Capt. Ross was wounded. He also heard at Mr. Youngs that Sizemore with his men of blood were out in the valley, that they were there on the hunt of Tom Miller last night. I trust dear Tom is beyond their reach.

April 23, 1865

With a feeling of delight I awoke this morning feeling it is the Sabbath and today I can go to the house of my God. We had rather a cool walk there having been quite a change in the air since yesterday. As we went along we had a few drops of snow. We passed on at Mr. Wax's we met up with uncle Doctor and cousin Joe — made inquiry for Mr. W, they thought him better.

25. George Etter married Nan Kinkead, and there are many references to George Etter in Margaret Lyons Smith's *Miss Nan: Beloved Rebel.*

April 24, 1865

Maria Wells called out a short time this evening to see me about a letter which Marietta had written to Miss Jones. She is a strong abolitionist I believe. O how little real concern does she feel for the souls of the poor Africans according to my views and understanding. She retreats from every argument by saying she has no will of her own, she desires the will of the Lord to be done. This I told her is the true feeling which every Christian should have, yet we have desires which we can make known to God pleading if it is his Holy Will to grant our request. I spoke to her of the fearful tendency of every thing which is now being exerted over the minds of our poor Negroes, that there was nothing good in it, that it was calculated to excite pride, haughtiness of spirit and every feeling contrary to the word of God and that it tended only to lead them down to hell. I said that I had no affinity for any people who could say "if the Bible sustain slavery we give it up for a higher law" to this she replied "Eliza I do not believe what I see in print on either side." I told her this was truth. I feel so sorry I did not say to her Maria you were once one of the warmest advocates for our Southern Church. How is it you are not with us today. We were not angry for this we both disapprove of and I feel I want people who I feel are Christians to tell me what views they have in a religious light of the horrible scenes which God from on high seeth day by day.

April 25, 1865

Another day of quiet has passed, the Lord is good. I have been much engaged planting a patch of corn and beans and cleaning out raspberry bushes aided at first by Cin and Nate, this evening by my dear Lizzie and Cin. After getting through with raspberries I trimmed up several of my apple trees. Tonight I feel much wearied.

Some paroled soldiers from Middle Tennessee passed by this evening from Middle Tennessee, they were on their way home, left with Sarah a copy of Gen. Lee's farewell address to his army and also a copy of Gen. Grant's letter proposing terms of surrender and a copy of his order as a passport for them through the Yankee lines. My heart grows sad when I see the noble soldiers, who have struggled for 4 years for independence with a people who have acted as though there was no Bible, no God, no hereafter, returning to their home overpowered but not defeated, not conquered in spirit but might for the time being overpowering right. But a thought comes stealing into my heart—it is the name of Union as it has been applied since this war began which in days to come will be so opprobrious that he who has borne it will be like Cain. He will feel his punishment is greater than he can bear. He has lifted his hand against a white brother in forming his hands in his blood to elevate to an equality with himself his black brother whom all nations feel to be an inferior race of beings.

The soldiers are bringing pretty much the same information—that there is some fearful foreboding of evil. There is posted up in Richmond printed bills asking the Confederate soldier to aid them against the French. The soldiers say they have been treated so respectfully by the Yankees since the surrender. They know that the blood of the South is nothing but patriotism. I fear they have gone so far with aggression, oppression and tyranny that the South can never feel for one moment she can again trustingly link her political destiny with such a people.

April 27, 1865

Yesterday I could not write as my spirit was overwhelmed within me. I felt so rebellious, I felt I could not submit to the thought of having to bow to the Union element of East Tennessee. The larger proportion of it is so degraded and even the respectable portion seem to have become so demoralized by its blighting influence I can have no affinity for or with them. I heard yesterday evening that Gen. Johnston was preparing to surrender his army and that Gen. Smith had disbanded his. This is Union news.

We were cheered last night by the sight of one of our dear noble boys. The children went to bed, our dogs began to bark so fiercely I felt some one must be coming and I do confess my heart grows sick at the thought of another scene such as I witnessed the 5th. The girls soon came downstairs saying somebody is coming. Liz went to the door. He spoke we knew it was some of our loved ones. He rode into the yard, dismounted and came in. It was no other than the noble Pete [Ernest] Fain. I was so glad to see him. The sight of one Reb although disarmed and helpless does me good. He and brother Hiram had arrived after dark. Pete brought home an old horse for us which I feel so thankful to my Heavenly Father.

Pete brought us news from some of my precious treasures. My dear husband and Sam are still with my good old uncle. My dear boy is improving; his wound is a flesh wound but I fear worse then we at first anticipated. Nick Fain and Mike McCarty are in Blountville. Powell at uncle Bob's and Sam Gammon in Virginia. My poor boy Ike with Ed Powel travelling somewhere in the more Southern land. We hear the dear boys who left us when Samuel left have struck out for South Carolina. My firstborn it is said is at Mrs. Lyons.

Pete came over this evening telling us Mr. Sizemore was in town with about 25 men. It is really so painful for any of us to hear of his presence. I am confident that no Rebel squad has left such a thrall of horror to the heart of any Union woman since the war began.

April 28, 1865

No enemy, as yet, has come to our dwelling. We heard that Sizemore had come to take a list of confiscated property. He has taken Col. Simpsons intent on appropriating it to his own use. He says he has the money to pay for it to the government. He has also made a list of Mrs. Clay's furniture. This was done on yesterday. Today he has been at the farm of George Powel and taken it for governmental use.

I much fear the tendency of the mind of the North to deep seated infidelity. Shall the Christian heart of the South give way, no no, never, never, never. God's hand has already given to us proofs of his love for in the very hour when they thought there was a consummation of all their hopes strikes terror to the soul by the removal of their president under the most harrowing circumstances—assassination by the hand of a man named John Wilkes Booth. This brings to the presidential chair a man whose character we have all regarded as a very dark one. Andrew Johnson was once sustained by the democracy of the state of Tenn.—had taken the highest political post in the state but this did not satisfy his unbounded ambition. The White House had ever been his acme of political aspiration. He has succeeded to this by being a traitor to his own native section. The North and the Union men of the South composed of a few Democrats but mostly of the other party and now his heart is in the hand of God who will turn as he pleases. The party who placed him there I do believe are trembling with anxious fear as he has done away with the taking (as I understand it) of that accursed oath which was an outrage upon the feelings of every Christian man. He may now seek to do something which will wipe away the stigma of traitor. Today Sallie closed her school having taught same three months in Rogersville.

May 1, 1865

The Yanks are in town and upon the road towards Dr. Shields—said to be ninth Tenn USA. I trust the Lord will restrain their wicked hearts and make them to do what is right. E. Ruth has just left, has been to the farm today attending to her sheep.

May 2, 1865

Mercy still surrounds us although our souls are so fiercely tried. Last night just as we were preparing for bed someone turned the knob of the door. At first we thought it had been done by Sallie as she passed by but soon discovered this was a mistake. The girls Mollie, Sallie and Lizzie were in their night dress. Liz asked in rather an imperative voice who is there. A voice answered it is me. Liz then asked who are you. The voice replied Mike McCarty but neither Mollie, Sallie nor I recognized the voice but Liz says it is Mike. She opened the door and there stood our manly boy sure enough. With trembling hearts we bid him welcome—sat and talked to him sometime asking many questions in reference to himself and the other boys. He told us he was anxious to go on but could do nothing on account of his horse having given out completely—that Powell's had also given out, that he turned back with Nick from Yadkinville N.C. He said that Powell, cousin Johnny Bachman and the others turned back from Mt. Airy, that after disbanding of the men by Gen. Echols every thing was confusion and disorder of the most frightful nature, that the wagons were all emptied drawn up together near Christiansburg preparatory to burning. We regard this as a very sore calamity. Had Gen. Echols retained his command in our judgment he could have moved right on through this part of the state without much interruption and made a junction with Gen. Johnston at some point.

I lay down before the girls retired and suppose I fell asleep directly as I knew nothing of when they went to bed (Mike came between 10 & 11). It was after 11 before I went to bed and before they had fallen asleep the repeated report of shot after shot awakened within each breast the most painful apprehensions. They awoke me, I got up, set upon the side of my bed and listened with intense feeling to some 4 or 5 shots. I felt I was unnerved and was going to have something close akin to an ague. Mollie says "Lord have mercy Aunt Liza what will we do." I told her all be still and all we could do would be to pray. I lay down on my bed and just one petition after another ascended to my father in the name of my dear Jesus for protection and deliverance. We momentarily expected an attack and knowing our dear Mike was here we did not know what would be the result should they come. Liz awoke Mike but he did not get up which I feel was so right. Had he attempted to have gone from the house they might have seen him. This agony of suspense was of more than an hour. Still no one came and we felt God was our deliverer, God our shield and protector.

As soon as Sallie was dressed next morning she went over to Sarahs to hear what it all meant. After she left I learned by Gus that they had been there last night, had turned out their horses and wanted Gus to get up and make the fence up. But Sarah prevailed on them to let him alone. When Sallie came back we learned from her that they came about 9 o'clock and asked for supper. Sarah gave it but the first thing they knew of anyone being about was an unearthly whoop or noise of some kind striking all with terror. They then knocked at the front door. Three came in there and one at the back. They spoke to Pete asking him several questions and looked at his parole, kept talking and laughing. Sarah and the girls Sallie, Dick and Lucy talked to them some but not much. They acted as though they had put up for the night but about 12 went out on the porch this way and began firing off their guns as they said at someone crossing the meadow. Mike thought he heard a bullet strike near the house. Mike had told us when he came that his uncle Richard was coming on.

Cousin Audley [Anderson] and Col. Walker[26] arrived about noon today, had been hurt by the disturbances of our peace and robbed of all they had that was valuable. Col. Walker had his watch taken which had belonged to his son Frank along with some of his best clothes and all of his money amounting to $600 in Confederate. Richard had between 2 and 300 in confederates. Cousin Audley had some but they did not take. They took Richard's clothing but missed his watch. They had met Hill who was on before in the wagon and had stripped him of his roundabout and cut it into fragments. They scared him badly.

May 4, 1865

This morning a company of some 60 or 70 Federals came out and rode up to Sarahs, made inquiry from Sarah about the road to Caney Valley. She directed, they turned and passed out by the shop; their conduct is so different from what it has ever been before.

26. Colonel John Walker was a native of Rogersville whose son, Frank Walker, was a Confederate officer killed in Georgia during the Civil War, according to R. Clay Crawford's "Reminiscences of Rogersville," published in the *Rogersville Herald* in 1901 and collected in a pamphlet privately printed in 1994 by Sheila Johnston. Eliza mentioned the death of Frank Walker in her diary entries of August 14, 1864, and September 28, 1864.

My heart has had another trial today in regards to Africa's poor child. About noon I was down about the stable giving some directions about a hog diseased when a Negro man came up. I did not know at first who he was but soon found out it was the last man belonging to Mr. David Lyons left on his place (Dave). I had some dinner prepared for him, as he was eating I talked to him and found out he had turned his back upon his home to seek for himself another place. My heart was troubled. I advised him to go back to his mistress and see if she would be willing to feed and clothe him and his family as she had done, for him to agree to it, that he had never known what trouble was until his little children would begin to cry for bread and he would have none to give them. I thought O the misery and wretchedness which this war has entailed upon these sable sons and daughters of the once fair, beautiful and sunny South. I just felt God will visit the destroyers of their peace with sorer judgments than they have ever felt. I could not prevail on him to go back. He said he would go to town and look around and see what he could do.

This morning Jennie McCarty, Kate Carmichael and Alice Huffmaster came out. They report the Feds as behaving quite genteelly. Orders had been read which were quite strict prohibiting all interference with anyone. Rebs to be protected as much as Unions. O this is so remarkable and so different from their policy heretofore when they had entire control of any section of our country. We poor Rebs move around with hearts it is true often heavy but with cheerful faces. They do not know that we feel any biliousness of spirit.

May 5, 1865
I went in company with Sarah, Mollie Ruth, Fannie, Ida and Lillie to town this morning to help E. Ruth pick wool. Mollie and Sallie brought back from Mr. Rileys, having staid there Wednesday night, an account of Mr. Rileys deep humiliation by Sizemore, of his keen feeling on account of it that death would be preferable if he was

only prepared, that one of Mr. Cane's sons had murdered Buly the murderer of his father and that young Cane had fallen by the hands of some of his barbarian associates under Sizemore. Truly the earth mourns when the wicked bear rule. We saw today what was not pleasant to us—the blue clothes occupying the place which we feel belongs to the gray.

May 7, 1865

We have had another peaceful Sabbath and was permitted to attend the house of my God in company with my dear S. After Sabbath School we had a prayer meeting that was refreshing to the crushed heart. Quite a number of Federal soldiers were present. Mr. Hicks conducted the service and Uncle Doct and Mr. Rogan prayed very excellent feeling prayers. I have felt sad today, the sight perhaps of my enemies may have had something to do with it, but I feel it has been produced more by the consequences which follow their achievements.

I heard today that it was said no Southern man can hold his home even should he take the oath.[27] If this be true I hope God our Father will put it into their hearts to lose all earthly possessions rather than sacrifice one principle of right.

In looking over my little book I find in December of 1860 I penned the following words: [space is blank]. My feelings tonight are the same as they were at that time. We have passed through a terrible revolution. Tonight our prospect is dark and gloomy, our home may be taken; but I feel man cannot do it unless it is our Father's good pleasure. I have ever believed the South was right in the principles she advocated—I think so yet. I feel I would rather surrender every thing of earth than take one step violating the deep sense of duty I feel this war has only increased.

27. In the end property rights were honored, and very few individuals lost their homes or farms (Groce, *Mountain Rebels*, 137). When the slaves were freed, their former owners were not compensated for their value. However, one could reclaim stolen property, such as a horse, so long as it could be positively identified.

May 8, 1865

I have been engaged today in washing. I feel so thankful bodily strength is given to me to do this for my dear family. Lizzie began teaching today at Amy's house—had but few scholars. I feel so anxious about my own little children. I feel willing to do anything to advance their interests. Sallie and Mary Martin have been cleaning the house. My dear daughter Fannie has not done much. I feel so troubled about her; fear she has imbibed such wrong notions about work she does not seem willing to do.

This evening my heart was made glad by seeing my first born son and yet I felt sad. The thought of his having to bow before the powers that are now in authority was to me painful. But Joseph was made to yield before his brothers but in the end his brothers bowed to him and thus it may be with the rebel of the South. They have rebelled against tyranny and oppression. Hiram had been to town and told me he was treated with much kindness by Capt. Colwell and others, even the poor wretched Sizemore seemed disposed to be very kind. Said he felt badly for treating me as he did on the 5th of April but whether he is sincere or not he is so wicked. May God have mercy on his soul is my prayer.

As Hiram was going down he met a scout of Yanks amongst them was Tom Sizemore. He accosted him with "are you a Fain?" Hiram answered "yes." He then asked him if he was Sam. He told no but Hiram. Tom then spoke of his determination to avenge the death of his brother. This is hard to bear from such as he is when he knows that through the intercession of Sam, Wyly Miller and Nick McCarty his father was saved. But this is the gratitude of such as he is when power as he thinks comes into his hands. I do think it is so important this low element of society should be disarmed and made to feel who they are and what they must be. This element will, I think, yet give trouble to those who have upheld them.

Yesterday when in town I called a few moments on my long loved friend old Mrs. Neill. She is much troubled in these calamitous days. She was telling me of the insolence of one of her Negro girls (Ellen) whom she had raised more like a child than a servant. She had asked her a question which she answered very impudently. Mrs. N. spoke kindly to her, after she left the room she began to abuse some fowls and swore. Mrs. N. reprimanded her sharply and told her she should not do so about her. She stepped up to her, knocked her fists together in her mistress face telling her she would do what she pleased. She gave Mrs. N a push and the old lady fell against a box. Neppie came out and she made war on her. This is the effect of Negro equality. This is the result of this fearful struggle. Can any Christian heart feel this will be tolerated in the land? What will be the result? They will either be reduced back to servitude or they will be exterminated. White men and women cannot bear such as this. May the God of Heaven have mercy upon these people. May he teach them what is their duty to those who have been so kind.[28]

May 11, 1865

O God have mercy, my soul is so troubled. Hours of darkness are growing darker and darker. Some of the paroled soldiers of Gen. Johnston's army came in yesterday. We seem to be almost bereft of military power but God our Father is till reigning. O will he give us up to be oppressed and down trodden by a people who have ever seemed to feel and act as though he had nothing to do in this mighty struggle.

I went to town yesterday with Mollie Ruth. My object was to see something about sending word to my dear husband to return home. I had hoped to see Mr. Kyle but he had gone to the river to see Col Parson's company with Lon Kyle and others. I learned when I got to town that my dear Powell was at Miss Rileys in

28. The end of slavery and the transition to freedom for female slaves resulted in the need for new domestic relationships. Caroline had simply left Eliza's home, but Ellen stayed and learned that her former owner did not yet comprehend the consequences of the end of slavery. These issues were common during this time, and similar experiences are cited by Marti F. Weiner in *Mistresses and Slaves: Plantation Women in South Carolina, 1830–80* (Urbana: Univ. of Illinois Press, 1998).

company with Capt. McCamie, Col. Bishop, Mr. Bryant and one or two others. Poor Rebs this is a day of great humiliation but with it God is blending great mercy. Our men are receiving kind and polite treatment. Before leaving home we heard Mike Mc was in town — had been brought in under guard also Col. Sam Powel and Capt. C. Lyons. This gave us a feeling of great sadness. The thought of those upon whom we have looked with feelings of so much pride being thus humbled is so trying.

We stopped at cousin Annis, where we found Col. Powel, Mr. Wax and Poats looking sad indeed. After conversing awhile I learned that Col Powel was under arrest charged with high treason and was sued for $40,000 dollars. He had to start to Knoxville next Saturday to appear before the great tribunal of American despotism.

Awhile after dinner I set out to see what I could accomplish in my business in coming to town. Went up to Nancys and from here I went to see Mrs. Mary Kyle to ascertain when Mr. Kyle would be back. With her I had a very pleasant conversation of a religious character. I love her, she may have many faults but I do believe she desires to be a Christian. She too has had her trials. She nursed tenderly for many long weeks her dear little Kity without any kind sympathy of her dear husband being manifested by his presence only by letter. From here I went back to Nancys and sent for Capt. Colwell. He came and seemed to be very respectful in his demeanor. I soon found out from him he had a heart rankling with bitter hatred towards all who bore the name of Rebel. He told me in the course of conversation that he wanted it distinctly under-stood he showed no kindness to them from any love he had for them but only from a sense of duty to an enemy in his power. I think the Captain is the bitterest man at heart I have ever seen. No northern Yank has ever exhibited to me such a demonstration of what the heart can take in. He blames the South with all the calami-ties now upon us — says this war has made him an abolitionist. He spoke of the tyranny of the South in suppressing men who came amongst us from speaking forth their sentiments on this vexed question. That he rejoiced to know and feel the hour had now come when the common men of the country could rise to eminence and distinction. That slavery was done away with and the South had done it. Often as he spoke his brow would knit and his face seem to grow dark from the workings of deep seated vindictiveness. I tried to talk to him as I have ever done to every soldier and every one since this war began on the great importance of doing right and of cultivating a right spirit. But I felt I was "casting pearls before swine." Eliza Ruth came in while we were talking. She cast in her effort to help, to defend our cause but alas it did no good. The only one present who seemed to throw upon the whole the least genial influence was Buena. She seemed to be able in mirthfulness but with decision to say more than anyone else.

Buena and Julia set out for Ruths and Dot Walters. As they moved on they saw the Yanks had moved their flag from the Heiskell house and placed it over the store door of Col. Simpsons. They avoided passing under it which caused quite an outburst of feeling from the soldiers. Some saying "three cheers for the Bonnie Blue" but on others it did not set quite so well. Afterwards Sallie Huffmaster passing along sought to avoid it when a Lt. by the name of the Northern came up to her and took her by the arm cursing her and saying you shall walk under that flag and she had it to do. Afterwards Annis Shaver came along. She also was going to take roundings when Capt. Colwell cried out "stop I tell you—stop I tell you or by the eternal God I will shoot you. You shall walk under that flag." Annis replied "never." He then told her to go back which she did. This is the gentleman who spoke so arrogantly of Southern tyranny this evening. This is a specimen of the men who would rule if they could, but thanks to God he is a subordinate. Although these things have occurred setting forth the deep seated malignity of the heart of man, yet we rejoice and feel it is from God's hand that the troops who are now here have been placed in our midst. Very few of them indeed can brook the idea of the Negro being placed on an equality with the whites and but few, very few indeed, have one particle of sympathy for them. The

Negroes are still slaves of a more despotic power than ever they had in any Master of the South. But I feel this is all from God, should he in his providence see best to reduce them to a state of servitude they will only be the more humble and better slaves.

I started Dicky this morning to see Mr. Kyle—wrote him a note. On the way he met my poor little soldier trudging homeward. They came; we all met him with feelings of gladness it is true, but O how sad to think of the noble soldier of the South laying aside his gun and coming home not a subjugated man but overpowered by a combination of forces from every land almost and last though not least the Negro soldiers whom they had to call to their aid. To me it seems there will be a dark record hereafter of this terrible struggle on the part of the North and all who have aided or abetted their cause in any way. While the South will stand forth to the world as a people noble, good and great for having opposed such oppression and cruelty which the North has been seeking to lay upon for many years. May God's will be done is my prayer. I do feel he will deliver us from shame and disgrace.

May 12, 1865
All peace, no person comes to molest or make afraid.

May 13, 1865
Still unmolested. Two soldiers names Mr. Johnson and Edmonds from Jefferson came this morning to get my wagon and oxen. I made some excuse saying they were all I had to work and I had a piece of ground I was anxious to finish breaking up. They rather insisted but with much politeness and good feeling saying wagons were so hard to get for hauling goods and supplies. I told them I would finish my piece of ground and then start, for them to wait at Mrs. McKinneys until after 11. But I failed in getting them from here by that time. Gus met the men on the way but they were very kind.

This evening as stitch and stitch went into the old garments my work was stopped for a short time by the entrance of a poor looking woman dressed in a style rather singular. She soon scraped up an acquaintance with me having known my dear sister and other dear friends of Blountville. She had called wanting to know if I would be willing for her to come back and stay all night. I said certainly and she is with us tonight. A great talker. May I be enabled to say words of kindness and truth which will impress her deeply that this world is not her home. O Lord have mercy on the poor and teach them thou art good.

May 14, 1865

Enjoyed today many precious privileges. I was permitted to leave home, after much religious conversation with poor Vina, in company with my dear children Fannie and Nannie. As I passed on I called a moment at cousin Audleys, had hoped to see him but he had left for Knoxville. Here I found a dear wife mourning in deepest anguish of soul on account of the ill treatment which her husband had received from the hands of a wicked man. She was filled with the most painful apprehensions for his future safety as she heard of threat after threat being made by men in the country. I tried to cheer by speaking words of comfort.

I passed on to the church and here I met my precious class. After Sabbath school closed in company with Neppie Neill and Mary Alexander I went to see Mrs. Neill and found the old lady looking as she has ever done so clean and nice. Here I had a pleasant conversation. Mrs. Neill has been relieved of her domestic trouble (Ellen) who went to Knoxville taking the younger child of a dead sister. Poor wretched girl she lost her best earthly friend when she turned her back on her mistress. From here we returned to church and enjoyed a pleasant prayer meeting. Mr. Rogan conducted the services and uncle Doct. prayed. Young ladies who have not been much in the habit of attending prayer meeting were there dressed very nicely. The appearance of one of them impressed me so deeply of the folly of vanity. She looked as though she felt she was some distinguished personage. Her towering head and haughty air induced within the thought has she felt she is a worm of the dust travelling to the judgment set of Christ. I hope she may become the devoted Christian.

After prayer meeting I met with Doct. Hampton and had much conversation on the great question which now agitates the mind of us all by the present arrangement of things. We have two classes of society turned loose as it were upon the great community—the lowest down element of whites and the Negroes. I told Doct. H. that I thought every man of any standing or influence in society belonging to the Union party ought to exert himself to the very utmost of his ability to suppress if possible the present movement of such men. That if it was not done he nor no other Union man would in a short time be any more secure than Mr. Poats (who was present) or any Southern man. He replied "I know it." I feel they have the greatest burden to contend with in the reconstruction of this government that any people have ever had.

From cousin A's I went to Mr. Hales and found kind friends who gave me such a cordial welcome. From Mary P. I learned I was a grandmother again. Bet having given birth to a little boy on Wednesday the 11th, both doing well. Mary P had come down on Saturday evening to see something about her horse which had been taken on Wednesday. I rather think she followed on after her beloved husband to see and know as far as she could about him, he having come on before on foot (I suppose) this far on his way to Knoxville. This morning he with many others, perhaps 100 altogether, were on their way. Amongst the number my dear boy Hiram.

May 15, 1865

This evening my beloved husband arrived at home again from uncle Isaacs, cousin Samuel Anderson with him. He had come to find if he could some horses taken by robbers who had also taken much clothing stripping my husband of his coat. He told me that one of them called him out of the house and said to him, "pull off that coat you old d—m rebel or I will shoot you." He had his pistol presented at him. These are all trials of our Christian character. How thankful we should be when enabled to bear them in a right spirit. He left my dear boy S. doing as well as could be expected. His wound is a much more serious one than we at first thought. How dark did this dispensation of my Father appear to me at the time it occurred. I had prayed fervently for the deliverance of the little band of men with whom he was connected that they might all get away safely without any of them being wounded or killed. And when I heard my own son was the only one upon whom any calamity had fallen my soul was so troubled. I felt there was something which I could not see into then and bowed submissively to my Father's will. But now all is so plain, I feel my darling soldier boy was stopped in his soul destroying career. That morning they had gotten some liquor and all had been drinking. He had broken his solemn resolve to never touch again the deadly poison. O my soul bless the Lord who in tender mercy heard my prayer for my sons salvation and not for his deliverance from the hand of man. Sam is now reading his Bible as he lays on his bed and feels his God stopped him in his downward career.

## May 16, 1865

At an early hour this morning Camel left intending to go out to Col. Parsons[29] headquarters at the river. Richard wrote a note by him

---

29. Colonel Joseph H. Parsons headed the Ninth Tennessee Cavalry (U.S.A.). On April 25 General George Stoneman ordered the unit to Rogersville to clear the country between the Holston River and the Cumberland Mountains of outlaws. Reports had reached him of the lawless conditions that guerrilla forces, such as Sizemore's band, had perpetuated. General Stoneman's order included the following: "The persons with whom you have to deal are outlaws so long as they are at liberty and should be treated as such. When taken prisoners they must be treated as prisoners, and are entitled to trial, which takes time and entails trouble and expense. Give them to understand that no false mercy will be shown them and no prisoners taken, and that every man found in arms under whatever pretense, and acting without authority from Federal officer or the legally constituted authorities of the State of Tennessee, will be treated as a public enemy and an outlaw and killed like a mad dog by anyone who meets him. See that your command does not interfere in any way, either in their persons or their property, with the peaceably disposed, and with those who stay and home and mind their own business." From the Web site "Tennesseans in the Civil War," http://www.tngennet.org/civilwar/usacav/usa9cav.html.

asking the Colonel to have his coat returned as the man who had taken it was brought to jail on Sabbath. Dick saw them and knew his fathers coat. Richard and Fannie walked down this morning and returned before dinner—Richard bringing his coat with him. I feel so thankful he was permitted to get it back. I feel it is a matter of such great gratitude to God our Father that he sent the troops to be with us who are here. Col. Parsons seems to be so kind and conciliatory in his feelings. Says he has no feeling of vengeance towards anyone—that he would not hurt a hair of any individual he knows. This sounds like the true gentleman and one who has some consciousness of right. No unbiased mind can look in calmness on the present condition of our country but must see that Southern integrity of character under the guidance of Almighty God is the only preserver of civil and religious liberty in our country.

Our enemies are in a great dilemma, they have now under their control two elements of human beings which if not restrained by God himself will give them trouble such as they have never had before. The lower class of society elevated by what they regard as a great victory to a place they cannot appreciate not having moral capacity to do it and the other our poor Negro turned loose upon society with no one to care for him at a time it is so difficult to maintain a family.

Cousin Camel returned about 2 o'clock bringing back a black mare—the one he was most anxious to get. We prepared him some dinner and after 3 he and my dear Sallie set out for his home. She going to nurse her brother and to ride the horse feeling it might be a protection to cousin C. This evening Frank Fulkerson came to see Richard. He had just returned from Knoxville and Mr. Kyle had urged him to see Richard and if not at home for him to urge me to send for him immediately so that he might come down while court was in session. He thinks they will have much trouble amongst themselves as the two parties are already beginning to show enmity—the copperheads and the abolitionists. Frank told us that he had heard while absent that Andy Johnson in a conversation with a particular friend had asked him what he thought ought to be the course to pursue with the Rebels. The friend replied they will have to make a choice between 3 things. One to kill all. To this Andy J. replied that will not do as all humanity and the whole civilized world would revolt at such a thought. Second to exile all and to this he said no. Third to conciliate and win them over by kindness and he replied this will do. If this is true of that man I feel from my inmost soul God has done it. He had his heart in his hand and he can do no more and go no further than the Father of the Southern Christian will permit him.

May 17, 1865

The dreaded hour has come. O how my soul has been wrung with anguish as I have looked forward to this sad moment when my beloved husband should say to us. I must leave you and go to Knoxville to take the oath. Can the heart be in it—if not O my God do open up a way of deliverance—do give to our noble Christian men something to allay the bitterness of soul which an oath falsely taken must give.

I feel the sacredness of an oath has been so tampered with during the last four years that men have ceased to regard it in its true light. For my own part I have been so troubled at the thought of trifling with anything so solemn. I have felt rather than do it I would lose life, property or anything rather than call on my God to witness what my soul did not believe. May God our Father help us to do our whole duty to our God, our country and our fellow beings. The first representation of the oath that was made to me was so revolting to every true principle of what I thought was right I just felt let me die or go with my family into exile rather than submit. But Frank Fulkerson tells me there are no requirements made of renunciation of principles excepting in reference to the slave question.

The oath binds to support the old constitution. I feel it is more important to administer this oath to our enemies than us as they are the ones who have torn to shreds this noble document of patriotic hearts. They are the ones who first violated its sacred compact, had this remained untouched by the unjust interference of wild fiendish fanaticism the South would have been true to the last. Should God our Father see best in the plenitude of his wisdom and mercy to bring us together again may each section be taught by this terrible struggle what is true in relation to slavery and may it be the means of forever settling this mortal question as to the right of slavery in the minds of all nations of the earth. It has caused the best blood of the South to flow. I believe the Bible teaches slavery is right. If this is true every soldier of the Confederate Army who has fallen is a martyr for the truth and no great truth of God's Holy Word has ever been sustained without the seal of the blood of the Christian being affixed.

May 19, 1865

After 11 o'clock at home with my two little ones Ellie and Lil. My other dear children Liz, Fannie, Powell, Dick and Nannie all at Sarahs enjoying a dance. Sarah has given Ernest leave to have a select company of young friends tonight and I suppose they are dancing. I cannot see how they can at this time enjoy an amusement of that kind when God's wrath seems to be pounding out. How can the heart be so light so unmindful of its great interests.

I heard this evening that my first born son and Mr. Hasson were sent to Nashville. Whether true or not remains to be seen. I was called on today by a neighbor of the order for belief of Dunkards. Mr. Samberg came to inform me that one of my sons was with Mr. Rhineheart and Kyle when his mare was taken. He told me he thought his mare was taken on the 10th of March or that Wednesday. I did not recollect what day of the month it was but remembered the day well it being the day Richard had left home to go up the country after our troops fell back. I told him I knew none of my sons were at home at that time. He seemed to think they were but I have made a record in my book which will exonerate them from blame. I find it was the 23th of March. I talked kindly to Mr. S and I told him none of my boys I did not believe would do anything of that kind to him and that I did not feel we should be held responsible for the acts of men whom we could not control. He said the man whom he took to be my son sat upon his horse and took no part in it only he acted as a guard with his pistol in his hand. I had a very pleasant conversation and hope he went back feeling more kindly than when he came. I feel my sons have done things which I disapprove and I do feel for these things we may suffer. But I always believed it was possible that sons of Southern mothers should whenever they could protect their own home but in a right manner. I believed it was right to tell the Union men of influence that they believed could suppress this robbery of horses if they would try and if it was not done that retaliation would be necessary. In this I may have been wrong and took too much out of the hands of him who hath said "vengeance is mine, I will repay saith the Lord."

May 20, 1865
From Liz or Lillie R. who came over and staid with us I learned that Mr. Hasson had returned home yesterday evening and from Buena I heard that our esteemed friend and good citizen Mr. Wyly Mitchell had bid adieu to earth on yesterday morning. He felt to the last that the dragging of him to Knoxville was what had shortened his days and that it was to no purpose. He was a rebel to the last, it moved him not in the belief of the right of our cause. When I say dragging him to Knoxville I mean by that he was urged contrary to his wishes and the desires of his heart.

May 21, 1865
This has been a day of great spiritual dearth. I awoke this morning, I felt all wrong—no spirit of prayer—no submission but a heart filled with murmurings, discontents and unhappiness. I attended Sabbath School this morning but not with the same delight I hitherto have done. I felt it was a great trouble to set out and walk but I did not yield to the tempter. With my little Lil for company I started but I

had no delightful thoughts. As I walked to the sanctuary I got in sight of Mr. Hale's clover field and my eyes beheld what my heart refuses to love the bluecoats in abundance pasturing their horses. As I walked on thoughts of this kind seized upon me—how strange that a God of truth, of love should permit such a people to overcome us. How strange that a people so lost to every feeling of humanity, truth and justice should be permitted to come and occupy the places of the loved ones of the Christian of the South that they be permitted to rule with such despotic sway as to drive from our pulpits our precious ministers who have labored so faithfully in our midst.

## May 22, 1865

I was busily engaged in washing this morning but was for a short time stopped by the coming of Lewis and Elieh.[30] They both seemed so glad to see me. Poor creatures how troubled I do feel when I see them. Although they at present greatly surpass in dress those who have once been over them, yet everything connected with their future looks so dark to me. I fear their souls are lost sight of. Elieh tells me they have many religious advantages yet there is great wickedness in their midst. He gave to poor Margaret some wholesome advice saying to stay here with Miss Liza and learn to do everything you can to be a useful woman. It is no place for women to be strolling from place to place and that he had seen many of them sent off from Knoxville.

The more I see the more deeply am I impressed each day of my life that God is pouring out his wrath upon the South on account of the amalgamated race who have been born in a state of slavery. O white man of the South has it ever entered in thy soul to count the cost of this terrible sin. Think of Manassas, Richmond, Shiloh, Franklin and many other bloody battlefields where the noble, the pure and good have fallen and then see what it is for a nation favored

30. Elieh was a former slave who had once belonged to Richard's brother John and then to Richard. However, he was sold prior to the Civil War. Lewis was a former slave who had left with Union troop two years earlier. Margaret, apparently, was a sister of Lewis who came to live with her mother, Polly, after slavery officially ended in April 1865.

of God as no other has been to mix blood with a race whom God for reasons unknown to us has doomed to a state of servitude. During the last few days my mind has dwelt much on the thought why should man, fallen rebellious man set up opinions contrary to the word of God in regard to slavery and speak of him as an unjust unholy being; because he for the good of mankind and for the carrying out of his holy law in regard to Adam's race should see best to enslave one portion—to organize the family relation, father, child and servant and make for that organization laws and precepts to govern every action of all which will promote the eternal well being of all the races. This to me seems so presumptuous—has the clay any right to say to the potter why didst thou form me thus?

June 20, 1865

This morning Richard went to town and returned before dinner bringing us the sad intelligence of the death of my brave noble cousin Harvey Galbraith.[31] Truly he was a noble boy as Sam Powel remarked in his letter bringing the news of his death. I feel he has been a sacrifice to a noble cause. Southern liberty has been gained not what the wild fanatics of the North would term Southern liberty but what the resigned Christian Master and Mistress of the South feel today as they bow submissively to the will of him who sitteth upon the throne. Our Father has recognized the servant as a part of the family from the time of the giving to Abram his blessing, until the writing of Revelation and until the present moment. Today the Negro is not free, no place but in this state does there seem to be such a breaking up of family regulations that we can hear from. No state has been to human vice so given up to bad men as rulers. Yet we do feel God our Father has so ordered all these things. They come not by chance, they spring not out of the ground but infinite wisdom is guiding and controlling all our great political machinery. Whether he intends to perpetuate our liberties or not we cannot now tell.

31. Harvey Galbraith enlisted in the Sixty-third Tennessee in 1862 and was captured at Petersburg on April 2, 1865. He died in the Point Lookout, Maryland, prison on May 31, 1865.

June 29, 1865

I have felt so unwell today. I moved around this morning making my first cheese this season and tending to churning. When through I felt so badly and came to the house, took a rest and a sleep. I have felt better this evening. How the body feels its decaying condition when sickness lays hold on us. Richard brought out yesterday the American Presbyterian the organ of the New School Assembly. In it I find nothing, no nothing congenial with the Southern heart. Their whole enthusiasm and care is lavished upon the African race regardless of the feelings of the white Christian brother or sister who may from his view of Bible teaching see fit to differ with them. They seem to have placed the idol of their hearts (the black man) upon the pinnacle of intellectual, physical and moral greatness. O that God in his mercy and wisdom might see fit to throw them into the Northern states that they who have so much sympathy with them might know more of the African character so that they might then more willingly award to Christian master and mistress what is justly due them. They know nothing of what their wild fanaticism is causing. The poor Negro is today in a condition which makes the tears start and the bosom heave with an emotion of sympathy no northern heart has ever felt. Listen to them as they go from house to house begging to get work or something to eat. Hear one who was once a servant kindly cared for by a mistress (who is in eternity) abusing and cursing her dear daughter until she (the servant) is driven from the house by her master with a preemptory order to not return and with 5 helpless children she leaves that masters house (where she has ever been kindly cared for with regard to the necessary wants of herself and children all supplied) to go forth on a cold hearted world. She drags around for a night and a day then comes back but her masters heart relents not. He tells her to go but one of her little children refuses to go. The master says to him you may stay if you wish. He tells him he is hungry and weary of such a life. O such liberty—Great God have mercy upon us and enable us all to live to thee. May the poor deluded child of Africa learn wisdom and choose slavery such as they had with us to a liberty which has in it no provisions for their soul or body.

July 16, 1865

This has been a peaceful day of rest. I have this day been at home the rain preventing my attendance at a place to me so sweet, so dear the Sabbath School and prayer meeting. Read the Observer of 22nd June and almost entirely the religious pages. I was struck with a feeling of sadness and sorrow as I looked over the article headed The New School Assembly.[32] I am startled at the displays of the horrid effects of a wild fanaticism and at the greediness with which the mis-representations of a man who of all others should have been at least truthful to the South were destined to and received from his statement in regard to Holston Presbytery. The following was a part of the mis-statement. "It appears that at a regular meeting of Holston Presbytery formerly in our connection three ministers were present all of whom are loyal men and desirous of a union again with this Assembly; but one of them who resides on the line and has been much exposed to much difficulty from his loyalty was afraid to vote for such action lest it should expose him to more trouble. No action was therefore taken." The reading of this called forth the remark from this man (who is a true servant I do believe of the Lord Jesus Christ) "Here is another of his lies." Mr. S.[33] also goes on in his address to the Assembly stating

32. The Civil War may have been over, but the Northern Presbyterians (or New School Presbyterians) would have nothing to do with the former Confederates unless they were willing to publicly confess their sin of having supported the Confederacy and to admit that slavery was wrong. Daniel Stowell, *Rebuilding Zion: The Religious Reconstruction of the South, 1863–1877* (New York: Oxford Univ. Press, 1998), 54.

33. "Mr. S." clearly refers to the Reverend Samuel Sawyer. The Presbytery of Holston had been constituted by the New School General Assembly in May 1865 with three members: the Reverend Sawyer, the Reverend Rufus P. Wells, and the Reverend Nathan Bachman. The Presbytery of Holston was "directed not to recognize or admit, as a member of their respective bodies, any minister known to be disloyal to the Government of the United States" (Thompson, *Presbyterians in the South*, 2: 124.). The Assembly went on to characterize ministers who had supported secession as grievous sinners against God, saying that they could only be admitted if they were willing to make a public confession and repent of their sin. Clearly the Northern Presbyterians were much harsher on secessionists than the federal government, which exhibited a forgiving spirit and willingness to promote reconciliation.

that the masses have already decided the question in regard to the Emancipation Proclamation of Abraham Lincoln. He says "I went up to the state constitutional convention at Knoxville and my vote went with the unanimous one which forbade all legislatures for the future to recognize in any way directly or indirectly property in man. This decree has been endorsed in a free election of the people by a majority of 30,000 votes legally taken. We are ready for the abolition of slavery. In the name of all that is patriotic, of all that is just and true we do not want our children to listen to the preaching of ministers who have been traitors to their country and if this Assembly should recommend their reinstallation I doubt if in Tennessee you could get a corporals guard to listen to them."

Now Mr. S. knew when he was saying this that falsehood was stamped on almost every word. He knew there was no legality in the voting. He knew that the whole Christian heart of the South with few exceptions stood with the South. Were God as swift in his punishment of an awful sin as he was in the days of Peter he would have been carried out from that assembly a dead man. But God is long suffering and I do hope will permit this erring man to repent of his sin and live for Jesus—Glory to God he is ruling, he is reigning; and could the men of the North whose spirits are not beleaguered by wild fiendish fanaticism see the condition of the Freedmen as are so called they would cry out what a liberty—what a liberty nothing but degradation, shame and poverty seems to be before them.

## July 17, 1865

O my God do keep my heart for I do feel there is in it much that is not right. I find there is bitterness and perhaps envy. I ask myself the question do I regret to see any of my fellow beings rising in the world and I cannot feel that I do yet there is some strange unaccountable struggle within I cannot comprehend. It may today have arisen within me because I have been reading some Union papers particularly the Knoxville Whig (Brownlow's organ).[34] I think it is so corrupt, so vile, so anything but what high souled Americans should be.

About 10 this morning I was seated on the porch reading, my dear husband near when we saw approaching a man whom we knew to be one of our brave Confederate soldiers. When he came up he spoke to my husband calling him by name then gave his name as Wallace. He said Mrs. Anderson had told him to call as he was passing. I learned he had been staying with cousin William Anderson for the last two months or more. He was trying to make his way home. His father lived in McMinnville near Athens. I liked his appearance and asked him about his family. I learned from him his parents were members of the Baptist Church. Thus it is with all of our noble soldiers with few exceptions. They or their parents are members of some branch of the Christian.

July 18, 1865

We were pleased this morning to welcome as a visitor to our home a dear friend for whom we have ever had a true regard — Tom O'Keefe.[35] He was captured in Polk Co. the latter part of the fall or first of winter in 63. Since which time he has not been in the Confederate line until now. His heart is with us and ever has been.

After dinner was over we had a call from Mr. W. C. Kyle and lady. These are Union friends I have always loved. I believe Alice is a Christian and for her I have warm feelings of love. We had much pleasant conversation. Mr. Kyle has liberal views and kind feelings. He censures the Southern government for its tenacity in holding on when there was a time just before the last presidential

34. Parson Brownlow was the editor of this paper, a rabid Unionist, and a skilled propagandist who headed the government of Tennessee after the Civil War.

35. In Johnston's *Blue and Gray from Hawkins County: The Confederates* (141), a Tom O'Keefe is listed as a second lieutenant in the Twenty-ninth Tennessee Infantry (C.S.A.) who had enlisted on January 25, 1861. He was promoted to regimental commissary on July 25, 1862, and resigned on October 26, 1863. If this is the same man to whom Eliza refers, he may have, if captured, taken an oath not to fight again, which could have secured his release from prison. Possibly, he remained in the North until the end of the war.

election when the Northerners whose sympathy was with the South were ready for almost any overtures of peace in which there could have been a restoration of the Union. He may be correct but Yankee ingenuity cannot be trusted. They have so often deceived us, they have so often promised to do and would not perform. We have fought them as long as we could. We have surrendered as brave, noble magnanimous citizens and as Christians are willing now to submit to powers that be. We wait now for the display of magnanimity to a fallen foe—who conscientiously felt and still feel they struggled for civil and religious liberty. I do believe God will give to us yet the high and glorious privileges of knowing that the South has been the preserver of American liberty. The bold stand they have taken against interference on the part of one section of the country with the other in regard to any of its local institutions must have its weight in our political history hereafter.

## July 31, 1865

Billy Carmichael came out this evening. He has been ordered to quit his home. No charge against him, only that he is a rebel. How deeply my heart pained to see such malice in the hearts of men who say they are for peace and the building up of a glorious country.

## Aug. 6, 1865

The past week has been to me a week of much trial. I have seen leave home two of the little black children over whom I have watched with almost a mothers care since the death of their mother my noble and trusty servant Mary. Jim left on last Monday and Linda [Cindy] on Thursday. We had advised Gus to hire them out knowing our circumstances would be so straitened we could not possibly clothe and feed them. I feel I so willingly surrender every claim I have upon them as property. The trial of seeing them thus leave me is great but nothing to compare with what it would have been to have seen them sold from me. Poor little Nate, he has been an object of special care since his mother's death. They seem to feel little affection now for any of us. This to me is a sad thought—bewildered by the vain delusions of their present condition it seems to have absolved every good feeling.[36]

August 20, 1865

After Sabbath School closed I went to Dr. Walkers to see a letter from our beloved minister. Found in the same envelope a letter from Mr. Wells to cousin J. Bachman (having been put there) in answer to one addressed by Cousin J. in regard to the high handed measures of Mr. Flagg ordering him to not preach in Rogersville again. The spirit of the letter was not what I thought and felt Mr. W would write. So different from the spirit of our dear minister. The contrast seemed so great. May God forgive Mr. W. and enable him to give his own heart a close examination and see whether or not he is making the standards of Christian excellence and character—loyalty to the civil government but not a strict adherence to the word of God.

August 31, 1865

This morning Nannie and Pete Powel came out from town bringing the painful statement that Mr. Camel was forbidden to preach last night by the controlling men of the time—Mr. Sizemore and Cain Lawson.

September 6, 1865

My poor heart has this day been wrung with anguish. I do feel all things are so much greater trials now than when war fierce, yea terrible war was everywhere abroad in the land. We of the South felt we had laid so freely on our country's altar the dear and loved ones of our hearts fighting as we believed for the maintenance of the purest principles of liberty both civil and religious. This was ever

36. The mother of these three ex-slave children—Jim, Linda, and Nate—was Mary, who died in 1858 and was married to Gus. It appears that Eliza had been helping Gus raise these children by providing their shelter, food, and clothing.

nerving us but of this hope we are now bereft. Men of the lowest character stalk through the land with the mostly lordly air defying God and his children. This is so dark, so mysterious we cannot comprehend why it is so but we still feel our Father reigns. He may for awhile veil that loveliness of his face but it is only to display with greater beauty and brightness.

Our sons have to leave the home of their childhood not from choice but because tyranny and oppression set their seals upon us as doomed victims which cannot be allowed the privilege of seeking by honest endeavor the means of a livelihood. My dear, my darling boy Nick[37] left us this morning to go I suppose to Illinois in company with Mr. Russell, Perry Powel, Jessie Powel and Mrs. Coffin and daughter who are going to Knoxville. I feel God my Father has in these hours of calamity raised up a friend who so cheerfully offers assistance to our dear children. Richard and I went up yesterday evening to Mr. Russells to see them and bid our dear friends goodbye. We found them quite busy. I always dislike to go in upon friends (unless I can be useful) on the eve of departure. I felt sad as I looked on the comforts which surrounded Mr. and Mrs. R and was led to feel so deeply the uncertainty of everything earthly.

September 15, 1865

Had a letter from my precious boy Nick from Nashville dated the 7th. They arrived there safely with Mr. Russell and Jesse standing the trip well. They remained there a day and night and expected to leave that evening in company with Capt. Wash for Louisville.

September 17, 1865

The Christian of the South has little to hope. How passing strange that the disciples of Jesus of the 19th century should feel thus. The minister of the New School body North appointed to enlighten the poor deluded heathen South preached yesterday in the New School

37. Nick later moved to Carrollton, Georgia, and never returned to Rogersville.

church. I did not go as we all thought it best to hold on to our precious prayer meeting claiming the sweet promise of our Father that where two or three are gathered together in my name there will I be. I humbly hope those who assembled at the other church had the same feeling.

As we went in this morning the blacksmith shop belonging to Mr. Netherland but now rented by some of the blacks or Sizemore was open. The bellows puffing briskly and a two horse vehicle stood at the door awaiting the repair. Thus it is with our country. War, desolating war has to human view blotted the Sabbath from the mind of many.

October 12, 1865

A space being left here which I had designed filling out with interesting details from October 10 to 27 1864 being so long neglected passed from memory under the crowding in of a multitude of other and stirring scenes. My pen has been but little used for some time having no material for the outlay of thought.

On the 27th of Sept. 1865, Samuel Gammon,[38] Mec Powel and her two little children turned their backs upon us to go to Illinois. We felt so sad to give them up under the trying ordeal through which we are all passing. Only the pleasing anticipation of being permitted to enjoy in a land of strangers what the land of their nativity withholds could have induced them to at this time make the sacrifice. We felt so sorry to say farewell. For we know not where or when our next meeting should be. Sam. G seemed to feel so deeply. He felt he was saying farewell to the early home of his childhood perhaps never to return again and if permitted to find it in strangers hands.

On Tuesday the 26th Richard & Fannie set out for Sullivan. Since which time we had some developments of what is felt

---

38. Sam taught for a year in Illinois, then moved to Memphis to practice law. He died in 1879. Some of the Powels settled in Jerseyville, located in southern part of Illinois just above St. Louis, Missouri. Eliza's son Dick later moved to the area, married a local girl, and lived there the rest of his life.

concerning us as a church and people. On the 1st Sabbath of this month Mr. Sawyer, Mr. Elliott and Mr. Root held a sacramental meeting in Rogersville. In the evening Mr. S. went across the knobs to a meeting which the Dunkards had in memory of Jesse Burton and [name blank]. Men whom all knew to be not what they ought to be. Here Mr. S. took great pleasure in showing forth his zeal not for the upbuilding of his Master's kingdom on earth but for the setting forth of every thing calculated to produce mischief and unkindness. But the Lord gave to the people, hearts to be disaffected with him and he returned feeling he could not accomplish much there.

Last night as we were quietly seated around our fireside a foot-step told us that someone was coming. The door opened and Ernest came in. Soon after he set down he drew from his pocket a large looking document saying you know what that it. He guessed he did as it bore on it the name of Andrew Johnson. R. opened it and it was his pardon.[39] As he read from a sheet of paper whose dimensions were I think 16 x 20 inches I must confess my blood was not very cool. The best men of the country compelled to ask and receive a pardon and for what. O for what, for sustaining the only true principles of civil and religious liberty. The day is coming in which every true hearted Southern man will stand before the world in his true character. May God help us to be faithful and to do our duty as humble Christians relying on the army of our Father God.

Mr. Starnes was here today and told Richard he had been in Kentucky. They were all one way there. The rebels were the men there who held the rule and those who were once Union were now with them in sentiment. He said they did not intend to give up their Negroes; that they had never been out of the Union.

39. Richard was one of some 13,500 individuals who received presidential pardons from Andrew Johnson. (See Jonathan T. Dorris, *Pardon and Amnesty under Lincoln and Johnson* [Chapel Hill: Univ. of North Carolina Press, 1953], 141.) The pardon restored his civil rights, prevented confiscation of his property, and provided political standing in Tennessee. The pardon and the envelope it came in are in the private collection of John and Ann Fain. Richard wrote a note on the envelope that he had received the pardon on October 11, 1865, and that he had notified William H. Seward, the U.S. secretary of state, about having received and accepted it.

Sample excerpt from the diaries of Eliza Fain in October 1865. Here she mentions Richard's receiving the official pardon from President Andrew Johnson. From the John N. Fain Collection, East Tennessee History Center.

The envelope in which Richard's pardon was sent. On the envelope, Richard noted that he received the letter on October 11, 1865, and had notified Secretary of State W. H. Seward by letter the next day. Richard's acknowledgment letter was delivered to the post office on October 13 by James McCarty, a son of Richard's sister. From the private collection of John and Ann Fain.

# ANDREW JOHNSON,

## PRESIDENT OF THE UNITED STATES OF AMERICA,

### TO ALL TO WHOM THESE PRESENTS SHALL COME, GREETING:

Whereas, R. G. Fain of Hawkins County, Tennessee, by taking part in the late rebellion against the Government of the United States. has made himself liable to heavy pains and penalties;

And whereas, the circumstances of his case render him a proper object of Executive clemency;

Now, therefore, be it known, that I, ANDREW JOHNSON, President of the United States of America, in consideration of the premises, divers other good and sufficient reasons me thereunto moving, do hereby grant to the said R. G. Fain a full pardon and amnesty for all offences by him committed, arising from participation, direct or implied, in the said rebellion, conditioned as follows:

1st. This pardon to be of no effect until the said R. G. Fain shall take the oath prescribed in the Proclamation of the President, dated May 29th, 1865.

2d. To be void and of no effect if the said R. G. Fain shall hereafter, at any time, acquire any property whatever in slaves, or make use of slave labor.

The first page of the pardon issued on October 2, 1865 by President Johnson to Richard Fain. This was one of 13,750 pardons that Johnson ultimately issued. Richard required a pardon because he was a graduate of West Point. From the private collection of John and Ann Fain.

3d. That the said *R. G. Fain* _____ first pay all costs which may have accrued in any proceedings instituted or pending against his person or property, before the date of the acceptance of this warrant.

4th. That the said *R. G. Fain* _____ shall not, by virtue of this warrant, claim any property or the proceeds of any property that has been sold by the order, judgment, or decree of a court under the confiscation laws of the United States.

5th. That the said *R. G. Fain* _____ shall notify the Secretary of State, in writing, that he has received and accepted the foregoing pardon.

**In testimony whereof,** I have hereunto signed my name and caused the Seal of the United States to be affixed.

Done at the City of Washington, this Second _____ day of October _____ A. D. 1865, and of the Independence of the United States the Ninetieth _____ .

*Andrew Johnson*

By the President:

*William H. Seward* Secretary of State.

Page 2 of the presidential pardon issued to Richard Fain. From the private collection of John and Ann Fain.

October 23, 1865

My heart is often so cast down and so disquieted within me when I think of the separation of my family. I was so impressed this morning with the thought of a peaceful home in Heaven where nothing can come to mar or disturb its peaceful beauty and quiet. O if I can only meet my precious family at the right hand of my Father in the New Jerusalem.

November 19, 1865

I had intended to reserve the occupied pages of this book for bank purposes to be examined if necessary hereafter by the legal author-ities—unwritten upon by myself but I find I have no means to secure any to put down my thoughts upon and feel if ever necessary what I have written will not interfere as I suppose banking business if ever presumed will require new books.

On yesterday I had what the children call the ringing of the death bell in my ear. I felt very solemn remarking to myself I shall hear of a death soon. The thought struck me what if it should be one of my beloved sons. I love my children. I fear I have had an ambitious love that they might be something more on earth than I should have been. I feel I have been guilty of desiring that they might become prominent actors in the great civil affairs of our country. When engaged in our country's service I desired them to be faithful soldiers. I believed what we were doing was right—I think so yet as the mighty problem is unsolved but I believe that our Father in his own good time and way will vindicate Southern character and bring us forth as one of the tried, refined and purified people of the earth, that he will set forth before the world the highest attainments of Christian excellence from the South ever known of earth which could never have been done had we as a military power been successful.

The spirit of the Northern church is so contrary to every thing which the Bible inculcates—it is so contrary to every view which has ever been taken by true Christian principles that even the most bitter political papers of the North denounce it. While with the South all is so different. The gentle resigned submission which seems to characterize the whole South tells we have been taught by God that the reverses which have come are from our Father's hand and he will take care of us. Slavery was right but its evils caused the withdrawal of his aid for its support.[40] My own impression is it is the amalgamated races in our midst.

November 28, 1865

These are hours of much sorrow to me through which I am now passing. My sons from home—pecuniarily distressed. Several of my children so very deficient in education but above all rises the darkness which hangs over our beloved Zion.

I received on last Saturday letters from my beloved sons N, S & I. The letter from Nick was to my soul a balm. The letter from my poor wild boy Ike was gloomy and disconsolate. The letter from Sam was one of anxiety and care as he feels his helpless condition. He writes that if he would have consented to sell liquor he could have gotten employment but that he would rather starve than do that.

Saturday night as we were quietly seated by our fireside a voice was heard. Lizzie went to the door and the familiar voice of cousin Joe Newland attracted my ear. I got up and went to meet him—but I could not rest in myself as I thought of the place whither he was bound. I hope an indignation may ever arise towards what I do regard this thing to be of dragging men to Knoxville who are the best and most law-abiding men of the country. Cousin Joe did not wish to travel on the Sabbath and neither did Richard but hearing on Saturday evening that the distinguished Col. C. W. had written to Mr. P.[41] by R. that he would take a forfeiture against all who were

40. The phrase "his aid" refers to God's assistance. Eliza was wrestling with the idea that God no longer supported slavery and that this was why the South had been defeated.

41. "Mr. P." is probably William M. Piper, the clerk of the circuit court for Hawkins County. It was before Piper that Richard had signed the oath of allegiance to the Union on November 21, 1965. A holographic copy of this oath is contained among the military papers of Richard Fain in the Fain Collection. The "ponderous document" referred to at the end of this paragraph is presumably Richard's presidential pardon.

not there on Monday. They did not know what was best for them to do. So early on Sabbath morning they set out, went to town and there Richard saw Mr. A. Kyle who kindly assumed the responsibility of his absence and left for Knoxville with the ponderous document. Richard and Joe were permitted to attend the sanctuary and we felt so thankful they did not have to travel on the Sabbath.

We returned home enjoying its peaceful hours and in the evening another one was added to the list of travelers: Mr. Robert Cooper a good orderly citizen. Treason, treason, infamy, infamy — may those who advocate in such strenuous terms this horrible abominable soul destroying radicalism be brought to their solemn senses is my great desire. On Monday morning the three culprits left for Knoxville according to Brownlowism. I trust no evil may befall them.

[Note added later] Reading this record on June 12, 1870 my heart is pained to see the bitterness which rankled in it upon that Sabbath of November 1865. God has since led me in a way I thought not of at the time.

December 31, 1865

Almost at the close of another year, to us of the South what an eventful year and one in which we still see our Father's hand so plainly manifested in guiding, protecting and upholding poor fallen sinful rebellious man. Our religious liberties under God still remain although in Tennessee and Missouri the greatest effort has been made to suppress the Southern Ministers.

We bow submissively and reverently to him who still sitteth as King of Kings and Lords of Lords feeling he cannot err in any thing which comes to pass. And yet our views concerning slavery as an institution of divine origin and one which the Bible recognized are today the same as when, in 61, we took our stand in our country's cause. We feel God our Father has not been pleased to perpetuate the system of slavery which then existed. Why we cannot know now but he does and this is all we deserve to know. We do believe that there have been sins and evils connected and growing out of the lax

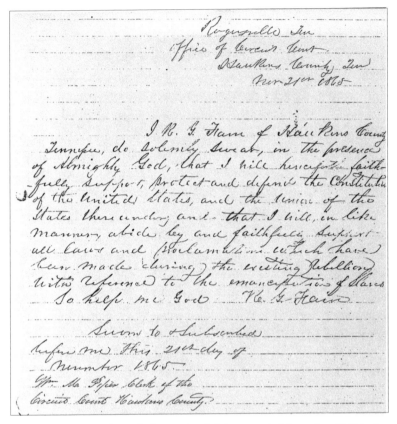

Holographic copy of the oath that Richard Fain swore in November 1865 before the clerk of the Circuit Court of Hawkins County. He was not required to ask forgiveness for supporting the rebellion but merely to affirm that slavery was dead. From the John N. Fain Collection, East Tennessee History Center.

discipline which was so prevalent in our Southern land and God's decree had gone forth that it must go down and the greatest of these to my eye has been the permitting of the mixing of the races. I do believe this violation of God's holy law should have been suppressed by the laws of our land with heavy penalties in every family. I have known of several families where the having a child of this kind resulted in the unfortunate being sold and driven from a home where she was happy. But it was a stain upon Southern character which the blood of Jesus can alone wipe out.

Amongst all the nations of the earth, so far as I can learn, there is towards the African race the feeling you are unmixed with any other race and are an inferior people. I this morning had a difficulty with one of the race which always troubles me. A boy named Hill[42] who had once been one of my family as a servant had been here during part of the Christmas holiday. I felt kindly disposed to him and anxious for him to do right, I had given him much counsel in what way he should act to secure him friends. I told him to be kind and obliging in his manner to everyone, to be a good boy and try to do right. Cousin Annie Poats with her little children Fannie, Walter, Nannie and Ellie with Dick to drive got into the wagon to go to town. I told Hill to go and open the gate for Dicky but this not suiting the young man's pleasure I had to speak harshly to him before I could get him to go and when he did he went to the first gate and came back. I was provoked as he had been here for several days and I had fed him and was willing for him to be with his mother but I just told him he had to go, that I would put up with no such conduct as that about me. Poor mortals what will become of them I cannot see.

---

42. Hill, aged twenty-six, was the son of Polly. Both were slaves belonging to Richard and Eliza prior to the end of the Civil War. Hill continued to work for the Fains after the war, and in 1874 Eliza comments that Ike sent Hill his photograph. Polly is listed as black in the 1860 census, while Hill is listed as a mulatto.

# Chapter 6

# The Desolations of Zion during Reconstruction: 1866–1885

Reconstruction in East Tennessee was an especially difficult period for those who had supported secession, as bitter passions continued to prevail. Parson Brownlow and his Radical Republican followers ruled with a desire for revenge for all they had suffered during the war. They also attempted to drive former Confederates from East Tennessee, but Eliza, for one, remained at her home near Rogersville. The persecution by Unionists, especially Bill Sizemore, continued in and around Rogersville, and for Eliza it culminated with the jailing of her son Ike in 1866 for his alleged role in the murder of William Bird. Ike's prison stay was short as he was released on bond. In 1867, however, he was arrested again, this time for his role in a riot in Rogersville. At this point, Ike took the hint and left town for good. The case never came to trial, and Ike was described after his death in 1917 as one of the most prominent citizens of Chariton, Iowa.

The worst parts of Reconstruction were essentially over by the end of 1869 in East Tennessee. Richard Fain was re-registered as a voter in Hawkins County on July 5, 1869.[1] Turning against Parson Brownlow and his Radical Republican coalition of mostly poor whites and freed slaves, the majority of the East Tennessee voters in 1869 elected conservative Republicans to office. Relative normalcy returned to Hawkins County and the rest of Tennessee.

Richard died in 1878, Hiram in 1869, and Sam in 1874. Eliza's three youngest daughters died of consumption in 1876, 1879, and 1882. Three of the remaining sons—Ike, Nick, and Dick—left East Tennessee, and they along with two of the Fain daughters—Sallie and Fannie—married during the period from 1867 to 1880. Powell married his first cousin in 1880 and eventually settled on the family farm. Shortly before the death of her husband, Eliza and Richard moved to Mossy Creek with her daughter Lizzie, where they lived mostly with Sallie and her relatively affluent husband, Sam Fain. Eliza remained in Mossy Creek until shortly before her death in 1892.

Using the labor of her sons and hired ex-slaves, Eliza tried to farm for a while after the war, but these efforts were not very successful for reasons that are unclear. After moving to Mossy Creek, she attempted to run a boarding house, but that venture failed as well. However, her religious faith was sustained. When the issue of uniting the Northern and Southern Presbyterian churches in Rogersville was raised in 1881, a local resident noted, "Rev. Cowan said he hoped that the members of the respective churches would lay aside all their hard feelings of the Civil War and they seemed willing. Mr. Cowan then read a letter from Aunt Eliza Fain. She urged the churches to unite and work for Jesus. 'Work, work, the time is so

---

1. This was a printed form (see page 375) in which only the county, date, and names were written by hand. Of course, since women were not allowed to vote at this time, the form pertained only to white males.

short and so much to be done for Christ.' Her message seemed to fall as a happy benediction for there were bowed heads and weeping eyes all through the congregation."[2]

Among the entries reproduced below, there are three brief passages—from 1870, 1884, and 1885—in which Eliza reflects on the Civil War. Clearly, she had accepted that slavery was gone and believed, to quote her own words, that the time had come to move forward as a "conquered but not crushed people." However she still maintained that the superior forces of the infidel North had overwhelmed the South and were responsible for the region's postwar poverty. It also appears that three of her sons married Yankee women, and the lore in one of those families was that Eliza never completely accepted them.[3] Eliza may have forgiven her former enemies, but she had not forgotten what they did to her and her family.

In 1884 the Democrats returned to power in Washington and things were looking up for the former Confederates. In 1887, when thirty-four of the most prominent white male citizens of Hawkins County were listed in *Goodspeed's History of Tennessee, East Tennessee Edition*, twenty-four of them gave their political affiliation as Democrat.[4] This suggests that there had been little change in class status as a result of the Civil War and that while the Republicans held political power, this was not necessarily so with regard to

2. Outside of the family papers, this is virtually the only reference I have been able to find to anyone mentioning Eliza in the postwar period. Taken from a woman's letter to her husband, the quotation appears in an article, "History of Rogersville Presbyterian Church," that was first published in the *Rogersville Review* on December 5, 1940. This article is reproduced on page 8 of the January 2000 issue of *Distant Crossroads*, a periodical published by the Hawkins County Genealogical and Historical Society.

3. In 1993 I received a letter from Mary Fain Hurley, the granddaughter of Eliza's son Dick, who had married a local woman after moving to Carrollton, Illinois. "My grandmother," Mary told me, "never was comfortable with daddy Dick's family. She felt to them she was a Yankee." Mary's letter is now in the Fain Collection.

4. *Goodspeed's History of Tennessee*, 1225–39.

economic power. However, no Fain was among these prominent citizens of Hawkins County, and today not one of Eliza's
descendants lives in Rogersville.

## February 21, 1866

Two weeks this evening my beloved husband and Sallie left home
for Mossy Creek.[5] To me it was the saddest parting I have ever felt.
My husband whose silver locks tell that much more than half of the
allotted period for man's life has already past—forced from dire
necessity to leave his home to seek employment elsewhere for the
support of his family.

## August 20, 1866

The dreaded scene has come. My precious darling boy [Ike][6] I fear
sleeps this night in a loathsome dungeon. My poor heart was
almost broken this evening when the announcement was first made

5. Richard had been working as a clerk for his cousin Sam Fain at Mossy Creek since the
end of the Civil War and would continue to do so until he was too feeble to work. Sallie,
aged twenty-eight, acted as a governess and teacher for the orphaned children of Sam
Fain's sister. Sallie married Sam in June 1867.

6. An article in William "Parson" Brownlow's *Knoxville Whig*, dated August 29, 1866, is
headed "Arrest of Young Fain." An excerpt reads as follows: "Isaac Fain, son of Col. Richard
G. Fain, a prominent and wealthy citizen of East Tennessee, was recently arrested and put
in prison at Rogersville, in Hawkins County, on the charge of robbing and MURDERING
several loyal citizens of East Tennessee. This arrest has been made the occasion of virulent
and outrageous editorials on the part of the rebel editors of this section. It has been *alleged*
that Fain was arrested in an irregular and illegal manner by a 'radical mob.' The letter below
from officer Sizemore, refutes the false charge of the Johnson organs."

   The letter was reproduced at the end of the article and addressed to Col. John B.
Brownlow, editor of the *Whig* and the son of William Brownlow, the Radical Republican who
was then the governor of Tennessee. The letter from Sizemore, the notorious ex-bush-
whacker, stated:

   I notice a short article in the Knoxville Commercial of the 25th
   inst., taken from the "State Line Gazette," a little, dirty, filthy rebel
   sheet, published at Bristol. Tenn., relative to the arrest of one Isaac
   Fain, son of Col. Richard G. Fain, which is a misrepresentation of
   the whole affair. Isaac Fain was arrested by me as an officer of
   Hawkins county, at or near Russellville, under a capias issued
   from the Circuit Court of said county, for being present, aiding and
   abetting in the murder of old man Wm. Bird during the reign of

but prayer has given peace. I humbly trust this night O Father into thy hands all that pertains to me and mine. Thou has deigned to hear thy poor erring child. I do feel all things shall work together for good to those who are thine. Give me Abrams faith, let me not waver. O may I lay my sons upon the altar as a sacrifice to gospel truth and civil and religious liberty. This was the feeling which predominated in my heart at the commencement of the struggle. It is the same tonight. Make me faithful, make me humble, my proud heart needs so much to be ever kept down. Discipline O my Father as thou pleasest but do not leave me for one moment.

He was arrested today at Russellville on his way to Bristol. Some word had been sent to Sizemore that he would be on train today. Cousin Sam came up with him today. I love him, he is a noble Christian. O my Father watch over my child this night, preserve him from every danger.

---

the rebels. He was brought here to Rogersville by me, and then bailed by his cousin Sam Fain, of Mossy Creek, and his brother Hiram Fain. He was then re-arrested for robbing, and is now in jail for that offence.

I would state for the information of all concerned and particularly for the little man of the "State Line Gazette" that no person rushed into the cars, that the prisoner was by me arrested as above stated, in a very orderly manner, and not by a posse of men.

Isaac is being well treated, and is visited every day by his mother and friends. As to who reported him as being on the train, I will state, that it was currently reported here on the streets, two days before he was arrested, that he was coming up on the train Monday, the day I arrested him. Now if the editor of the Gazette thinks he can make capital for the rebel cause out of this . . . he is welcome to do so. I think he had better keep quiet, if he is a friend of Isaac and let the law take its course.

WM. O. SIZEMORE
Const. And Special Dept. Sheriff for Hawkins Co.

The death of William Bird is mentioned in Eliza's diaries on December 26, 1861, and March 26, 1862. Ike was there and part of a home guard rather than a regular military unit. In *Mountain Rebels* (136–40), Todd Groce points out that almost none of these suits by Unionists were successful in either civil or criminal courts.

August 22, 1866

O my God do not leave, do not forsake me, do not give me into the hands of the wicked but O my father say thus far and no further canst thou go. Thou has given comfort this morning from thy holy work. Thou hast been my shield, my helper, my protector, my everlasting defense in the many hours of darkness through which my soul has passed during the last five years. O do not in my hours of greatest calumny leave me. On yesterday morning I went in quite early in the wagon with my loved Mollie H. and her precious little child. I found my child still an inmate of his horrid cell; had hoped I should find him released. I found he had been kindly and tenderly cared for by the loved sister E. and Aunt Nancys dear daughters. An hour or more after getting in Mr. James White came in. I saw him and he assured me he would do all he could for my dear boy; thought it best not to act to precipitantly. Mr Beal the sheriff was absent and his loyal sons would not assume so great responsibility as to act without his sanction. I went to the jail — never before have I had such feelings and O my God may I never again have to pass the same ordeal. I found Major Lawson who had been a Federal soldier of the fourth infantry under Col Stover. His manner was kind and sympathizing and as he drew near the cell door. Mrs. Fain I feel sorry for you to have to see your son in such a place. Human sympathy in such an hour is sweet, refreshing and coming as it did from the heart of one for whom I had been so deeply interested spiritually; seemed to be an evidence that he had an appreciation of my feelings and a confidence in the religion of Jesus. He unlocked, I entered. O my soul groans sick as I think of what met my eyes. My son, my darling boy looking through an iron grate. The fountains of grief were dried, the heart heaves with an emotion such as I never knew before. My whole frame shook from agitation — my son spoke "howdy mama." I blessed him through the cold bars and asked my God to bless him. I then gave utterance to exhortations to him to be a Christian. I tried to impress on his mind the thought that God was disciplining him in such a severe manner to bring him to bow to Jesus. O My God if this shall be the result, my soul will bless thee through all eternity for thy love. I addressed the other prisoners 9 in number on the importance of being Christians.

The interview closed and I kissed my child thinking I would come home after the door closed upon him. I with much difficulty restrained a burst of grief—leaned up against the wall—asked Major Lawson to have patience for a few moments which he so kindly gave. After a moment or two I regained my composure— bade him good morning earnestly entreating him to be a Christian. While in the room containing the barred cell where my precious treasure was so unjustly confined Mr. White and John Wolfe came in. Mr. White offered so kindly to assist Ike in any way he could and John, may God bless him and make him the humble follower of Jesus Christ. I can never forget him, he was so kind and has been from the first. I turned from the place retracing my steps to sister N's who was with me in my deep affliction in heart and body. After I got back Liz and Powell came home. I remained—after awhile I concluded to go to see Mr. Kyle. My kind brother George Powel went with me and he too seemed to feel so much for my boy. Sent his word that he would come and see him but felt it was best for him to not go as it might involve him in trouble from some of those who feel the weight of our great government rests on their shoulders. After dinner Buena, Jennie Walker, Bob Blevins, Ella & Fannie Walker, Ella and Silla Fain and self set out with dinner for my child. When we get to the jail Major was not there, Bob hunted him up.

They soon came and once more we entered the terrible room. O my God give me grace, a shudder passes over me as I write these lines. I carried with me a Bible and some newspapers. After we got in Mr. Lawson, the jailer came in, seemed in a bad humor, was very snappish and uncourteous. I asked him if I might remain with my son an hour or two feeling his mothers presence would help his loneli- ness, but he answered "Mrs. Fain you can't stay. I am surprised at so many being in here now." I meekly replied very well sir and we soon left the place.

August 26, 1866

I felt so calm this morning made my visit to my sons cell with his breakfast. Selected a portion of God's word for him to read. Found him as comfortable as I could hope for him to be. The prisoners very kind and Major Lawson very kind to him indeed. After returning to Nancys I soon set out for Sabbath School. Felt I was going to meet my precious class under trying circumstances but was anxious because I wanted them all to pray for my Son. When I went in I found several present had pleasant converse, but when Mr. Hicks began the opening exercises my heart ran over. I could scarcely refrain from loud lamentations. At prayer fell on my knees feeling I could not only bow my spirit but my body into the very dust before him who ruleth in the Heavens and in the earth. After prayers with a heart so full of the abounding grace of God I proceeded to the examination of my class. Our lesson was the trial of Abraham's faith in regard to Isaac. I felt it was a singular coincidence and my heart I do believe was prepared by the same God to offer up my darling boy. Not as Abraham did his looking by the eye of faith through the long period of over 1800 years to the coming Messiah who was to be sacrificed upon that same mountain (as is supposed by most Bible readers, I believe), but in looking back over 1800 years with a most perfect confidence in the power and the efficacy of this great atoning sacrifice which had come, which was offered for mans redemption through whose precious merits my beloved child could by faith be presented before the father. I feel this was one of the most impressive lessons to me and I do hope to my class.

September 3, 1866

All in circumstances of mercy. My dear, my beloved husband has again bid me goodbye. I find this separation is becoming so irksome, so trying to me when I bade him goodbye. During his soldiers life my heart was so borne up with the mighty cause for which I felt we struggled it seemed to be a sustainer. But now he goes forth borne down with much anxious care for the maintenance of this family. The thought of which seemed not to trouble us during the four long years of struggle.

## May 7, 1867

This day we returned from New Providence[7] having gone up on the Sabbath. My dear husband coming up late Saturday night having had that day to be present at a trial for my noble red horse which had been taken on the 5th April by a set of dark hideous monsters.[8] I do feel my Father in Heaven has given him back to my possession. On Sabbath morning mounted on this horse, my husband on one from Mr. Fulkersons, we set out early. Reached the place just as services began. The congregation was singing *"Homeward Bound."*

## August 1, 1867

Today I draw near the 51st anniversary of my life. My thoughts turned upon the great events of this day in the political issues of our state government. My heart is troubled as we appear to be standing upon a rather roaring volcano which seems to threaten the complete overthrow of the mighty fabric of American liberty. Will there be brought upon this country a war of races. Will this wild fanatical element be permitted to draw into their net the poor deluded outcasts of Ham and have them all sacrificed to the demon of war. This is the day which tests the election for governor in the state. Etheridge the Conservative — Brownlow the Radical candidate. We as a people so far as I know stand for the conservative

7. New Providence refers to the Presbyterian church located in Surgoinsville, Tennessee. Within two years, Eliza's oldest son, Hiram, would be buried in a marked grave in the cemetery beside this church.

8. The reference is to the raid by Sizemore's band of lawless guerrillas. Since the group was not part of an authorized Union force, there was no justification for theft of a horse.

believing that they are the party now rising in the government who will stand shoulder to shoulder with us who have borne the burden and heat of the day for sustaining constitutional liberty as was once enjoyed by us as a people. My feeling is I never want to see the black race now in our midst enslaved for this I believe has been one of the causes of our defeat. Last week was one of stirring interest in this part of the state. On Tuesday the 23 [of July] Mr. Etheridge spoke at a place which had been prepared for him and Mr. Maynard one of Brownlow's satellites was also to stand forth. The crowd divided.

The white man standing with the white man for the sustaining of the principles of true liberty. The black man in heart standing with the black in skin for the pulling down of every thing which had been reared upon the foundations laid by the Fathers of the past. All passed off quietly until in the evening as the radicals were returning from the stand where they had listened, as I understood, to language calculated to excite the bad feeling of the human heart. The whites taking their position as they will ever wish to do in the front of the black (except when shell and shot threaten) passed through without any outburst of applause for the great Mogul. After which came the poor deluded beings of Northern fanaticism led on by a white man, whose name will not occupy an enviable position hereafter, he pulling into the ranks of the formidable procession little boy children. After getting about the center of town he took off his hat, threw it around and called for cheers to Brownlow. Of course the sable cloud let forth a heavy shower. Many whites were standing upon the sides of the streets watching the maneuvering, amongst the number some of those upon whom the radicals take great pleasure in venting spleen. Ike and Mike McCarty were standing near each other; a large yellow radical drew down upon them and let go his shot striking near the head of Mike. This was as I understand the first shot; this was the signal. A general encounter took place the whites who formed the advance guard fled in great disarray leaving the poor African to his fate. After a few shots they fled in terrible fright seeking shelter wherever one could be found. A white man by the name of York (a conservative) was killed and a man by the name of Roy, both of whom were Federal soldiers, was severely wounded in the shoulder. He too was a conservative and some four or five Negroes were wounded as well. I have no doubt but that many of them would have been killed had the whites tried to shoot them but the Southern heart who has ever had sympathy for the poor Negro still felt it and felt more like taking vengeance on the white man who was the instigator and executor of their plans.[9]

In the evening the conservatives held the town as quiet and peaceably as though nothing had occurred. But this was not the end to the Reb who dared to raise his head (Ike). On Thursday evening Nick went to town. Mr. Beal the sheriff, a sworn officer to keep the peace, arrested him under the pretext it was Ike and had him disarmed. Nick at first refusing to give up his pistol on the grounds that he had no right to disarm him telling him who he was but this would not do. Beal called around him some four or five armed sentries and took his pistol. Nick came on out home and told Ike he had better be making preparations to leave. We got through a supper and he began to prepare to start. We were busy hunting his clothes; Nick, Powell and Dick having gone over to Hirams to get his saddle bags. Bug was with us—had talked of going over but Ike said stay and help me.

9. In *Blue and Gray from Hawkins County: The Battles* (69–71), Sheila Johnston describes this event as one of the largest battles fought in Rogersville during the Civil War era. It was, in fact, a politically and racially charged riot between the conservatives and the radical Unionists. The one man killed was Jessie York of Russellville, a former Union soldier. Eight men were wounded in the riot, which was alleged to have started when a mulatto fired into the crowd, resulting in a dozen or more pistol shots from the whites. The blacks allegedly responded by firing into the crowd and killing York. General firing then ensued, and the blacks retreated to a hill outside of town where they were attacked and disarmed by a group of former Union soldiers agitated by the death of their comrade. Several men were arrested and charged with disturbing the peace and harming Daniel Hord, a black man, who lost his leg in the riot. Johnston lists at least ten other men besides Ike Fain who left the county and never returned after this riot.

When news came they were after him Ike started to run out the back of the house but they were there and called to him to halt. He ran back into the house and went upstairs and took refuge in the garret. Joe Wright was the soldier and a man by the name of Dempsey his deputy assisted by Amperdia Anderson, Sam Beal, the Marshall and a Negro. Wright asked me if Ike was here; I told him he had left that evening. The fear of man overcame, I did not know but they might attempt to kill him. I deceived, this made me tremble like the aspen leaf. I could not get rid of the fearful feeling they will get him. Mr. Wright told me he had a capias [writ] to serve upon him. I could not tell for what neither could he. He said he thought it was for violating his bond. I could not see how it had been a violation of his bond but felt I was ignorant in legal matters. After sometime Mr. Wright thought of going when he was informed by some of those who came in on the rear that Ike had been out then this made Mr. Dempsey quite anxious to search. He asked me if they might. Here I lost all the right I had; the prerogative was mine to say no but I did not know it and said yes. The search began and he was found, brought out under a cocked pistol by Mr. Dempsey from his retreat (he surrendered when he found he was so near being found). Although I do not think Mr. D. had seen him. They marched him downstairs and then made arrangements to take him to town. Nick went with him. Mr. Wright and Mr. D. promised me he should not be put in jail. Such a night I have never passed in all my life. The terrible thought ever and anon crossing the mind that I had lied unto God and he might deliver my son into his enemies hands. I prayed almost the whole night; I thought of Peter and of Jacob but this was but little comfort to the Christian of the 19th century. Such an agonizing time. I feel now that God's hand was in it all, I feel his infinite mercy is so great.

My son was taken to town and contrary to the promises and I believe the wishes of Mr. Wright he was made the inmate of the iron cage and slept that night in the prisoners cell. Father as I write give me Christian grace for my soul revolts with horror at the usurpation of power in this Government which is said to be peace. On the 24th of June in cold blood Sizemore murdered a man by the name of Webster whose only crime was that he said he was a conservative.[10] Sizemore was put under arrest but a guard of friends came around him from whom, as I have understood, he quietly walked out saying good evening gentlemen (this I have heard but do not say it is true) and made his escape. He was not seen on the street publicly until the 4th of July. The blacks had a supper and I hear he officiated in his official capacity taking charge of things and giving directions as to behavior. I have no doubt many blacks present felt themselves disparaged by the association. Some of the true and noble who still live (although they have in days gone by sought our destruction but feeling now war is over and they want the peace they fought to obtain the restoration of the union as it was) stepped forth and took the law in their own hands saying to Mr. Beal you have either to see this man gives a good bond or be sent to jail. (As I understand this was not a bailable case but I suppose they thought no one could be found who had property or character who would stand for him—as to property I do not know what the bailers have, as to character God is their judge not me.) He has a bond of $4,000 for murder, cold hearted deliberate murder and my son was required to give a bond of $10,000 for being with a squad of men during the war although he was not present when the murder was done. This man was in arms arrayed against us; the capias upon which he was last confined, for which to be released he must give a bond of $1,000, was a presentment by the grand jury for taking 3 horses from a man by the name of William Alvis.[11] When that man knows he never took them, was along the night they were

10. According to Johnston (*Blue and Gray from Hawkins County: The Battles*, 67), newspaper reports of the era stated that James Webster was killed in a Rogersville hotel during a "drunken fight" by William Sizemore. Webster, aged twenty-eight, had been a Confederate soldier who served in Company E of the Twenty-ninth Tennessee from August 13, 1861, to August 12, 1862.

11. William N. Alvis, born in 1844, enrolled in a Union cavalry regiment on January 1, 1865, but was absent since January 11, 1865, having joined Sizemore's band. The federal government denied a pension to his widow, claiming that he deserted on March 15, 1865 after serving seventy-four days.

taken during the war but afterwards, perhaps the next day, rode 27 miles with him and brother to George Fains introducing him to the commanding officer and asking I have no doubt that he might get them back. This is liberty which makes the one who has an innate consciousness of what true American liberty is boil at times.

February 9, 1868

My heart has been so troubled this day. I have again bid my own dear boy Ike farewell. He left yesterday to go out as a stranger in a strange land far away from home and home loved ones.[12] He attended for two weeks the Circuit Court—no call for his suit. He felt he was released from the bonds for his appearance and left yesterday evening on horseback.

My heart is so sad. I have loved him so tenderly. The persecution to which he has been subject for almost the two last years has rendered him an object of such special care. I know he has a wayward heart fond of life, fond of all its pleasures, fond of worldly gain and I may say worldly favor but he has a kind heart and I love him. He has a temper which is hard to control but I have often found a soothing word from his mother has calmed the tempest. At other times silence with a look of disapprobation has left its impress.

July 21, 1870

This day has been one of commotion and excitement in Rogersville — having been appointed as a day for a mass meeting. Andrew Johnson the prominent political speaker is there. These things do not interest or affect me as they once did. Our country is ruined unless God in

12. On this occasion, Ike left Rogersville for good and went to Chariton, Iowa, where his brother-in-law owned some tracts of bounty land. Ike married Mattie James of Chariton in 1876, and they had four children. His obituary in the *Rogersville Journal and Tribune* of January 12, 1917, stated, "Mr. Fain was a native of Hawkins county and was widely and prominently connected in the county. He had been very successful at Chariton where ever since the Civil War he had been among the town's most prominent citizens." See Fain Collection.

Voter registration form for Richard Fain issued on July 5, 1869. Richard was not re-enrolled as a voter in Hawkins County until almost four years after he received his presidential pardon. From the John N. Fain Collection, East Tennessee History Center.

his infinite mercy to us will incline the hearts of our people to that which is right. It is his prerogative to cast down and to build up. I have felt for many years the South was her own destroyer. We were so hot headed, so impetuous that the cool calculating North stripped us of our strength by the firebrands of party strife. O may we remember this and stand together. My family are well represented in town—husband, 4 sons, and daughter (Nannie) and brother George. I trust they may all act as men who fear to do wrong.

November 15, 1884
On the 4th of this month Gov. Grover Cleveland was elected. We are so thankful for this victory. How often during the four years of terrible conflict did we feel our cause must succeed for we felt the Bible was the book to which we turned as the lamp to our feet and the light to our path. When we heard of others saying (in the

North) if the Bible sustains slavery; we set it aside for a higher law. Our system of slavery has passed away and I for one would never be willing to see its shackles upon us again, but our Bible is the same. We feel it has indeed been a lamp to our feet and the light to our path. During the long years of what has been to us oftentimes humiliating times we have ever turned to our Bible and there found a solace to all our troubles. If our wishes have been thwarted we have found the words of a dear Saviour precious and been made to feel in all this there was a needs be for the glory and honor of our blessed Master and the good of all his disciples.

February 22, 1885
Loved ones permitted to go to Sabbath school today. I do love to see them go. This is the anniversary of the birth of our noble Washington whom God raised up to be a leader to our people in the establishment of a free government; and over which he our God has been watching; and upholding for more than a century permitted the development of a grand republic. Having passed through a severe civil struggle and the South having sustained herself as conquered, but not a crushed people. Our God has not forsaken us, he is beginning to see the heavy clouds of despotism which have been so long heavy over her drifting away; and a brighter day dawning upon us.

GEN. Richard G. Fain, of Rogers-ville, died at Mossy Creek, in Jefferson county, last week. Gen. Fain was in the 67th year of his. In 1832 he graduated at West Point, accepted a commission in the U. S. army and served a campaign in the North West against the Indians. Resigning his place in the army he came home—where he lived a life of remarkable activity. He was a soldier again in the Cherokee war, then he was a merchant, a Bank officer, Clerk and Master of the Chancery Court, Rail Road President, &c. When the late war broke out he again took up his sword and served about two years in the Confederate army. When the war closed i found him broken in health and broken in fortune, but he struggled on manfully until death came and relieved him of all the cares and sorrows of life. We hope he has found rest "over the river."

Mrs. Eliza R. Fain.

On January 19, 1892, in Rogersville, Tenn., there passed away from earth a true mother in Israel. Mrs. Eliza R. Fain, or "Grandma," as she was called by almost the entire congregation, was born in Blountville, Tenn., August, 1816, and at the age of seventeen, united with the Presbyterian church at that place. In December, 1833, she married Gen. Richard G. Fain, and moved to Rogersville, where she lived till the time of her death.

For over a half century, she went out and in among that people, manifesting in all things the power of the grace of God; and few have been better known and honored by all, as a quiet, earnest, saintly woman.

She was of Scotch Irish parentage, and inherited a zeal and faith and love for the Church of the living God, which never weakened nor wavered. Only when the infirmities of age forbade, was her seat vacant in the sanctuary, and her visits of mercy and ministration stopped.

Well instructed in the word of the Lord and the doctrines of her Church, she was always in full sympathy with the messenger of God as he taught the people from Sabbath to Sabbath. Her presence in the congregation was always an encouragement; for, as the minister looked into her face and eyes, often dimmed with tears, he was conscious that her prayers were for him, that he might rightly divide the word of life to a dying people. Others might criticise; she never would. She was strong in faith, and there were few who had greater longings for the "kingdom of God to come." The enlargement of Zion was to her a matter of continual rejoicing.

The end of such a life was hardly dying. It was only departing to be with Him whom her soul loved, and to have fellowship with the great multitude around His throne.

To her large family and a multitude of relatives and neighbors, she has left a precious legacy in so many years of godly living.

He hath given his beloved sleep and rest.

AN OLD PASTOR.

Copies of newspaper obituaries for Richard and Eliza Fain that were found among the family papers. From the private collection of John and Ann Fain.

**Privileges**

**347** SAFE IN THE ARMS OF JESUS   7. 6. 7. 6. D. with Refrain

William H. Doane, 1870

1. Safe   in   the arms of   Je - sus,   Safe   on   His gen - tle breast,
Cho.—*Safe   in   the arms of   Je - sus,   Safe   on   His gen - tle breast,*

There   by   His love o'er - shad - ed,   Sweet-ly   my   soul shall   rest.
*There   by   His love o'er - shad - ed,   Sweet-ly   my   soul shall   rest.*

Hark! 'tis the voice of   an - gels,   Borne in   a   song to   me,

O - ver the fields of   glo - ry,   O - ver the Jas - per   sea. . .

Used by permission of the Biglow & Main Co.

2 Safe in the arms of Jesus,
 Safe from corroding care,
 Safe from the world's temptations,
 Sin cannot harm me there.
 Free from the blight of sorrow,
 Free from my doubts and fears;
 Only a few more trials,
 Only a few more tears!

3 Jesus, my heart's dear refuge,
 Jesus has died for me;
 Firm on the Rock of Ages
 Ever my trust shall be.
 Here let me wait with patience,
 Wait till the night is o'er;
 Wait till I see the morning
 Break on the golden shore.

233             Fanny J. Crosby, 1868

"Safe in the Arms of Jesus" was one of the three hymns sung at the funeral for Eliza Fain, according to her son-in-law Sam Fain. This hymn was written by Fanny J. Crosby, one of the most famous hymn writers of the nineteenth century. It is reproduced here from *The New Psalms and Hymn Book*, published in 1901 by authority of the General Assembly of the Presbyterian Church in the United States. From the private collection of John and Ann Fain.

Copyright 1871, by W. W. Bostwick & Co.

The cover of a four-page brochure (six by nine inches) found among the diaries of Eliza Fain. It was issued in 1874 by the Bostwick Company, acting as agents for the Lee Memorial Association, to promote the sale of a "life-size Steel Engraved Portrait of General R. E. Lee, to raise money in furtherance of the object of this Association, namely: To the erection of a monument to his memory at the Washington and Lee University, Lexington, Va." The Lee monument was eventually erected but bears no resemblance to the picture. Instead, the recumbent statue of Lee, sculpted by Edward Valentine, was placed in an addition to the back of the chapel of Washington and Lee University. From the private collection of John and Ann Fain.

# Epilogue

Eliza continued to make entries in her diaries until shortly before her death on January 19, 1892. Her funeral was conducted in the Rogersville Presbyterian Church, and she was buried in the church cemetery. Today an imposing monument marks her resting place alongside that of her husband. A eulogy written after her death by someone identified as A.R.H. says:

> For seventy five years Mrs. Fain bore the burdens of this mortal life and as to the weight and magnitude of hers it may be sufficient to say, that she had been the mother of 13 children, the wife of a man whose circumstances were at no time affluent, that she had buried in the prime of manhood two sons and in the flower of maidenhood three daughters, and lastly her husband. She was also the center of a large circle of nieces and nephews to many of whom she supplied the place of a missing mother. One in particular, whom she reared with her own family and loved as a son, whose genial nature and ready wit made him the favorite of every social circle and whose name will ever be linked in honor with the Bar of Tennessee, wrung her poor old heart, as only Mother hearts can know—when he came home to die in her arms, in the

darkness of delirium and without the Hope which
was to her the "Anchor of the Soul."

When the country was rent by Civil War
and her fortunes were attached to the losing side, she
not only met with benediction and generous hospitality the enemy who were brave enough to meet her
sons upon the field of battle, but even the skulking
marauders, who invaded her defenseless home to
haunt her with her helplessness, she turned away in
shame by the gentleness of her bearing and the mild
dignity of her replies.

The curse of strong drink which has written
its blasting history upon so many families in this fair
land did not spare her, but as if she had been selected
by Providence to illustrate how much one woman
can bear, she was called upon to drain this cup too.
Yet through all this long and varied career of suffering, neither under the petty exactions and trials
which the rearing of a large family in straitened circumstances must have imposed, nor beneath the
heart breaking sorrows which befell her in later life,
did any words of complaint or repining escape her.

This eulogy was discovered among the family papers and,
along with supporting information on genealogy and related
matters, can now be found in the John N. Fain Collection of the
McClung Historical Collection, East Tennessee History Center, in
Knoxville, Tennessee. The nephew referred to was Samuel Rhea
Gammon. The curse of alcohol appears to have especially blighted
the life of Eliza's son Sam, who died in 1874, and possibly her son
Powell, as well as her son-in-law Amos Smith.[1] While none of

1. Writing in 1874 in the *Atlantic Monthly*, George Cary Eggleston, a former Confederate soldier
from Virginia observed, "The real sorrows of war, like those of drunkenness, always fall most
heavily on women." This was true for Eliza, and when men are alcoholics, they spend what

Eliza's five sons or her husband died during the Civil War, two of her sons died within nine years after the hostilities ended. Times were hard for returned soldiers in a divided community where economic and political power now resided with those who had fought for and supported the Union.

money they can get their hands on for alcohol, leaving little for the women and children in their lives. Eggleston further stated that "the men came home moody, worn out, discouraged and but for the influence of woman's cheerfulness, the Southern States might have fallen into lethargy." The poverty and privation that befell many former Confederates was especially the lot of Eliza and her family, and Eggleston's comments in 1874 were probably applicable to the Fains at that time. However, Eggleston was a born romantic, and it is unlikely that women like Eliza were able to maintain cheerfulness throughout Reconstruction. (Eggleston's memoir was published in book form as *A Rebel's Recollections* in 1875 and reprinted several times since then, most recently in 1996 by Louisiana State University Press. The above quotations, taken from the 1959 edition [Indiana University Press], are found on pages 84 and 93, respectively.)

# Selected Bibliography

## Archived Papers

Calvin M. McClung Historical Collection, East Tennessee
    History Center, Knoxville
        Frank B. Fain Collection
        John N. Fain Collection
East Tennessee State University, Archives and Special
    Collections, Johnson City
        Fannie Rhea Fain Diary
Hawkins County Public Library, Rogersville, Tenn.
        Merrimon Family Papers

## Books and Articles

Ash, Stephen V., ed. *Secessionists and Other Scoundrels: Selections from Parson Brownlow's Book*. Baton Rouge: Louisiana State Univ. Press, 1999.

Bailey, Fred Arthur. *Class and Tennessee's Confederate Generation*. Chapel Hill: Univ. of North Carolina Press, 1987.

Bible, Donahue. *From Persia to Piedmont: Life and Death in Vaughn's Brigade*. Mohawk, Tenn.: Dodson Creek Publishers, 1995.

———. *Their Eyes Have Seen the Glory: East Tennessee Unionists in the Civil War*. Mohawk, Tenn.: Dodson Creek Publishers, 1997.

Burr, Virginia Ingraham, ed. *The Secret Eye: The Journal of Ella Gertrude Clanton Thomas, 1848–1889.* Chapel Hill: Univ. of North Carolina Press, 1990.

Chapla, John D. *50th Virginia Infantry.* Lynchburg, Va.: H. E. Howard, 1997.

Clinton, Catherine. *The Plantation Mistress: Woman's World in the Old South.* New York: Pantheon Books, 1982.

Coppock, Helen M., and Charles W. Crawford, eds. *Paul R. Coppock's Mid-South.* Vol. 2. Memphis: Paul R. Coppock Publication Trust, 1992.

Coulter, E. Merton. *William G. Brownlow: Fighting Parson of the Southern Highlands.* Chapel Hill: Univ. of North Carolina Press, 1937.

Crawford, R. Clay. *Reminiscences of Rogersville.* Edited by Sheila Johnston. Rogersville, Tenn.: Privately published, 1994.

Crofts, Daniel W. *Reluctant Confederates: Upper South Unionists in the Secession Crisis.* Chapel Hill: Univ. of North Carolina Press, 1989.

Cummings, H. F. *Report to the General Assembly on the condition of the railroads in Tennessee.* Nashville: E. G. Eastman, 1859.

Dorris, Jonathan T. *Pardon and Amnesty under Lincoln and Johnson.* Chapel Hill: Univ. of North Carolina Press, 1953.

Douglass, Elisha P. *The Coming of Age of American Business: Three Centuries of Enterprise, 1600–1900.* Chapel Hill: Univ. of North Carolina Press, 1971.

Draper, Mary G. "The Powel Family." *Distant Crossroads,* October 2000, 122–23.

Dunn, Durwood. *An Abolitionist in the Appalachian South: Ezekiel Birdseye on Slavery, Capitalism, and Separate Statehood in East Tennessee, 1841–1846.* Knoxville: Univ. of Tennessee Press, 1997.

Eggleston, George Cary. *A Rebel's Recollections.* 1875. Reprint, Bloomington: Indiana Univ. Press, 1959.

Fain, John N. "The Diary of Hiram Fain of Rogersville: An East Tennessee Secessionist." *Journal of East Tennessee History,* no. 69 (1997): 97–114.

Fain, Max. *Nicholas Fain of Tennessee.* Atlanta: M. Fain, 1980.

Faust, Drew Gilpin. *Mothers of Invention: Women of the Slaveholding South in the Civil War.* New York: Random House, 1996.

Faust, Patricia L., ed. *Historical Times Illustrated Encyclopedia of the Civil War.* New York: Harper & Row, 1986.

Fisher, Noel C. *War at Every Door: Partisan Politics and Guerrilla Violence in East Tennessee.* Chapel Hill: Univ. of North Carolina Press, 1997.

Foley, Edward F. *The Descendants of Matthew "The Rebel" Rhea of Scotland and Ireland.* Bowie, Md.: Heritage Books, 2000.

Foote, Shelby. *The Civil War, a Narrative.* 3 vols. New York: Random House, 1958–74.

Fox, William F. *Regimental Losses in the American Civil War.* 1898. Reprint, Dayton, Ohio: Morningside Bookshop, 1974.

Govan, Charles E., and James W. Livingood. *The Chattanooga Country, 1540–1951.* New York: E. P. Dutton, 1952.

Groce, W. Todd. *Mountain Rebels: East Tennessee Confederates and the Civil War, 1860–1870.* Knoxville: Univ. of Tennessee Press, 1999.

Haynes, Stephen. *Noah's Curse: Race and the American Imagination.* New York: Oxford Univ. Press, 2002.

Hewett, Janet B., ed. *Roster of Confederate Soldiers, 1861–1865.* 16 vols. Wilmington, N.C.: Broadfoot Publishing Co., 1995–96.

———. *Roster of Union Soldiers, 1861–1865: Kentucky-Tennessee.* Wilmington, N.C.: Broadfoot Publishing Co., 2000.

———. *Roster of Union Soldiers, 1861–1865: Ohio.* 4 vols. Wilmington, N.C.: Broadfoot Publishing Co., 1999.

"History of Rogersville Presbyterian Church." *Distant Crossroads,* January 2000, 8. Reprinted from *Rogersville Review,* December 5, 1940.

Hoehling, A. A. *Women Who Spied.* New York: Dodd, Mead & Co., 1967.

Johnston, Sheila Weems. *The Blue and Gray from Hawkins County, Tennessee, 1861–1865: The Battles.* Rogersville, Tenn.: Hawkins County Genealogical & Historical Society, 1995.

————. *The Blue and Gray from Hawkins County, Tennessee, 1861–1865: The Confederates*. Rogersville, Tenn.: Hawkins County Genealogical & Historical Society, 1995.

————. *The Blue and Gray from Hawkins County, Tennessee, 1861–1865: The Federals*. Rogersville, Tenn.: Hawkins County Genealogical & Historical Society, 1995.

Judd, Cameron. *The Bridge Burners: A True Adventure of East Tennessee's Underground Civil War*. Johnson City, Tenn.: Overmountain Press, 1996.

Lindsley, John Berrien, ed. *The Military Annals of Tennessee, Confederate: First Series: Embracing a View of Military Operations*. Nashville: J. M. Lindsley, 1886.

Marvel, William. "The Battle of Saltville: Massacre or Myth?" *Blue and Gray*, August 1991, 10–19, 46–60.

Mathews, Donald G. *Religion in the Old South*. Chicago: Univ. of Chicago Press, 1977.

Mays, Tom. *The Saltville Massacre*. Fort Worth: Ryan Place Publishers, 1995.

McGuffey, Charles D., ed. *Standard History of Chattanooga, Tennessee*. Knoxville: Crew & Dorey, 1911.

McPherson, James M. *Battle Cry of Freedom: The Civil War Era*. New York: Oxford Univ. Press, 1988.

Mendenhall, Marjorie S. "Southern Women of a Lost Generation." In *Unheard Voices: The First Historians of Southern Women*, edited by Anne Firor Scott. Charlottesville: Univ. Press of Virginia, 1993. First published in *South Atlantic Quarterly*, 1934.

Mims, Edwin. *The Advancing South: Stories of Progress and Reaction*. New York: Doubleday, Page & Co., 1926.

Moore, John Trotwood, and Austin P. Foster. *Tennessee: The Volunteer State, 1769–1923*. Vol. 4. Nashville: S. J. Clarke, 1923.

Noe, Kenneth W., and Shannon H. Wilson, eds. *The Civil War in Appalachia: Collected Essays*. Knoxville: Univ. of Tennessee Press, 1997.

Patton, James W. *Unionism and Reconstruction in Tennessee 1860–1869.* Chapel Hill: Univ. of North Carolina Press, 1934.

Piston, W. G. *Carter's Raid: An Episode of the Civil War in East Tennessee.* Johnson City, Tenn.: Overmountain Press, 1989.

Rothrock, Mary, ed. *The French Broad–Holston Country: A History of Knox County, Tennessee.* Knoxville: East Tennessee Historical Society, 1946.

Scott, Anne Firor. *The Southern Lady: From Pedestal to Politics, 1830–1890.* Chicago: Univ. of Chicago Press, 1970.

Scott, J. L. *36th and 37th Battalions Virginia Cavalry.* Lynchburg, Va.: H. E. Howard, 1986.

Silver, James W. *Confederate Morale and Church Propaganda.* Tuscaloosa, Ala.: Confederate Publishing Co., 1957.

Smith, Margaret Lyons. *Miss Nan: Beloved Rebel.* Johnson City, Tenn.: Overmountain Press, 1994.

Snell, William R., ed. *Myra Inman: A Diary of the Civil War in East Tennessee.* Macon, Ga.: Mercer Univ. Press, 2000.

Stowell, Daniel. "'A Family of Women and Children': The Fains of East Tennessee during Wartime." In *Southern Families at War: Loyalty and Conflict in the Civil War South,* edited by Catherine Clinton. New York: Oxford University Press, 2000.

———. *Rebuilding Zion: The Religious Reconstruction of the South, 1863–1877.* New York: Oxford Univ. Press, 1998.

Sutherland, Daniel E., ed. *A Very Violent Rebel: The Civil War Diary of Ellen Renshaw House.* Knoxville: Univ. of Tennessee Press, 1996.

Taylor, Oliver. *Historic Sullivan: A History of Sullivan County, Tennessee.* Bristol, Tenn.: King Printing Co., 1909.

Temple, Oliver P. *East Tennessee and the Civil War.* Cincinnati: Robert Clarke Co., 1899.

*Tennesseans in the Civil War.* 2 vols. Nashville: Civil War Centennial Commission of Tennessee, 1964.

Wash, William A. *Camp, Field and Prison Life: Containing Sketches of Service in the South, and the Experience, Incidents and Observations Connected with Almost Two Years Imprisonment at Johnson's Island, Ohio.* St. Louis: Southwestern Book Publishing Co., 1870.

*War of the Rebellion: A Compilation of the Official Records of the Union and Confederate Armies.* 128 vols. Washington, D.C.: U.S. Government Printing Office, 1880–91.

Weiner, Marti F. *Mistresses and Slaves: Plantation Women in South Carolina, 1830–80.* Urbana: Univ. of Illinois Press, 1998.

Wink, Amy L. *She Left Nothing in Particular: The Autobiographical Legacy of Nineteenth-Century Women's Diaries.* Knoxville: Univ. of Tennessee Press, 2001.

Woodward, C. Vann, ed. *Mary Chesnut's Civil War.* New Haven, Conn.: Yale Univ. Press, 1981.

Woodward, C. Vann, and Elisabeth Muhlenfeld, eds. *The Private Mary Chesnut: The Unpublished Civil War Diaries.* New York: Oxford Univ. Press, 1984.

Worsham, W. J. *The Old Nineteenth Tennessee Regiment, C.S.A.* 1902. Reprint, Oxford, Miss.: Guild Bindery Press, 1992.

Wyatt-Brown, Bertram. "Modernizing Slavery: The Proslavery Argument Reinterpreted." In *Region, Race, and Reconstruction: Essays in Honor of C. Vann Woodward*, edited by J. Morgan Kousser and James M. McPherson. New York: Oxford Univ. Press, 1982.

## Newspapers

*Brownlow's Knoxville Whig and Rebel Ventilator,* February 20, 1864.
*Knoxville Whig,* August 29, 1866.
*Rogersville (Tenn.) Journal and Tribune,* January 12, 1917.

# Documents on Microfilm

National Archives and Records Administration, Microfilm
Publications, Washington, D.C.
  *Compiled Service Records of Confederate Soldiers Who Served in
    Organizations in the State of Tennessee,* RG109, M268
      Hiram and Richard Fain, Roll 347
      Isaac Fain, Rolls 52, 347
      Nick Fain, Rolls 197, 338
      Powell Fain, Roll 338
      Sam Fain, Rolls 52, 197, 347
  *Eighth Census of the United States, 1860,* RG029, M653
      Free Schedules, Hawkins County, Tennessee, Roll 1255
      Slave Schedules, Hawkins County, Tennessee, Roll 1282
  *Case Files of Applications from Former Confederates for Presidential
    Pardons, 1865–1867* ("Amnesty Papers"), RG094, M1003
      Roll 49 (Tennessee, Ea-Jo)
Tennessee State Library and Archives, Nashville
  Confederate Pension Applications — Widows, Case 5520,
    Roll W30

# Online Sources

"The American Colonization Society Website."
  http://ourworld.cs.com/ceoofamcolso/id24_m.htm.
Brown, David E. "5th Regiment Cavalry, United States Colored
  Troops." http://mywebpages.comcast.net/5thuscc.
"Peter Alexander Selkirk McGlashan." From "Kyreb and
  Bootneck's Scots in the Civil War." http://www.scots-in-the-
  civil-war.net/mcglashan.htm.
Shepherd, Henry E. "Narrative of Prison Life at Baltimore and
  Johnson's Island, Ohio." Univ. of North Carolina at Chapel
  Hill Libraries. http://docsouth.unc.edu/shepherd/shepherd.html.
"Tennesseans in the Civil War."
  http://www.tngennet.org/civilwar/usacav/usa9cav.html.

# Index